# GIDEON'S ARMY

VOLUME I · THE COMPONENTS OF THE DECISION

# *Gideon's army*

## CURTIS D. MacDOUGALL

*Professor of Journalism, Northwestern University*

*Introduction by*

## H. H. WILSON

*Professor of Politics, Princeton University*

MARZANI & MUNSELL · NEW YORK

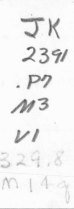

Copyright © 1965 by CURTIS D. MACDOUGALL

Printed in the United States of America.

FIRST EDITION

Library of Congress Catalog Card Number: 65-18683

# CONTENTS

# INTRODUCTION

## H. H. WILSON

The events of recent months, indeed of recent years, have led millions of literate people throughout the world, and many thousands in the United States, to question both the motives and the efficacy of United States foreign policy. Few people outside the United States take seriously our claim that we are defending freedom against Communist expansion on behalf of the people in Vietnam or the Dominican Republic. They believe the Johnson Administration has made it obvious that we are simply interested in establishing American power and furthering what are defined as American interests. Despite the fact that within the United States opposition to this foreign policy appears to be more extensive and more broadly based than any previous protest in this generation, there is no visible evidence that it is having any effect on the Administration's hazardous course. Recently the foreign editor of the London *Sunday Times* observed that "so far as one can see, nothing—and nobody—is going to deflect the United States from its course." (Los Angeles *Times,* June 13, 1965)

Against this background Professor Curtis MacDougall's meticulously documented and infinitely detailed history of the 1948 Progressive party seems almost prophetic. For whatever the swirling confusion, the calculated distortions of its opponents, the mistakes of Progressives, the personality conflicts that bedeviled contemporary comprehension of the Wallace movement, this history enables us to understand this "Quixotic Crusade" as a desperate attempt to reverse the tide which, less than twenty years later, has brought us to the brink of disaster.

Professor MacDougall is convinced that the defeat of Henry Wallace for the Vice Presidential nomination in 1944 made a third party all but inevitable. Many, and not only future Progressives, feared that this defeat marked the end of the New Deal. With the death of Franklin D. Roosevelt and Truman's assumption of the Presidency, this fear turned into a virtual certainty. More than ever, Wallace became, for millions of people, the legitimate heir of Franklin Roosevelt—the personification of an on-going New Deal. More important, after April, 1945, it seemed to many that the "Roosevelt approach" in foreign policy was to be jettisoned as well. Concern with what was considered to be a new direction in foreign relations —a "get tough" policy toward the Soviet Union coupled with an increased sidetracking of the United Nations—was from the start an important element in the growing dissatisfaction with the major parties.

Originally, third party talk in the labor movement stemmed from dissatisfaction over domestic issues, especially Truman's seizure of the coal mines, his threat to draft striking railroad workers, his request for anti-labor legislation, and his appointment of Wall Streeters, corporation officials and military men as replacements for New Dealers. This initial labor support was subsequently undercut by Truman's veto of the Taft-Hartley Bill, which was a major factor in destroying the possibility of an effective third party coalition. Many labor leaders became convinced that they could continue to gain concessions from the Democrats despite the Republican-Southern conservative bloc.

In the end, pressure for third party action persisted primarily among those elements in the society which were mainly preoccupied with foreign policy issues. The crucial question was whether it was possible to coexist with the Soviet Union, to settle differences by negotiation and compromise. Though many individuals, including Republican and Democratic Senators, had spoken out against the Truman-Byrnes policy—especially after Churchill's "Iron Curtain" speech at Fulton, Missouri, in March, 1946—it was the analysis of international affairs, presented by Wallace at Madison Square Garden, September 12, 1946, that sharply delineated the issues.

The violent reaction to Wallace's speech by conservatives long hostile is understandable, since it constituted a direct challenge to their basic premises about dealing with the Soviet Union and their conception of the proper role for the United States as *the* world power. But in reading the speech today one finds little justification for the denunciation by liberals that it advocated appeasement or was pro-Soviet in tone. As a matter of fact one understands more readily why the *Daily Worker* and American Communists were less than enthusiastic about its content. Read in the light of the past nineteen years of history, the speech, at the very least, sounds reasonable in analysis and often prophetic.

Wallace stressed that the price of peace for all nations is giving up prejudice, hatred, fear and ignorance. The United States must not hitch its foreign policy to Great Britain, a warning given by many American political leaders, and he warned that British policies in the Middle East might well provoke a Soviet reaction which could lead to war. "To prevent war and insure our survival in a stable world it is essential that we look abroad through our own American eyes . . ." Policy must not be guided by those who want war with Russia—that does not mean appeasement. "We want peace with Russia—but we want to be met halfway. We want cooperation." His acceptance of spheres of interest, the recognition that Eastern Europe was going to be primarily a concern of Russia, was criticized for undermining world unity, yet it was and is a fact of life not likely to be altered. He argued that the Soviet Union must be assured that German industry can never again be converted to military power against her, and the West must be convinced that the Soviet's Germany policy will not be directed against Western Europe. Failure to resolve this issue and the active remilitarization of West German are not insignificant elements in the East-West tension today. Finally, it was argued that the United Nations must be strengthened as rapidly as possible, even though it is apparent that we are not yet ready for world federation. "Realistically, the most we can hope for now is a safe reduction in military expense and a long period of peace based on mutual trust between the Big Three."

This, Wallace believed, was the basic issue for the 1946 Congressional campaign and the Presidential election in 1948.

No one can conclusively prove that a less hostile approach by the United States would have produced Soviet moderation, but the results of twenty years of the "get tough" policy seem visible enough: it is hard to believe that the security of the United States or the peace of the world has been much enhanced since 1945. Many reputable scholars believe that the United States' refusal to even consider a Soviet request in 1945 for a loan and the abrupt termination of lend-lease after V-E Day intensified suspicions, and convinced Soviet hard-liners that aggressive action was essential to its national security. This is the kind of evaluation on which reasonable men should be able to differ without acrimony, but in the climate created by the Cold War in the United States it became increasingly dangerous to question the bipartisan premises of the "get-tough" policy, a fact soon to be learned by Henry Wallace and many of his followers.

Measured by the number of votes recorded, 1,156,103, the Wallace-Taylor campaign was a dismal failure. It was overwhelmingly defeated, even when allowance is made for Progressive votes which were never counted. Only in three states was the Progressive vote large enough to enable Dewey to win, and in no other state did the party affect the outcome of Presidential or Congressional races. In the spring of 1948 many, including some professional politicians, had estimated that the Progressives might get as many as ten million votes, and Henry Wallace had always said that three million votes would justify the campaign. After the Philadelphia convention, support faded, and by mid-August polls reported that only five percent of the electorate would support Wallace-Taylor.

Understandably, some leaders of the Progressive party made quite excessive claims for the effectiveness of their campaign, claiming to have slowed down the reactionary trend in domestic politics, forcing the major parties to examine the bipartisan foreign policy, and stimulating voter interest in an otherwise dull campaign. One may discount this as partisan enthusiasm, but a distinguished historian, Prof. Ray A. Billington, has said the Progressive party was the most influential third party in American history. Traditionally, a third party has influenced major parties over a period of years by attracting enough support so that its program was gradually absorbed by the major parties. In this instance, Truman moved immediately to appropriate Progressive domestic planks, a phenomenon noted by the *Wall Street Journal:*

> It is said by political commentators that Mr. Wallace made a bad showing because he got few votes. What they neglect is that Mr. Wallace succeeded in having his ideas adopted, except in the field of foreign affairs. From the time that Mr. Wallace announced he would run for President, Mr. Truman began to suck the wind from the Wallace sails by coming out for more and more of the Wallace domestic program. Now these promises are in Mr. Truman's platform and the men who see eye to eye with Mr. Wallace on domestic, economic and social questions are

among those who can rightfully claim a share of the credit for Mr. Truman's victory. We have not any modified New Deal. What we have is the New Deal in its most extreme form . . .

Many believe that Truman never could have staged the upset victory had he persisted with his 1946 program. Inadvertently the existence of the Progressive party benefited Truman by drawing the Red-baiting normally directed against the Democrats. ". . . By contrast with the three preceding Presidential election campaigns, it wasn't Republicans who were yelling 'Red' at Democrats, rather it was Democrats yelling 'Red' at Progressives, while the Republicans smugly enjoyed the spectacle in the firm belief that nothing could prevent their victory."

As already noted, it was in the area of foreign policy that the Progressives failed most signally to have any effect. Not only were they unable to shake the bipartisan stance toward the Soviet Union, but increasingly Soviet actions seemed geared to doom their appeal for moderation in foreign policy. The Czechoslovakian coup in February and the Berlin blockade in June, 1948, caused many to question whether it was possible to achieve normal diplomatic relations with the Soviet Union. Many potential supporters now concluded that Progressive proposals for negotiations with the USSR were either futile, or evidence of soft-headed appeasement.

The demise of the Progressive party also meant the collapse of the only movement that might conceivably have made a contribution in keeping alive a genuine discussion of foreign policy alternatives. Professor MacDougall points to three basic weaknesses within the party which hastened its fall. First was the fact that the movement was built around, and became dependent upon, a single personality. All previous third parties developed over a period of time, and derived from dissatisfactions on bread-and-butter issues which directly affected a large number of people. Having a broad base, previous protest parties gradually developed leadership, but were rarely, if ever, dependent upon a single person. Secondly, the Progressive party support came primarily from middle-class professional people, liberal dissenters with faith that problems could be solved without radical transformation either of institutions or ideas. They lacked unity of purpose, were not accustomed to the unspectacular drudgery of organized politics, and MacDougall also feels that many were prima donnas, who departed when they were defeated on a pet issue. Finally, there was the role played by the Communists.

It appears, from the evidence presented by MacDougall, as well as by other scholars, that it is simply wrong to give Communists credit either for creation of the party or for significant influence on its policy as of 1948. Their greatest contribution was a tremendous energy, and hard work in particular districts. Over a period of time, this was to change, as more and more non-Communists withdrew, the result both of Soviet intransigeance, which appeared to justify the hard-line policy, and of social pressure, stimulated by Red-baiting and the distortions of the mass media. Though many Progressives felt at the time, and continued to feel, that a firm non-Com-

x

munist declaration might have saved the situation, I am more skeptical. Perhaps, had the Communist party run its own candidates and its own campaign, the effect of Red-baiting might have been minimized. Certainly, denial and even repudiation of Communist support didn't protect the La Follette movement from Red-baiting in 1924, and the vehement anti-Communism of Americans for Democratic Action had done little to dissuade its enemies. Moreover, MacDougall concludes that "given Wallace's views toward the world situation it would have been impossible for him to have repudiated the Communists in the way that his critics demanded." He was convinced, and undoubtedly at the time a majority of non-Communist Progressives agreed, that to have done so would further undermined civil liberties and destroyed the basis of his criticism of American policy. To believe that the passage of the Vermont Resolution at the Philadelphia Convention would have significantly changed the atmosphere or led to honest news coverage of the Progressive party is unrealistic. Wallace had long since gained the active enmity of powerful political leaders, North and South, because they really believed he meant to restore the New Deal, suspended since 1938, and implement its ideals. They had defeated him in 1944, and nothing would have altered their determination to drive him from public life.

This examination of the Communist issue reinforces the conclusion that the Progressive party fell victim not merely to its internal weaknesses but to the national mood. A climate had developed by 1948 in which criticism, dissent from official assumption, or even the discussion of alternative policies was not only deemed heretical but un-American and traitorous.

How did this climate of doubt, suspicion, and fear come to dominate? The approved explanation holds that it was the dawning realization that the Soviet Union was out to conquer the world and in order to do so had created a vast, diabolically clever international conspiracy. So clever, in fact, that its minions were assumed to be able to manipulate individuals and organizations to Soviet ends without the awareness of those involved. For those satisfied by this fantasy, it was sufficient justification for any measures taken in the name of national security. One cannot exaggerate the impact on the United States of this reaction to a world in revolution. The logic of the Cold War and the resulting policies have affected every aspect of American life. It may be seen in the distortion of science, the merging of educational institutions with the state apparatus, and the undermining of traditional democratic safeguards against concentrated arbitrary power. In the name of security we have discouraged dissent, opposition, political debate of alternative policies. We have come increasingly to justify official deceit.

Though the Truman Administration introduced the loyalty program, both Republican and Democratic administrations have contributed to the anti-Communist phobia. House and Senate committees have for twenty years provided a steady stream of "documents" which lend credence to the wildest fears and charges. A major role in sustaining the fear has been played by J. Edgar Hoover, who has consistently exaggerated the importance of domestic Communism, praised and cooperated with the various Congressional committees, and given moral support to those who attack defenders—including the Supreme Court—of civil liberties. The plain fact is that, since 1938, the "disease theory" of Communism has been used to discredit the New Deal, as well as every continuing movement for social betterment in the country, from civil rights to "socialized" medicine. The thesis that there had been Communists in various agencies during the 1930-40 period was elaborated to claim that they had determined policy and infected the whole government. Ultimately expanded to include all institutions in the society and in other countries, the theory of Communists as "Typhoid Marys" served both to justify the violations perpetrated by Congressional committees, the loyalty programs, and American interventions in the affairs of other governments. Most tragically, a frightened liberalism succumbed to the same paranoia, a fact clearly demonstrated in the savage attack by liberals on the Progressive party. Because there were Communists in the party, every conflict, mistake, or disapproved policy position was seized upon as evidence of Communist control, and proof of the existence of a Kremlin-inspired conspiracy. Anyone reading this record may see the pattern it set for the McCarthy era and understand better why liberals were ineffectual in resisting. They had long before accepted and acted upon McCarthy's premises, and were therefore reduced to wringing their hands over "his methods."

It may be that it is impossible to build a party, or a political movement, on foreign rather than domestic issues. There is a strong tendency for people either to ignore world problems, or to strongly support any action taken by an administration. American political institutions are simply inadequate for the democratic control or direction of foreign policy. The Progressive party was an attempt by some of the ablest, most conscientious and devoted Americans to make the country aware of the implications of Cold War policies. They attempted to keep the channels of communication and public debate open. Their failure meant that some of the ablest critics of foreign policy and American society were politically immobilized and ultimately silenced. The absence of a viable Left, providing a fundamental critique of society and of national policy, has led to a deterioration in the quality of political discussion. In fact, we have now reached the point where discussion itself is suspect. A recent Harris Poll reports that, of those people aware of the teach-ins on our foreign policy in Vietnam, "the weight of public opinion, by a 3 to 2 margin, views the campus-originated debates not as a healthy sign . . . but as a harmful activity while U.S. troops are fighting abroad." (Los Angeles *Times,* June 21, 1965)

It may be appropriate to conclude by making explicit my own response to the Progressive party in 1948. Though emotionally attracted by the idea of third party action, and convinced of the inadequacy of the major parties, I did not participate. The decision was difficult because I agreed with much of the Progressive analysis, and continued to remain skeptical about Harry S. Truman. Further, many for whom I had great affection and respect became deeply involved at great personal sacrifice. I agreed with Professor Ray A. Billington's propositions: "first, that in a nation politically constituted as is the United States, third parties are vitally necessary for progress; and second, that in the past they have proved more influential in securing progressive change than have the established parties." But I was convinced that there was insufficient time to build an effective organization. I thought A. Philip Randolph was right in insisting that an intensive educational program was an essential prerequisite, and that the absence of labor and farm support would render the effort futile. A second factor in this decision was the conviction that Henry Wallace did not have the personal attributes necessary for a party leader. Highly intelligent, perceptive in his analysis of likely world developments, principled in his concern for mankind, he was in many ways a prophetic spokesman for all that is best in the American conservative tradition. At the same time, he seemed totally lacking as a politician; perhaps as much because of his virtues as his weaknesses, he had no political "feel." (Professor MacDougall concludes that Wallace never made a decision for "political reasons.") He also failed to provide firm leadership where it would have clarified vital issues within the party.

I was, rightly or wrongly, convinced that Wallace could make his greatest contribution by repudiating any personal political aspirations, while continuing his appeal to reason in foreign affairs. In effect, this might have meant not a third party, for the Progressive party was peculiarly the creation of Henry Wallace, but rather a political movement which might have had time to mature without the early trauma of shattered hopes and heroes. A political movement can devote its energy to education, to presenting its analysis of issues, to stimulating debate, arousing controversy, and building support. It need not have become involved in the expense in time and energy of building the many-tiered structure essential to a political party. Not directly challenging politicians seeking office, it may still exert considerable influence on those pursuing votes. Currently, one might cite the Right Wing or the civil rights movement, which remain powerful, though not as one usually judges a political party—by its ability to elect officials. Of course, a political movement may, if it broadens its appeal and gains committed supporters, become a party.

Historians will be grateful to Professor MacDougall for what surely must be the most extensive treatment of a third party published in this country. They will find invaluable this detailed chronology of events, from the time Henry A. Wallace was rejected for the Vice Presidential nomination in 1944 to the demise of the Progressive party. These volumes are based on contemporary reporting, private records and, most important, hundreds of interviews with almost everyone of importance to the movement, including many who opposed the decision to form a third party. Though MacDougall was an active participant, running as Progressive candidate for the United States Senate in Illinois, he has achieved a remarkable degree of objectivity in reporting the most controversial issues, evaluating the principal personalities, and weighing strengths and weaknesses, successes and failures, of the movement. He may well have come as close to "the truth" as is humanly possible.

# FOREWORD

Much historical writing suffers because it is done a generation or more after the key figures have died and valuable records have been lost. It is based on written records, minutes, reports and the like which often do not reveal the debates and in-fighting that took place before resolutions or motions were put into the final form available to the researcher.

The Progressive party of 1948 is now part of American history and already a dozen master's theses and doctoral dissertations have been written about it and around it. With rare exceptions they contribute little new knowledge. The master's theses (they are called essays at Columbia University) are usually rewritings of the *New York Times*. Doctoral dissertations are usually attempts to prove certain hypotheses, so that much of the content is selected to buttress preconceived conclusions. They include references to relevant books and sometimes an interview or two. Primarily, however, they too rely heavily on that newspaper of record, the *New York Times*.

No one respects the *Times* more than I do, but it is not infallible and, particularly in its coverage of the 1948 campaign, it was swayed by the historical passions of the times. Further, its reporters had the same difficulty in getting news sources to talk as plagued others. I have endeavored to fill the gap by interviewing nearly everyone of any importance who was connected with the formation of the Progressive party and its campaign in 1948, including many prominently opposed to the venture. My interviewing took place early, while memories were fresh and documentary material was still intact. I know of nothing of importance that was withheld from me except in the few instances mentioned in the text.

As a participant in the 1948 campaign, some historians may argue, I disqualify myself. No one, the tenet runs, can write objectively about events in which he is involved. There is merit to this argument, but there is equal, if not greater, merit to a counter-proposition, to wit, that no one who was *not* a part of those events could have gathered and understood much of this material. I acted as an open-minded reporter who does his fact-finding first and makes his hypotheses or conclusions later, on the basis of his discoveries. The overwhelming majority of those interviewed were unknown to me in 1948 and I was ignorant of most of the material in this book until I uncovered it.

My credentials are those of both a social scientist and journalist. I have worked for six newspapers and a press association as reporter, editor, and editorial writer, and have edited an almanac and a news map. My Ph.D. was in social psychology and I have taught journalism in three universities over the past 35 years. Since 1942 I have been professor of journalism at Northwestern University. I belong to a number of scholarly organizations and have some ten books to my credit as well as numerous monographs and articles in scholarly journals. Whatever passions may have swayed me 18 years ago have mellowed with time. Today I have no axe to grind and my motivations are presented here so that the reader may judge for himself.

1. *To preserve the record.* The Progressive party of 1948 was an episode in American political history. I have explained the unreliability or rather the incompleteness of written records and opine that unless I or someone else undertook this task at this time, it could not be done later.

2. *To provide a case study in political behavior.* The sheer details of how the Progressive party originated and ran its campaign ought to cast light on political behavior as a whole. Most political treatises are general, stressing theories and principles. The literature describing detailed operations is limited.

3. *To "place" the party in historical perspective.* Roughly, the chronological period covered by the narrative is from the end of World War II (or the death of Franklin Delano Roosevelt) to the outbreak of the Korean War in 1950. Nevertheless, it is necessary to consider events both before and since that time span to give perspective to it. There have been a number of third party attempts throughout American history; how does this attempt fit into the tradition?

4. *To record something of the "feel" of the movement.* What did it mean to the thousands who worked slavishly for it? Why did so many risk or sacrifice so much? What kind of people were they? No matter what evaluation the historians or cultural anthropologists of the future may put upon the movement, its "spirit"—meaning the prevailing attitudes and opinions of its members—is important to know.

5. *To discover any "lessons" that the episode provided.* Those in labor and liberal circles, who have thought of the possibility of an eventual new political party will be most interested in any such lessons. The question is posed: Why did the Wallace movement fail so badly? What mistakes should any group in the future avoid?

Throughout the book I have cited the names of many who cooperated with me in my fact-finding, usually in connection with use of material so obtained. A complete list of those who helped—by granting interviews, conducting them for me, correspondence, providing records, clippings and the like, copying from microfilmed material and in other ways—would run into the hundreds.

Because there were scores of others who requested to remain anonymous, any list would be inadequate or misleading as an index to my source material. To all who assisted me, therefore, I extend my heartfelt thanks. And to the Louis H. Rabinowitz Foundation my deep appreciation for a timely grant without which this history probably would not have been completed or published.

CURTIS D. MACDOUGALL

Evanston, Ill.
July 1, 1965

# THE STORY OF GIDEON

*According to chapters 6 to 8 inclusive, of the Book of Judges, Gideon was an Israelite farmer who led a successful revolt in the 12th century B.C. against the Midianites, who had ruled his people for seven years. Obeying the commands of an angel, Gideon destroyed an altar of Baal and assembled an army of 32,000. Of these, 22,000 departed when Gideon asked only the fearless to remain. Then he reduced the remaining 10,000 to 300 by noting whether they remained alert while drinking from a stream. He equipped each of them with a trumpet and a pitcher containing a lamp. In the dark the Midianites were routed by the sound of the trumpets, the breaking of the pitchers and the light of the lamps which surrounded them. They fled in confusion, fighting among themselves, and Gideon became ruler of Israel for 40 years.*

# I

## THE COMPONENTS OF THE DECISION

# ¶1 THE BEGINNING. *Henry A. Wallace's failure to win renomination for Vice President in 1944 indicated the intensity of the liberal-conservative split in the Democratic party and made likely, if not inevitable, a splinter third party in 1948.*

On the evening of Thursday, July 20, 1944, my wife and I sat with about 25,000 others in the Chicago Stadium, waiting for the fourth session of the Democratic national convention to begin.

Neither of us was a delegate, but I was the Democratic candidate that year for the United States House of Representatives from the old 10th Illinois congressional district. Consequently we had excellent seats, about forty feet to the right of, and slightly above, the speakers' platform.

The highlight of the session was the acceptance speech of Franklin Delano Roosevelt, made by radio from his railroad car in the naval reservation at San Diego, California. With only 90 dissenting votes out of a total of 1174, FDR had been renominated on the first ballot that afternoon.

The political battle at that 1944 convention was over the Vice Presidency. For days the papers had been full of speculative articles on the progress of the "stop Wallace" movement and it was obvious that Vice President Wallace was fighting for his political life. The big city bosses— Edward J. Kelly of Chicago and the Bronx's Edward J. Flynn especially —and such conservative Democratic bigwigs as Edwin W. Pauley, national treasurer; George Allen, Frank Walker and especially National Chairman Hannegan were dead set against his renomination. FDR seemed to be playing an ambiguous role.

The convention had opened on Wednesday, July 19. At the afternoon session on Thursday, July 20, Sen. Samuel D. Jackson of Indiana, the permanent chairman, read a letter from the President:

Hyde Park, N. Y.
July 14, 1944

My Dear Senator Jackson:

In the light of the probability that you will be chosen as permanent chairman of the convention, and because I know that many rumors accompany all conventions, I am wholly willing to give you my own personal thought in regard to the selection of a candidate for Vice President. I do this at this time because I expect to be away from Washington for the next few days.

The easiest way of putting it is this: I have been associated with Henry Wallace during this past four years as Vice President, for eight years earlier while he was Secretary of Agriculture, and well before that. I like him and I respect him and he is my personal friend. For these reasons I personally would vote for his renomination if I were a delegate to the convention.

At the same time I do not wish to appear in any way as dictating to the convention. Obviously the convention must do the deciding. And it should—and I am sure it will—give great consideration to the pros and cons of its choice.

Very sincerely yours,

FRANKLIN D. ROOSEVELT

The same day, however, Hannegan had confirmed the rumors, originating largely from hints he himself had dropped, that there was a second communication from the President. This letter, which Hannegan had mimeographed and rushed to the headquarters of all the state delegations, read as follows:

July 19

Dear Bob,

You have written me about Harry Truman and Bill Douglas. I should, of course, be very glad to run with either of them and believe that either one of them would bring real strength to the ticket.

Always sincerely,

FRANKLIN ROOSEVELT

That afternoon Henry A. Wallace, in seconding the nomination of Franklin D. Roosevelt, had proved his statesmanship and political courage when he said in part:

6

The strength of the Democratic Party has always been the people—plain people like so many of those here in this convention, ordinary folks, farmers, workers and businessmen along Main Street. Jefferson, Jackson and Woodrow Wilson knew the power of the plain people. All three laid down the thesis that the Democratic Party can win only if and when it is the liberal party.

Wallace then went on to challenge those Democrats who for six years had united with Republicans to block many New Deal programs and who, four years later, were to be known as Dixiecrats with their own Presidential candidate. This is what he said, as given in the *Official Proceedings*, with the delegate reaction:

The future belongs to those who go down the line unswervingly for the liberal principles of both political democracy and economic democracy regardless of race, color or religion (applause and cheers). The poll tax must go (applause and cheers; boos). Equal educational opportunities must come (applause and cheers). The future must bring equal wages for equal work regardless of sex, or race (applause and cheers).

Milburn P. "Pete" Akers, then political editor of the *Chicago Sun,* tells me that the eminent columnist Thomas L. Stokes, tears running down his cheeks, leaped from his place in the press section, applauding wildly and declaring, "It's wonderful; it's marvelous; it's beautiful. But, goddamn it, it isn't smart politics!"

As the evening began there were few placards and banners bearing the names of any candidates. As FDR's acceptance speech drew to a close, however, some Truman placards began popping up. And then, just when it seemed that the opportunity was to be lost, it came—the Wallace parade, with placards, banners and signs. And mostly, the Wallace cheers. It was contended, of course, that the galleries had been packed by the Wallace supporters, meaning chiefly the Political Action Committee of the Congress of Industrial Organizations (CIO-PAC). That was not so. Those galleries were packed by the Cook County (Kelly) Democratic machine. CIO-PAC had been given exactly 100 tickets for that session and there were about 25,000 persons in the Stadium, with about half as many more in the streets outside. CIO-PAC *had* prepared a demonstration which it hoped would come off, but the meager $100 which the leader of demonstrators outside the building had been given, to use in case there was difficulty getting by the gatekeepers, was not needed.

Furthermore it was not the CIO-PAC, leaders or rank-and-filers, who started the demonstration when it came. Rather it was a small group led by Sen. Claude A. Pepper of Florida. In a letter to me dated Dec. 12, 1954, he described what happened:

After President Roosevelt had accepted the nomination and the audience was uplifted by his stirring words, a group of us decided to start a parade for the nomination of Henry Wallace for Vice President. With the Florida standard and several of us in the vanguard, the parade started and was joined immediately by many other enthusiastic supporters of Wallace. Pretty soon the aisles were filled with the marching enthusiasts. After we had been around three times, as I recall, I stepped up on my chair by the middle aisle where I sat as chairman of the Florida delegation and looked over the parade to see the strength of it. I was surprised by the number of state standards and Wallace placards in the parade, as well as by the evident enthusiasm, not only of the marchers, but of many other delegates and of the galleries.

After I had surveyed the scene for a little while it occurred to me (knowing as I did of the conflicting letters which had come in from President Roosevelt about the Vice Presidential nomination and of the efforts being made to defeat Wallace's nomination) that if Wallace were to be nominated Vice President at all it would have to be then, and we should have to get the convention to proceed to the nomination of a Vice President at that time.

Of course, I knew that that event had not been scheduled for that evening. However, I began to wave my banner and to shout for recognition from the chairman. However, struggle as I might I could not get his recognition. I was confident, however, that he had seen me and no doubt divined what I had in mind.

Finally I pushed my way up the middle aisle to the gate leading to the platform. Fortunately this was manned by an old friend of mine who readily let me on the stairway leading to the platform. When I got near the top of the stairway the chairman suddenly recognized someone standing near him who made a motion that the convention should then adjourn. The chairman quickly put the question and although the noes obviously overwhelmed the ayes the chair declared the ayes to have it and the convention adjourned. This action was followed by loud booing from a considerable part of the audience.

In *The Man of Independence* (J. B. Lippincott, 1950) Jonathan Daniels wrote that Major Edward J. Kelly of Chicago gave orders to allow the demonstrators to enter the Stadium "to give them their fling."

Well, I suppose I was a Kelly machine man myself inasmuch as I was endorsed by the regular Democratic organization. I yelled "We want Wallace" until I was hoarse and later I met many of those clerks, bailiffs, elevator operators and other patronage recipients who are the backbone of the Chicago Democratic political machine; they confessed they were as hoarse as I was that night. I had seen them, led by ward committeemen whom I knew, filling those gallery seats earlier in the evening, and it was they who put on the best part of the show, not the handful of CIO-PAC paraders who were let in on orders from Kelly. The demonstration, in other words, was genuine. Those people *did* want Wallace, just as the Gallup and other polls had shown 65 per cent of the registered Democrats did.

According to the *Official Proceedings,* at the conclusion of President Roosevelt's radio address the chairman remarked, "Ladies and gentlemen of the convention, we are packing these aisles until it is becoming dangerous. This has been a great day for the party, a great day for the country.

"I recognize Delegate David Lawrence from the State of Pennsylvania for the purpose of making a motion."

Then Boss Lawrence said, "Mr. Chairman, I move that this fourth session of the Democratic national convention recess until tomorrow, Friday, July 21, 1944, at 11:30 a.m."

Reads the *Proceedings:*

"The Chairman: As many as favor will signifiy by saying 'aye.' Contrary 'no.' The 'ayes' have it. The meeting is recessed, to reconvene at 11:30 o'clock Friday morning, July 21, 1944.

"The meeting recessed at 10:55 p.m."

These "proceedings" are of little help to a research scholar who wants to know what went on. The same, of course, goes for most other printed "official proceedings" for all political parties, including the Progressive party; and for the minutes of labor organizations, businessmen's associations and liberal groups; in fact, I'd say for organizations of all sorts. At least, I know of no exceptions.

During the space of time supposedly covered by the portion of the *Proceedings* I have quoted, there was bedlam in the Chicago Stadium. Wallace signs were everywhere. The organ was playing "Iowa" and everyone was singing as much of it as he knew, usually only the last line, "That's where the tall corn grows." Daniels says the organist changed the tune only when someone, under orders, threatened to cut the wires from his instrument to the public address system. The galleries were in an uproar; rank and file Democratic workers were grabbing the signs and banners which the Wallace supporters had distributed and were using them. Unless delegates and spectators were just demonstrating out of sheer exhilaration, if a vote—an honest, unbossed vote—had been taken of the entire house that night, Henry A. Wallace would have been renominated in a landslide.

Claude Pepper says he heard someone make a motion and Senator Jackson call for a vote. The Florida senator was on the stairway leading to the platform at the time. I was about forty feet away and I heard no motion or vote. All that most of us who were there knew was that suddenly the chairman banged his gavel and walked off the platform, followed by his entourage, leaving it vacant. Slowly the tumult died down and we all started for home.

The next day Senator Jackson said (in essence) to Senator Pepper:

"Claude, I hated to do what I had to do to you last night. I knew,

9

of course, for what purpose you were seeking the platform. But it had been agreed by the authorities governing the convention that the Vice Presidential nomination should be postponed until the next day, and I felt it my duty as chairman to see that that determination was carried out. I hope you understand."

In the Sept. 14, 1944 issue of *Social Action*, a publication of the Congregational Christian Church, Wilfred E. Binkley, leading political historian, wrote:

> Every element in the convention reminiscent of the Jacksonian Democratic tradition—the interest of the common men—shouted for Wallace. So irresistible were they that the will of the delegates had to be overwhelmed by intrigue, manipulation and main force on the part of the interests that could not tolerate the idea of Wallace as President of the United States.

On Friday, July 21, 1944, I was unable to attend the afternoon (fifth) session of the convention, but I had expected to return for the evening (sixth) session. Shortly before the dinner hour I began listening to the radio reports. The voting on the Vice Presidency was in progress, and the radio announcers revealed that it had been decided to keep the convention in continuous session without recess. Otherwise, those holding tickets for the afternoon session alone would be ineligible and those with tickets for the evening would be able to take their places. Those evening ticket holders were the same Democratic party rank and file who had defied their bosses the night before to join the Wallace claque. They had to be kept out at all cost. When I heard the news by radio I naturally knew it would do me no good to go to the Stadium, so I remained before the receiving set. Out of 1,176 votes on the first ballot, Henry A. Wallace had 429½ and Truman 319½, the rest being scattered among "favorite son" candidates.

On the second ballot, at one point Wallace reached a high of 484, which was still far short of the 589 needed to win. After Senator Bankhead of Alabama withdrew as a candidate and announced that the Alabama vote should be changed to 22 for Truman and two for Wallace, the rest of the voting was anticlimactic. At the end, Wallace still had 105 diehard votes, Truman had 1,031 and 27 were scattered.

Reminiscing, Mark Sullivan wrote in the *New York Post* for April 16, 1945: "Defeat of Henry A. Wallace for nomination was more than just the defeat of a candidate . . . It was the interruption of the New Deal as, so to speak, an ideological dynasty."

That Friday afternoon, July 21, 1944, however, Sullivan and nearly everyone else did not realize what later became obvious: that in the Chicago Stadium *a new national political party to the left of the Democratic party had become inevitable in 1948.*

Several liberal analysts attempted to be comforting by seeking the dark cloud's silver lining. In *PM* for Aug. 1, 1944, Max Lerner wrote:

10

I suppose . . . that the hardest blow to progressives during the past few years has been the defeat of Henry Wallace at Chicago. But I think it is a mistake to regard it as an unalloyed defeat. The heartening thing to me is how close a man like Wallace came to sweeping a hard-boiled convention. Don't forget that some pretty powerful forces were arrayed against Wallace. Don't forget that he had expressed the most candidly progressive ideas of any man in high public life. No fight is lost which can afford either that daring or that integrity. The fight over Wallace was not a rear-guard action, but a vanguard action in which we fought for something new, in a new spirit and didn't quite make it. Some day we will.

And in "The Liberals After Chicago," in the Aug. 7, 1944 *New Republic,* Bruce Bliven wrote:

Actually, liberalism showed more strength at the Chicago Democratic Convention than it has ever done before in normal times in American politics. It was able to veto Jimmie Byrnes for Vice President. It showed so much strength that at one time the bosses were badly frightened by it . . . Indeed, with a little more skill, a little more preliminary work, the liberals might have won on their most important issue, the renomination of Henry Wallace.

Despite the treatment he had received, Henry Wallace campaigned for the Roosevelt-Truman ticket throughout 1944. As a reward FDR offered him the position of Secretary of Commerce, which he asked Jesse Jones to resign. He did so, however, in such a seemingly ungracious manner that liberals were astounded and inclined to regard Wallace as more truly representative of their interests than FDR. According to both Grace Tully, FDR's long-time secretary, in *FDR, My Boss* (Charles Scribner's Sons, 1949), and Samuel Rosenman, for years FDR's chief speech writer, in *Working With Roosevelt* (Harper, 1952), FDR's uncharacteristic letter indicated his declining health. It read:

Dear Jesse:

This is a very difficult letter to write—first, because of our long friendship and splendid relations during all these years and also because of your splendid services to the government and the excellent way in which you have carried out the many difficult tasks during these years.

Henry Wallace deserves almost any service which he believes he can satisfactorily perform. I told him this at the end of the campaign, in which he displayed the utmost devotion to our cause, traveling almost incessantly and working for the success of the ticket himself, he gave of his utmost toward the victory which ensued.

11

He has told me that he thought he could do the greatest amount of good in the Department of Commerce for which he is fully suited. And I feel, therefore, that the Vice President should have this post in the new administration.

It is for this reason only that I am asking you to relinquish this present post for Henry and I want to tell you that it is in no way a lack of appreciation for all that you have done and that I hope you will continue to be part of the government.

During the next few days I hope you will think about a new post—there are several ambassadorships which are vacant or about to be vacated. I make this suggestion among many other posts, and I hope you will have a chance, if you think well of it, to speak to Ed Stettinius.

Finally, let me tell you that you have my full confidence and that I am very proud of all that you have done during these past few years.

With my warm regards,

Always sincerely,

FRANKLIN D. ROOSEVELT

To Wallace-ites that seemed most ungracious, as it put the appointment entirely on a political basis. Since then Grace Tully and Samuel Rosenman have opined that getting Jesse Jones out of the cabinet was more in Roosevelt's mind than getting Henry Wallace in; the reason being that FDR was convinced of the veracity of the reports he had received of Jones' behind-the-scenes opposition to both his third and fourth terms. The references to Wallace's political loyalty were "digs" at Jones' apostasy. Unofficially FDR used to refer to his Secretary of Commerce opprobriously as Jesus H. Jones.

When he received his dismissal letter, composed hastily on inauguration day, Jan. 20, 1945, on the eve of FDR's departure for Yalta, Jones showed his pique by releasing both it and his reply to the press. The pertinent paragraphs of that answer were the first two:

Dear Mr. President:

I have your letter of today, asking that I relinquish my post as Secretary of Commerce which carries with it the vast financial and war production agencies within the Reconstruction Finance Corporation and its subsidiaries so that you can give it to Henry Wallace as a reward for his support of you in the campaign.

You state that Henry thinks he could do the greatest amount of good in the Department of Commerce and that you consider him fully suited for the post. With all

12

due respect, Mr. President, while I must accede to your decision, I cannot agree with either of you.

Four days later, Jan. 24, 1945, Jones elaborated his thesis that Wallace was not competent to direct the lending agencies, which extended from $30 to $40 billion worth of credit annually to American corporations. The huge investment in war plants and materials, Jones argued, "should not be made the subject of careless experimentation." He added, "Certainly the RFC should not be placed under the supervision of any man willing to jeopardize the country's future with untried ideas and idealistic schemes."

Following Jones before the Senate Commerce Committee, Wallace said of his critics, "You know and I know that it is not a question of my 'lack of experience.' Rather, it is a case of not liking the experience I have." It took a whole page of the *New York Times* to print Wallace's prepared statement and more than another page for the highlights of his cross-examination. Two days later, the committee voted 14 to 5 in favor of the bill, proposed by Sen. Walter George of Georgia, to separate the lending powers from the Department of Commerce; at the same time, by an identical vote, they recommended that the nomination of Wallace for the cabinet position be disapproved by the Senate

The sharpness of the political lines that were being drawn was discernible in the statements of leaders in and out of government. On the one hand there was the opinion of Sen. Harry Byrd, who had received 89 of the 90 votes cast against the nomination of Franklin Roosevelt at Chicago: "Mr. Wallace is the leader of the most radical group in America. He is the close friend and close co-worker of Sidney Hillman and the extreme elements of the CIO. The maintenance of free enterprise means the preservation of our American way of life. It may well be that the action of the United States Senate on this appointment will have a decisive effect on the future of the free enterprise system."

By contrast James Loeb, Jr., executive secretary of the Union for Democratic Action, predecessor of Americans for Democratic Action, declared, "The 14 members of the Senate committee who voted against Wallace stand condemned before the American electorate for having betrayed the people's will. The fight is not for Henry Wallace the man but for the ideals for which he stands." At the time, I was recording secretary of the Chicago UDA chapter and in thorough agreement with Loeb. By mid-1948, as will be related, Loeb spoke quite differently when he tried to stampede the Platform committee at the Progressive party convention.

In his book *I Was There* (Whittlesey House, 1950) Admiral William D. Leahy, President Roosevelt's military aide, recalls that at least two messages reached President Roosevelt while he was at sea bound for the Yalta conference, urging his intervention in the fight to win Wallace's confirmation. The first was signed by Judge Samuel Rosenman on behalf of Secretary of the Treasury Henry Morgenthau, Jr., Mrs. Eleanor Roosevelt and others; it asked the President to issue an executive order to separate the functions of the Federal Loan Agency from the Department of Commerce to facilitate the confirmation. The second was from Mrs.

Roosevelt alone, asking her husband to do something in behalf of Henry Wallace. Commented Leahy, "The idealistic attitudes of Mrs. Roosevelt and Mr. Wallace were at that time not very different and appeared to me to be about equally impracticable." FDR, he said, did not seem much disturbed by the messages and, as far as is known, did nothing about the requests for help. A letter, written Feb. 2, 1945 from Yalta by FDR to his wife, explained that his failure to answer was because the ship was under "radio silence" owing to the proximity of an enemy submarine. The letter is included in Vol. II of *FDR, His Personal Letters*, edited by Elliott Roosevelt.

It was not until March 1, 1945 that the Senate confirmed Wallace, by a 56 to 32 vote; this was only after the George bill had passed the Senate 74 to 12, on Feb. 2, and the House, 399 to 2, on Feb. 17. Five Democrats were among those who voted against Wallace to the end: Byrd of Virginia; McCarran of Nevada; McKellar and Stewart of Tennessee; and O'Daniel of Texas.

March 1 was also the day that Franklin Roosevelt reported on the Yalta conference to a joint session of both houses of Congress and simultaneously by radio to the people of the United States and the world. A harbinger of things to come was the fact that the weakened President remained seated while he spoke, but to many who listened it seemed that his was the voice of prophecy, expressing the hopes and aspirations of all mankind; more than that, he was reporting on the first steps toward creation of the practical machinery to realize the dreams of a war-weary world:

> I come from the Crimean conference, my fellow Americans, with a firm belief that we have made a good start on the road to a world of peace . . . Days were spent in discussing these momentous matters and we argued freely and frankly across the table. But at the end, on every point, unanimous agreement was reached. And more important even than the agreement of word, I may say we achieved a unity of thought and a way of getting along together.

There was the essence of what seemed to old New Dealers to be important as regards Yalta: not just a new United Nations without the organizational weaknesses of the old League of Nations but *a new spirit of cooperation* between the leading nations, regardless of the differences in their forms of government or their social, economic and political ideologies.

When I asked Mayor Kelly why FDR had agreed to the dropping of HAW in 1944, his explanation was in essence: "He was not certain that he would live out his fourth term and he became convinced that Wallace, no matter how good he was, couldn't hold the Democratic party together after his death. With nobody able to predict in July, 1944 how long the war would continue, FDR believed that the best interests of the country and of the world required that the Democratic party remain united."

It was, of course, Kelly and others like him who caused FDR to reach

14

such a conclusion. Opinion differs sharply as to just when that occurred. In *27 Masters of Politics* (Funk & Wagnall, 1949) Raymond Moley wrote: "On the political front the demise of the BEW [Board of Economic Warfare] meant two things: that Mr. Wallace was not to be renominated and that the ideology of the New Deal had suffered a serious setback."

According to Presidential Secretary Jonathan Daniels in *The Man of Independence* (J. B. Lippincott, 1950), after the Jones-Wallace fracas of August, 1943 over the BEW, David Niles, another one of the secretaries "with a passion for anonymity," predicted Wallace never would be renominated. Nevertheless, Grace Tully insists that FDR had little or no use for Jones and wanted Wallace to continue in office. "I know because I heard him say so many times," she wrote. About three weeks before the convention, former Georgia Governor Ellis Arnall revealed in *The Shore Dimly Seen* (J. B. Lippincott, 1946), FDR told him he wanted Wallace renominated, declaring, "Henry is a great man, though some people don't understand him. He has courage and loyalty. Nobody has been more loyal." On June 27, 1944 the President told a small group, "Of course, everybody knows I'm for Wallace," according to Daniels, who says he was there. Nevertheless Rexford Guy Tugwell, then Governor of Puerto Rico, tells me that three or four days before the convention was to start, FDR advised him to stay away; the reason given was that "You won't like what's going to happen," meaning the ditching of Wallace.

Jonathan Daniels expressed doubt of Russell Lord's statement, in *The Wallaces of Iowa* (Reynal & Hitchcock, 1947), that FDR virtually gave in on Wallace at a conference in January, 1944 with Democratic leaders. Daniels, however, gives the most detailed account of how those bosses worked on FDR for well over six months. They obtained the cooperation of Gen. Edwin "Pa" Watson, FDR's military aide, to "screen" FDR's visitors so that only anti-Wallace party leaders got to see him. Early in the year, Democratic leader Flynn discloses, FDR asked him to tour the country, partly to sound out party leadership sentiment as to Wallace. Upon his return Flynn says he reported that, even with CIO support, Wallace would doom the ticket if renominated.

Instigator and chief promulgator of both the anti-Wallace and the pro-Truman drives was Robert E. Hannegan; he became national chairman of the Democratic party in January, 1944, at which time the *St. Louis Post-Dispatch* editorialized that the appointment boosted Truman's chances for the Vice Presidency. This was so because of Truman's stubborn insistence in 1942 that Hannegan be named Collector of Internal Revenue in St. Louis and, in 1943, United States Commissioner of Internal Revenue, putting him in political debt to Truman.

In the *New York Times* for April 7, 1946, Rosenman stated categorically that Harry S. Truman was the personal selection of FDR. In an article entitled "Franklin Roosevelt: One Year After," he wrote: "Harry S. Truman was picked by Franklin Delano Roosevelt and by no one else. I make this statement not on information or belief or hearsay. I make it as a matter of personal knowledge." Rosenman's book makes clear that he had in mind a meeting in late June, 1944 between FDR and Hannegan, at which the President declared his disinclination to "go through a convention like 1940 again." Rosenman, however, was *not present* at what he and others say was the decisive session July 11, 1944; it was attended by Hannegan; Kelly; Frank Walker; Flynn; George Allen; John Boettiger, FDR's son-in-law; and—Daniels says—also by Anna Boettiger, the President's daughter; and most importantly, by Edwin W. Pauley.

At that meeting, everyone agrees, it was taken for granted that Wallace was to be dropped and the political strength of all other potential candidates was discussed in detail. Leading and most aggressive contender at the moment was James F. Byrnes, who, however, was considered ineligible because of opposition from labor, especially the CIO, and Negroes; also because of his early conversion from Catholicism to Protestantism, which, some thought, would count against him with Catholic voters. At the end of the conference, which agreed, as Flynn put it, that Truman "just dropped into the slot," Rosenman says FDR asked Walker to inform Byrnes that he could not be supported. Nevertheless, Flynn relates, when he arrived in Chicago four days later Hannegan excitedly told him, "It's all over. It's Byrnes." Kelly, he said, had agreed to stop agitation for Illinois Senator Scott Lucas, but Byrnes insisted that FDR had given him the "green light." Harry Truman authorized William Hillman to say in *Mr. President* that this was Byrnes' contention on July 14, 1944, when he phoned Truman to ask him to make the nominating speech in his behalf at the convention.

In *All in One Lifetime* (Harper, 1958), Byrnes declared that his confidence was based on a telephone conversation on June 12 or 13 with FDR, in which the latter told him, "You are the best qualified man in the whole outfit . . . You must not get out of the race. If you stay in you are sure to win."

"There is no doubt in my mind that President Roosevelt did say to many men that the convention in Chicago would be an open one," Flynn wrote. However, the encouragement that he gave Byrnes, which caused the South Carolinian to remain in the race almost up to the time the balloting began, was nowhere near as confusing as his attitude toward Vice President Wallace.

Apparently FDR remained indifferent for many months to the entreaties of the Democratic leaders whom Hannegan and others sent to see him and Watson admitted. Finally, however, the pressure became so great that, as Kelly told me, FDR became convinced that Wallace was too unpopular with the party leaders to be a wise choice. In June, 1944 the Vice President had gone to China as FDR's emissary to Chiang Kai-shek— "to see if I could persuade him to do a little fighting," Wallace told me —and he was due back about a week before the convention was to open. Rosenman details in his book the effort he made, at FDR's request, to meet Wallace somewhere in the Western part of the United States and accompany him back to Washington, so that he could break the news to him that the President wanted him to withdraw as a candidate for renomination. Wallace's office staff evidently became suspicious and did not cooperate in contacting Wallace. Finally Wallace wired Rosenman that he wanted to see FDR first. It happened that his plane was forced down in Canada because of the illness of one of the pilots, after which it flew home nonstop.

Accompanied by Harold L. Ickes, who to Rosenman's regret had persuaded FDR to allow him to join in making contact with Wallace, Rosenman had a breakfast conversation with Wallace on Tuesday, July 11, the day after the Vice President's return to Washington. Although he stated the case in very strong language, he got nowhere. Instead Wallace said, "Sam, I've just come back from a country where people are dying by the hundreds of thousands because of lack of food. They and their children and grandchildren have nothing to look forward to in the future but a continuance of that kind of life—whether there is war or peace. In the face of my experience in China, I have no interest now in discussing political matters. I shall do so eventually with the President."

Wallace did intimate that if convinced that FDR wanted him to step down, he would do so. He refused, however, to commit himself to Rosenman or any other intermediary. Maybe the presence of Ickes, who had been Wallace's bitter enemy through many long years in the cabinet —which fact the *Ickes Diaries* (Simon & Schuster, 1954) eloquently verify —had a dampening effect. Anyway, even before the breakfast in question, Wallace had been invited to lunch at the White House. It was a two-hour affair and there is only one living person who knows what happened. He is Henry A. Wallace, who has never chosen to make public a complete statement. Rosenman relates that FDR was evasive when questioned about the session. At subsequent meetings with the President on July 12 and 13, Wallace presumably acquainted FDR with the results of Gallup polls, which showed approximately 65 percent of registered Democratic voters favoring his renomination, while only 2 percent were for Truman. Also, HAW was able to report that Harold Young, his administrative assistant and political advisor, was certain that close to 300 delegates were already pledged to him. At this, Russell Lord says, FDR blurted, "I'll be damned." At Wallace's request, FDR wrote the letter to Senator Jackson (reprinted earlier). Lord confirms what Wallace also told me, that his most vivid recollection of his visits that week with Roosevelt was the President's placing his hand on his arm and saying, "I hope it's the same team again, Henry."

That may have been—in fact probably was—FDR's real feeling. It seems to me that, although he felt compelled to give in to Hannegan, Flynn, Kelly and the other party leaders to the extent of writing the second letter, he secretly hoped that Wallace would be able to defeat them at the convention. Anyway, here were two letters, written not more than 48 hours apart, giving both sides support and thus virtually removing Roosevelt from the final decision-making; it was a Pilate-like gesture.

Maybe the two letters were written the same day. Rosenman says that Hannegan remained after the July 11 conference to ask for a Presidential letter saying "It's Truman"; when he came down from FDR's study he whispered to Frank Walker, "I got it." The next morning, July 12, Hannegan returned to the White House to have Grace Tully type a copy on White House stationery. According to Rosenman, the original handwritten note now is in the possession of Hannegan's widow.

Grace Tully has complicated the task of the fact-finder by writing that the original letter, eventually typed by Dorothy Brady, one of her assistants, named Douglas ahead of Truman and that the letter was re-

17

written in Chicago three days later, after Hannegan conferred with the President in his railroad car there. She says Hannegan himself told her FDR wanted the letter rewritten, to put Truman's name first, and that was done. Elliott Roosevelt accepted Miss Tully's account in a footnote on page 1524 of *F.D.R., His Personal Letters, 1928-1945,* Vol. II (Duell, Sloan, Pearce, 1950). Rosenman, however, rather vigorously denies it, and Daniels quotes Pauley as declaring the letter wasn't written in Washington at all, but was scribbled by FDR on an envelope in the railroad car in Chicago and later typed up, either by Miss Tully or someone else. Flynn implied that it was written even later, while FDR was en route to the West Coast, after Kelly insisted on seeing a written statement from the President that Truman was his first choice. Walker confirms Hannegan's story. Leahy wrote that after the train left Chicago, the President told him that he had recommended Truman, and that was the first intimation that close advisor of FDR had of his preference. On the other hand, Robert Sherwood in *Roosevelt and Hopkins,* Vol. II, page 529 (Harper, 1948), quotes an even closer advisor, Harry Hopkins, to the effect that FDR decided on Truman very early.

If all of this weren't confusing enough, Elliott Roosevelt included in the published collection of his father's letters one dated July 17, 1944, to former Sen. George W. Norris of Nebraska, which contained the following:

"I am honestly trying to keep out of the Vice Presidential contest, which includes a score of active candidates and another score who have their lightning rods up and would like to be struck. The only thing I have done is to write a letter to Senator Jackson, the permanent chairman, expressing my close friendship for Wallace and telling the convention that if I were a delegate I would vote for him."

All of which confirms the fact that often the Strong Man in politics, deliberately or otherwise, puts even his closest associates in the positions of the blind men studying the elephant. It also suggests the question: How important is it to ascertain the detailed facts of any historic occasion? In this project I am attempting to do just that, largely by means of the eyewitness accounts of persons who helped make the history concerned. There still is a better chance to do that, it seems to me, by accumulating the testimony of the living, rather than waiting until a generation or a century after they are dead. In this particular instance, since the result was the same, it makes little difference whether you believe Miss Tully or Hannegan, but in others it might matter a great deal.

As regards the part he played in bringing about his own nomination, Harry Truman's own version—as related by Rosenman *with a statement that Truman had read the passages and called them factually correct* and as told in *Mr. President* (Farrar, Straus, 1952)—is that he played "hard to get" until after Roosevelt was renominated on July 20. Then, from a room in the Blackstone hotel, with Walker, Flynn, Kelly and Truman present, Hannegan talked long distance with FDR in San Diego. Upon being informed that the Missouri Senator was being mulish, both accounts say, the President declared that such an attitude was endangering the future of the Democratic party and the country as a whole in wartime. According to this story, then and then only did Truman consent to be a candidate; presumably, Hannegan then hastily mimeographed and distributed the Roosevelt letter which, though written some time earlier, was dated July 19.

To put it mildly, Robert E. Allen and William V. Shannon were extremely skeptical regarding Truman's disclaimer of having been a candidate at an earlier date. In *The Truman Merry-Go-Round* (Vanguard, 1950) they wrote:

> The story of Truman's nomination for the Vice Presidency has been told many times. But the full story will never be known. One myth connected with it, however, should certainly be dispelled.

> This is the fiction that Truman received the nomination with no effort on his part and that, indeed, he took it with considerable reluctance and regret. Actually, he battled for it furiously and, in his way, very effectively . .

> Truman was feverishly active on the floor of the convention, backstage, in hotel lobbies and elsewhere, buttonholing and cajoling political bosses, cabinet officers and just plain delegates for their votes. When the nomination came to him, Harry Truman was a very proud, happy and self-satisfied man.

Two persons who were there told me that a day or two before the convention opened on July 19—that is, either on Monday the 17th, or Tuesday the 18th—Harry Truman went to the suite of CIO president Philip Murray, in the Hotel Morrison, to solicit his support for the Vice Presidential nomination. He was told abruptly that the CIO had only one candidate, Henry Wallace, so abruptly that Senator Truman didn't even sit down.

Harry Truman had known for some time that he was being considered. Daniels relates that on March 20, 1944, Truman, Sam Rayburn, Pauley, Senators Kilgore and Wallgren discussed the possibility of a Truman candidacy in Truman's hotel room in San Francisco and that, a week later at St. Louis, Rayburn proposed Truman. A July 4, 1944 entry in *The Forrestal Diaries* (Viking, 1951) is to the effect that on that day Truman told James V. Forrestal, Secretary of the Navy, that he was being urged to accept the Vice Presidential nomination. Forrestal wrote: "I told him it was his duty to take it in view of the fact that the alternative would be Henry Wallace. This alternative he regarded with the same misgivings as myself but still felt he did not want to take the nomination." In view of this it seems strange that Truman should have been "flabbergasted" when told July 20 by Hannegan that he was first choice, as related in *Mr. President*.

At dinner a week before the convention Murray and Sidney Hillman, chairman of the CIO Political Action Committee, had informed Hannegan that Byrnes was decidedly unacceptable to them as a candidate, which probably pleased Hannegan, who had Truman not too far up his sleeve.

Nevertheless, at that conference Hannegan hinted broadly that Byrnes had White House approval. In an article, "Henry Wallace: A Divided Mind," in the *Atlantic Monthly* for August, 1948, Gardner Jackson declared that a few months before the 1944 convention, C. B. Baldwin, assistant director of CIO-PAC; Clark Foreman, secretary of National Citizens PAC; and Sidney Hillman were ready to ditch Henry Wallace, but that Philip Murray refused to go along. This Baldwin denied, as regards himself and Foreman, in the same issue of that magazine. As for Sidney Hillman, however, the charge was by no means groundless, despite the fact that Hillman never openly deviated from the CIO line: Wallace and no second choice.

What Hillman did behind the scenes is another matter. On Sunday, July 16, occurred what might possibly be one of those seemingly small incidents on which the course of history depends. It was at a private breakfast between Hillman and Truman. As Daniels tells it, Truman tried to solicit Hillman's support for Byrnes, for whom he intended to give the nominating speech. "No," Hillman declared, "we're for Wallace but we might accept two other men. Our second choice after Wallace would be Douglas. I'm looking at our first choice now."

It is doubtful if Hillman ever told Murray about his breakfast with Truman. Despite the "front" they presented, the two men were intensely jealous of each other. Those who were close to Hillman in 1944 may have differed on some other details, but they all agreed that he was a constant and skillful maneuverer. As head of the CIO's new political arm, he thought it most important to "play ball" with the professional politicians. Murray, on the other hand, was adamant in his support of Wallace, whose nomination in 1940 he had helped considerably by persuading the Pennsylvania delegation to cast its votes for him. The night before the convention began, Murray asked Baldwin to inform Hannegan that if Wallace were not renominated he would cause every CIO member who was a convention delegate to withdraw. Hannegan, however, never got that message because Baldwin, despite strenuous efforts, was unable to contact him.

After the Hannegan managerial group had the convention "in hand," Hillman was the first labor leader to know what was in the wind. This was the "clear it with Sidney" convention, which meant that, on FDR's instructions, Hannegan conferred with Hillman on the Vice Presidential matter (although Hannegan denied FDR ever used the phrase which the Republicans quoted so widely). Hannegan further insisted that all FDR ever suggested be taken up with Hillman was the single matter of the Vice Presidency, after labor's strong opposition to Byrnes became known. (In his *New York Times* column for Oct. 16, 1957 Arthur Krock finally admitted he had been wrong in starting the "clear everything with Sidney" rumor in 1944.) So Hillman burst in on a group of CIO and CIO-PAC leaders, in a Congress hotel room waiting to learn what was going on, and jubilantly announced, "We've stopped Byrnes!"

"And what are we getting?" asked Lee Pressman, CIO general counsel; Kermit Eby, CIO educational and research director; J. Raymond Walsh, CIO-PAC director of research; Baldwin and Murray, almost simultaneously.

"Harry Truman of Missouri, it is rumored," was the reply.
Pause.

Then, "And who in hell is Truman?"

Further pause, after which Walsh turned to Murray to ask, "Phil, what do you think about it?"

"We stopped Byrnes, we lost Wallace and we got Truman," sarcastically epitomized the president of CIO.

To this day the surviving CIO leaders and others are divided as to whether it would have been possible to have brought about the renomination of Henry Wallace. As the convention opened, Baldwin reported to a strategy meeting of CIO leaders and several other Wallace supporters, including Senators Claude A. Pepper of Florida, Joseph Guffey of Pennsylvania and James Murray of Montana, that the maximum convention strength possible for Wallace on any ballot just fell short of 500. This represented a considerable gain: when the pre-convention jockeying began a week earlier, there were fewer than 200 delegates pledged to Wallace. It seemed imperative to reach President Roosevelt by long distance telephone and several, especially Senator Guffey, tried in vain to do so. The best person to perform such a task was Hillman. He never did and his excuse to Baldwin was that Wallace had asked him to refrain from making the effort. This Wallace has denied, to both Baldwin and me. The closest he came to such a statement, he says, was to surmise that the call probably would do no good; but he decidedly did not forbid its being made. Possibly it would have made a difference, possibly not.

Either because he was confident that FDR's letter to Senator Jackson would be sufficient to insure his renomination, or because of political ineptness, or for some other reason, Wallace had no personal organization at Chicago. He had not, in fact, even planned to attend the convention, until implored to do so by long distance calls from Baldwin; Jake More, the Iowa Democratic leader; and others. He had no headquarters except those provided for him by CIO-PAC and it was by pure accident rather than design that Wallace went to the Sherman hotel, where that organization was already holding forth. Wallace had no floor manager of his own; whatever contacts he had with state delegations were made for him by the CIO boys.

The big demonstration on Thursday night, July 20, was CIO-planned and financed and might have succeeded if the strategy of quick adjournment had not been enacted by the Democratic leaders. Overnight the Wallace forces picked up 45 or 50 votes, but these were not enough to offset the losses occurring through the strenuous efforts of Pauley and others, who were promising jobs and patronage and threatening reprisals against delegates, in an almost frenzied spurt of activity. Anecdotes are told of delegates who burst into tears upon informing the Wallace people that they had found it impossible to withstand the tremendous pressure being applied.

The only leader, labor or otherwise, who had any chance of changing the situation was Sidney Hillman and he did not make the attempt. Daniels relates that someone quoted Hannegan as saying that before he died he wanted his epitaph to indicate that he was the man responsible for preventing Henry Wallace from becoming President. Maybe it was Sidney Hillman who deserved that epitaph.

# ¶ 2 TRUMAN CHANGES FDR's POLICY. *From almost his first day in office, the new President adopted a strong anti-Russian stand which seemed to be an abandonment of the One World dreams of Franklin D. Roosevelt and Wendell Willkie.*

About six weeks after the death of Franklin Delano Roosevelt, the two leading officials of the National Citizens Political Action Committee —Elmer Benson, acting chairman; and C. B. Baldwin, executive director— went to see his successor in the White House.

Even before they arrived they had an awareness of change. Before April 12, 1945 it had required only a telephone call, often a last-minute one, for any higher-up of the NC-PAC, or of its sister organizations, the CIO-PAC and the Congress of Industrial Organizations, to obtain a conference with the President. A five days' wait and a call to Robert E. Hannegan, chairman of the Democratic National Committee, had been necessary before the new appointment secretary, Matt Connelly, had been able to find a spot for Benson and Baldwin on President Harry S. Truman's appointment calendar.

For both men, accustomed to entering that office in different capacities for at least a decade, the experience was traumatic. Knowing FDR was dead was one thing; actually seeing his place occupied by another was something else. As Baldwin relates it:

"The sense of loss was terrific. FDR was crippled and never could rise to greet you. Nevertheless, rooted to his chair he created an impression of greater strength than Harry Truman did, alert and lively, striding to meet us with his hand out."

The first few minutes of the interview were pleasant. Mr. Truman began the conversation by recalling the day, early in 1936, when Elmer Benson took his seat in the United States Senate as a Farmer-Labor appointee, to fill out the unexpired term of Thomas D. Scholl of Minnesota. Republican Leader Charles L. McNary had approached him to remark, "We'd like to have you over on this side of the aisle, Senator," but the new third-partyite had replied, "I think I'll sit over here," and had plumped himself down next to Democratic Senator Harry S. Truman of Missouri.

Other pleasantries out of the way, Minnesota's former Governor and Senator came to the point of their visit:

"Mr. President, we're worried about the situation in agriculture, about the Secretary of Agriculture."

The smiling response was immediate. "I agree with you. There's going to be a change there very soon, and you both will be pleased."

"Well, as a veteran of World War I," Benson continued, "I'm also worried about the Veterans Administration."

"Again," replied the Chief Executive, "I agree. There's going to be a change over there too, in just a few days and you'll both be pleased."

(The changes were: Clinton Anderson for Claude Wickard as Secretary of Agriculture and Gen. Omar Bradley for Brig. Gen. Frank T. Hines as Director of VA, neither of which pleased either Benson or Baldwin overly much.)

So the conversation continued.

Benson—"We're planning a trip across the country very shortly. We already know that a great many of our people are disturbed and we want to know what to tell them. There are a great many rumors coming from San Francisco [where the United Nations founding conference was in session]. Averell Harriman seems to be doing a lot of spouting off." The reference was to rumors that Harriman had held a press conference of leading American editors and publishers, at which he declared American policy was to be vigorously anti-Soviet. There also had been rumors, later confirmed, that Truman had had a stormy scene with V. M. Molotov, Soviet foreign minister, when the latter called on him in Washington while en route to San Francisco.

Truman: "You mean our attitude toward the Soviet Union?"

Benson: "That's exactly what I mean."

Truman: (Banging his fist on the desk) "We have got to get tough with the Russians. They don't know how to behave. They're like bulls in a china shop. They're only 25 years old. We're over 100 years old and the British are centuries older. We've got to teach them how to behave."

Benson: "Maybe so, but if there is to be peace we are going to have to learn to get along with the Soviet Union. They are an important nation."

Truman: "That is right."

Except for a prediction by Baldwin that, if the apparent nationwide dissatisfaction with the way things were going continued, there'd be a strong Republican upswing in 1946, that was about all of their conversation. Its effect was to convince Benson and Baldwin, months or years before the rest of the country became aware of the fact, that "get tough" was to be the Truman administration's policy vis-à-vis the Soviet Union. So-called bipartisan champions of that policy have always contended that the administration made a long and valiant effort to continue the Rooseveltian policy, until the Soviet Union made it impossible to do so any longer. They point to the undeniable attempts of the Russians in the spring of 1945 to influence the outcome of elections in Rumania and Bulgaria; their interference with the affairs of Iran in early 1946 and their frequent use of the veto in the United Nations Security Council, as early evidences of intransigence. In this book it is impossible to go into detail regarding all of these matters, as each is worth a book in itself. What is attempted here is to explain what the world picture looked like to those who were to become the founders, a few years later, of the Progressive party.

As Benson and Baldwin left the White House, one of them—neither remembers which—remarked that maybe it would become necessary to have a new political party to continue the policies of FDR, as they understood them to be. In "Report to the President" in the Oct. 8, 1945 *New Republic,* Baldwin summarized his and Benson's findings during their six weeks' nationwide tour. To Mr. Truman he wrote, "Everywhere we went we found you had amazing support, but there were questions." Some of these pertained to personnel changes that had occurred at high levels in the Federal Government, causing some progressives to "question some of the support you have been receiving from queer circles." Especially mentioned were the appointment of FDR-hating former Sen. Bennett Clark of Missouri to the U.S. Circuit Court of Appeals and the resignation of Henry Morgenthau, Jr. as Secretary of the Treasury.

In state after state, Baldwin warned, staunch New Deal Democrats were beginning to feel stranded because of apparent lack of White House support: an example being California, where the favoritism shown conservative millionaire oilman Edwin W. Pauley, in preference to such proven liberals as Robert Kenny, seemed puzzling.

On April 29, 1945, Mark Sullivan had predicted in the *New York Herald Tribune* that Truman would end the power of New Deal intellectuals: "It is not that President Truman will make any head-on drive against the New Deal," he wrote. "Far from it. Many features of the New Deal are accepted by everybody. But the intellectuals who felt at home during the Roosevelt administration will not feel so under President Truman."

Five years later, in their *Truman Merry-Go-Round* (Vanguard Press, 1950), Robert S. Allen and William V. Shannon reported: "In the history of Washington the period 1945-47 will be known as the years of the flight of the intellectual."

The consequence, as seen by liberals of all shades, was that summarized editorially by *The Progressive,* organ of the Wisconsin La Follettes, in its issue of July, 1948: "He has surrounded himself, barring two or three distinguished exceptions, with dull mediocrities and more than a few reactionaries."

Within three months Truman fired Francis Biddle, Claude Wickard, Frank Walker, Henry Morgenthau, Frances Perkins and scores of others, substituting members of the "Missouri gang." These were personal friends and associates of Harry Truman, some of the most important acquaintanceships dating from World War I days, when they served with Captain Truman in Battery D, 129th Field Artillery, AEF. Among those who got "closest to the throne" were: Harry Vaughan, promoted to brigadier general and made Presidential military aide, whose name later became associated with "5 per centers" and deep freezes; General Wallace Graham, the President's personal physician, later revealed as a grain-market speculator presumably using information not available to the general public; Jacob Vardaman, president of two St. Louis banks, who became Presidential naval aide and a member of the Federal Reserve Board; Donald Dawson, personnel expert and political liaison man; Charles Ross, press secretary, more charitably remembered for his 40 years as a newspaperman before he took the White House job; Admiral Sidney Souers, who became executive secretary to the National Security Council; Matthew Connelly, who later served a prison sentence for influence peddling; and Clark Clifford, assistant naval aide and later a Presidential secretary and speech writer. Many of these appointments helped to fulfill a prophecy which Baldwin made to Henry A. Wallace early in 1946 and which Wallace, a few years later, told Baldwin he had recorded in his diary at the time. It was that the Truman administration would be remembered as one of the most corrupt in American history.

All of the new Truman intimates were conservatives or reactionaries: men such as George Allen, who became known the country over as a sort of court jester. Under Truman he became head of the Reconstruction Finance Corporation and so frustrated the attempts of Wilson Wyatt, veterans housing expediter, that the former Louisville Mayor finally quit in disgust. Similarly obstructive to the furtherance of the so-called Fair Deal liberal policies of the Truman administration was John Snyder, former Arkansas and Missouri banker, who first became Director of War Mobilization and Resources, and then Secretary of the Treasury. Dr. John R. Steelman, "sycophantic, Old Guardish and a jealous self seeker," according to Allen and Shannon, became the leading White House economic advisor.

Then there was Edwin W. Pauley. One of Harry Truman's first important acts, on April 26, 1945, was to rescind FDR's appointment of Isador Lubin as head of the American delegation on the Anglo-American Soviet Reparations Committee and to replace him with Pauley. Among those who accompanied Pauley to Moscow on that mission was the attorney for a leading California oil company, whose identity was concealed by a State Department announcement that he was just a small-town lawyer from Ashland, Ky. I am told that one of the first, if not the first, indications the Kremlin had that the wartime honeymoon between the US and the USSR was over was obtained by observing Pauley's activities in Moscow in mid-summer, 1945; not, as is sometimes supposed, at San Francisco or when the atom bomb was used in Japan, in order to achieve the ambition which (James V. Forrestal wrote in his diary on July 28, 1945) James F. Byrnes had, of getting the war against Japan over before the Russians had a chance to enter it. In the *Saturday Review of Literature* for March 8, 1947, Robert R. Young, then chairman of the board of the Chesapeake & Ohio Railroad, wrote: "We are kidding ourselves if we believe the atomic bomb was dropped on Japan. There is evidence that fully eight months earlier Japan was ready to capitulate. If the purpose of the bomb was to save American lives, then a fair warning before Okinawa would clearly have saved more . . . No, the atom bomb was dropped not militarily but diplomatically upon Russia . . ." Fuller treatment of this theme was contained in *Fear, War and the Bomb* (Whittlesey, 1948), by the Englishman P.M.S. Blackett, 1948 Nobel prize winner in the field of physics. On page 139 he epitomized his argument: "So we may conclude that the dropping of the atomic bombs was not so much the last military act of the second World War, as the first major operation of the cold diplomatic war with Russia now in progress." At the Potsdam conference where, on July 17, 1945, he learned of the successful atomic tests in New Mexico, President Truman remarked, "If it explodes, as I think it will, I'll certainly have a hammer on those boys," according to Jonathan Daniels in *The Man of Independence*. Wrote Daniels: "He seemed to be referring not merely to the still unconquered Japs but to the Russians with whom he was having difficulty in shaping a collaboration for lasting peace." This interpretation was confirmed by Byrnes when he appeared in a documentary film, "The Decision to Drop the Bomb," produced by the National Broadcasting Company in January, 1965.

Three outstanding public servants of the Roosevelt era who were given more important positions by Truman were James F. Byrnes, James

V. Forrestal and W. Averell Harriman. What they had most in common was a disbelief in FDR's hope for post-war collaboration with the Soviet Union. Under the date of April 20, 1945, Forrestal wrote of Harriman, "He stated his strong apprehensions as to the future of our relations with Russia unless our entire attitude toward them became characterized by much greater firmness." Of his concurrence with this viewpoint Forrestal left no doubt. Nor did Byrnes in his *Speaking Frankly* (Harper, 1947). Disregarding the rightness or wrongness of their thinking, it is indisputable that the policy which they and others almost immediately succeeded in making that of the Truman administration was not the one which Franklin Roosevelt had at least hoped would be the post-war American foreign policy. As evidence of this fact there is Elliott Roosevelt's *As He Saw It* (Duell, Sloan & Pearce, 1946) which was condensed in *Look* magazine beginning with the issue of Sept. 3, 1946. In the very first installment, the late President's son, who had accompanied him to almost all of the important international conferences, wrote:

> I know what conditions Franklin Roosevelt predicated for the structure of world peace. I know what conversations led to them, of the bargains and promises.
>
> I am writing this then to you who agreed with me that the path Franklin Roosevelt charted has been grievously— and deliberately—forsaken. I am writing this in the hope that it will be of some service in getting us back on that path. I believe it is possible. I am fearful of the alternative road.

Likewise Judge Samuel I. Rosenman wrote, in *Working With Roosevelt* (Harper, 1952), of his impressions of FDR's attitude on the way home from the Yalta conference:

> The President made it clear, not only when we were working alone on the speech, but in luncheon and dinner conversation, that he was certain that the Yalta conference had paved the way for the kind of world that he had been dreaming, planning and talking about. He felt that he understood Stalin and that Stalin understood him. He believed that Stalin had a sincere desire to build constructively on the foundations that had been laid at Yalta; that Stalin was interested in maintaining peace in the world so that the Soviets could make the industrial and social changes he thought necessary.

As noted New Dealers departed government service in a continuous stream, military and big business men arrived to take many of their places. Commented the semi-official *Army and Navy Bulletin* on Jan. 18, 1947:

> Today the army has virtual control of foreign affairs, commencing on the home front with General Marshall . . .

26

The chain of control in diplomatic hot spots, both in execution of basic policy and in the formulation of ad hoc arrangements, lies almost totally in the hands of the military authorities.

Similarly, David Lawrence wrote in the *United States News* for March 21, 1947:

> Never before have the Army and Navy been so powerfully placed in governmental controls. And never before has the United States adopted so stern a foreign policy. The group as a whole has been operating as a team.

Among the most outstanding appointments of military men by Truman to high positions were the following: Maj. Gen. Philip Fleming, administrator of the Office of Temporary Controls; Maj. Gen. John Hilldring, assistant secretary of state; Gen. Thomas Holcomb, Ambassador to Belgium; Gen. Douglas MacArthur, Governor of Japan; Gen. George C. Marshall, Secretary of State; Brig. Gen. Kenneth Royall, Secretary of War; Brig. Gen. Charles Saltzman, assistant secretary of state; Lt. Gen. Walter Bedell Smith, Ambassador to the Soviet Union; Adm. Lewis L. Strauss, U.S. member, United Nations Atomic Energy Commission; Comdr. James K. Vardaman, Jr., member Federal Reserve Board of Governors; Lt. Gen. Albert Wedemeyer, Special Commissioner to China; and Col. Clarence Young, Civil Aeronautics Board.

As conservative a source as the *Chicago Sunday Tribune* headlined a story from Washington in its May 2, 1948 issue: "Wall Streeter Is Edging Out the New Dealer." The detailed story proper began:

> The Wall street influence is the most important force in Washington.
>
> The New Dealers are out and the Wall streeters are in. The most important programs in the government are in the hands of men who came from the nation's financial center.
>
> The defense program, the State Department and the Marshall plan are in the hands of Wall streeters. Men with financial backgrounds are in key positions in other departments . . .

Three Truman dismissals on the very eve of the 1948 campaign caused particularly caustic criticisms from liberal quarters. They were: (1) the last-minute withdrawal on Dec. 30, 1947 of the reappointment of James M. Landis as chairman of the Civil Aeronautics Board; (2) the demotion on Jan. 27, 1948 of Marriner S. Eccles, from chairman to mere member of the Federal Reserve Board; (3) the demotion on Feb. 14, 1948 of Dr. Thomas Parran, as Surgeon General of the United States Public Health Service.

The nomination of Maj. Gen. Laurence S. Kuter to replace Landis was generally credited to pressure from the large commercial airlines, exercised through Averell Harriman; it stemmed from their displeasure with Landis' attempts to encourage the growth of small independent airlines, many of them operated by veterans who had learned to fly during the war, and from his concern, as the Air Line Pilots declared, for "safety ahead of the dollar." Harriman is supposed to have advised Truman to disregard his promise (presumably made to Democratic House Leader Sam Rayburn) to reappoint Landis, former dean of the Harvard Law School, because he had long wanted the CAB to become a unit of the Department of Commerce, which Landis resisted. Because Congress refused to allow him to retain his army pay, Kuter never assumed office. J. J. O'Connell Jr. then got the job. Harold Ickes on Jan. 10, 1948 almost two years after he had quit over the Pauley appointment, wrote in his syndicated newspaper column:

> If there ever was a case of a lobbyist "bringing home the bacon" it was the successful manipulation of President Truman by his personal "friends" who were also the friends of the big airlines, to persuade him not to reappoint James M. Landis . . . An administration from which able men have been leaving in droves and which is "down to the dregs and getting dreggier" will now lose self-respecting men who can get out . . .

Eccles, a millionaire Utah banker, had received three four-year appointments as chairman of the Federal Reserve System. He could not be fired as a member because his term had until 1958 to run. His demotion, generally believed to have been engineered by Snyder and Vardaman, came because he wanted to control the nation's interest rate by requiring the banks to put up special reserves against loans, mostly in the form of government bonds, which would have prevented a rise in the interest rate on the public debt. The conservative *Kiplinger Washington Letter* for Jan. 31, 1948 began:

> *Truman's demotion of Eccles* as head of the Federal Reserve System is stirring up an awful ruckus . . . with controversy over Truman's motive.

> *Eccles has been anti-inflation* . . . most vigorous of all officials. He's the ONLY one who has really DONE anything, while others just talked.

After explaining that Truman had not abandoned his anti-i stand, the letter continued:

> *But politics enter here.* The bankers have never liked Eccles. He didn't consult them much. He fixed policies and passed down the word. He ruled the Board, and the Board ruled the regional Fed. Reserve banks. He believed

in controlling credit . . . easy credit at certain times in past, tighter credit at such a time as the present, when inflation is running. The bankers resented the control . . . they thought THEY could tighten credit without any "dangerous" intrusion from the Reserve System, from gov't.

*So New York bankers got to Truman last week . . .*

In *PM* for Feb. 15, 1948, Albert Deutsch called Truman's failure to reappoint Dr. Parran "not only a stunning blow to the public health of America, but the final touch, the convincing symbol of the President's callous disregard for greatness in public service and his peculiar drive to rid the Executive Dept. of Roosevelt appointees."

The year 1945 was a crucial one in the history of this country and of the world. It is not too wild to conjecture that, because of the decisions made by world diplomats, future historians may consider it the most important of all times.

The widespread awakening, in the labor and liberal ranks which had provided the "backbone support" for Roosevelt's New Deal, to the fact that fundamental changes in policy had occurred in Washington was in two steps: (1) in March, 1946 when Winston Churchill spoke at Fulton, Mo., with Harry S. Truman on the platform; (2) in May, when Mr. Truman seized the coal mines, threatened to call out the Army to break up a railroad strike and asked Congress for anti-labor legislation which even Sen. Robert A. Taft considered too drastic.

From then until after the Democrats renominated Mr. Truman in July, 1948, these labor and liberal elements—regardless of how badly split they became over the Progressive party and other issues—had little that was good to say about Harry S. Truman. Months before the Republican sweep of Congress in November, 1946, he was called a betrayer of Rooseveltian policies, either deliberately or because he was too lightweight for the heavy job of President; he was almost unanimously branded a hopeless liability for the Democratic party. In fact, up to midnight of Nov. 2, 1948, about the only person who thought Harry S. Truman had a chance of being elected President of the United States in his own right was Harry S. Truman.

Simultaneously with adverse criticism of President Truman, well in motion less than a year after he was catapulted into office, there began rumblings from numerous sources about the need for a realignment of political forces: to an increasing number, this came to mean a new political party.

According to Jonathan Daniels in *The Man of Independence* (J. B. Lippincott, 1950), Mr. Truman invited Mr. Churchill, then vacationing in Florida, to speak at Westminster College as a personal favor to Maj. Gen. Harry Vaughan, an alumnus of this small school which almost nobody else had ever heard of. Mr. Truman told Daniels he had not read the former Prime Minister's manuscript but knew in essence what Mr. Churchill intended to say.

Most quoted line from the Fulton, Mo. speech was: "From Stettin in the Baltic to Trieste in the Adriatic, an iron curtain has descended across the continent," although Mr. Churchill used the phrase at least once before: on Aug. 16, 1945, in the House of Commons. This suggested the general theme: that it was unlikely the Soviet Union could be trusted in the post-war world. Although Mr. Churchill did not believe Russia wanted war, he deplored her "expansive and proselyting tendencies" and charged that Communist fifth columnists were active and influential almost everywhere else in the world except the United States and Great Britain. His solution, which he said would strengthen rather than weaken the United Nations, was a "fraternal association of the English-speaking peoples." Specifically this meant "joint use of all naval and air force bases in the possession of either country all over the world which would perhaps double the mobility of the American navy and air force."

Under the heading "How American Newspapers Viewed the Churchill Speech," Rep. Adolph J. Sabath of Illinois extended his remarks in the March 13, 1946, *Congressional Record*. "Mr. Speaker," he began, "it is gratifying to all honest-to-God Americans that American newspapers were not misled by the shrewd efforts of Britain's Winston Churchill in his Fulton speech to inveigle America into saving England's tottering empire, as we have saved her national existence twice already." After quoting the wartime Prime Minister's famous remark of Nov. 10, 1942, "I have not become the King's first minister to preside over the liquidation of the British Empire," the Illinois congressman declared, "Presumably he hopes to avoid that liquidation with our help." Then Congressman Sabath quoted and summarized the views of a number of newspaper columnists and editorial writers, all adversely critical of the Churchill proposal. Typical was the following from the *Chicago Sun:* "To follow his standard, raised by this great but blinded aristocrat, would be to march to the world's most ghastly war." The *Detroit News,* a Scripps-Howard paper, warned that a military alliance "would insure an armaments competition with the Russians far more likely to lead to war than to anything else." Eleanor Roosevelt wrote that Churchill advocated power politics which "lead sooner or later to war."

Three New Deal Senators—Claude Pepper of Florida, Harley Kilgore of West Virginia and Glen Taylor of Idaho—immediately issued a joint statement which read:

> Mr. Churchill's proposal would cut the throat of the United Nations. It would destroy the unity of the Big Three, without which the war could not have been won and without which the peace cannot be saved. It is shocking to see Mr. Churchill, who rose to power on the repudiation of Chamberlain, align himself with the old Chamberlain Tories, who strengthened the Nazis as part of their anti-Soviet crusade.

In Philadelphia five days after the Fulton speech, James Roosevelt, oldest son of the late President, who had recently become national director of the Independent Citizens Committee of the Arts, Sciences and Professions, announced that Harold L. Ickes had been named executive chairman of that group. In an unsigned news story for March 11, 1946, the *New York Times* said that this appointment "was interpreted as showing the intention of the committee to join with other liberal groups in trying to force a return by the national administration to the Roosevelt policies, both foreign and domestic."

Four nights later, before 1,000 people who dined at the New York's Commodore Hotel to celebrate his new position, Ickes demanded that President Truman "stand up aggressively for the foreign policies of President Roosevelt." The American people, he said, "do not feel comfortable with the sniping at Russia which is being indulged in. They know that without Russia we would still be fighting the war. They cannot envision a peaceful future without an understanding with Russia. They do not want any trucking to the Soviet Republic, but they do want an agreement based firmly upon mutual concession and a willingness to give and take. Moreover, the people of America do not regard the atom as a plaything for the armed forces."

On the same program James Roosevelt declared that, whereas Winston Churchill at Fulton had ably presented the British point of view, he questioned whether "our government or our President have attempted truly to represent the Russian point of view to the people of this country." Sen. Glen Taylor added: "Mr. Churchill's proposal would in effect serve notice on Russia that the English-speaking people have banded together to perpetuate the age-old game of European power politics, which has started the two world wars of our time."

CIO unions, which had provided strong backing for Franklin D. Roosevelt, recognized that changes in fundamental policy had occurred and expressed their disapproval.

*The People's Program for 1946,* an official pamphlet edited for the CIO-PAC by Joseph Gaer, declared:

> The people want peace. That is why the United Nations was created. Our nation and its people must support the United Nations wholeheartedly.

> The key to the strength of the United Nations is the warborn unity of Great Britain, the Soviet Union and the United States. Any effort to break or weaken the unity of the Big Three is a threat to the existence of the United Nations.

> We reject all proposals for American participation in any bloc or alliance which would destroy the unity of the Big Three. We repudiate all efforts calculated to weaken the collaboration among the Big Three . . .

Virtually the same wording was used in the resolution on foreign policy adopted at the Nov. 18-22, 1946 national convention at Atlantic City.

In April, 1946, "on the basis of the decisions of the Atlantic City convention and the problems that were referred by the convention," the International Executive Board of the United Automobile Workers declared:

> The UAW-CIO reaffirms its consistent stand for the defense of our country. All of contemporary history proves clearly that the defense of our country rests on the solid foundation of collective security by the peace-loving nations. The Winston Churchills and William Randolph Hearsts who are trying to divide the United Nations are thus striving to lead our country to disaster. We favor independence for all colonies, the outlawing of peacetime military conscription and support world-wide economic cooperation. We urge the Big Three—Britain, Soviet Russia and the USA—to iron out their differences and work unitedly to defeat fascism as during the war.
>
> On this issue we stand on common ground with international labor organized in the World Federation of Trade Unions. We wholeheartedly endorse the WFTU and we shall do all in our power to induce our government to secure representation of the WFTU on the Economic and Security Council of United Nations.

At its convention in Atlantic City, on April 24-27, 1946, the Textile Workers of America passed resolutions recommending that the United States turn over its newly-acquired Pacific island possessions, seized from the Japanese, to the United Nations for trusteeships; opposing any unilateral action outside the UN; calling for an end to diplomatic relations with Franco Spain.

At the last national convention presided over by Sidney Hillman, May 6 to 10, 1946, the General Executive Board of the Amalgamated Clothing Workers of America declared:

> Since the partnership of the United States, Russia and Britain is the cornerstone of peace, then it is the partnership of all three which must be maintained and strengthened.
>
> We recognize that there are reactionary forces in our own country which oppose and work against this basic policy. They seek to use our nation's great strength, not for unity and peace, but to wrest world domination for themselves. These forces must be isolated and defeated; for their path is the path to war . . .

Considerable applause, according to the convention proceedings, greeted Delegate Salerno when, speaking for the resolution, he said, "We must stop this 'Hate Russia' crusade, for if we have united nations for war, we must learn the need to have united nations for peace."

Sidney Hillman's last important statement on foreign policy also delivered at this time, included the following quotations:

"We either have united nations or divided nations. United Nations spell peace and plenty; divided nations mean war and fascism and nazism and bigotry. In order to make the United Nations effective, we must strain all our efforts to keep the unity of the Big Three secure." Hillman called for American leadership to bring about disarmament, warned against the atomic bomb, said all traces of fascism must be eliminated in Germany and in Franco Spain, and declared this nation cannot permit fascism to grow in Argentina. He concluded:

"You know, some people, not very many, want this to be what they call the American Century and not an American century for peace, so why shouldn't American big business exploit the rest of the world? This is not what America wants. This means war."

Hillman's use of the phrase "American Century" obviously was in reference to an editorial by that title which Henry Luce wrote for the Feb. 17, 1941 issue of *Life,* almost a year before Pearl Harbor. In it he contended that regardless of the extent of American participation in the war, when peace came only the United States would be in a position to assume world leadership. He called American isolationism as dead as the strength of the British Empire, even though the British might muddle through to victory in World War II. His editorial was a plea for the USA to "take over" and to run the world as successor to John Bull.

This editorial is probably one of the three clearest and most influential statements of basic American foreign policy as it has developed since 1945. The other two statements were Winston Churchill's speech at Fulton, Mo. and the X article in the July, 1947 issue of *Foreign Affairs,* reprinted in *Life* for July 28, 1947. There was little attempt to disguise the true author: George F. Kennan, head of the Planning division of the Department of State. The article was entitled "The Sources of Soviet Conduct" and contained a brilliant analysis of the development of Russian leadership psychology as regards the rest of the world. Its general conclusions can be deduced from a few quotations:

> It is clear that the U.S. cannot expect in the foreseeable future to enjoy political intimacy with the Soviet regime. It must continue to regard the Soviet Union as a rival, not a partner, in the political arena . . . It would be an exaggeration to say that American behavior unassisted and alone could exercise a power of life and death over the Communist movement and bring about the early fall of Soviet power in Russia. But the U.S. has it in its power to increase enormously the strains under which Soviet policy must operate, to force upon the Kremlin a far greater degree of moderation and circumspection than it has had to observe in recent years and in this way to promote tendencies which must eventually find their outlet in either the breakup or the gradual mellowing of Soviet power. For no mystical, Messianic movement—and particularly not that of the Kremlin—can face frustration indefinitely without eventually adjusting itself in one way or another to the logic of that state of affairs.

In addition to these three statements, some say, for a proper understanding of post-war American policy there must also be considered the address on "Capital Needs of Industry for National Defense," delivered on Dec. 10, 1940 by Virgil Jordan, president of the National Industrial Conference Board (an affiliate of the National Association of Manufacturers), at the annual convention of the Investment Bankers' Association of America in Hollywood, Fla. This pre-Pearl Harbor address was not essentially different in content from the Luce editorial, but is significant because of Mr. Jordan's position as spokesman for American Big Business. In a key passage he said:

> Whatever the outcome of the war, America has embarked upon a career of imperialism, both in world affairs and in every other aspect of her life, with all the opportunities, responsibilities and perils which that implies. This war inevitably involves a vast revolution in the balance of political and economic power, not only internationally but internally. Even though, by our aid, England should emerge from this struggle without defeat, she will be so impoverished economically and crippled in prestige that it is impossible she will be able to resume or maintain the dominant position in world affairs which she has occupied so long. At best, England will become a junior partner in a new Anglo-Saxon imperialism, in which the economic resources and the military and naval strength of the United States will be the center of gravity. Southward in our hemisphere and westward in the Pacific the path of empire takes its way, and in modern times of economic power as well as political prestige, the sceptre passes to the United States.

Contrast this declaration of naked imperialism with President Roosevelt's vision: "I think I speak as America's President when I say that America won't help England in this war simply so that she will be able to continue to run roughshod over colonial peoples," Elliott Roosevelt in *As He Saw It* quotes his father as saying, on the eve of his first meeting with Churchill, in August, 1941 off the coast of Newfoundland, when the Atlantic Charter was concocted.

In 1944, to explain why he did not publicly protest British actions in Greece to liquidate the wartime anti-German underground, a story fully related by Leland Stowe in *While Time Remains* (Knopf, 1946), FDR optimistically said, according to Elliott, "The point is, we are going to be able to bring pressure on the British to fall into line with *our* thinking. It's all tied up in one package: the Dutch East Indies, French Indo-China, India, British extraterritorial rights in China. We're going to be able to make this the 20th century after all, you watch and see."

One of Henry Wallace's favorite stories pertained to a wartime meeting between Roosevelt, Churchill and himself. The British Prime Minister had been advocating the necessity for unity between the English-speaking people and the President asked Wallace to comment. He did so by referring to the close ties existing between North and South America, saying, "It seems to me we first have to establish a bond with our other American brothers." Then Churchill, described by Wallace as livid, declared, "I am not just a government leader, I am also a painter, and I tell you that when you mix colors you get only a dirty brown."

The leader in the United State Senate in opposing the Truman "get tough" foreign policy was Claude Pepper of Florida. He began his attack on anything except the Rooseveltian idea of Big Three collaboration even before FDR died. On Jan. 10, 1945 Sen. Arthur H. Vandenberg, Michigan Republican, made "a speech heard round the world," to use the appellation given the chapter discussing it in *The Private Papers of Senator Vandenberg* (Houghton Mifflin, 1952), edited by Arthur H. Vandenberg Jr. It purported to be a challenge to FDR to reveal his policies on the eve of his departure for the Yalta conference, growing out of a fear on the part of the former leading isolationist that there might result "an unjust peace and a demand for the United States to underwrite such a peace through the United Nations." As his son explained, "What was really in Vandenberg's mind was the future position of Russia."

Against the earnest pleas of Sen. Alben Barkley, Democratic majority leader, that he should not do so, Pepper spoke on Jan. 15. Ostensibly it was in answer to a three-hour speech by Sen. Burton Wheeler of Montana, who had not abandoned his isolationist views; Wheeler attacked the policy of unconditional surrender as "brutal, asinine," accused the Soviet Union of bad faith and termed the Dumbarton Oaks conference, to prepare the outline of the United Nations charter, "a plan to underwrite tyranny."

Pepper entered the debate by frequent heckling questions to Senator Wheeler and then went on with a positive statement:

"When an able Senator, who has a national reputation, upon the floor of the Senate holds out hope of terms more favorable than unconditional surrender to the enemy, attacks our allies and makes it clear that he does not favor our entering into any effective organization to keep the peace of the world, I cannot refrain from stating at least that those are not my sentiments and I believe they are the sentiments of very few, if any other Senators, upon this floor."

At first it seemed that Pepper was endorsing Vandenberg's speech of a few days before, as he cleverly pointed out that the Republican leader had suggested that the United States' refusal to join the League of Nations had been a contributing factor in causing World War II. According to one present, however, Vandenberg turned gray as it became increasingly clear that Pepper was answering him as well as Wheeler.

It was the United States Senate, not President Woodrow Wilson, which was responsible for this country's isolationist policy between the wars, Pepper recalled. So he challenged both Wheeler and Vandenberg to come up with positive programs of their own, rather than merely state their suspicions of or opposition to the policies of Franklin Delano Roosevelt. Certainly both the Montana and Michigan Senators were included in this barb: " . . . I shall always believe that those who delayed the repeal of the Neutrality act in the United States Senate in 1939 also contributed dangerously to the probability of this war."

And there was no mistaking his viewpoint when he declared:

"We cannot have a foreign policy without the approval of the United States Senate. I do not think it is proper to sit here, divided as we appear to be, without clarification of our own sentiments and ideas, and not give the chief executive any general charter of authority or indication of policy which we will back up but, instead, send him off on a mission around the world to meet with other world leaders and make commitments upon which we base a hope for future peace."

When FDR returned from the conference, Pepper saw the Crimean accords as "the greatest step toward lasting peace that has ever been taken." In the fall of 1945 he went abroad and on Sept. 14 he saw Premier Josef Stalin. His own story of the interview appeared in the *New York Times* for Oct. 1, 1945. Insisting that his country needed time and assistance to repair the tremendous damage caused by the war, the Russian leader informed Pepper that his government's request, six months earlier, for a $6 billion American loan had not even been acknowledged. Stalin termed "ridiculous" charges that such a loan would be used for military purposes and Pepper believed him. At the Senator's request the Russian premier sent a message to the American people: "Just judge the Soviet Union objectively. Do not either praise us or scold us. Just know us and judge us as we are and base your estimate of us upon facts and not rumors."

Some time later Pepper told a newspaperman, who interviewed him in my behalf, that he believes the cold shoulder the Soviet Union got from us regarding its loan request, and the sudden termination of Lend-Lease after V-E day, plus the "ineptness of the Truman government at that time" were reasons why the so-called Cold War was accelerated.

Pepper's denunciation, with Kilgore and Taylor, of the Churchill speech at Fulton, Mo. has been mentioned (See page 30). On March 20, 1946 Senator Pepper delivered what the *New York Times* described as "the strongest defense of the Soviet Union yet heard in Congress in the recently darkened world scene. He argued in effect that the Russians were justifiably afraid of this country and of Britain." Pepper charged that it was fear that had brought about a "tension comparable to the days before Munich or on the eve of either of the last wars" and denounced Vandenberg as "the most vigorous and powerful advocate of the newest form of isolationism" which advocated "the exclusive possession of the atom bomb by the United States and the effective control of atomic energy by the military." He described as "blind alleys" the pursuit of "unilateral nationalism" and a "program of 'get tough'," or of two power alliances, and said a fog of distrust and fear could be driven away only by a "full scale conference of the Big Three."

The *CIO News* for Sept. 16, 1946 reported that Pepper was "loudly applauded" the week before at the Milwaukee convention of the United Electrical, Radio and Machine Workers, when he said:

"The American people don't want to fight anybody. They don't want to drop atomic bombs on anybody. But we've drifted too far back to the imperialist policy of McKinley.

"If Roosevelt were alive we'd be getting on better with Russia. The liberal wing of the Democratic party is scarcely, if ever, consulted on our foreign policy . . . It is not our duty to join any old western European power to say Russia can't get into the Mediterranean."

He warned that the United States should not become "a guarantor of western European imperialism anywhere in the world."

Senator Pepper was not alone in his distrust of Truman's foreign policy. There were Democrats, such as Kilgore and Taylor, and Republicans, such as Sen. George D. Aiken (Rep., Vt.).

On a National Broadcasting Company forum July 6, 1946, Aiken declared, "We have been following the British lead entirely too closely. Britain and Russia have been opposed to each other for 200 years. We should steer clear of this conflict and work instead to bring the two nations together." On the same program Sen. Glen Taylor (Dem., Ida.) said, "I'm afraid our foreign policy has been definitely pro-British. Take the case of Trieste. We followed the British lead there. It was the French, not ourselves, who proposed a conference acceptable to both the Russians and British." And Rep. Charles R. Savage (Dem., Wash.) added: "So we'll drift from the one-world stage to the two-world stage and then perhaps to a no-world final curtain."

The issue these Senators presented was whether it was possible to "bury the hatchet" and "do business" with the Russians after World War II. Almost from the moment he became president, Harry S. Truman firmly believed the answer was "no." Throughout the first year of his presidency, however, there were a great many individuals and groups— a few of them mentioned in this chapter—who disagreed and said so, while Henry A. Wallace generally remained silent. Most of them later were either to change their minds or to become silent, but it is 1945 and 1946 of which we have been writing.

# ¶ 3  TRUMAN DISAPPOINTS FDR's LABOR BACKERS. *The President is condemned by union leaders and groups for cracking down on strikers and for apparent lack of vigor in promoting liberal domestic policies.*

The alarm over the course American foreign policy was taking, expressed by certain CIO unions, was minuscule compared with the furor which developed in mid-1946 over the labor policies of the Truman administration.

In his State of the Union message in January, 1944, President Roosevelt had proclaimed what the nation's post-war domestic objectives should be, in a form which came to be called the Economic Bill of Rights. It represented what New Dealers considered their "unfinished business," interrupted by the war. The "rights" enumerated by FDR were:

37

The right to a useful remunerative job in the industries, or shops or farms, or mines of the nation;

The right to earn enough to provide adequate food and clothing and recreation;

The right of every farmer to raise and sell his products at a return which will give him and his family a decent living;

The right of every businessman, large and small, to trade in an atmosphere of freedom from unfair competition and domination by monopolies at home or abroad;

The right of every family to a decent home;

The right to adequate medical care and the opportunity to achieve and enjoy good health;

The right to a good education;

The right to adequate protection from the economic fears of old age, sickness, accident and unemployment.

"All of these rights spell security," FDR said, "and after this war is won, we must be prepared to move forward, in the implementation of these rights, to new goals of human happiness and well-being."

In its Pamphlet-of-the-Month No. 11, *The People's Program for 1946,* by Joseph Gaer, the CIO-PAC summarized what, by mid-1946, had become the prevailing viewpoint among labor leaders: "The coalition of poll-tax Democrats and reactionary Republicans has set itself out to destroy the gains made under President Roosevelt and to prevent his Bill of Rights from being realized."

On Sept. 6, 1945, President Truman made his first proposals for legislation on the domestic front. His 21-point legislative program, as he submitted it to Congress, was summarized by Paul R. Leach in the *Chicago Daily News* for Sept. 6, 1945 as follows:

ONE—Act immediately to provide a maximum of $25 a week for 26 weeks for displaced war workers seeking peacetime jobs.

TWO—Substantially increase the 40-cent hourly minimum wage rate and write in general coverage to include agricultural processing workers.

THREE—Extend the President's second War Power Act to continue such controls as are necessary, such as food rationing and rent control.

FOUR—Hold off Congressional proclamation of war's end, which would terminate war powers and war agencies

38

"before we are ready." Pass permanent legislation giving him blanket authority to reorganize a topheavy government.

FIVE—Enact quickly full employment laws.

SIX—Enact permanent fair employment practice laws.

SEVEN—Terminate the War Labor Board soon, strengthen the Labor Department; support collective bargaining and a "truly effective system of conciliation and voluntary arbitration."

EIGHT—Continue federal control of the U.S. employment service.

NINE—Carry out price support commitments to farmers.

TEN—Encourage voluntary enlistments; continue drafting 18- to 25-year-old men for two years service to meet occupation requirements.

ELEVEN—Encourage private capital to invest $6,000,-000,000 to $7,000,000,000 annually in new housing; assist in slum clearance; quicken rural housing.

TWELVE—Create a single federal scientific research agency.

THIRTEEN—Pass a transition tax bill with "limited reductions" in 1946 removing barriers to speedy reconversion.

FOURTEEN—Provide a single surplus property disposal administrator.

FIFTEEN—Provide "adequate protection and encouragement" of small business.

SIXTEEN—For war veterans, pass amendments clarifying and liberalizing provisions relative to hospitals and medical care, vocational training, education, loans, life insurance, right of reemployment; assure veterans social security credit for their service years.

SEVENTEEN—Return to a sound conservation policy for all natural resources, improve roads and highways, provide funds for river, harbor, and flood control projects held back by the war.

EIGHTEEN—Settle our wartime lend-lease relations; repeal the Johnson Act prohibiting loans to countries in default on First War Loans. Appropriate $550,000,000 now obligated and $1,350,000,000 more for United Nations relief.

NINETEEN—Increase Congressional salaries.

TWENTY—Provide for early sale of excess cargo ships.

TWENTY-ONE—Provide a stockpile of strategic materials necessary for defense.

Primary blame for failure to enact this or a similar program, of course, rested with the 79th Congress, in which the Democrats controlled both houses. Before the end of 1945, however, there were strong rumblings in labor and liberal circles that although Harry Truman spoke liberally he, to put it mildly, lacked "follow-through."

Predictions that such would be the case had, in fact, been made even before Franklin Roosevelt was buried. For example, Paul R. Leach wrote for the *Chicago Daily News* of April 13, 1945:

The New Deal died with Mr. Roosevelt.

That may be proved a partial overstatement as Harry S. Truman settles himself more definitely in his services as President of the United States.

But left wing New Dealers themselves believe they and their extremist ideas are gone. None other than Roosevelt could carry them, they think.

Conservatives in Congress expect broad political changes in government domestic policies . . .

In the same newspaper the next day Charles C. Miller wrote from Washington: "The nation will find a strong champion of individual enterprise and vigorous private industry in their new president, Sen. Harold Burton (Rep., Ohio) predicted today. He is squarely in President Truman's corner, confident that the nation can count on the Chief Executive to give it leadership of the highest order."

In the same article Sen. Homer Ferguson (Rep., Mich.) was quoted as saying of Truman, "I believe his policy will strongly favor re-establishment of vigorous private industry after the war."

Wrote Lou Schneider in the *Chicago Daily Tribune* for April 18, 1945: "President Truman's administration will be built around James F. Byrnes—in whom the President places the utmost of confidence."

In October, 1945 at Caruthersville, Mo., Truman made an unfortunate remark, from the standpoint of his own public relations, to the effect that some strikers should "cut out the foolishness" and go back to work. At the time, organized labor was pressuring Bowles and whatever other New Dealers were still around. Instead, despite the pro-labor views he expressed publicly, he seemed to be consistently taking the advice of John W. Snyder, John R. Steelman and others. In the *Chicago Sun* for Dec. 12, 1945, Willard Shelton declared Harry Truman's "besetting weakness" to be "a lack of a clear-cut doctrinal comprehension of the times in which we live."

The *Congressional Newsletter* of the Union for Democratic Action, in its Jan. 1, 1946 issue, concluded its summary of what had happened to Mr. Truman's 21 proposals of Sept. 6 as follows: "What does this tragically negative record in an era of profound issues mean? Truman came to power hailed as the old legislator who would know how to work cozily with Congress. The glad-hand approach was worked to a fare-thee-well. Results: almost nil. When it comes to a constructive, forward-looking social program, evidently it means little to Congressmen whether they call the Executive 'Harry' or 'that man.' Buttering won't work with a Congress resolved on 'legislative business as usual.' "

One of the most uncomplimentary reviews of Harry Truman's first three years as President was contained in the issue of the *New Republic* of May 17, 1948, entitled "Truman as Leader." The record as regards four leading post-war issues—reconversion, cost of living, homes for veterans and labor relations—was one of talking liberally and then capitulating to conservative or reactionary counsel.

William H. Davis and Chester Bowles wanted the President to use the War Production Board to break production bottlenecks and direct scarce raw materials into needed products for domestic consumption. Instead, Truman listened to J. A. Krug and John W. Snyder and lifted restraints on business, with the result that luxury items began to appear first. Bowles was relieved of his duties as Price Administrator and shifted to Director of Economic Stabilization when Steelman was attempting to overcome his opposition to a price breakthrough. When the White House itself began granting price increases, Bowles quit that job. His resignation was announced the same day the Senate, 47 to 23, passed a compromise bill extending the Office of Price Administration for another year with curtailed powers. Bowles said the new bill would "serve to legalize inflation" and urged the President to veto it.

That Mr. Truman did, just 37 hours before the old bill was due to expire on June 30, 1946. When the House vote of 173 to 146 was 38 votes short of overriding the veto, it stood and price controls ended. Three weeks later, however, Congress passed virtually the same bill and on July 24 President Truman "reluctantly" signed it. During the two months to follow, under the powers of the new law, the OPA "dealt out price increases hand over fist" to use the language of an Associated Press dispatch from Washington dated Aug. 23, 1946. In September there occurred a market strike by Western cattlemen and hog raisers, who kept their animals off the market in an attempt to force the lifting of price controls on meat. It worked. On Oct. 14, the eve of the 1946 election, President Truman did so, and four days after election day he eliminated all remaining controls except those on rents, rice and sugar.

"President Truman abandoned the Roosevelt planned economy tonight in favor of the law of supply and demand," the *Chicago Tribune* jubilantly reported. It based its claim on Mr. Truman's message, which included the following: "Manufacturers, thinking of their future markets, will hesitate to raise prices unreasonably. In short, the law of supply and demand operating in the market place will, from now on, serve the people better than would continued regulation of prices by the government."

When the steel industry refused his own suggestion that labor be granted an 18½¢ per hour wage increase, President Truman did not seize the steel industry. Nor did he seize the automobile industry when it refused to accept the recommendations of a Presidential fact-finding board for a 17 per cent wage increase. However, when the coal miners struck on May 21, 1946, the President seized the coal mines, and four days later he appeared before a joint session of Congress to make perhaps the most violently anti-labor speech that any President of the United States ever made.

A half hour before the President delivered his message, a threatened railroad strike had been averted by agreement between the operators and the railway brotherhoods. Mr. Truman had been advised of that fact and interpolated mention of it in his address. Nevertheless, he proceeded to ask of Congress emergency power to break strikes in any specified industry and to draft strikers into the armed services if necessary. He called for deprivation of rights under the National Labor Relations Act and the Railway Labor Act for any worker failing to return to work when requested to do so by government, and the possible use of a federal injunction to restrain violators. Labor leaders who failed to cooperate in ending strikes would be subject to fine or imprisonment.

Within two hours, an almost hysterical House of Representatives passed the legislation asked by the President, by an overwhelming 306 to 13 vote. Mostly as a result of the leadership provided by Sen. Robert A. Taft, however, the Senate instead passed the Case Bill, 49 to 29; this was a measure which had originated in the House under the sponsorship of Rep. Francis E. Case of South Dakota. In doing so the Senate, 70 to 13, struck from the bill a provision to permit the drafting of strikers. A few days later the House acquiesced to the Senate version of the bill. By then Harry Truman had cooled down and so he vetoed the Case Bill, and his veto stuck.

Labor leaders were aghast and used almost identical language, including the appellation "slave labor bill," to characterize Truman's proposals. As one whose union was most directly affected, A. F. Whitney, president of the Brotherhood of Railway Trainmen, immediately declared political war on the President, saying he would use the entire union treasury of $47 million, if necessary, to defeat him in 1948. At his Brotherhood convention on Sept. 17, 1946, he also called the 79th Congress the worst of all time.

To Michael Quill, president of the Transport Workers of America, President Truman had become "the Number 1 strikebreaker of the American bankers and railroads." He accused Mr. Truman of having committed treason against the American people "under instructions from American Fascists." Said Mr. Quill: "It is unfortunate we got President Truman in the first place as the result of an accident. Truman has committed treason against the people of the United States. Yesterday it was the railroad workers and unless we act quickly it will be the maritime workers tomorrow and the automobile and steel workers in a week or two. He has become the Number One strikebreaker of the American bankers and railroads. In one 15-minute speech to Congress he did more to break labor than the Pinkertons and Pearl Bergoffs did in 70 years."

The *New York Times* for June 4, 1946 quoted William Green, president of the American Federation of Labor, as saying, "Please, Mr. President, get rid of your advisors, at least some of them. They ill-advise and mislead you. You have fallen victim of the hysteria cooked up by the enemies of democracy."

Before the House Labor Committee on Feb. 25, 1947, Whitney angrily shouted that labor was under a propaganda attack not equaled in his 57 years in the labor movement and was "fighting in almost its last ditch before Congress to save democracy." He denied that there was any public demand for restrictive labor legislation. "It comes," he said, "from Wall street and through the columns of the press. Labor proved itself by its work in the war. Labor died by the thousands overseas."

No better summary of labor's case against the Truman administration could be cited than that released on June 4, 1946 by the International Executive Board of the United Automobile Workers at a special session in Cleveland. A summary of accumulated grievances, it began:

> When Harry S. Truman took the oath of office as President of the United States, he pledged that his administration would carry out the program and policies of Franklin D. Roosevelt.
>
> He has violated that pledge.
>
> President Truman's un-American legislative proposal to Congress May 25 was the climax of a series of surrenders by the Truman administration to the demands of reactionary industrialists to make peacetime strikes illegal and impose a fascist system of involuntary servitude upon American workers, including millions of veterans of the nation's victorious war against fascism. Truman's proposal makes complete the surrender to demands of the same forces that the trend of progressive social and economic legislation established by the Roosevelt administration be reversed . . .

On July 11, 1946, the National Farmers Union, through James Patton, president, announced that it had broken with the Truman administration. "The union has lost confidence in the Truman administration's doing anything about legislation we consider important," the statement read. Patton accused the President of not putting up a fight for public health, rural housing, river valley authorities, federal aid to education and permanent Farm Security Administration legislation.

Patton announced that the NFU, which had 400,000 members in 32 states, was starting a "grass roots mobilization" for "the economic M-day we feel is coming." He was careful to add, however, that this action did not presage the formation of a third party, although he admitted it "might grow into an independent movement."

Such a disavowal of the intention to start or encourage any third party movement was characteristic, at this time, of many who were outspoken in their adverse criticisms of the Truman administration. Philip Murray, CIO president, argued against the advisability of a new party in the *New York Times* Sunday Magazine for April 11, 1946. Nevertheless, third party talk was already rife in organized labor circles, as Louis Stark had reported in the same paper on March 28 and 31, 1946. In recognition of this fact was the Political Action Resolution adopted by the Executive Board of the United Automobile Workers in April, 1946, containing the following statement:

"That we work toward the eventual formation of a broad third party based on the thinking and interests of millions of the labor, farmer, professional and other progressive people of our nation. Such a movement can succeed if it is not prematurely launched on a narrow base."

Similarly, the Textile Workers, during its convention at Atlantic City on April 24-27, 1946 declared on the subject of political action:

"Whereas this power must be mobilized in the most practical and realistic manner. We do not believe that at the present time independent political action by labor can be taken through the medium of a third party. At the same time we do not close the door to such action if and when the full powers of labor and all other liberal elements in our nation can be mobilized behind it."

And the International Fur and Leather Workers Union, at its 16th biennial convention on May 24, 1946 at Atlantic City, resolved: "that our incoming International Executive Board and our representatives to the CIO give their full support to the establishment of an independent political party of labor and progressive people at the opportune and appropriate time."

The attitude of David Dubinsky, president of the International Ladies Garment Workers, AFL, was decidedly defeatist when he spoke on June 5, 1946 to the convention of the United Hatters, Cap and Millinery Workers, AFL, in New York. Obviously meaning A. F. Whitney among others, he belittled the "threats" by various union leaders to defeat President Truman or members of Congress because, he said, organized labor had no machinery by which to do it. He had no kind words for either major party, but he denounced labor "statesmen" whose "main object is to bore from within the existing parties." Questioned later, he told reporters that "only an independent labor party is the solution." Ten days later, at a New York Liberal party convention, however, he opposed the attempt of others to forbid coalition with other parties. "I'm for a third party," he said, "but I am not one of those who believe that a third party can be built by dreams."

Nevertheless, on May 26, when, at a meeting of CIO shop stewards, Michael Quill called for an end to labor support for candidates "who play both sides of the street" and advocated more independent labor action in politics, the *New York Times* reported, "This advocacy of third party tactics evoked a new burst of applause from the delegates." Also, at the conclusion of the United Automobile Workers convention on March 27, 1946 at Atlantic City, the newly elected president, Walter Reuther, declared that "all liberal elements should work toward a realignment to draw together the best elements of both parties" into an eventual new third party; however, he doubted if this could be done in time to be effective in the 1948 campaign.

At its convention on June 3-7, 1946 in Montreal, the United Packinghouse Workers of America resolved: "The United Packinghouse Workers of America has joined in the support of candidates of the Democratic party for the office of President since the advent of Franklin Roosevelt upon the American scene. President Truman's unwillingness or inability to bring to reality the principles for which Franklin Roosevelt stood and on which he was elected creates grave problems as to the role we will play in future Presidential contests."

Perhaps the most significant statement during this period by a national labor leader was that of Daniel J. Tobin, president of the International Brotherhood of Teamsters, the largest AFL union. Tobin, who had been chairman of the labor division of the Democratic party in all of FDR's campaigns, wrote in the July, 1946 issue of *The International Teamster:*

> Democrats have a substantial majority in the Congress of the United States, but there are only 100 congressmen out of 435 who stand up and vote for the workers when adverse legislation is aimed at them.
>
> The average worker then measures the facts, weighs the results and he simply decides one party is no better than the other, and while he won't vote for a reactionary Republican or for a reactionary Democrat, he will simply stay away from the polls and eventually it may lead to a massing together of the toilers of the nation in all organizations of labor so that united action will prevail.

Tobin hinted at the dwindling differences between Democrats and Republicans in public office. As early as March 10, 1946, none other than FDR's oldest son James had gone even further. At a Philadelphia meeting of the Independent Citizens Committee of the Arts, Sciences and Professions, of which he was then national director, James Roosevelt said:

"It takes courage and persistence to be independent. The labels of the Democratic party and the Republican party are meaningless as far as the responsibility to carry out platforms and pledges of each party is concerned. Any student is aware that a coalition of Southern Democrats and Republicans work hand in hand. Progressive and liberal Republicans often join with liberal Democrats.

"The time must come if our democracy is to succeed when a fundamental realignment of the political parties is accomplished. The timing of such a reform is the only open question."

Five days later, at the New York dinner honoring him upon his assumption of the executive chairmanship of the ICC-ASP, after lambasting Churchill and Truman as reported in the preceding chapter (see page 31), Harold L. Ickes declared, "In desperation people sometimes think we ought to organize a third party. I do not agree with this at the moment." He cited the difficulty a new party would have in getting on the ballot and the danger of splitting the liberal vote which it would entail. He added, however, that even if not practical, such a party might become necessary.

One who considered a new party not only necessary but inevitable was A. Philip Randolph, long-time president of the Pullman Porters, AFL. His threat of a wartime March on Washington by a large mobilization of Negroes pressured FDR into issuing his Executive Order 8805, calling for fair employment practices. On April 7-8, 1946 Mr. Randolph called together a group of more than 100 labor and civic leaders from 16 states, at the International House on the campus of the University of Chicago, to establish a national education committee. It was not intended to be a new political party in itself, but was to undertake the long-range educational program which would be an essential background when a new People's party arose. Said the statement made public after the second meeting of the group, on May 4, 1946 in Detroit:

> We did not at our Chicago conference nor do we intend to, at this time, start a new party. We have organized simply for the purpose of carrying on an educational campaign for a People's party and for the principles upon which a party should be based.
>
> If and when a new People's party does arise it will arise as the action of organized labor, farmers, white collar, professional and small business men who will join together in a People's party against the threat of monopoly capitalism to economic plenty, freedom and peace.
>
> The committee is not opposed to the CIO-PAC despite charges to that effect in the *New York Daily News* and the *Daily Worker*. The PAC is a direct electoral instrument which endorses candidates of various political parties. Our group is an educational committee which is helping to build sentiment for a new party when the time is ripe.

Clayton Fountain, public relations man for Walter Reuther, attended the Detroit meeting and Reuther's remarks the month before were recalled. John Dewey, the aged philosopher who had helped organize a League for Independent Political Action in the late '20s, and James Patton, president of the National Farmers Union, were said to be interested. Few other names were mentioned in any announcements concerning the organization. Mr. Randolph explained to me that his purpose was never to seek a cross-section of big names; rather, he preferred to lay the groundwork with "only little people."

After President Truman's message in connection with the railroad strike, Randolph stated publicly, "President Truman's anti-strike program may open the eyes of labor, farm and cooperative leaders to the responsibility of continuing the worn-out tradition of a two-party system in which neither party serves the interest of the people." At a Conference on Human Relations on Nov. 23, 1946, sponsored by the Catholic Interracial Council, the Jewish Labor Committee, the Negro Labor Committee and the Presbyterian Institute of Industrial Relations, he called both the Democratic and Republican parties "bankrupt" spiritually in their economic program and called for CIO and AFL unity to fight reaction and totalitarianism.

In his conversation with me more than seven years later, Mr. Randolph said that his movement failed because it was "engulfed" by the growing demand for immediate action which culminated in the formation of the Progressive party. If this had not happened, there would have been a series of large meetings all over the country to educate people to the fact that neither major party truly represented their interests. Mr. Randolph still believes in the necessity for such an educational program. He said that we still have some progressive capitalism (using Henry Wallace's term), but it is becoming steadily less progressive. In order to avoid cataclysmic results when the time comes and to make possible an orderly change to a form of mixed economy, an enlightened labor class will be essential. Randolph, who is socialistically inclined in his thinking, was trying to develop an alternative to communism. He was extremely critical of attempts to interpret discontent among working class people, especially in colonial areas, as resulting only from Russian propaganda and fifth column activity.

Indisputably, growing out of displeasure with both the foreign and domestic problems of the Truman administration, there was quite a bit of new political party talk in the air as early as 18 months before Henry A. Wallace announced his independent candidacy for the Presidency, on Dec. 29, 1947. The Progressive party, however, did not simply develop out of these haphazard complaints and suggestions. It had distinct organizational forebears, of which the most significant was the National Citizens Political Action Committee. Before proceeding with this story, some background regarding that organization is necessary. This involves at least brief mention of two of its predecessors: Labor's Non-Partisan League and the CIO-PAC (Congress of Industrial Organizations Political Action Committee) of which the NC-PAC was an offshoot.

Although George L. Berry, president of the International Pressmen's Union, AFL, was chairman of the Non-Partisan League, the organization really was the personal political tool of John L. Lewis. He started the League in 1936, to help in the first reelection campaign of Franklin Delano Roosevelt. Within a year Lewis began to cool on FDR. Some, such as Frances Perkins, charged that Lewis was disappointed not to be given some official government position, possibly even that of Secretary of Labor or Vice President. Most others say the cause was FDR's "plague on both your houses" statement, at the time of the Detroit automobile sitdown strikes, when Lewis wanted the President to lend the full weight of his office to bringing the operators into line.

Anyway, according to *John L. Lewis*, by Saul Alinsky (Putman, 1949), by early 1937 Lewis was publicly questioning whether the New Dealers were any better than the Republicans. On Feb. 1 of that year at a dinner sponsored by *Common Sense* magazine, he came out for a third party based on a popular front of workers and farmers. On April 1, 1940 at Monogah, W. Va., Lewis threatened to call a convention of such delegates "to formulate a program that each and every American can support." He did not do so, undoubtedly because he failed to obtain the support of any other outstanding labor leader. All summer long, in fact, Sidney Hillman, president of the Amalgamated Clothing Workers of America and one of the CIO's founders, followed Lewis around the country to reply to, or at least offset the effect of, his anti-FDR speeches. On Oct. 25, 1940 Lewis endorsed Wendell Willkie over a nationwide radio hookup paid for, Ralph Barnes revealed, by William Rhodes Davis, millionaire oilman with friendly German connections.

The only support that Lewis obtained for his third party ideas in 1940 came from the Communists within the CIO, with whom at the time John L. was aligned, both in regard to internal CIO policy and in criticism of America's definitely pro-British foreign policy. This was the period of the "phony war." Following the non-aggression pact between Nazi Germany and the Soviet Union of Aug. 29, 1939, the American Communist line was that World War II was just another imperialistic struggle. So they were isolationists at this juncture. Lewis was also an isolationist, but the Old Guard Republican variety. Politics, it is bromidic to repeat, makes strange bedfellows, but Lewis also had found it necessary to play ball with the Communists in the early days of the CIO. They were the hardest workers, the strongest believers, and possessed the most experienced rank-and-file leaders. Many authorities have concluded that without the Communist manpower there never would have been a CIO. As a base from which to launch a third party movement, however, they were of doubtful value.

The idea for the CIO-PAC, as far as Sidney Hillman was concerned, originated with Philip Murray, CIO president. During a meeting of the CIO Executive Committee in July, 1943, Murray broached the subject to Hillman privately. Later the same day, the other members of the committee greeted the idea of establishing a political action committee, to support FDR and work for favorable labor legislation in Congress, with enthusiasm. Public announcement was made on July 11, 1943 and included the following:

"We are opposed to the organization of a third party at this time because it would divide the forces of the progressives throughout the nation. We are here to mobilize our power for political action now—not to wait until a few months before the election of 1944."

What had disturbed labor and liberal leaders was the fact that, whereas 48.8 million had voted in 1940, only 28 million did so in 1942. As a result, according to their interpretation, the 78th Congress was much more conservative and many of the New Deal gains were in jeopardy. At the CIO convention on Nov. 1-5, 1943, Murray and Hillman had no difficulty in obtaining endorsement of the CIO-PAC, with promises of $700,000 to be contributed by the individual unions to finance its operations.

The next political step was for Hillman to take over the American Labor party in New York. The story of his big fight has been fully related by Matthew Josephson in *Sidney Hillman: Statesman of American Labor* (Doubleday, 1952). The battle, which ended in an overwhelming Hillman victory in the March 28, 1944 primary, followed long attempts by Hillman, President Roosevelt and Mayor Fiorello La Guardia of New York to persuade David Dubinsky, and others who at the time controlled the ALP, to "broaden the base" by permitting proportionate representation to all elements in the labor movement. The redbaiting charges and smear tactics that reactionaries used against Hillman and the CIO-PAC later in 1944 hardly surpassed those used by Dubinsky, Adolf Berle, George Counts and others of the old leadership who, after their defeat, promptly resigned from the ALP and organized the American Liberal party. Thus, the ALP came into existence in 1936 as an outgrowth of Labor's Non-Partisan League, at least with President Roosevelt's blessing if not, as some say, at his request. It helped to carry New York State for the Democrats that year and to elect La Guardia as Mayor of New York in 1937. It suffered from left-right factionalism during the phony war period of 1939-41. In 1944 the right wing controlled the state organization, but the left was stronger in New York City.

Once in control of the American Labor party through election as state chairman, Hillman proceeded to make the CIO-PAC into a big thing. At least he succeeded in making it a leading campaign issue in 1944, with the opposition spokesmen, including the press, screaming "Communist!" and "Clear it with Sidney." Rep. Martin Dies of Texas, original chairman of the House Committee on Un-American Activities, took out after the CIO-PAC on Jan. 26, 1944; a few weeks later he demanded to examine all of the new organization's records and expense accounts. Then Dies issued a 215-page blast against Hillman and the CIO-PAC as a Red front. Hillman stood his ground, refusing to appear before Dies, and both CIO and AFL leaders quietly persuaded 30 per cent more eligible voters than ever before to register in Dies' constituency of Beaumont County, Texas. In May, Martin Dies announced he would not be a candidate for re-election.

Even Gov. Thomas E. Dewey, Republican candidate for the Presidency, often acted as though he were running against Sidney Hillman instead of Franklin Delano Roosevelt. He talked of the "Roosevelt-Hillman-Browder plot" to rule America. A popular Republican slogan was: "Sidney Hillman and Earl Browder's Communists have registered. Have you?" The $371,000 which the CIO-PAC actually spent up to July 23, when its remaining $298,000 was frozen (put in escrow), was exaggerated into a slush fund numbering into the millions. Hillman's Lithuanian origin and his Jewishness were cited, mostly through a whispering campaign, although Clare Boothe Luce, then running for Congress in Connecticut, cracked, "If my head is to roll in a basket, at least it's a more American head than Sidney Hillman's." On Aug. 28, 1944 Hillman and other CIO-PAC leaders appeared before the House Campaign Expenditures Committee, which, despite the earnest desires of some of its members, could find no irregularities in their handling of the PAC's finances.

This was because the Smith-Connally Act, forbidding labor union contributions in connection with elections to Federal offices, had been circumvented by the freezing of CIO-PAC funds after the political conventions and state primaries and, with the blessing of the CIO Executive Board, by the creation on June 18, 1944 of the National Citizens Political Action Committee, to be financed by individual contributions only. This had no official connection with the CIO and made its appeal primarily to middle-class and non-labor groups. Its director was Clark H. Foreman.

Contributions to the NC-PAC were on an individual basis; no trade union money was acceptable. The torrent of campaign literature put out by the CIO-PAC and the NC-PAC in 1944 can hardly be described by an impartial student of political public relations except as "terrific." Joseph Gaer gathered some of it together in book form as *The First Round* (Duell, Sloan & Pearce, 1944). Among the leading titles of the popularly written pamphlets were: *Jobs for All, What Every Canvasser Should Know, A Woman's Guide to Reaction, Radio Handbook, Speakers' Manual* and *A People's Program for 1944.* Altogether, over 80 million pieces of literature were distributed. At least one CIO leader of the time, however, was extremely skeptical regarding its effect. He was Kermit Eby, then CIO director of education and research, who pointed out that, according to the best estimates, about 71 per cent of all registered CIO members voted Democratic. On the other hand, about 68 per cent of all AFL members did so also, and the AFL engaged in virtually no pamphleteering. "Since such a percentage is well within the statistical margin of error," Eby said, "the truth probably is that the printed matter had no effect at all."

Through its own publicity and that which others, including its political and journalistic enemies, gave it, the NC-PAC attracted 18,000 members. It may seem odd, but this response was embarrassing to some, alarming to others. It was not desired at that time to develop a mass movement. A number of persons were opposed to such an undertaking, for a variety of reasons. In New York State, American Labor party leaders, principally Rep. Vito Marcantonio, did not want to see a rival hierarchy of ward and precinct clubs organized by either the CIO-PAC or the NC-PAC. Nevertheless, one important and highly successful attempt to organize community clubs in support of FDR was made under the independent leadership of Mrs. Elinor Gimbel, wealthy widow of a scion of the department store Gimbel family who was killed while serving in the wartime Air Transport Command. Her recruits were mostly internationally-minded Republicans who believed in the re-election of the wartime President. Probably she was inspired by Bernard "Barney" Conal of the Voters Research Institute, who in 1942 had conducted a political survey for CIO in New York, breaking down its membership in the (then) approximately 3,500 election districts and recommending that community councils of CIO members be organized by districts. He discovered that already a large number of workers were active campaigners in these districts for one of the political parties, principally the Democratic party. Conal, whose scientific approach to politics had often been used by the Democratic national committee, compiled the first political street guide to New York. He used ethnic maps and data regarding the industrial, racial, religious and other characteristics of a political district to determine areas for concentration in any campaign and to provide clues to what kind of campaign appeals should be made in different places.

Another reason why no mass membership was sought for the NC-PAC was the fear, on the part of some, of Communist infiltration. Hillman had fought for a Popular Front approach, which would include Communists, when he had ousted Dubinsky, Berle, Counts and the rest from American Labor party leadership; but once on top he was content to keep his corporation a closed one, with direction from the top rather than from any

ass roots. Hillman was eager to use the ALP as a means of pressuring
e Democrats, as it possessed the balance of power in New York. Because
oth it and the two PACs were too close to CIO, however, the kind of
people Mrs. Gimbel attracted to her clubs would never have joined and
us would never have been formal participants in the 1944 campaign.
wo years later, it was her clubs which formed the nucleus of the Progres-
ve Citizens of America in New York.

The major reason why post-election development of the NC-PAC was
owed down, however, was neither of those already given. Rather, it was
ecause of the splitting of the CIO family into two camps, caused by ex-
tence of the CIO-PAC and the NC-PAC, with headquarters in New York
ther than near the CIO itself in Washington. Some uncharitably believe
at, when Philip Murray appointed Sidney Hillman head of the PAC, he
ought he was "burying him" as a rival for power and prestige within
e CIO. Whether this is so or not, there is no doubt that Murray soon
ecame more than worried over the tremendous success of the enterprise.
isregarding any personal envy which may have developed because of
e world-wide prominence Hillman received in his new position, Murray
ever ceased being an Old School trade unionist. He was sincerely alarmed
ver anything which tended to overshadow what he considered the basic
aison d'être of the CIO: collective bargaining for better economic condi-
ons. So there rapidly developed an internecine warfare. The "Murray fac-
on" remained in Washington and the "Hillman faction" was in New
ork. Neither trusted the other and each tried to outdo the other. Eby
ld me of how he wheedled more money out of Murray for special proj-
cts by declaring that if his department didn't do the job the New York
roup doubtless would. Right after the CIO-PAC was formed, it was con-
dered a great triumph for Eby to be able to place before each member
f the board of directors at its first meeting a *Political Primer,* written in
Washington. Eby got an appropriation to enable him to prepare a mailing
st, which he had long wanted. When finished, it contained 150,000 names
1 54 categories, and was used thereafter for all CIO mailings. Murray gave
by a letter stating that no one, including Hillman, could use this list
ithout Murray's own permission.

James Carey, who became the CIO's secretary-treasurer after being
usted from the presidency of the United Electrical, Radio and Machine
Vorkers of America in 1941, had the perspicacity to realize that the
olitical wind was veering to the right. With such statements as, "Last
ime we fought with the Communists to defeat the Fascists; this time we
hall fight with the Fascists to defeat the Communists," he added more
han a few huffs and puffs to that wind, to help make it the mighty
urricane of reaction it has become. Carey would engage Eby in lengthy
elephone conversations, telling him what a bright future he would have
n the CIO if he remained true to the right faction.

On Nov. 23, 1944 after a 14-minute ovation for Hillman, following
is report on CIO-PAC activities, the CIO convention unanimously voted
o continue its political arm—making it clear, however, that it had nothing
ike a third party in mind. Nothing, of course, could be decided regarding
he NC-PAC, since it was not an official CIO agency. On March 23, the

51

executive committee of the NC-PAC met in closed session at New York Hotel Commodore and later announced that Hillman had been authorize to appoint a committee to draw up plans and programs for continuation a a permanent organization. Among the committee members whose attenc ance at the meeting was publicized were: Dorothy Parker, the novelis Freda Kirchwey, publisher of *The Nation;* Louis Weiss, attorney for Mai shall Field, publisher of the *Chicago Sun* and the *New York PM;* Micha Nisselson, later Hillman's appointee as president of the Amalgamated Ban of New York; Mrs. Edward M. Warburg.

On May 12, 1945, the election of Elmer A. Benson, former Minnesot Governor and Senator, as acting chairman and chairman of the NC-PA national executive council was announced Frank Kingdon, a vice-chai man, explained that Sidney Hillman, who was in San Francisco at th time, had too many other duties to continue as acting chairman. "W didn't exactly clear it with Sidney, but what we have done meets with h approval," Kingdon was quoted as saying in the *New York Times* fo May 12, 1945.

That wasn't exactly the truth; as a matter of fact, it was just abou the exact opposite. The important meeting to decide the NC-PAC's futur had been in the form of a caucus in December, 1944 at the Washingto home of Gifford Pinchot, former Pennsylvania Governor. It was attende by Benson; Baldwin; Philip Murray; Weiss; Clark Foreman, presider of the Southern Conference for Human Welfare; James Patton, presider of the National Farmers Union; and possibly others. Foreman and Patto were among the NC-PAC's many vice-chairmen, others being A. F. Whitney president of the Brotherhood of Railway Trainmen; James C. McGill, o the McGill Manufacturing Company of Valparaiso, Ind.; Bishop R. I Wright Jr. of the African Methodist church; Mrs. Emmons Blaine c Chicago; Dr. Robert C. Weaver, prominent Negro leader; Mrs. Verda Barne of Idaho. Dr. J. Raymond Walsh, former Harvard professor, had becom chairman of the New York committee.

At the Pinchot meeting, presumably coached by Murray, Patton spok up for the replacement of Sidney Hillman as chairman of the NC-PA( and the removal of the national office from New York. Hillman, he arguec had become too controversial to enable the NC-PAC to expand into mass-membership organization and it could not survive with a narrow bas When Patton finished speaking, Philip Murray declared, "I agree wit Patton." Benson pleaded that no action be taken in Hillman's absence, bu in vain. At the Cosmos Club bar after the meeting, Patton "let the ca out of the bag" when he exclaimed, "You don't think Philip Murray ca be second fiddle all the time, do you? He's got his pride."

Murray's choice to replace Hillman was Pinchot, who, however, re fused to accept until he had spoken to Sidney. He did so by a long distanc call to Arizona, where Hillman was vacationing. Although Hillman cor sented to stepping down, he was furious and Pinchot refused to be chairma

After the May meeting, at which Hillman was formally deposec Murray delegated Baldwin to notify Sidney. Unable to talk Murray int performing the disagreeable task himself, Baldwin reluctantly did i His reluctance, however, was not due to any strong desire to have Hillma

emain as chairman, as he had become convinced that Sidney was ready
> put both the CIO-PAC and the NC-PAC "on ice." The breach which
1e action created between Hillman and Murray never was healed.
Iillman died on July 10, 1946.

Almost all of the important organizational leaders of the Progressive
arty in 1948 had held similar positions in either the CIO-PAC or the
JC-PAC, mostly the latter. Most important, from start to finish, was Cal-
in Benham Baldwin, whom everyone called "Beanie." For ten and a
alf years, Beanie had worked with the New Deal in Washington, where
e was called on May 23, 1933 by Paul Appleby to become an assistant
> Henry A. Wallace, then Secretary of Agriculture. Appleby had known
aldwin in Radford, Va., where the former ran a newspaper and the latter
'as a successful businessman. Later, Beanie became assistant Farm Se-
urity administrator and for three years, before he quit on Nov. 23, 1943 to
ecome assistant to the chairman of the CIO-PAC, he had been FSA ad-
1inistrator. On May 12, 1945 Clark Foreman became fulltime executive
:cretary of the Southern Conference for Human Welfare and Baldwin
:signed his CIO-PAC position and took over the running of the NC-PAC.

Beanie has told me several times that the idea of a third party did
ot come to him suddenly. Rather, his New Deal experience of more
1an a decade had convinced him that a day of reckoning was coming.
What was called the New Deal," he once said, "was one of the most un-
asy coalitions of liberalism ever held together, first by the depression and
1en by the threat of fascism. FDR was close to the liberals and pro-
ressives but at the same time he had Jones, Byrnes and others like them
'ith whom he never broke. It never would have worked if it hadn't been
or the personal power FDR possessed. The forces of reaction always were
lose by, waiting for the opportunity to get control."

What Beanie Baldwin tried to do after the death of FDR was to
eep together a core of New Dealers. He conscientiously did his utmost
> persuade the Truman administration to follow the Roosevelt tradition.
Ie kept after Robert E. Hannegan, national Democratic party chairman,
omplaining about bad appointments, statements and actions, trying to ex-
rcise what weight he could to bring about a reversal of the trend
>ward the right.

Although his office was in New York, he made weekly visits to Wash-
1gton and organized a series of luncheon meetings of members of Con-
ress and others who had been considered staunch New Dealers. Most of
1ese were held at the Hays-Adams house and received little or no public-
y, because they were private affairs. Among the most frequent in attend-
1ce were Secretary of Commerce Henry A. Wallace; Senators Claude
'epper, Elbert Thomas and Glen Taylor; Representatives John Blodgett,
Ielen Gahagan Douglas and Chet Holifield of California, Henry M. Jack-
>n of Washington, George G. Sandowski of Michigan and Walter K.
iranger of Utah.

In his *Frontiers on the Potomac* (Macmillan, 1946), Jonathan Daniels
:lls of meeting Baldwin and Benson in Seattle during their summer, 1945
ationwide tour. He writes:

Baldwin needs more attention from the country, which
may have been paying too much attention to Tommy
Corcoran. He is out of government too. Though younger,
he understands his way around in it, I think, at least as
well as Corcoran does. But there is a continuity of purpose to his pushing from the outside which Corcoran's
law practice seems to lack.

Beanie, as everybody calls him, grins as he goes and I
suspect that at least some of his grinning in pressure
grows from the remembrance of the pushing around some
conservative Democrats gave him while he was director
of the Farm Security Administration. I do not know the
exact direction of Beanie's liberalism or how far to the
left it has taken him. But in pressure he seems at least
as native as his native Virginia.

Any third party movement needed a strong labor representation. S
as a harbinger of events to come, I was intensely interested in Louis Ho
lander's statement to me as to what labor's attitude was during 1946. H
said that at the time of the railroad and coal strikes, members of othe
unions did not feel particularly affected. Those were fights of only th
unions involved, he said. He added that furthermore there was wide
spread feeling among working people that, when you tie up the railroad
you are really striking against the American government. In Teddy Roose
velt's day, the attitude was the same as regards the coal mines, he said.

"The Truman period will rank in history with that of Andrew Jack
son," Hollander told me in his office on July 13, 1953.

# ¶4 TRUMAN FIRES WALLACE

*When he said publicly what many labor and libera*
*leaders were saying about American foreign policy, th*
*Secretary of Commerce became a private citizen.*

The mass meeting and money-making techniques which were a phe
nomenon of the 1948 Progressive party campaign were developed mostl
by the NC-PAC in 1945-46 and by the Progressive Citizens of Americ
in 1947.

The first of a scheduled series of 19 dinners in as many large cities
to begin mobilizing support for the 1946 congressional campaigns, wa
held on June 21, 1945 in New York's Hotel Commodore; it met witl
what, judged by later standards, was moderate success. The approximatel
1,000 who were there, ostensibly to honor Hillman, just back from
World Federation of Trade Unions meeting abroad, and Benson, newl

lected acting chairman, contributed approximately $40,000. The principal peaker was Republican Sen. Charles W. Tobey of New Hampshire, who ɪbeled as "dangerous and ill-considered" efforts to arouse public opinion gainst the Soviet Union.

"It is an attitude which may well spread against other nations," Tobey warned. "It is an attempt to create prejudice against our allies in this rucial time while we are working for cooperation and harmony and it s liable to seriously injure the great efforts being attempted at San Franisco and in the Senate."

Hillman warned that the defeat of Germany militarily did not mean he end of fascism in the world: "Powerful forces in our country have a ɪifferent answer and they will be unscrupulous in their attempt to impose : upon us and upon the world . . . American reaction fully understands hat its mad dream of an 'American Century' will never be fulfilled if the Jnited Nations—and particularly the United States and its British and ʲoviet allies—continue to work together in the peace as they fought toʲether against the common enemy."

To which Benson added: "We must be united in our demand that he American foreign policy be the fulfillment of the aspirations of the ʲeople. We have no interest in the preservation of doddering pre-war emʲires or in the construction of imperial schemes of our own country."

At other similar meetings throughout the country, Mrs. Eleanor ʲoosevelt, Harold L. Ickes, Henry Morgenthau Jr. and other old New ʲealers were the headliners. At Milwaukee on Feb. 4, 1946, Morgenthau harged that, in permitting the fascist regimes of Spain and Argentina to ɪain in power, the United States was marching down a road that would ʲad the world to imperialism and war. He accused the Truman adminisration of lacking a forthright policy in regard to those two nations.

On Jan. 31, 1946, a "full dress discussion" of American foreign policy ɪttracted over 1,000 guests to the Hotel Commodore. Max Lerner, columʲist for *PM*, was chairman of the invitations committee and presided. Col. ʲernard Bernstein, formerly director of the finance division of the Office ʲf Military Government and of its division of investigation of cartels and ʲxternal assets of Germany, charged that the United States and Great ʲritain had not done as good a job of living up to the Potsdam agreement ɔ demilitarize, decentralize and de-nazify Germany in their zones as the ʲussians had in theirs. Rep. Helen Gahagan Douglas, of California, adʲocated international cooperation through the United Nations as the only ʲrotection against atomic annihilation. Michael Straight, editor of the ʲew Republic, and Dr. Frank Kingdon seconded her remarks.

In the evening's principal address, Claude Pepper again lambasted ʲsinister and reactionary forces," which he said were destroying Roosevelt's ʲlans for peace. He scored those who were opposing a proposed loan to ʲreat Britain because the British possessed a Labor government; said that ʲtrong elements of fascism continued to exist in Spain, Portugal and Argenʲina as well as in Germany and Japan, and lamented the almost-daily press ɪttacks on the Soviet Union.

The only non-fund-raising affair of this period was the impressive ʲemorial service to Franklin Delano Roosevelt on April 12, 1946, the first anniversary of his death. Senator Pepper's remarks on that occasion were a reaffirmation of the ideas expressed in his Senate speeches (see pages 35-36). Similarly, Frank Kingdon declared:

> In the international field we seek security and justice under law. To this end we pledge support to a foreign policy which will put all our national strength back of the United Nations. We repudiate the theory that we cannot work with Russia or Great Britain or any other nation. We are a full and free association of all nations in the adventure of peace.

And Henry Wallace, the principal speaker, waxed optimistic:

> There is not going to be any war with Russia. Russia has too much sense just as we have too much sense . . . For, aside from language and a common literary tradition, we have no more in common with imperialist England than with communist Russia. We should take only the side of world unity, only the side of making the United Nations an equitable instrument for a just and enduring peace.

It was quite a turnout that applauded these words. Henry Morgenthau Jr. was chairman and every member of FDR's cabinets, even from New York governorship days, was asked to be a guest of honor. Only two of those who had been serving at the time of FDR's death were absent: Harry S. Truman and Harold L. Ickes. FDR's widow, Mrs. Eleanor Roosevelt, was there, as were Franklin Jr. and Elliott, his sons. Sixty dignitaries were arranged on a triple dais, from which they were visible to about 2,000 others. Frances Perkins spoke, as did Associate Justice Hugo A. Black, Mayor O'Dwyer, Herbert Lehman, Sen. Robert F. Wagner, Judge William Hastie, Orson Welles and others. Nobody seemed to be worried about whether, at some future date, he'd be considered guilty of something or other for having associated with the others under NC-PAC auspices. Although there was no fund raising, Nathan Strauss, the owner of station WMCA, was so impressed that he contributed $10,000 to the NC-PAC that night.

With the overwhelming success of each undertaking, the next became even more ambitious. Although attendance was limited to 500 the School of Political Action Techniques, sponsored by the NC-PAC in Washington on June 26-29, 1946, was the most important sounding-board up to that time for criticisms of the Truman administration and for third party talk.

A total of 39 courses were offered through five departments: political strategy; political organizations and administration; political groups; political research and public relations. The faculty and advisers totaled more than 80 and included, in addition to a number of CIO, CIO-PAC and NC-PAC leaders, such headliners as Henry Hoke, author of *Blackmail* (Readers Book Service, 1946), and *It's a Secret* (Reynal & Hitchcock, 1946).

56

Louis Bean, statistical analyst; Dr. L. M. Birkhead, director, Friends of Democracy; Elmo Roper, director, Citizens Research Bureau; Prof. Samuel A. Stouffer, Harvard sociologist; Dr. Hadley Cantril of Princeton University, director of the Office of Public Opinion Research; and Thomas . Brandon, president of the Public Affairs Films Production Company.

Postmaster General Hannegan, chairman of the Democratic national committee, and Republican Sen. Wayne L. Morse of Oregon addressed the opening session on "The Significance of the 1946 Elections." Each insisted that his party could be used as a vehicle for progressivism.

Claude Pepper made an unscheduled appearance and warned that, if reactionary forces captured the Democratic party and filibustered the passage of anti-poll tax legislation to the detriment of the party's "liberal destiny," creation of a third party would be forced. Even more unexpected was the appearance of Secretary of Commerce Henry A. Wallace, whom Beanie recalls having induced to leave his office on the spur of the moment. Wallace's talk was impromptu and consisted of a confession that the Democratic party needed a "rebirth," but was still "ten times more likely to serve a progressive cause than the Republican party." After 12 years in office, he said, any party loses some of its original zest and needs a little "chastening."

As Baldwin listened to all of the oratory and learned instruction for two and a half days, he considered it excellent but lacking in concreteness. To what purpose was all this knowledge to be put? The objectives liberals sought were clear, but the means of achieving them were unclear.

The night before the final session of the school, Beanie told me, he tossed about in bed; unable to sleep, trying to make up his mind what to say when his turn came the next day. Beanie evidently felt that to send the 500 amateur politicians, who had come from all over the country, home without a ringing call to arms would mean failure for the entire effort. On the other hand, there was still only a small minority, himself included, who wanted immediate action toward development of a third party.

If there was to be a third party, obviously the best person to lead it was Henry A. Wallace, but up to that time Mr. Wallace had given little indication that he might be sympathetic to the idea. At the April 12 rally, he had been introduced by Morgenthau as "the one who more than anyone else is carrying on the spirit of the late President," and there had been loud applause and cries of "Wallace in '48." The preceding day, however, before the Senate Interstate Commerce Committee, Wallace had said he favored the two-party system and recalled that in 1938 he had opposed FDR's attempt to "purge" the Democratic party of anti-New Dealers. He made these statements in answer to questions concerning a speech he had made a month earlier, on March 18, 1946, to the National Democratic Women's Club, when he had suggested that Democratic congressmen who refused to support administrative policies should be disciplined by the party. While a number of Southern Democrats, and James Forrestal, fussed and fumed over that one, President Truman at his March 21, 1946 press conference indicated he agreed with his Secretary of Commerce.

Nevertheless, four days later, 12 Southern members of both houses of Congress boycotted the annual Jackson-Jefferson Day banquet in

57

Washington because Wallace was a listed speaker. Actually, Wallace's speech at that time was conciliatory. He warned the Democrats that, although Jefferson had given the party its philosophy and spirit, it was Jackson who first put the belief into practice and that when, after Jackson's time, the party became lazy in promoting the people's interests, they turned to the newly formed Republican party which had a true believer in the people, Abraham Lincoln, as its candidate. Wallace's tongue must have been in his cheek at the time, but he praised Harry S. Truman for attempting to carry on FDR's policies. Afterwards Rep. Adolph J. Sabath was quoted as saying, "Mr. Wallace helped a great deal by being tactful and welcoming all the Democrats back into the fold instead of trying to read them out of the party as some feared he might do."

The helpfulness, of course, was to the Democratic party, to maintain a facade of unity to conceal the deep internal splits which had developed.

But Wallace had discouraged third party talk on other occasions. As early as Aug. 19, 1934, in an article, "If War Should Come" in the *New York Times,* he had written that old party tags had become meaningless and a political realignment of conservatives versus liberals was badly needed. Nevertheless, at the Union for Democratic Action testimonial dinner to him on Jan. 29, 1945, when FDR still was alive, he had declared, "I still hope and pray for a united progressive Democratic party. The strategy of the enemy is to break the Democratic party in two. They want to push you and me into the futility of a third party. I don't think we shall have to have a third party. I think we can win within the framework of the Democratic party. I hope that we are not now in for a political realignment like that which substituted a Republican party for the Whig party nearly a century ago. There will be far less trouble in this country if the progressives can find full and free expression in the Democratic party."

More recently, on Feb. 8, 1946, under NC-PAC auspices in New Haven, he had applauded the "need—an indispensable need—for political action independent of organized political parties," but as for himself he had declared, "I am here tonight still fighting for the things Franklin Roosevelt fought for—and supporting President Truman in his fight for the progressive legislation that will continue to make the Democratic party the party of progress in this country. I will keep up the fight as long as the Democratic party remains the people's party." On April 18, 1946, at Los Angeles, he had repeated his blast at "a recalcitrant minority of the Democratic party which fails to support administrative policies in Congress." Four days later, at San Francisco, he said, "A congressman who is against his party's program should not expect his party to make him chairman of a committee which has the power of life or death over legislation sponsored by his party."

Introduced by Sidney Hillman at the 10th anniversary dinner of the American Labor party, on May 24, 1946, as the "symbol of the people's movement for the common man," Wallace expressed opposition to formation of a national third party because the election laws of many states would guarantee a heavy reactionary vote by dividing the progressives. On June 14, 1946, under CIO-PAC auspices at St. Louis he elaborated on this theme, saying, "It would be simply impossible for a third party to get on the ballot in enough states to make anything approaching an effective challenge . . . It is time for the third party advocates to stop kidding themselves." That year Wallace publicly endorsed Johannes Steel, ALP candidate for Congress, against Democrat Arthur G. Klein in New York's 19th C.D.

Knowing all this, Beanie Baldwin nevertheless decided to extend his political neck as far as he could. He boldly told the 500 students that it was not beyond the realm of possibility that they would be the pioneers in establishing a new political party. He said frankly that he disagreed with Wayne Morse that the Republican party ever could be used by liberals. Rather, he labeled the GOP as "the party of reaction" which was "still controlled by the vested interests." Henry Wallace, he said, was on sounder ground when he said it still was possible to use the Democratic party as a liberals' political vehicle. However, he pointed out that Wallace had not told the group how it was to overcome the "unholy coalition of forces between the two parties." If Wallace had been renominated in 1944, Beanie opined, "I think our position here today might be decidedly different." Nevertheless, the situation as he saw it was that there were not more than 20 progressives in the Senate at that time and not more than 100 in the House of Representatives—"if we stretch things a bit." He said he would prefer not to have a third party, but emphasized that it might become necessary if the Democrats "continue on the road to reaction as in the past 18 months." Then, he said, "There will be a third party whether Mr. Truman likes it, or whether Mr. Hannegan likes it, or whether Henry Wallace likes it." So he sent the students at the school home with this message: "Through the organization of progressive groups throughout the country you are building a machine: a people's machine which can be used to make the Democratic the more progressive party, perhaps to help slightly in that direction in the Republican party; but if leadership is not responsive to the needs of the people, the same machinery can be used for a third party."

That was about as plainly and honestly put as anyone could possibly put it. The next day Henry Wallace met Beanie and, grinning, remarked, "Maybe you're right."

In 1946, U.S. Sen. James M. Mead received the nominations of three political parties—Democratic, American Labor and Liberal—as a candidate for governor of New York, against Republican Thomas E. Dewey. Likewise, former Gov. Herbert H. Lehman was the three-party candidate for the U.S. Senate, against Republican Irving M. Ives. The NC-PAC endorsed Mead and Lehman and, in the late spring, rented Madison Square Garden for a Sept. 12, 1946 rally in their behalf, with the ICC-ASP as co-sponsor. Wallace accepted an invitation to be one of the speakers at least three months ahead of time, but the subject matter was left for a later decision. Then, about Aug. 1, a young lawyer in the office of Harold Young, solicitor in the Department of Commerce under Wallace, confided to Baldwin that on July 23 HAW had sent a letter concerning the United States' foreign policy to President

Truman. Off the record, he allowed Baldwin to see a copy of the letter, and it was an exciting experience for Beanie, who had had no prior knowledge that any such communication was being contemplated. Without betraying any confidence, Baldwin inquired shortly thereafter of Young what kind of speech Wallace intended to make at the Sept. 12 rally. He was informed that Wallace wanted to talk about the record of the 79th Congress, as he evidently agreed with Baldwin's characterization of it, on Aug. 1, as having made "the worst record of any in several years." Baldwin replied he wanted Wallace to speak on foreign policy and Young suggested that Beanie see HAW about it personally. Beanie did. Wallace repeated that he wanted to talk about Congress. Beanie said he wanted Wallace to talk about peace. Then Wallace realized Beanie had seen his letter to Truman, although he had never himself shown Baldwin a copy of it. Finally, Wallace acquiesced and at a subsequent meeting it was agreed that the Sept. 12 speech would cover the same general ground as the July 23 letter to the President.

Then Beanie raised the question of clearance for the speech, recalling the rule that Roosevelt had put into effect that whenever any high government official intended to talk on a subject not under his own jurisdiction there must be White House clearance. What happened in such cases was that the White House routinely sent the manuscript around to the offices most likely to be interested, for their comment.

"If the usual method of clearance is followed, you'll never get to give that speech," Beanie told Wallace. When the latter asked what he should do, Baldwin said, "Why don't you go over and clear it personally with the President?"

At the time of this conversation not one word of the speech itself had been written. Because, in late 1940, Vice-President-elect Wallace had attended the inauguration of Manuel Avila Comacho as President of Mexico, he had been invited to visit Mexico City again, to hear Comacho deliver his report on his six years in office, on Sept. 1, 1946. He was to leave just a few days after his conversation with Beanie and would not return until Sept. 9. So Wallace phoned the White House to make an appointment to see the President on Tuesday, Sept. 10.

I have heard Henry Wallace tell of that interview numerous times and so have many others. According to him, it lasted over an hour. He held one copy of the speech while the President patiently read another. There were frequent pauses in the reading for questions and brief discussion. The most important interruption came when President Truman banged his fist on the desk and exclaimed, "By God, Henry, that *is* our foreign policy!" This was right after the sentence which read: "In this connection I want one thing clearly understood. I am neither anti-British nor pro-British, neither anti-Russian nor pro-Russian."

"May I quote you as saying so?" Wallace then asked. The answer was affirmative so, two nights later, Wallace followed that sentence with: "And just two days ago, when President Truman read these words, he said they represented the policy of his administration."

When he returned to his office after his interview in the White House, Wallace told some of his colleagues of Truman's approval of the

mpending speech. Then he roguishly added, "But I don't think he under-
tood it."

Copies of Wallace's speech were distributed in advance of President
Truman's press conference on Thursday morning, Sept. 12. On Saturday,
Sept. 14, amidst the furor that the speech caused, Truman called in
eporters and, without permitting any questions, read them the following
rief statement:

> "There has been a natural misunderstanding regarding the
> answer I made to a question asked at the press conference
> on Thursday, Sept. 12, with reference to the speech of the
> Secretary of Commerce delivered in New York later that
> day.
>
> "The question was answered extemporaneously and my
> answer did not convey the thought that I intended it to
> convey.
>
> "It was my intention to express the thought that I ap-
> proved the right of the Secretary of Commerce to deliver
> the speech.
>
> "I did not intend to indicate that I approved the speech
> as constituting a statement of the foreign policy of this
> country.
>
> "There has been no change in the established foreign
> policy of our government. There will be no significant
> change in that policy without discussion and conference
> among the President, the Secretary of State and Congres-
> sional leaders."

Then, however, reporters referred to the stenographic transcript of
he Sept. 12 interview which showed, as such transcripts always do,
he President's replies paraphrased because of a White House rule that
he must not be quoted directly without his permission. The transcript
vent as follows:

> "Reporter—'In a speech for delivery tonight Secretary of
> State—I mean Commerce—Wallace says that—'
>
> "The President broke in to ask if the reporter said the
> speech is to be delivered.
>
> "Reporter—'Yes.'
>
> "The President said he could not answer questions on any
> speech that hadn't been delivered yet.
>
> "Reporter—'Well, it's about you, that's why I asked you.'
>
> "The President asked what the question was, adding that
> maybe he could answer it.

61

"Reporter—'In the speech he says, "When President Truman read these words he said that they represented the policy of the administration." '

"The President replied that this was correct.

"Reporter—'Does that apply just to the paragraph or to the whole speech?'

"The President replied that it applied to the whole speech."

That ended that in the press conference.

The near-pandemonium that the Madison Square Garden speech created was due primarily to the fact that at the moment Secretary of State Byrnes, accompanied by the two outstanding exponents of bipartisanship in foreign policy—Sen. Arthur H. Vandenberg, Republican of Michigan, and Sen. Thomas Connally, erstwhile Democratic isolationist from Texas—was in Paris attending a meeting to draft peace treaties for Italy and the Balkan countries. Furthermore, six days earlier, on Sept. 6, Byrnes had gone to Stuttgart, Germany, to deliver one of the most important policy speeches of the post-war period. In essence it was a strong bid to woo German sympathies for the United States and away from the Soviet Union. Although Byrnes agreed that the Saar should go to France, he opposed giving Germany's ancient enemy the Ruhr or more of the Rhineland. He opposed heavy reparations, reminding his listeners—1,500 American Army officers and 150 German officials—that the United States had not made demands on Germany for payments. He endorsed de-Nazification and demilitarization but called for a unified, democratic German government instead of continued partition and prolonged occupation by foreign troops. He charged that carrying out the Potsdam Agreement had been obstructed by failure of the Allied Control Council to take the necessary steps to enable the German economy to function as an economic unit. In several different ways, he declared that American isolation is dead forever.

Byrnes' Stuttgart speech was taken to be a reply to the hour-long criticism that Russian Foreign Minister Vyacheslav M. Molotov had made on July 9, 1946, in Paris, of Byrnes' prior proposal for a four-power 25-year treaty to keep Germany disarmed. He objected because the plan would have meant the evacuation of troops from Germany before the $10 billion worth of reparations that the Soviet Union demanded of Germany had been paid. He said that Lt. Gen. Lucius D. Clay, American deputy military governor in Germany, had acted unlawfully in suspending reparations deliveries from the American zone. Byrnes had replied at the time that the deliveries were stopped because Germany had not become an economic unit and the United States was paying $200 million annually to maintain its zone.

Rereading Wallace's Madison Square Garden speech four years later Jonathan Daniels revealed in *The Man of Independence* (J. B. Lippincott 1950) that he was amazed to realize how much criticism of the Soviet Union it contained. To my knowledge the truth has never been told as to why Wallace omitted a few passages which had been included in the advance copies of the address. This led Dwight MacDonald to charge, in *Henry Wallace, The Man and the Myth* (Vanguard, 1947), that Wallace was lacking in moral courage because, he said, the deletions were made after some of the sentences just preceding them had been booed. This version has become the popularly accepted one, but it is incorrect.

There were boos, all right, from a small segment of the audience, at a few harsh statements regarding the Soviet Union. The deletions, however, were not made as a result of them. Rather, they had been made about an hour and a half before the speech was delivered, as a result of pressure applied by left wingers within the ICC-ASP; they had been made aware of what Wallace intended to say by the *Daily Worker,* which had received a copy of the speech that morning at the same time that other newspapers had gotten theirs. In an early-evening meeting with Wallace they urged him to make even further deletions. Observers tell me that these same persons who booed later lustily cheered other parts of the speech.

Because the Madison Square Garden speech resulted, a week later, in Wallace's dismissal from the Cabinet (after which, in my opinion, there was never any chance of preventing his running for President in 1948); because, in other words, it was the most eventful speech of Wallace's long public career, and because it stirred up an international debate over American foreign policy, there is herein reproduced that portion of the speech which became controversial. At the proper place the deletions which Wallace made—*before,* not *after,* he took to the platform—are indicated.

> Tonight I want to talk about peace—and how to get peace . . . Never have the common people of all lands so longed for peace. Yet, never in a time of comparative peace have they feared war so much.
>
> During the past year or so, the significance of peace has been increased immeasurably by the atom bomb, guided missiles and airplanes which soon will travel fast as sound. Make no mistake about it—another war would hurt the United States many times as much as the last war.
>
> We cannot rest in the assurance that we invented the atom bomb—and therefore that this agent of destruction will work best for us. He who trusts in the atom bomb will sooner or later perish by the atom bomb—or something worse.
>
> If modern war can cost us $400 billion, we should be willing and happy to pay much more for peace. But certainly, the cost of peace is to be measured not in dollars but in the hearts and minds of men.

The price of peace—for us and for every nation in the world—is the price of giving up prejudice, hatred, fear and ignorance.

Let's get down to cases here at home.

First we have prejudice, hatred, fear and ignorance of certain races. The recent mass lynching in Georgia was not merely the most unwarranted brutal act of mob violence in the United States in recent years; it was also an illustration of the kind of prejudice that makes war inevitable.

Hatred breeds hatred. The doctrine of racial superiority produces a desire to get even on the part of its victims. If we are to work for peace in the rest of the world, we here in the United States must eliminate racism from our unions, our business organizations, our educational institutions, and our employment practices. Merit alone must be the measure of man.

Second, in payment for peace, we must give up prejudice, hatred, fear and ignorance in the economic world. This means working earnestly, day after day, for a larger volume of world trade. It means helping undeveloped areas of the world to industrialize themselves with the help of American technical assistance and loans.

We should welcome the opportunity to help along the most rapid possible industrialization in Latin America, China, India, and the Near East. For as the productivity of these people increases, our exports will increase.

The Republican party is the party of economic nationalism and political isolationism—and as such is as anachronistic as the dodo and as certain to disappear. The danger is that before it disappears it may enjoy a brief period of power during which it can do irreparable damage to the United States and the cause of world peace.

Gov. Dewey has expressed himself as favoring an alliance of mutual defense with Great Britain as the key to our foreign policy.

Certainly we like the British people individually, but to make Britain the key to our foreign policy would be, in my opinion, the height of folly. We must not let the reactionary leadership of the Republican party force us into that position. We must not let British balance-of-power manipulations determine whether and when the United States gets into war.

Make no mistake about it—the British imperialistic

policy in the Near East alone, combined with Russian retaliation, would lead the United States straight to war unless we have a clearly defined and realistic policy of our own.

Neither of these two great powers wants war now, but the danger is that whatever their intentions may be, their current policies may eventually lead to war. To prevent war and insure our survival in a stable world, it is essential that we look abroad through our own American eyes and not through the eyes of either the British foreign office or a pro-British or anti-Russian press.

In this connection, I want one thing clearly understood. I am neither anti-British nor pro-British—neither anti-Russian nor pro-Russian. And just two days ago, when President Truman read these words, he said they represented the policy of his administration.

I plead for an America vigorously dedicated to peace —just as I plead for opportunities for the next generation throughout the world to enjoy the abundance which now, more than ever before, is the birthright of man.

To achieve lasting peace, we must study in detail just how the Russian character was formed—by invasions of Tartars, Mongols, Germans, Poles, Swedes and French; by the Czarist rule based on ignorance, fear and force; by the intervention of the British, French and Americans in Russian affairs from 1919 to 1921; by the geography of the huge Russian land mass situated strategically between Europe and Asia and by the vitality derived from the rich Russian soil and the strenuous Russian climate.

Add to all this the tremendous emotional power which Marxism and Leninism give to the Russian leaders— and then we can realize that we are reckoning with a force which cannot be handled successfully by a "get tough with Russia" policy. "Getting tough" never bought anything real and lasting—whether for schoolyard bullies or businessmen or world powers. The tougher we get, the tougher the Russians will get.

Throughout the world there are numerous reactionary elements which had hoped for Axis victory—and now profess great friendship for the United States. Yet, these enemies of yesterday and false friends of today continually try to provoke war between the United States and Russia. They have no real love for the United States. They only long for the day when the United States and Russia will destroy each other.

65

We must not let our Russian policy be guided or influenced by those inside or outside the United States who want war with Russia. This does not mean appeasement.

We most earnestly want peace with Russia—but we want to be met half way. We want co-operation. And I believe that we can get co-operation once Russia understands that our primary objective is neither saving the British Empire nor purchasing oil in the Near East with the lives of American soldiers.

We cannot allow national oil rivalries to force us into war. All of the nations producing oil, whether inside or outside of their own boundaries, must fulfill the provisions of the United Nations charter and encourage the development of world petroleum reserves so as to make the maximum amount of oil available to all nations of the world on an equitable peaceful basis—and not on the basis of fighting the next war.

The real peace treaty we now need is between the United States and Russia. On our part, we should recognize that we have no more business in the political affairs of Eastern Europe than Russia has in the political affairs of Latin America, Western Europe and the United States.

We may not like what Russia does in Eastern Europe. Her type of land reform, industrial expropriation, and suppression of basic liberties offends the great majority of people of the United States.

But whether we like it or not, the Russians will try to socialize their sphere of influence just as we try to democratize our sphere of influence. This applies also to Germany and Japan. We are striving to democratize Japan and our area of control in Germany, while Russia strives to socialize eastern Germany.

As for Germany, we all must recognize that an equitable settlement, based on a unified German nation, is absolutely essential to any lasting European settlement. This means that Russia must be assured that never again can German industry be converted into military might to be used against her—and Britain, Western Europe and the United States must be certain that Russia's German policy will not become a tool of Russian design against Western Europe.

We know what Russia is up to in Eastern Europe, for example, and Russia knows what we are up to. We cannot permit the door to be closed against our trade in Eastern Europe any more than we can in China. But at the same time we have to recognize that the Balkans are closer to Russia than to us—and that Russia cannot permit either England or the United States to dominate the politics of that area.

China is a special case and although she holds the longest frontier in the world with Russia, the interests of world peace demand that China remain free from any sphere of influence, either politically or economically.

However, the open doors to economic development in China are meaningless unless there is a unified and peaceful China—built on the co-operation of the various groups in that country and based on a hands-off policy of the outside powers.

Russian ideas of social-economic justice are going to govern nearly a third of the world. Our ideas of free enterprise democracy will govern much of the rest.

*Note: The words enclosed in [brackets] in the following two paragraphs were given by Mr. Wallace to the press but omitted from his oral delivery of the speech.*

The two ideas will endeavor to prove which can deliver the most satisfaction to the common man in the respective areas of political dominance. But by mutual agreement this competition should be put on a friendly basis [and the Russians should stop conniving against us in certain areas of the world just as we should stop scheming against them in other parts of the world]. Let the results of the two systems speak for themselves.

[Meanwhile, the Russians should stop teaching their form of Communism must, by force if necessary, ultimately triumph over democratic capitalism—while] we should close our ears to those among us who would have us believe that Russian Communism and our free enterprise system cannot live, one with another, in a profitable and productive peace.

Under friendly, peaceful competition, the Russian world and the American world will gradually become more alike. The Russians will be forced to grant more and more of the personal freedoms; and we shall become more and more absorbed with the problems of social-economic justice.

Once the fears of Russia and the U.S. Senate have been allayed by practical regional political reservations, I am sure that concern over the veto power would be greatly diminished.

Then the United Nations would have a really great power in those areas which are truly international and not regional.

In the world-wide, as distinguished from the regional field, the armed might of the United Nations should be so great as to make opposition useless.

Only the United Nations should have atomic bombs and its military establishment should give special emphasis to air power. It should have control of the strategically located air bases with which the United States and Britain have encircled the world.

And not only should individual nations be prohibited from manufacturing atomic bombs, guided missiles and military aircraft for bombing purposes, but no nation should be allowed to spend on its military establishment more than perhaps 15 percent of its budget.

Practically and immediately, we must recognize that we are not yet ready for world federation. Realistically, the most we can hope for now is a safe reduction in military expense and a long period of peace on mutual trust between the Big Three.

During this period, every effort should be made to develop as rapidly as possible a body of international law based on moral principles and not on the Machiavellian principles of deceit, force and distrust—which, if continued, will lead the modern world to rapid disintegration.

In brief, as I see it today, the world order is bankrupt—and the United States, Russia and England are the receivers.

These are the hard facts of power politics on which we have to build a functioning, powerful United Nations and a body of international law. And as we build, we must develop fully the doctrine of the rights of small peoples as contained in the United Nations charter.

This law should ideally apply as much to Indonesians and Greeks as to Bulgarians and Poles—but practically, the application may be delayed until both British and Russians discover the futility of their methods.

In the full development of the rights of small nations, the British and Russians can learn a lesson from the good neighbor policy of Franklin Roosevelt. For under Roosevelt, we in the Western Hemisphere built a workable system of regional internationalism that fully protected the sovereign rights of every nation—a system of multilateral action that immeasurably strengthened the whole of world order.

I believe that peace—the kind of peace I have outlined tonight—is the basic issue, both in the Congressional campaign this fall and right on through the Presidential election in 1948.

How we meet this issue will determine whether we live, not in "one world" or "two worlds"—but whether we live at all.

Probably also through newspaper channels, an advance copy of this speech reached the State Department in mid-afternoon and was the object of considerable excitement, of which a garbled account appears in *The Forrestal Diaries* (Viking, 1951). Regardless of that, no later than 6 p.m. Will Clayton, Acting Secretary of State, talked to Press Secretary Charles Ross at the White House, regarding the imminent speech. There was still plenty of time to try to persuade Wallace to make additional changes, had the President wanted to do so.

If Harry Truman really believed that there was nothing inconsistent between the views of Henry Wallace and Jimmy Byrnes, he soon found out that he was the only person who did. Most newspapers and many political and other leaders said that Wallace had raised issues which needed careful consideration, but few engaged in much consideration of them. Instead, those who didn't like Henry Wallace anyway—and that meant most newspapers and professional politicians—took literary swats at him. However, they were even more severe in what they had to say about President Truman, for either willfully or stupidly "pulling the rug" out from under Byrnes. At the time the fact that, nine months earlier, Truman had considered his Secretary of State "too easy" in his relations with the Soviet Union was not generally known. It was generally supposed that the "get tough" policy which Byrnes had been following had Presidential approval. Consequently, many saw in Truman's endorsement of Wallace's speech merely a political trick to hold left wing Democratic votes in the November, 1946 election. The confusion that the Presidential act was bound to create all over the world, as to understanding what American foreign policy was, however, was roundly deplored and Truman was widely charged with having committed an irresponsible act. When *Mr. President* appeared, it was revealed that Truman and Byrnes had been feuding for nine months and that Byrnes had submitted his own resignation on April 16, 1946, to take effect July 1. He had stayed on at Truman's insistence. In *Collier's* for April 26, 1952, Byrnes vigorously denied that Truman ever read him the letter dated Jan. 5, 1946, which is included (with a partial facsimile of it) in *Mr. President*. He also denies having gotten the "riot act" from Truman on Dec. 29, 1945, on the presidential yacht *Williamsburg*. Nevertheless, the fact that the two men had cooled by September, 1946 seems indisputable.

Acting Secretary of State Clayton refused to be drawn into a discussion of the merits of Wallace's proposals. At a press conference the day after the Madison Square Garden speech, he admitted he did not understand President Truman's endorsement of the speech but, as far as he was concerned, the policies of the Department of State continued to be what Secretary Byrnes said they were. In Paris, Byrnes himself maintained a public silence, leaving it up to Senators Vandenberg and Connally to make formal statements. That they did. On Sept. 14, Vandenberg said:

> The authority of American foreign policy is dependent upon the degree of American unity behind it. Rightly or wrongly, Paris is doubtful of this unity this morning.

> Our bipartisan foreign policy during the last 18 months has had overwhelming bipartisan support in the behalf of the unselfish aim for which we fought the war. Though differing in some points, most Republicans have been glad to join with most Democrats in thus presenting a united American front to the world. This is the only road to organized peace and collective security.

> Those who leave this road jeopardize the very objective which they profess to embrace.

> I am sure most Republicans, despite inevitable differences in some aspects, will be glad to continue to seek unity with the administration in bipartisan foreign policy on a sound American basis which rejects dictatorship by anybody, which is neither hostile nor subservient to any other power on earth, and which defends human rights and fundamental freedom.

> But the situation equally requires unity within the administration itself. We can only co-operate with one Secretary of State at a time.

Connally's viewpoint was similar: "There must be no division behind the lines." According to the *Chicago Tribune* for Sept. 21, 1946 James A. Farley conferred with Byrnes in Paris and urged strong action.

In *Speaking Frankly* (Harper, 1947), Byrnes relates that he avoided representatives of other countries throughout the hectic week that ensued. He also made public in his book the text of the message he sent President Truman on Sept. 18 and his side of the teletype conversation he had with the White House on Sept. 19. Very succinctly, Byrnes' ultimatum was: either shut Wallace up permanently or I quit at once. In the meantime, on Monday, Sept. 16, Wallace had reaffirmed his position in a press conference, saying, "I stand on my New York speech," and indicated that he intended to speak again, on Sept. 23, to the East-West Association in New York and on Sept. 24 at Providence, R. I., under NC-PAC auspices. In October, he had been booked for 15 campaign speeches by the speakers bureau of the Democratic national committee.

On Tuesday, Sept. 17 came a new "blockbuster": publication of the full contents of Wallace's July 23 letter to the President. This came about when some newspapermen learned that the noted columnist Drew Pearson possessed a copy and intended to use it the next day. So they beseiged both Wallace and Charles Ross, White House press secretary, for copies for themselves. Without waiting to consult the President, Ross gave Wallace permission to release the letter. When Truman learned of the action it was too late to rescind the permission, as the copies were already out. How Drew Pearson obtained his copy was at first an object of controversy. In a formal statement, Wallace said a copy "was filched from the files and is in the hands of a newspaper columnist." Pearson threatened to sue for libel, saying he had come into possession of his copy "in open and above-board fashion from sources which had no connection with his department." Then it was learned that the "leak" had been in the State Department, where several copies of Wallace's letter had been floating around, and Wallace apologized to Pearson.

Wallace had written his July 23 letter at President Truman's request, following a Cabinet meeting a few days earlier. It was too long to quote fully here, but can be obtained in a Pamphlet Press book, *The Fight for Peace,* published by Reynal & Hitchcock in October, 1946.

Writing as Secretary of Commerce, Wallace pointed out that approximately 80 per cent of Truman's proposed budget for fiscal 1947 was to pay for wars: past, present and future; no reduction would be possible without a cut in military appropriations. "Thus, even from a purely dollars and cents standpoint," he wrote, "American business and the American people have an interest in organizing a peaceful world in which the completely unproductive expenditures on national defense could be reduced." A more important reason for wanting a peaceful world, however, was because an atomic war "will undoubtedly be directed primarily against civilian populations and may well mean the end of modern civilization." He added that the huge military expenditures, the Bikini tests of atomic bombs, the plans to arm Latin American countries with our weapons, production of B-36's and the effort to secure air bases spread over half the globe "must make it look to the rest of the world as if we were only paying lip service to peace at the conference table."

Wallace challenged the military concepts of "predominance of force" and "defensive attack" as impractical in atomic warfare and declared that, even if we succeeded in destroying all Russian industrial centers, we would be faced with the necessity of also destroying most of the other cities of Western Europe, as the Red Army would immediately overrun the continent.

What turned out to be the most controversial part of the Wallace letter was his attack on the American plan for international control of atomic energy, which had recently been presented to the United Nations Atomic Energy Commission. This was the so-called Baruch plan and was an interpolation of the earlier Acheson-Lilienthal proposals. The scheme's defect, according to Wallace, was that of "arriving at international agreements by 'many stages,' of requiring other nations to enter into binding commitments not to conduct research into the military uses of atomic energy and to disclose their uranium and thorium resources while the United States retains the right to withhold its technical knowledge of atomic energy until the international control and inspection system is working to our satisfaction.

"In other words, we are telling the Russians that if they are 'good boys' we may eventually turn over our knowledge of atomic energy to them and to the other nations. But there is no objective standard of what will qualify them as being 'good' nor any specified time for sharing our knowledge. Is it any wonder that the Russians did not show any great enthusiasm for our plan?"

Although the nature of the conversation was not revealed, on Sept. 18, the day after the release of the letter, Bernard Baruch saw Truman. Six days later, he sent the President a long memorandum answering Wallace's criticisms. There followed quite a hassle between Baruch and Wallace. The former charged that, during a conference in New York's Empire State Building, Wallace admitted he "obviously had not been fully posted as to the facts" and promised to sign a statement pointing out his mistakes. This promise, Baruch charged on Oct. 3, Wallace refused to keep. Wallace responded publicly that Baruch had prepared a "fantastic" statement which was tantamount to an "admission of inaccuracy and a full endorsement" of Baruch's ideas. Rather, Wallace said, "Nothing in the recent statement of Mr. Baruch would cause me to revise the basic tenets in my letter to President Truman concerning the way to peace and atomic energy control."

It should be recalled that Henry Wallace was an original member of the commission, appointed by President Roosevelt late in 1939, to investigate the use of atomic energy for military purposes. By the end of 1941, the project was under the direction of a group of eminent scientists headed by Dr. Vannevar Bush. Wallace was on the general policy group, which also consisted of Stimson, Marshall, Bush and Dr. James Conant, president of Harvard University. It was this group which recommended the transfer of the major part of the program to the War Department; Maj. Gen. Groves was appointed by Stimson to direct the project.

Wallace has told me that his participation, from 1941 on, was mostly directed at keeping FDR's interest alive and making certain enough money was available for the experimental work. He was not consulted in 1945, however, over use of the bomb; he knew nothing of the successful experiment in New Mexico, or of the Hiroshima and Nagasaki raids, until he read of them in the newspapers like everyone else.

Forrestal, to put it charitably, was an inaccurate scribe; but he was probably correct in recording that, at Cabinet meetings early in 1946, Wallace objected to the Bikini tests being under strict military control. On March 12, 1946, Wallace publicly opposed the Vandenberg proposal to allow a military committee to "advise and consult" with the Atomic Energy Control Commission as they affected military usages. This, Wallace said, would deliver the nation into the hands of "military fascism." In his diary for March 14, 1946, Vandenberg called Wallace's charges "fantastic nonsense," but the scientists shared it and Vandenberg, to get his proposal through, had to revise it to limit the military committee's authority to "military applications" only, rather than "common defense and security." According to his son, Vandenberg learned a lesson from this setback and thereafter sidestepped obstacles, "instead of crashing into them."

The most grotesquely inaccurate entry in the Forrestal *Diaries* is that related to the Sept. 21, 1945, Cabinet meeting, at which the question of secrecy regarding the atomic bomb was discussed. Wallace, according to the *Diaries,* was "completely, everlasting and wholeheartedly in favor of giving it to the Russians." Forrestal wasn't content to leave this notation for posterity. Instead, he immediately "leaked" information to Felix Belair of the *New York Times.* In the Sept. 22, 1945, issue of that newspaper appeared a signed article by Belair which began, "A proposal sponsored by Secretary of Commerce Wallace that the United States, Britain and Canada reveal the secret of the atom bomb to Russia was discussed at President Truman's Cabinet meeting today and brought about a pointed debate that ended with no decision after having caused the longest Cabinet session of the present administration."

The story contained quite a few alleged quotations from Wallace's remarks at the Cabinet meeting. Immediately it appeared, Wallace told me, he went to see President Truman to protest that, unless the nature of Cabinet discussions was kept private, he would consider it impossible to speak up during them. Two days later, the *New York Times* contained an article relating President Truman's denial that Wallace had recommended that the atomic bomb secrets be turned over to the Soviet Union. In the same statement, the President declared that he would accept full responsibility for the future development of the atomic bomb. Included in *Mr. President,* by William Hillman, is a memorandum dated Sept. 24, 1945, from President Truman to Senator Connally, stating that he had been quoted inaccurately in the newspaper accounts. "The statement that was made was that I would assume full responsibility for the recommendation to be made to the Congress on the policy," he explained. "Of course the policy will have to be finally determined by the Congress . . . "

It was only after the *Diaries* appeared in 1951 that Wallace was certain of what he had always suspected: that it had been Forrestal who was responsible for the tip to Belair. Just as Vandenberg thought he was faced with the "ill-informed and ill-tempered" criticism of only one man, whom he didn't like, until Senator Brian McMahon and others of his colleagues joined the scientists in support of the Wallace position, so also Forrestal fixed on the views—which he then distorted—of a man whom he disliked and feared, namely, the same Wallace.

The utter inaccuracy and unfairness of the Belair story and the Forrestal diary entry were proven with the publication of *On Active Service in Peace and War* (Harper, 1948), by Henry L. Stimson and McGeorge Bundy. It reveals that it was the Secretary of War on the day of his retirement, which was also his 78th birthday, who, at the Sept. 21, 1945, Cabinet meeting proposed sharing the atomic bomb secret with the Soviet Union. Two sections, which Stimson later told his collaborator were the "heart" of the memorandum he wrote on the subject under the date of

Sept. 11, 1945, are italicized in the Stimson-Bundy book. They are as follows:

> *Those relations may be perhaps irretrievably embittered by the way in which we approach the solution of the bomb with Russia. For if we fail to approach them now and merely continue to negotiate with them, having this weapon rather ostentatiously on our side, their suspicions and their distrust of our purposes and motives will increase.*

> *I emphasize perhaps beyond all other considerations the importance of taking this action with Russia as a proposal of the United States—backed by Great Britain but peculiarly the proposal of the United States. Action of any international group of nations, including many small nations who have not demonstrated their potential power or responsibility in this war would not, in my opinion, be taken seriously by the Soviets.*

All of this was not much different from what Wallace said in his July 23, 1946, letter to Truman:

> We may feel very self-righteous if we refuse to budge on our plan and the Russians refuse to accept it, but that means only one thing—the atomic armament race is on in deadly earnest.

> I am convinced therefore that if we are to achieve our hopes of negotiating a treaty which will result in effective atomic disarmament, we must abandon the impractical form of the "step-by-step" idea which was presented to the United Nations Atomic Energy Commission.

Several months earlier, on Jan. 31, 1946, Wallace had appeared before the Senate Committee on Atomic Energy, to denounce secrecy in regard to the Manhattan project and to elucidate three principles as "the only possible alternative to an atomic arms race and ultimate chaos." They were:

> It must provide for civilian control in complete harmony with our international policy.

> It must provide the basis for a free international exchange of basic scientific information and the exchange of technical information when international arrangements make that possible.

> It must provide for the early development of the best possible techniques of inspection, which this country can then offer and propose to the United Nations.

74

The Stimson-Wallace view was also consistent with that of most of America's leading atomic scientists. On Oct. 9, 1945, Dr. Harlow Shapley, director of the Harvard observatory, told a Senate military-commerce subcommittee that it would be "unwise" to try to keep atomic knowledge secret "for any appreciable time." On Oct. 18, 1945, Dr. Harold Urey of the University of Chicago and Dr. H. J. Curtis of Oak Ridge, Tenn., who participated in the Manhattan project, called the administration bills to control atomic energy an invitation to a world-wide bomb armament race. Dr. J. Robert Oppenheimer, who also had helped make the first bombs, expressed a similar view. On Nov. 2, 1945, Dr. James B. Conant, president of Harvard University, told the same committee that hopes of outlawing the bombs were unrealistic. Four days later, Soviet Foreign Commissar Molotov, at a celebration of the Bolshevik revolution, said there were no technical secrets involved in the atom bomb and that it would not be long before the Soviet Union had one.

On Wednesday, Sept. 18, 1946, the day after the July 23 letter became public, Wallace had an afternoon session with Truman which was clocked, by the approximately 150 newspapermen who waited outside the White House, as lasting 2 hours 20 minutes. There was remarkable agreement in the accounts of what happened when the Secretary of Commerce finally emerged. From penciled notes he read a short statement:

"The President and the Secretary of Commerce had a most detailed and friendly discussion, after which the Secretary reached the conclusion that he would make no public statements or speeches until the foreign ministers' conference in Paris is concluded."

He then made it clear he meant the current meeting of 21 nations working on the peace treaties, which supposedly would end about Oct. 15, not the foreign ministers' conference which would follow.

"Are you standing on your Madison Square Garden speech?" a reporter asked.

"Absolutely," was the reply.

"Was any telephone call put through to Byrnes at Paris during your discussion?"

"There were no telephone calls whatever."

"Why did you make this decision?"

"The reason for making the decision is because all the hungry wolves are here. That's the way the press determines things," said Mr. Wallace, leaving his questioners bewildered as to his meaning. In later dispatches it was conjectured that he thought the question pertained to why he was making any statement to reporters.

"What led to your conclusion that you should make no more public statements?"

"The fact that I'm an honest man," Wallace replied, evidently meaning he intended to live up to his promise.

"What did the President say that led to your conclusion that you would refrain from further discussion of foreign policy?"

"The President was very confident about peace with Russia."

According to I. F. Stone in the Sept. 22, 1946 PM, Truman persuaded

Wallace to declare his month's moratorium on speech-making by promising that if Byrnes failed at Paris, he would negotiate directly with Stalin.

Perhaps the most widely discussed entry in *Mr. President* was the "Mr. X" comment, dated Sept. 19, 1946:

> Mr. X spent two and a half hours talking to me yesterday. I am not sure he is as fundamentally sound, intellectually as I had thought. He advised me that I should be far to the "left" when Congress was not in session and that I should move right when Congress is on hand and in session. He said FDR did that and that FDR never let his "right" hand know what his "left" hand did.
>
> X is a pacifist 100 percent. He wants us to disband our armed forces, give Russia our atomic secrets and trust a bunch of adventurers in the Kremlin Politburo. I do not understand a "dreamer" like that. The German-American Bund under Fritz Kuhn was not half so dangerous. The Reds, phonies and the "parlor pinks" seem to be banded together and are becoming a national disgrace.
>
> I am afraid they are a sabotage front for Uncle Joe Stalin. They can see no wrong in Russia's 4½ million armed force, in Russia's loot of Poland, Austria, Hungary, Rumania, Manchuria. They can see no wrong in Russia's living off the occupied countries to support the military occupation.
>
> But when we help our friends in China who fought on our side it is terrible. When Russia loots the industrial plants of those same friends it is all right. When Russia occupies Persia for oil, that is heavenly, although Persia was Russia's ally in the terrible German war. We sent all our supplies, which went to Russia by the southern route through Persia—sent them with Persia's help.

Harry Truman refused to identify Mr. X after reporters checked to determine that his only two-and-a-half-hour visitor on Sept. 18, 1946 had been Wallace. On his part, Wallace said that if Truman ever did confess it was he who was meant he would bring action for libel.

In his July 23 letter, Wallace had written:

> There is a school of military thinking which recognizes these facts, recognizes that when several nations have atomic bombs, a war which will destroy civilization will result and that no nation or combination of nations can win such a war. This school of thought, therefore, advocates a "preventive war," an attack on Russia now before Russia has atomic bombs. This scheme is not only immoral but stupid.

Immediately after the conclusion of the White House session between Truman and Wallace, Secretary of War Patterson and Secretary of the Navy Forrestal made public a joint statement declaring:

> There is no basis for this statement. There is no such military thinking in the War and Navy departments. We know of no responsible officer in the Army or Navy who has ever advocated or even suggested a policy or plan of attacking Russia.

In his account of the day's proceedings, which appeared in the *Chicago Sun* for Sept. 19, 1946, Thomas F. Reynolds interjected his own comment:

> Although no responsible Army or Navy officer ever has advocated such a policy of preventive war in public, there are few well-informed newspapermen in Washington who haven't heard the suggestion from officers in both services, responsible or otherwise, supporting such an idea.

Six days earlier, on Sept. 13, 1946, the same newspaper had used the following Associated Press item, datelined New Orleans, Sept. 12:

> John Stelle, National Commander of the American Legion, would not comment today on the possibility of war, but he said in an interview with the *New Orleans States,* "We ought to aim an atomic rocket at Moscow—and save one for Tito, too."
>
> He said Russia was holding up the peace conference at Paris with the attitude that "no country can have international relations except Russia."

In late 1942 Stelle, then lieutenant governor, for a few months became Governor of Illinois, following the death of Gov. Henry Horner.

On Thursday, Sept. 19, 1946, Truman and Byrnes had their twenty-minute transoceanic teletype conversation, his side of which Byrnes revealed in his book. On Friday morning, Sept. 20, 1946, Truman called in the newspapermen and read them the following statement:

> The foreign policy of this country is the most important question confronting us today. Our responsibility for obtaining a just and lasting peace extends not only to the people of this country but to the nations of the world.
>
> The people of the United States may disagree freely and publicly on any question, including that of foreign policy, but the Government of the United States must stand as a unit in its relations with the rest of the world.
>
> I have today asked Mr. Wallace to resign from the Cabi-

net. It had become clear that between his views on foreign policy and those of the Administration—the latter being shared, I am confident, by the great body of our citizens—there was a fundamental conflict. We could not permit this conflict to jeopardize our position in relation to other countries. I deeply regret the breaking of a long and pleasant official association, but I am sure that Mr. Wallace will be happier in the exercise of his right to present his views as a private citizen. I am confirmed in this belief by a very friendly conversation I had with Mr. Wallace on the telephone this morning.

Our foreign policy as established by the Congress, the President and the Secretary of State remains in full force and effect without change. No change in our foreign policy is contemplated. No member of the executive branch of the Government will make any public statement as to foreign policy which is in conflict with our established foreign policy. Any public statement on foreign policy shall be cleared with the Dept. of State. In case of disagreement, the matter will be referred to me.

As I have frequently said, I have complete confidence in Mr. Byrnes and his delegation now representing this country at the Paris Peace Conference.

Mr. Byrnes consults with me often and the policies which guide him and his delegations have my full endorsement.

President Truman broke the news to Wallace by telephone earlier that morning. The Secretary of Commerce was conferring at the time with Harold Young. his solicitor, firm in the belief that the agreement reached on Wednesday afternoon was final.

"Henry," the President said over the phone, "I am asking for your resignation."

"If that's your decision, Mr. President, I'll be very happy to comply."

Within half an hour there was delivered to President Truman the following message:

Dear Harry:

As you requested, here is my resignation. I shall continue to fight for peace. I am sure that you will join me in that great endeavor.

Respectfully,

H. A. WALLACE

That night Wallace made a brief radio speech over a nationwide hookup, the complete text of which follows:

Winning the peace is more important than high public office. It is more important than any consideration of party politics.

The success or failure of our foreign policy will mean the difference between life and death for our children and our grandchildren. It will mean the difference between the life or death of our civilization. It may mean the difference between the existence and the extinction of man and of the world. It is therefore of supreme importance, and we should every one of us regard it as a holy duty, to join the fight for winning the peace. I, for my part, firmly believe there is nothing more important that I can do than work in the cause of peace.

The action taken by the President this morning relieves me of my obligation of last Wednesday. I feel that our present foreign policy does not recognize the basic realities which led to two world wars and which now threaten another war—this time an atomic war. However, I do not wish to abuse the freedom granted me by the President this morning by saying anything tonight which might interfere with the success of the Paris Conference. But I do feel it proper to clear up some points about which there has been widespread misunderstanding of my Madison Square Garden speech.

I don't have to tell anyone who has followed my views on international affairs that I began talking about "one world" more than fifteen years ago. I do not believe in two worlds. I have continuously and wholeheartedly advocated the principles of living in one world. We cannot have peace except in "one world."

I wish to make clear again that I am against all types of imperialism and aggression, whether they are of Russian, British, or American origin. Also I wish to emphasize that the one world concept must be held steadfastly; and that any regionalism necessary to give practical form to world economic and political realities must take into account the rights of small nations just as the nations of the Western Hemisphere have done under Franklin Roosevelt's Good Neighbor Policy.

The success of any policy rests ultimately upon the confidence and the will of the people. There can be no basis for such success unless the people know and understand the issues—unless they are given all the facts—and unless they seize the opportunity to take part in the framing of foreign policy through full and open debate.

In this debate, we must respect the rights and interests

of other peoples, just as we expect them to respect ours. How we resolve this debate, as I said in my New York speech, will determine not whether we live in "one world" or "two worlds"—but whether we live at all.

I intend to carry on the fight for peace.

According to Beanie Baldwin, in many conversations during the preceding year and a half Henry Wallace had told him that if he ever left the cabinet he wanted it to be on a foreign policy issue. This was in part his excuse for not quitting at the same time Harold Ickes did, to the displeasure of Ickes. From several who were close to Wallace at the time, I have become convinced that there had been no visible friction or tension between Truman and Wallace in the preceding months. Wallace felt he was in a position to influence Truman and believed that he had a chance to succeed in the effort. That Baldwin hoped the Madison Square Garden speech would end as it did—with Wallace's firing—I do not believe and I am thoroughly convinced that his dismissal was a great surprise and shock to Wallace.

Comment was what might have been expected. Those who had always disliked Wallace, and had opposed his renomination in 1944 and his appointment to the cabinet in 1945, said "At last" and "Good riddance." Others more soberly declared that, having gotten himself into the kind of predicament he did, through his own blundering, Truman had no alternative but to choose between Wallace and Byrnes. Even before the firing, the New York Liberal party on Sept. 17 denounced Wallace for his Madison Square Garden speech. Through its chairman, Dr. John L. Childs, the party charged that Wallace "has departed from the cause of democratic liberalism" and that "in matters of foreign policy we can no longer follow him." For the NC-PAC, Frank Kingdon and C. B. Baldwin lamented, "The progressives and independents have lost their one strong voice in the administration . . . It underscores the extent to which Truman has drifted from the policies and programs of Franklin D. Roosevelt, a program which he was pledged to support."

"More than any other since Franklin Roosevelt, Henry Wallace has now served his country by pointing up the gigantic issues which we, as a people, must face and debate," declared the *Chicago Sun* on Sept. 19, 1946, in an editorial which generally supported Wallace's position.

"His speech and his letter have raised issues far too fundamental simply to die away into the silence which Mr. Truman doubtless fervently desires," editorialized the *Chicago Times* the same day.

"He has asked too many of the disturbing questions which uneasy Americans have been asking themselves for many months simply to try to ignore them into oblivion."

And that, of course, is what he kept on doing, throughout the rest of 1946 and until the middle of 1950.

# ¶5 WALLACE IN 1946 AND BEFORE. *What Henry Wallace said and did after World War II was consistent with his background from World War I to that time.*

Whenever he was questioned in later years about the origin of the Progressive party, Henry A. Wallace recalled that when he left the cabinet in September, 1946, he said peace was the overpowering issue of the times and that he intended to take part in the 1948 campaign.

I have been unable to find any newspaper or other periodical reference to any such quotation by Mr. Wallace at the time, but I have no doubt that that is the way he felt. In fact, he told me so on several occasions. J. W. Gitt, publisher of the York (Pa.) *Gazette and Daily,* says he had no doubt of Wallace's intentions after HAW spoke in York on April 28, 1946, at a Jefferson-Jackson Day dinner in which he said, "Certain people who represent a narrow sectional interest and oppose the national interest are doing their utmost to wreck the economic stability of the whole nation."

If Wallace's motives had been political in the usual sense, they would have been understandable and even considered admirable in most political circles. Whatever anyone thought of Wallace's ideas as he expressed them at Madison Square Garden, he couldn't deny that Truman gave Wallace a pretty raw deal. This was the same Truman, furthermore, who had beaten Wallace in July, 1944 for the Vice Presidential nomination of the Democratic party, which meant robbing him of the Presidency itself.

If politics is your business you reform your lines after a couple of such shellackings and plan your strategy to "get" your enemy the next time. The motivation is not revenge as the term is used in non-political matters. It's just part of the Great Game of Politics as it is played. You're respected if you play it that way and belittled if you don't.

The difficulty in using this orthodox formula to explain Henry Wallace and the Progressive party is that Henry Wallace never was a politician and revenge was not a *conscious* motive, as he spent the last three months of 1946 and all of 1947 building himself up for a Presidential try in 1948.

Dr. Samuel Rosen, physician, neighbor and longtime personal friend of Henry Wallace, who is also a student of semantics, has warned me that any attempt to determine Wallace's motives in 1948 would be speculative "at a high level of abstraction." Human motivations are always complex, Dr. Rosen said, but most people are not persuaded to do things against their will. I value and agree with this advice and I do not believe it inconsistent to express one of the firmest opinions I have regarding Henry A. Wallace: that throughout his entire public life, he never weighed carefully the political consequences of any important decision or act.

After a meeting in December, 1947, at which a delegation from Massachusetts urged Wallace to announce his independent candidacy, Leon Mohill, Pittsfield businessman, lingered for a personal chat with Wallace. Mohill asked Wallace bluntly why he wanted to run. At first the answers were in the form of the usual arguments related to the political issues of the moment. When Mohill persisted, however, Wallace finally blurted: "Harry Truman is a son-of-a-bitch."

Even this anecdote and several others I could relate of occasions on which Wallace made similarly blunt remarks concerning Harry Truman do not convince me that revenge was Wallace's motive. He had a great amount of company from coast to coast in his opinion of Harry Truman; in his judgment, it was not good for the United States for such a person to be President.

Henry Agard Wallace served longer than any other member of Franklin Delano Roosevelt's original New Deal Cabinet. He arrived in Washington in March, 1933, to become Secretary of Agriculture throughout the first two Roosevelt administrations, from Des Moines where he had been editing *Wallace's Farmer*. That paper had been founded in 1895 by his grandfather, "Uncle Henry" Wallace (as he was widely known throughout Iowa), a militant speaker and writer in behalf of the farmers' rights after he quit the United Presbyterian ministry because of poor health. "Uncle Henry," whose "Sabbath School Lessons" previously had made him widely known, adopted "Good Farming, Clear Thinking, Right Living" as the masthead for his new paper. At first he militantly attacked the railroads but later toned down his opposition, both because of pressure from advertisers and others on his business partner and because the screaming tactics of the Populists were distasteful to him. He served on President Theodore Roosevelt's Country Life Commission, and probably could have been Secretary of Agriculture if he would have accepted. Instead he boosted his old friend, James Wilson, for the position in the cabinets of Presidents McKinley, Theodore Roosevelt and Taft. He died in 1916 when his grandson, Henry Agard Wallace, was 28 years old. Russell Lord, author of *The Wallaces of Iowa* (Houghton Mifflin, 1947), and other biographers agree that the third Henry Wallace was more influenced by his grandfather than by his father, who served as Secretary of Agriculture under Presidents Harding and Coolidge. Henry C. Wallace, who died in office suddenly in 1924, was a taciturn man who wrote and spoke little in public. Nevertheless, he supported the McNary-Haugen bills for agricultural relief, which President Coolidge twice vetoed, and bitterly opposed Secretary of Commerce Herbert Hoover on many economic issues in Cabinet meetings.

In 1929, while Henry Agard Wallace was abroad, other members of his family made an unwise business move when they purchased a competing farm paper, to combine it with *Wallace's Farmer*. Three years later the family lost financial control of the publication, but Wallace continued as editor. In fact, throughout his eight years as Secretary of

Agriculture, his name continued to appear on the masthead as editor-on-leave.

To backtrack a bit, Henry Agard Wallace was born on Oct. 7, 1888 on a farm in Adair county, Iowa, the first of six children. His mother's maiden name was Carrie Mae Brodhead and she lived until May 12, 1948, the middle of her son's campaign for President of the United States. Wallace attended State College at Ames, Iowa, where his father was a member of the faculty, and in 1910 was granted the degree of Bachelor of Science in Animal Husbandry On May 30, 1914, he married one of his college classmates, Miss Ilo Browne of Indianola, Iowa, They had three children: Henry, born in 1915; Robert, born in 1918; and Jean, born in 1921.

The financial setback to *Wallace's Farmer* did not ruin Wallace, although some of his closest associates differ widely regarding his financial status when he went to Washington in 1933. According to Russell Lord, he had about $3 million at that time. This Beanie Baldwin disbelieves emphatically, saying that HAW was for all practical purposes "broke" in 1933, saddled with considerable personal debt because of the mishap to the family paper. Shortly thereafter, however, he began to derive a substantial income from the Pioneer Hi-Bred Corn Company, which he personally established in 1926 and which, in 1948, he said was doing an annual business of $10 million. In the *Chicago Daily News* for Sept. 21, 1946, George Thiem estimated that Wallace's annual income was between $150,000 and $200,000 from the Pioneer Company, of whose stock he and his wife owned about 40 per cent.

That company, the first to produce hybrid corn successfully, was the outgrowth of Henry Agard Wallace's personal scientific experiments. Even those who are most opposed to Wallace's political views admit that he deserves respect and admiration for his experimental work in agricultural economics. This scientific interest was inspired in part by George Washington Carver, the great Negro agriculturist, who was at Iowa State College when Henry A. was a boy; Carver took him on walks to study various aspects of nature and taught him his first lessons regarding crossbreeding when he was only eight years old.

The anecdote is always told of how Henry Wallace as a lad questioned the judgment of the judges of corn at a county fair. It was the finest looking ears that always got the blue ribbons. Young Wallace contended that beauty was lost on pigs and was told by his indignant elders to test the results himself. That he did, and he not only proved his point but also worked out the first ratio charts for forecasting the course of the corn and hog markets, which are still in wide use.

Wallace's scientific experimentalism led him up a lot of side alleys, some of which, after he got into politics, caused him a lot of trouble. His interest in the effect of weather on agriculture caused him to study not merely astronomy, but astrology and other forms of mysticism as well. At various times he experimented with different types of diet, some of which probably were correctly called food fads. Either because— or in spite—of this careful attention to nutrition or his love for the outdoors, he certainly kept himself in first-class shape physically. He has always been able to outwalk anyone else and more than once answered inquiries as to whether he wasn't exhausted from his energetic campaigning by doing a couple of dozen pushups from the floor, tossing his questioner in a bout of Indian wrestling, or challenging someone to a game of tennis. In Washington he used to walk to work, play quite a bit of tennis (one familiar anecdote tells of how he once removed his shoes and returned to his office barefoot) and, after studying the thermodynamics involved, throw the boomerang. The last enterprise got him nationwide publicity, when he allowed news pictures to be taken in order to prevent the distribution of other pictures of him asleep in a barber's chair. He once broke a rather rare Australian boomerang, which a guard had loaned him from the Smithsonian Institution. Vandenberg mentioned in his papers that he once accompanied Wallace on a boomerang-throwing expedition, but didn't repeat the experience for fear of being beheaded. On automobile caravan trips, it was not uncommon for Wallace to descend and walk for miles at a time, just to limber up, while the rest of his exhausted entourage caught snoozes in the slow-moving cars.

Valuable as Henry Wallace's scientific interests might have been in their own right, they didn't condition him to be a good politician. Although science may have destroyed some old absolutistic religious views, it hasn't destroyed absolutistic thinking itself. In Wallace's case, a lifetime of scientific pursuits has made him an abstract thinker and a stickler for the truth as he sees it, without compromise or consideration of its effect, upon himself or anyone else. A great obstacle to Wallace's ever becoming a practical politician is his geneticist view of mankind. He loves people in the abstract, and his championing of the cause of the common man was not feigned. Angus Cameron once pointed out to me the fundamental difference in the ways Wallace and Harry Truman regard people. Whereas the latter loves and is intensely loyal to individuals and is almost completely lacking in any perspective as regards mankind as a whole, the former loves man as a species but has little or no feeling for any one individual.

Similarly, almost everyone who ever gave loyal service to Henry Wallace has felt that Wallace was lacking in gratitude and let him down. Lew Frank relates the anecdote of a walk with Wallace on which the latter suddenly exclaimed, "How wonderful it would be if we could practice genetics on people. We could turn out a beautiful golden race." Wallace's interest in people is curious and intellectual and he may be incapable of really deep affection. Several persons have told me that they never saw him display any when he met members of his family after long absences.

I know of no one who claims to have been really close to Henry Wallace. Several who traveled with him day and night, and endured much pain and sorrow with him, say they never felt they knew the man. Gardner Jackson, in the August, 1948, *Atlantic,* said that working with Wallace gave him an "eerie" feeling; he always felt HAW wasn't listening when he talked to him, even about serious matters. Forrestal related in his *Diaries* that he never learned how to talk to Wallace, and

84

Jonathan Daniels has written several times that Truman always considered Wallace strange and impossible to understand. Admiral Leahy, in *I Was There* (McGraw-Hill, 1950), related how he phoned Wallace upon his return from Vichy to extend to him the greetings of a Spanish friend, only to get the impression Wallace wasn't a bit interested. Grace Tully wrote in *FDR, My Boss* (Scribner's, 1949) that, whereas other Cabinet members and persons who came to see the President would stop to chat with her, Wallace never did. She once had the delightful surprise, upon being seated next to him at a dinner party, to discover him to be an intelligent and pleasant human being. Corliss Lamont speaks of a feeling of "trepidation" regarding Wallace. Russell Lord told me of another longtime associate of Wallace's who said, after visiting him at Farvue, his South Salem, N. Y. farm, "I like Henry, but he certainly makes it hard to do so." Lord thinks it was tragic that Henry Wallace's father insisted that he be declared essential to the newspaper and draft-exempt in World War I. It might have done Wallace good to have served as a buck private. It might have taught him how not to be lonely in a crowd, made him capable of some small talk and able to know whom to trust at what time. One difficulty his advisors had with him, from the time he went to Washington all the way through the 1948 campaign, was to keep him awake during serious discussions. There are innumerable anecdotes of his having dozed off. I have been a witness to it myself. One leading Progressive has told me that Henry Wallace once confided that he felt as though he had a cold snake curled up inside him whenever he was in a small group. The alternative to going to sleep would be to get up and leave the room, and I have seen that happen also.

These personality traits are not those which endear an office seeker to professional politicians. In *Frontier on the Potomac* (Macmillan, 1946), Jonathan Daniels quoted Harry Truman as saying:

"Well, while Garner was Vice President there was hardly a day when at least half of the members of the Senate did not see him in his office or talk to him somewhere around the Capitol. In the past four years I doubt if there are half a dozen senators all told who have been in the Vice President's office. You can draw your own conclusions."

Only Edward J. Flynn, Democratic boss of the Bronx, of all the city Democratic bosses, apparently ever liked Wallace. Flynn explained in *You're the Boss* (Viking, 1947) that he considered Wallace a good administrator in the Department of Agriculture. At the 1940 Democratic convention, a great deal of the opposition to accepting Roosevelt's choice of Wallace as his running mate came from the fact that Wallace had been a registered Republican until 1932 and because he had not "played ball" with anyone as to patronage. Lord related how he gave a laconic "No" to a businessman who wanted a favor which would have been lucrative for him. Then Wallace lectured the man regarding what his sense of social responsibility should be. In politics, a successful person is one who listens to your troubles and does what he can to help you with a recalcitrant bureaucrat, or to influence the vote of a congressman. Throughout his 12 years in Washington, Wallace had no such friends and was not that kind of friend to anyone else. Presumably politicians have both public and private lives. With Wallace there was no such dichotomy; he acted the same on all occasions.

Wallace never understood the meaning of personal loyalty to him. A great deal of his apparent callousness isn't that at all. Prepared to make sacrifices for principle himself, he can't understand why others don't do likewise. When his followers in 1948 began to suffer through losses of jobs or in other ways, Wallace was indignant because such a state of affairs existed in the United States, but he never had a feeling that the martyrs were doing it for him. Rather, it was for the cause and consequently he never felt any obligation to assist anyone, except in the interest of a common cause. It is said that a word from him probably would have obtained a Federal Reserve Board appointment for Paul Appleby, perhaps his most steadfast assistant in the Department of Agriculture. When it was brought to his attention that Harold Young, his solicitor and right hand man while he was Vice President and Secretary of Commerce and thereafter until early 1948, was financially embarrassed because of serving at comparatively low pay, Wallace was uninterested. When Young packed up and returned to Odessa, Texas, after six years of association, Wallace never asked where he was. At the end of the 1948 campaign he never thought to thank anyone. When the name of Sen. Glen Taylor, who ruined his political career by running with Wallace as Vice Presidential candidate, came up in one of our conversations, Wallace remarked, "He was a nice fellow. I wonder whatever became of him?"

It probably is correct to say—and it has been said—that whereas Henry Wallace was *for* the common man, he never was *of* him. Perhaps exactly the opposite can be said of Harry Truman and many another politician. Every once in a while, however, Wallace would sneak off from a gathering of his political cronies, usually to be found some time later talking to some farmer or other person able to discuss corn, chickens, or eggs. Once, a frantic search in a restaurant ended when Wallace was found negotiating a sale of his Westchester County chickens to the chef. Often these disappearances from the table were interpreted as attempts by Wallace to avoid picking up the tab, for close associates are agreed that Wallace was unmercifully tight in money matters. "I never saw him put his hand in his pocket," more than one has told me. Or, if he did lay down a sum of money, saying he thought it would cover his share of a bill, it would be woefully short. When speech writers or others went to Farvue to confer with Wallace, they often were not offered lunch or refreshment. Personally, I never encountered this stinginess. Quite the contrary, on my last trip to Farvue I came away with a car loaded with the best tomatoes and cantaloupes my family or I have ever tasted and a gorgeous, full blossomed bouquet of gladiolas for a sick daughter.

Some of the best reporting of Henry Wallace—or of most anything else in official Washington during the past quarter century—was by Edwin A. Lahey of the *Chicago Daily News*. In mid-May 1947, Lahey accompanied Wallace on his speaking junket from Chicago to the West

Coast and back. Some of his accounts are memorable, not merely because his impartiality was such a contrast to that of most other reporters, but because they were journalistic gems in setting down how Wallace spent his time while not on the platform or in formal conferences. Much of that time he spent with Lahey, taking walks (Lahey says he himself was always steps behind, puffing to catch up) and eating in out-of-the-way places, "not flossy places but crummy little holes," as Lahey put it. In an article datelined Kansas City, over which his paper put the headline, "Wallace Meets Common Woman," in its issue of May 29, 1947, Lahey told of the visit he and Wallace made to a Mexican saloon and restaurant in Denver.

"Never in his years as a member of the Cabinet or as Vice President had he encountered a crisis quite like the situation presented by Helen," Lahey wrote.

"Unwilling to be rude to the girl, he finally said:

" 'Maria Magdalena, adios.'

"This, I gathered was a gentle Mexican rebuke to a woman of dubious virtue. Wallace had to say it twice. Then I had to whisper a less gentle hint into Helen's shell-like ear, and she departed, still full of good will toward us."

Lahey still howls with delight as he recalls the incident.

Another time a waiter turned out to be an ardent Wallace fan and lavished attention far beyond that required in the line of duty on the candidate and his party, which on that occasion included Mrs. Wallace. At the end she had to remind her husband to leave a tip and to say goodbye to the waiter.

In July, 1950, when a series of meetings was being held to settle on the Progressive party's statement on the Korean situation, Wallace drove up to Lillian Hellman's place in an old car, with a basketful of strawberry plants. Jack McManus of the *National Guardian* observed a workman emptying them. When Jack asked if the plants wouldn't spoil, he received the answer, "Yes, I guess they will, but Mr. Wallace wants the basket back."

Henry Wallace was always scornful of suggestions that he consider political expediency in anything he did. I believe he would have hated anything he won by resort to the usual methods of political chicanery. Seeing anyone praised for obtaining an honor which he had connived to receive rather than having it bestowed gratuitously disgusted him. Certain that any course he took was right, he thought others should follow, and there is no doubt that after the disastrous results of November, 1948 he felt a terrific letdown and betrayal. All of which, of course, suggests a strong egotism, but the explanation is not that simple. It is much closer to say that this attitude, disastrous and ungenerous as it may have seemed to be at times, suggests a strong amount of integrity. Henry Wallace was so ruggedly individualistic and true to his own convictions that he expected everyone else to be the same and despised any other method of operation. Russell Lord quoted Paul Porter as having once remarked regarding Wallace, "Don't it beat hell; he's a Christian." Until Beanie Baldwin, with the aid of Mrs. Anita

Blaine, stopped him, Wallace was accustomed to talking about himself as being dispensable.

The absolutism which I have said his scientific background caused in Henry Wallace was fortified, paradoxically, by his strong religious beliefs. On one occasion his personal secretary, Mabel Cooney, convinced a Southerner that Wallace was not a Communist by escorting him to the stateroom of the sleeping car, where she pointed to the open Bible Wallace had left when dropping off to sleep the night before. Henry Wallace is deeply religious and a Biblical scholar. He started life as a Presbyterian, but changed later to high Episcopalianism. His speeches and writings are replete with Biblical references and quotations, especially from such minor prophets as Amos and Hosea, noted for their humanitarianism. His Ever Normal Granary idea, advanced when he was Secretary of Agriculture, is a direct steal from the plan Joseph developed in the Egypt of the Pharaohs, although Wallace got the idea from reading a Columbia University thesis about "The Economic Principles of Confucius," who evidently also believed in governmental stockpiling of surpluses in good years to provide for famine years.

I know of no quicker way to obtain an understanding of Henry Wallace's philosophy than to reread his *Statesmanship and Religion* (Round Table Press, 1934), which consists of the three Alden-Tuthill lectures he delivered in January, 1934, at the Chicago Theological Seminary and a talk given before the Federal Council of Churches in December, 1933. Many have wondered whether Wallace did not consider himself a divinely appointed 20th century prophet, after perusing such passages as the following:

> Of course, the outstanding characteristic of the prophets which is lacking today is that intensity of conviction which enabled them to say, "Thus saith the Lord." Frankly, I see no reason why there should not emerge today men who are the modern equivalents of the prophets of old . . . The stage is being set for a social battle astonishingly similar to that which raged in Judah and Israel from the time of Solomon until Judah went into capitivity . . . I trust we shall never have to have a prophet like Elisha who stirred up Jehu to bloody revolution . . . But we will need men who are willing to think more fervently and vigorously than most of our leaders have hitherto . . . A modern Isaiah, seeing the possibilities of modern transportation and communication and observing the national barriers imposed by the nations against each other since the war, would cry out against international injustices. He would go to the people of the different nations with his message and call for a New Deal among nations. He would do this with vigor and immense earnestness even though from an immediate practical point of view his message might be premature . . .

Somewhat in the same vein, though more earthy, was Henry Wallace's article, "Spiritual Forces and the State," which appeared in the June 1934 *Forum*. In its issue of April 23, 1941, *The Christian Century*, which was then isolationist and pacifist, editorialized regarding what it considered Wallace's efforts to make World War II seem a holy crusade. It said that his Episcopalian views were not much different from those of the Catholic church: that the state is ultimately an expression of the will of God. Wallace's thought, the nondenominational Protestant organ said, "runs in these well worn authoritarian grooves. The survival of the state, so important to this point of view, appears to him to be gravely threatened by outside forces."

As David T. Bazelton put it, in the April 1947 *Commentary*: "Wallace is scientific as to the techniques of manufacturing things but he is religious and abstract in relation to human beings."

\* \* \* \*

During 1948, it was frequently charged that Wallace was expressing ideas which originated not with him but with left-wing advisors and speech writers. As a matter of fact, as regards both foreign and domestic issues, Wallace's public statements in 1948 were consistent with, and often identical to, what he had written and said long before he became the wartime spokesman for American international idealism.

In the early days of the New Deal, he was the target for a great deal of conservative and reactionary criticism because of the alleged radicalism of the Administration's agricultural relief program. Unfriendly cartoonists liked to depict him ploughing under rows of corn and killing little pigs just for the fun of it. Perhaps the best answer was that which he and others gave at the time: "You'd think people raised pigs for pets." Actually, the killing of 5 to 6 million little pigs not only reduced the tonnage of pork to be marketed later, thus raising the income of farmers, but also provided food for reliefers through the Federal Emergency Relief Administration; it was done in accordance with a policy no different from that of any manufacturer, who curtails production when there is an unsalable surplus.

During his eight years as Secretary of Agriculture, Wallace was actually far from radical in most of his policies. Even his severest critic, Dwight MacDonald, wrote in the Summer, 1948 *Politics* that for 13 years Wallace was a conformist and his policies were "cautious and conservative" on the domestic front. In February, 1935, he gave in to Big Farmer pressure applied through Chester C. Davis, AAA administrator, to get rid of Jerome Frank, Alger Hiss, Lee Pressman and some others in the department. In the *Progressive* for July, 1948, Fred Rodell charged that even when Secretary of Commerce, Wallace surrounded himself with Big Business advisors and let monopolists influence him on many matters. On the other hand, it is a matter of public record that he greatly increased the department's service to small business and issued several warnings against the dangers of monopoly.

At the same time, in his public utterances and articles he was advocating expansion of governmental planning and spending, and curbs

89

on monopoly, in order to save the capitalistic system from self-destruction; and he was warning against too much confidence in half-way measures. Typically, to the National Education Association on Feb. 28, 1935, at Atlantic City, he said:

> Individualism was a splendid thing to emphasize when it gave us much of the power that enabled us to conquer the continent in record time. Now the continent has been conquered and certain other forms have become manifest which also are inherent in capitalism, the tendency of different regions and classes to go out and get all they can. Once the conquest of new areas comes to an end, we come to the point of fighting between regions and classes, each for its own maximum profit. Then the disintegration forces come in. I feel that the social effect of teaching of the survival of the fittest has been profoundly unfortunate.

Although Wallace did not use the phrase "progressive capitalism" at that time, he preached the necessity for social and economic planning on both a national and international level as essential in the 20th century. His *Democracy Reborn* is a collection of his speeches and articles from March 10, 1933 to May 15, 1944. They show the influence upon him, which he has admitted, of his early reading of Thorstein Veblen's *The Theory of the Leisure Class* and *The Theory of Business Enterprise,* and of *Revolutions of Civilization,* by W. M. Flinders Petrie, the Egyptologist. Although impressed by Petrie's description of the rise and fall of civilizations, Wallace was more optimistic about the possibility of preventing cyclical decay.

Wallace's *America Must Choose,* a pamphlet published in 1934 by the Foreign Policy Association and World Peace Foundation, was the best epitome of his thinking as regards the need for a planned economy, instead of an economic laissez-faire system. In it he wrote:

> If we insist upon selling without buying we have to lend our surplus to foreign countries, and never take it back. It stays abroad. But we think we still own it, and that makes us figure out ways and means of keeping the investment safe. We must have some security that transcends the good faith of the borrower. There is no surer path to war.

At many a farm picnic in Iowa in the '20s, Henry Wallace had argued that the farmers' interests required that in the post-war period the United States act as the creditor it had become, rather than as a debtor nation. That meant lowering tariff barriers to accelerate international trade. He later came to believe that the world-wide depression of the '30s was caused in large part by the failure of this country to act in that way. Wallace's internationalism, in other words, was born of his belief that it was the only hard-headed practical policy, not only for the United States but for every other nation in the world. In the

'20s he was president of the Non-Partisan League of Nations Association and, with his grandfather, a strong supporter of Woodrow Wilson's one world dreams.

That the Soviet Union should be a full partner in that one world seemed thoroughly natural to Wallace, and any other situation appeared to be fraught with danger. Furthermore, he saw no reason why the Soviet Union and the United States could not get along with each other. In his first important speech on the subject on Nov. 8, 1942, at a Madison Square Garden rally of the Congress of American-Soviet Friendship, he said, "It is no accident that Americans and Russians like each other when they get acquainted. Both peoples were molded by the vast sweep of a rich continent. Both peoples know that their future is greater than their past. Both hate sham." He quoted the French author de Tocqueville of over a century earlier that the two nations "seem to tend toward the same end although they start from different points." He declared that both nations had learned the impossibility of isolationism and said, "The new democracy, the democracy of the common man, includes not only the Bill of Rights but also economic democracy, ethnic democracy, educational democracy and democracy in the treatment of the sexes." Then he explained that both countries had something to learn from each other as regards all types.

By this time, Henry Wallace's most famous speech was six months old. That was his "A Century of the Common Man" address, delivered on May 8, 1942, before the Free World Association in New York.

> Everywhere [Wallace said] the common people are on the march. Thousands of them are learning to read and write, learning to think together, learning to use tools. . . . The march of freedom of the last 150 years has been a long-drawn-out People's Revolution. In this great revolution of the people there were the American Revolution of 1775, the French Revolution of 1792, the Latin-American revolutions of the Bolivarian era, the German Revolution of 1848 and the Russian Revolution of 1917. Each spoke for the common man in terms of blood on the battlefield. Some went to excess. But the significant thing is that the people groped their way to the light.

This was the speech which was interpreted as meaning that Wallace wanted to give a quart of milk daily to every Hottentot. The charge grew out of the following passage:

> Modern science, which is a by-product and an essential part of the People's Revolution, has made it technologically possible to see that all of the people of the world get enough to eat. Half in fun and half seriously, I said the other day to Mme. Litvinov, wife of the Russian ambassador, "The object of this war is to make sure that every-

91

body in the world has the privilege of drinking a quart of milk a day."
She replied:
"Yes, even half a pint."

Strange as it may have seemed just a few years later, at the time they were uttered these words were acclaimed by liberals of all shades as charting the only sane course for the world after the war's end. Organizations and even newspapers reprinted and distributed hundreds of thousands of copies of the Century of the Common Man address. When, almost a decade later, President Truman expounded his Point 4 program for aid to underdeveloped parts of the world, Wallace claimed that the idea was stolen from him.

Only slightly less popular in liberal circles was Wallace's Dec. 28, 1942 broadcast, in commemoration of the 86th anniversary of the birth of Woodrow Wilson. In it he sounded the first call for what became the United Nations, as a permanent post-war council so set up as to avoid the blunders which led to the failure of the League of Nations. Parts of that speech were almost identical to the Madison Square Garden address of Sept. 12, 1946, which caused his firing from the Cabinet. Just prior to the speech's delivery, Wallace spent an hour and a half in consultation with FDR.

"Globaloney" was the appellation applied by Clare Boothe Luce, in her maiden speech as a congresswoman on Feb. 8, 1943, to some of the ideas Wallace propounded in an article, "What We Will Get Out of the War," in the *American Magazine* for March, 1943. She criticized particularly Wallace's plea for freedom of the air as comparable in importance to freedom of the seas. She warned against making any post-war plans until those of the Soviet Union were known because, in her opinion, the future of the world would be decided by Stalin. She expressed pity for FDR and Churchill who, she said, were floundering in a sea of uncertainty.

In the article which provoked this attack Wallace had argued, not merely for a network of globe-girdling airways and internationalized airports, but also for the "mental disarmament" of the people of aggressor nations, an end to cartels, international student exchanges and improved transportation of all sorts, as "the key that will unlock the resources of the vast undeveloped regions of the world. We may expect the history of those regions in the next 100 years to parallel our own history in the last 100 years." He also advocated utilization of the Tennessee Valley Authority idea on a worldwide scale.

At a Conference on Christian Bases of World Order, on March 8, 1943, at Ohio Wesleyan University, Delaware, Ohio, Wallace warned:

We shall decide some time in 1943 or 1944 whether to plant the seeds for World War No. 3. That war will be certain if we allow Prussia to rearm either materially or psychologically. That war will be probable in case we double-cross Russia. That war will be probable if we fail to demonstrate that we can furnish full employment after this war comes to an end and fascist interests motivated largely by anti-Russian bias get control of our government. Unless the Western democracies and Russia come to a satisfactory understanding before the war ends, I very much fear that World War No. 3 will be inevitable. Without a close and trusting understanding between Russia and the United States there is grave probability of Russia and Germany sooner or later making common cause.

In what was generally labeled the beginning of his campaign for renomination as Vice President, on July 26, 1943 at Detroit, shortly after his Board of Economic Warfare row with Jesse Jones, in a speech which FDR was said to have approved, Wallace said, "I believe in our democratic, capitalistic system, but it must be a capitalism of abundance and full employment. If we return to a capitalism of scarcity such as that which produced both 1929 and 1932, we must anticipate that the returning soldiers and displaced war workers will speak in no uncertain terms." He declared that the capitalism of scarcity is caused by holding inventions out of use, holding up prices and cutting down production during the early days of a depression. "No business prospers without prosperous customers," he said.

Other Wallace speeches of the period were in similar vein. And then, on Jan. 22, 1944, at a Jackson Day dinner, shortly after President Roosevelt had told a press conference that "Dr. New Deal" had departed and had been replaced by "Dr. Win-the-War," Wallace boldly declared:

The New Deal is not dead. If it were dead the Democratic party would be dead and well dead. But the Democratic party is not dead and the New Deal has yet to attain to its full strength. The New Deal is as old as the wants of man. The New Deal is Amos proclaiming the needs of the poor in the land of Israel. The New Deal is New England citizens dumping tea in Boston harbor. The New Deal is Andrew Jackson marching in the 20th century. The New Deal is Abraham Lincoln preaching freedom for the oppressed. The New Deal is the New Freedom of Woodrow Wilson fighting the cartels as they tried to establish national and international fascism. The New Deal is Franklin Delano Roosevelt.

In the *New York Times* for April 9, 1944, in an article entitled, "The Dangers of American Fascism," Henry Wallace warned:

Fascism is a worldwide disease. Its greatest threat to the United States will come after the war, either via Latin America or within the United States itself . . .

Fascism in the postwar era inevitably will push steadily for Anglo-Saxon imperialism and eventually for war with

Russia. Already American Fascists are talking and writing about this conflict and using it as an excuse for their internal hatred and intolerances toward certain races, creeds and classes.

On March 8, 1946, Wallace expressed "complete accord" with the statement of Senators Kilgore, Pepper and Taylor in criticism of Winston Churchill's speech at Fulton, Mo. (see page 30). "Mr. Churchill undoubtedly is not speaking either for the American people or their Government. I am against taking any steps which would lead to war, whether with Russia, with Britain or with any other country," Wallace said.

Before the Foreign Trade subcommittee of the Senate Small Businessmen Committee considering renewing and broadening the reciprocal trade law, on April 17, 1945, Wallace clashed with Sen. Alexander Wiley (Rep., Wis.). The Secretary of Commerce attributed the unemployment of the '30s to the tariff policies of the '20s and predicted trouble again if the law was not liberalized.

"If you open the floodgates from Europe you'll not be helping the American working man," Wiley declared.

"Senator, you're just talking for a third world war," Wallace replied.

"That's the hell of an answer. You're getting cockeyed; that's the trouble with you," was the Senator's rejoinder.

Five days later, Wallace had a similar set-to with Rep. Harold Knutson (Rep., Minn.), before the House Ways and Means Committee, considering the same legislation. Wallace declared that liberalization of the tariff laws was necessary to insure 60 million jobs, whereupon Knutson asked how he expected to provide them by destroying "so-called inefficient industries." Wallace retorted:

"I'm not beating my wife any more."

"That should go in the society columns," Knutson commented.

When Wallace blamed World War II in part upon bad economic policies of the '20s, Knutson declared, "Isn't it nice to have an alibi. You know, I envy your naiveness."

"I pity yours," retorted Wallace, exhibiting more quick-wittedness than he usually displayed in such situations.

In a colloquy with another committeeman, Rep. Bertrand W. Gearhart (Rep., Calif.), Wallace said:

"God grant that men of your thinking never get into power again as they were in the 1920s. If you do, the same pattern will be followed: a new Fordney-McCumber tariff law, a new Smoot-Hawley tariff law and the same depression and war."

In September, 1945, there appeared Wallace's *Sixty Million Jobs,* in which his approach was substantially that of the Full Employment Bill then pending in Congress. He advocated prime reliance upon private enterprise, backed by a government program to maintain full production and employment, and denied that the expense would be prohibitive.

To a group of 200 businessmen at a dinner sponsored by the NC-PAC on Sept. 13, 1945, Wallace said:

On the side of management, it is vitally important that genuine collective bargaining be accepted as the only practical and constructive means of removing the causes for industrial strife. It should be perfectly clear that without the acceptance of genuine collective bargaining as a starting point there is not even a basis for discussion.

On June 4, 1945, Wallace received the seventh annual *Churchman* award "for the promotion of good will and better understanding among all peoples." Before 2,500 at the Waldorf-Astoria, he called those who deliberately stirred up trouble between the United States and the Soviet Union "enemies of peace" and declared that the safety of this country and the peace of the world required the American government to go "all out" for full production and employment.

On March 19, 1946, he clashed with W. Averell Harriman, at a New York dinner given in Harriman's honor by the American Society for Russian Relief. Harriman had charged the Soviet Union with failure to fulfill "certain agreements as we understand them." Wallace replied that the Russians were taking what they conceived to be the "only road to peace and security" and had great fears of "capitalist encirclement" and war. "But," he declared, "granting that Russia is wrong on every count, I still say that the United States has nothing to gain but, on the contrary, everything to lose, by beating the tom-toms against Russia."

That these, and numerous other public statements by Wallace were causing embarrassment to Secretary of State Byrnes long before Wallace's Madison Square Garden speech was confirmed by an April 19, 1946 entry in the Forrestal *Diaries*. After a Cabinet meeting, Forrestal wrote, Byrnes "cited specifically Iceland where our efforts to get air bases had been aborted to a considerable degree by the statements and speeches of Secretary Wallace and Senator Pepper; Wallace's in particular having been quoted by the premier of Iceland as robbing him of any success in the advocacy of bases for the United States."

After Wallace was dismissed, the Alsop brothers, in their column for Sept. 18, 1946, declared that statements by Wallace regarding Iran had embarrassed Byrnes during the winter of 1945-46. They blamed Wallace for having caused Iceland to break off talks regarding air bases there, and said Wallace also had talked too much about Palestine. On page 239 of *Speaking Frankly,* Byrnes wrote, "His statement was effectively used by the Communists in Iceland and it had obstructed the efforts of the State Department to secure an agreement important to the defense of this hemisphere."

Wallace's statement on Iceland, on March 12, 1946, was to the effect that American troops should be withdrawn from that country, especially since Russian troops had been removed from the Baltic island of Bornholm. Otherwise, he said, the Russians would consider American occupancy of Iceland bases as aimed at them.

In view of the record of consistency in his views, regarding the economic bases for peace, from World War I on, Henry Wallace's public statements after he left the Cabinet do not seem surprising in retrospect. If any criticism were valid, it would seem to be that he failed to modify his views as world conditions changed, not that he suddenly espoused new ones.

\* \* \* \*

When aroused on the platform, Wallace could become evangelical in his fervor. Albert J. Fitzgerald and others who appeared often with him tell of his slouched, indifferent attitude before he took the platform in 1948; of how, while discussing domestic issues, he kept his eyes glued to his manuscript; but how, when he got to the parts in which he was interested—those related to peace—he raised his eyes, lifted his voice, stood on tiptoe and gave forth excitedly. Several of his closest associates believe that Wallace had a messianic complex, that he thought he was a modern Isaiah. I have heard, from one of his closest associates when he was in the Department of Agriculture, that he gave indications of agreeing with a fan who described him as a second Jesus. Perhaps, in 1948, he did think a modern miracle would be performed to elect him, but he was far from being alone in engaging in what Lee Pressman calls "a hell of a lot of romanticizing" at that time. After Nov. 5, 1948 he did feel dreadfully let down, but any persecution complex he may have developed could be explained in other than religious terms.

During the 1948 campaign, Henry Wallace learned to drink and like beer. When offered anything else he would take it, lift it to his lips, but not imbibe. In 1943, or 1944, his birthday was being celebrated by the Mexican Embassy at the Mayflower hotel in Washington. When his abstinence was noticed, he replied that he liked only one drink: the famous Mexican beer, Carta Blanca. When, not too many minutes later, some of that beverage was obtained from the embassy, the Vice President was really caught. Once initiated he came to enjoy it. To the best of my knowledge, however, his scientific interest has never led him to indulge in any form of tobacco and he is strait-laced as to conversation. He doesn't tell or like to hear off-color jokes and often he fails to understand them, or any other funny stories told in his presence. He is known for his natural "double take," an example being his belated reaction to a remark by his 1948 fund-raiser and eminent wisecracker, William S. Gailmor. A short while before, there had been a very serious discussion about the use of radiation in tomato raising. Shortly thereafter, the Wallace group passed a callipygous young lady on the street. "Radiated tomato," said Bill, but Henry didn't get it until they had gone two blocks farther. Then he guffawed.

On another occasion, in a hotel room, Wallace asked Vito Marcantonio how he was doing in his congressional district. Marc replied in very graphic terms, "I'm doing all right. I never have taken any shit from anyone and I'm not going to take any shit from anyone this time." After some more of the same, Marc departed and Wallace inquired, "Don't you think Vito uses picturesque language?"

Not only was Henry Wallace incapable of hanging around in smoke filled rooms, lifting a jug with fellow "statesmen," but he also refused to have anything to do with the mechanics of political organization. An illustration, typical though more recent than the 1948 campaign, was a note Wallace appended to a copy of a letter from a follower; it criticized an article by Marcantonio, in the *New York Compass*, regarding some proposed change in congressional rules in January, 1950. In forwarding the letter to Beanie Baldwin for reply, Wallace wrote, "The enclosed illustrates why I don't want to have anything to do with party affairs at the operating level."

That a man with an attitude like that never possessed anything resembling a political machine is not surprising. In order for him to campaign, the organization had to be provided entirely by others.

\* \* \* \*

Simultaneously with his firing of Wallace, Truman issued an order thereafter forbidding members of the executive branch of the Federal Government from making statements critical of American foreign policy without his approval. Also, Rep. John J. Sparkman of Alabama, director of the speakers bureau for the Democratic National Committee that year, announced that the speeches Wallace was to have given during the fall campaign would be canceled. Sparkman muttered something about not being willing to offer the Communists sponsorship for a private citizen.

In Miami Beach to speak at a Brotherhood of Railway Trainmen convention on Sept. 17, Sen. Claude Pepper denounced Truman, demanded a "turnabout" of American foreign policy and called Henry Wallace "a great American statesman." A. F. Whitney, the brotherhood president, seconded these views. Three days later, when Sparkman's edict against Wallace was extended to include him, Pepper really let loose. He denounced the Truman censorship order which, he said, "makes it obvious that if any of us in Congress dare to discuss what's being done we'll be subject to the most severe denunciation from certain places." He said he was shocked at the effort to suppress free speech and that he thought Wallace had "done a great service to the country in sacrificing a place in the Cabinet in an honest effort to make the people realize how important are the decisions being made by a few men in Paris to the peace of the nation and the world."

This was not surprising because, although Wallace had gotten the headlines, it was Pepper who had given the more radical speech on Sept. 12 in Madison Square Garden. Pepper had said:

> With conservative Democrats and reactionary Republicans making our foreign policy as they are today, it is all we can do to keep foolish people from having us pull a Hitler blitzkrieg and drop our atomic bombs on the Russian people. It is not so far from "get tough" to "get rough." I think we ought to remember, however, that the last two fellows who tried to get rough

97

with the Russians—you may remember them from their first names, Napoleon and Adolf—did not fare so well.

You and I know that today the reason we have got so much Republican unity behind the foreign policy is because there is so much McKinley imperialism in our foreign policy. What do you expect in a foreign policy which really meets the approval of Senator Vandenberg and John Foster Dulles?

In Chicago, on Sept. 22, 1946, Robert E. Hannegan, chairman of the Democratic National Committee, quickly declared that Sparkman's comments had been unofficial. "As far as I am concerned Senator Pepper still is on the list of available speakers," he said. "Any group that requests Senator Pepper will get him throughout the campaign."

In early 1945, Pepper had been floor leader to get Henry Wallace confirmed as Secretary of Commerce. He had helped him out with friendly questions before the Commerce Committee and he had been rough on Jesse Jones. When Wallace was given the *Churchman* award on June 4, 1945, Pepper made the presentation and called the recipient "the greatest living spokesman of Rooseveltianism" and "one of the really great men of our times." The voice of Henry Wallace, he said, "is not a voice crying in the wilderness. It is the call to the faithful for the pilgrimage. Behind such men has the race always moved forward. Behind such men shall we move on yet further and higher." In June, Pepper led the fight against Truman's emergency labor legislation and in August he was quoted as saying he would prefer Henry Wallace to Harry S. Truman as the Democratic nominee for President in 1948.

Henry Wallace's first public appearance after his Madison Square Garden speech was on Oct. 24, 1946, in Los Angeles; he went there upon the invitation of James Roosevelt, state Democratic chairman, and over the protests of two men: Will Rogers Jr., Democratic candidate for the U.S. Senate; and Gov. Earl Warren, winner of both major party primaries, who cried "presumptuous." Speaking in Olympia auditorium under the auspices of the ICC-ASP, the CIO-PAC, the Progressive AFL Committee for Political and Legislative Action, and the Southern California Railroad Brotherhoods Joint Legislative Council, Wallace said he wanted to make five things clear, namely:

1. I am still a Democrat.

2. More than ever before I am a progressive.

3. I am very happy that the prospects for a peaceful world have brightened greatly during the past month.

4. I want to do everything I can to elect progressive Democrats to Congress.

5. If the Democrats fail to control the 80th Congress there is only one way in which they can get control again and that is by becoming more progressive.

Wallace's encouragement regarding the international situation had been occasioned by Secretary of State Byrnes' radio speech upon his return from the Paris peace conference, which Ernest Bevin praised Oct. 22 in the House of Commons, and President Truman's address the day before, at the opening of the General Assembly of the United Nations.

What encouraged Wallace in Byrnes' report of Oct. 18, 1946 were such statements as the following: ". . . the development of sympathetic understanding between the Soviet Union and the United States is the paramount task of statesmanship . . . We must cooperate to build a world order, not to sanctify the status quo, but to preserve peace and freedom based upon justice . . . We will continue to seek friendship with the Soviet Union and all other states . . . We must . . . guard against the belief that delays or setbacks in achieving our objective make armed conflict inevitable."

During the Congressional campaign, Wallace spoke on behalf of liberal Democratic candidates for Congress in other West Coast cities and in Minneapolis, Madison, Wis., Chicago and Detroit. He warned against electing "Soviet-baiters" to Congress, called for a decrease in armaments spending and advocated acceptance of Molotov's overtures for a disarmament conference. He deplored Churchill, Col. Robert R. McCormick and all who talked about dropping atomic bombs on Moscow.

To wind up the campaign, on the last weekend Wallace and Pepper appeared together in New York, at several rallies sponsored by the American Labor party, the ICC-ASP, the NC-PAC and some left wing unions. Conjectured Warren Moscow, in the *New York Times,* for Nov. , 1946:

> The Wallace-Pepper engagements presented the possibility of future importance. Both men were brought to the city under the auspices of left wing groups independently of the Democratic command of the state. The leftist character of the last minute drive was emphasized particularly in the case of Senator Pepper whose appearance was announced by Irving Potash, manager of the Furrier Joint Council. Mr. Potash is a member of the National Executive board of the Communist party. Such activity appears to threaten the continuation in future elections of the Democratic party's alliance with the American Labor party though it should not affect the alliance with the Liberal party.

On the eve of his departure for abroad in early September, James A. Farley, former postmaster general and chairman of the Democratic National Committee, had declared that, "The Democratic party is now in the throes of trying to rid itself of the Communist and Communist fellow traveler element which attached itself to the party for its own subversive ends. Leadership which continues to play ball with that

99

un-American element faces rejection by the rank and file of the Democratic party and make no mistake about it."

After the election resulted in a nationwide victory for the Republicans, with their "Had enough?" slogan, several commentators declared that resentment of Old Guard Democrats against the alliance with left-wingers had been a factor in causing them to put forth less than a maximum effort and had kept others at home. The organizational Democrats were stung by the red-baiting, which the Republicans had been engaging in for 14 years, but against which there was no longer any Franklin Roosevelt to stand up. During the campaign, Dewey had charged that the Democratic party was the "captive of left wing splinter groups," and the Farley element, which had vigorously opposed the candidacy of James Mead in the primary, was out to answer the charge by admitting its validity and purging itself.

Only 73 of 318 candidates supported by the CIO-PAC and the NC-PAC won on Nov. 5, 1946 and only five of their senatorial preferences. The explanation given by the left wing elements, however, was quite different from that of either the Republicans or the Farley Democrats. The people, they said, had "had enough": not of New-Dealism, of which they considered themselves the real champions, but of the abandonment of Roosevelt policies by Harry Truman. Under the two-party system, the only way voters had to express their displeasure was by voting Republican. Actually, however, millions of them used another method: non-voting. Some have called what happened a prodigious sit-down strike on the part of former New Deal supporters and the figures tend to bear out this viewpoint. Only 34 million, or 37.5 per cent of those eligible to do so, voted in 1946 and the total Democratic vote dropped from 25 million to 15 million, whereas the Republican vote dropped only from 22 million to 18 million. Thus, there was no Republican landslide in the sense of a widespread shift of allegiance. Furthermore, the margins of victory were narrower than they had been for 15 years.

It was not only the so-called left-wingers who gave that kind of explanation.

In the *New York Times Sunday Magazine* for Jan. 19, 1947, Louis Bean, author of *Ballot Behavior* and *How to Predict Elections*, whose record for correct political forecasting excels that of anyone else in our generation, declared that it was not a change of heart as regards New-Dealism but worry because of inflation, food and other shortages and reduced purchasing power that caused voters, unwilling to vote Republican, to stay home.

Louis Hollander, CIO state president and a vigorous anti-Communist, blamed the election outcome on "the weakness displayed by the Truman administration in giving way to the monopolists and the reactionaries" and warned that, unless the Democrats returned to the policies of the New Deal, the pressure for a third party would increase. If labor decided to launch such a party, he said, it soon would become the first party, as had happened in England.

In his "President's Column," in the *United Automobile Worker* for November, 1946, Walter Reuther wrote:

> This election was a revolt against indecision, bungling and appeasement by the 79th Congress and the great capacity of the Truman administration to conform to those policies . . . Roosevelt is gone and this election has proven that our task is to build a broad people's political movement based on an understanding of the economic and political facts of life.

Jack Kroll, CIO-PAC chairman, in a National Broadcasting panel discussion with Wallace and Pepper on Nov. 10, 1946, called the Republican vote "not an affirmative vote. It was rather a negative vote . . . People were tired of the lack of results coming out of this 79th Congress and in an old American tradition they simply were against the party that they felt was responsible for this lack of action." On this NBC program, Wallace declared that "The Democratic party cannot win an election in the United States unless it is a forthright, clear-cut, liberal party with a forthright, clear-cut, liberal program"; he added, "Frankly, speaking as a realist, I don't think there is a ghost of a show for a progressive winning in 1948."

At an NC-PAC luncheon the day before the election, Wallace had told 1,500 that "I don't mean that the day after tomorrow we are going to form a third party, but I do say that new currents will be forming. What turn they will take I cannot now say but events will tell." At the final rallies there were shouts of "Wallace in '48" and in Harlem Rep. Adam Powell introduced Wallace as "our next President." There Wallace declared that he was fighting desperately to save "blind capitalists from communism in spite of themselves."

Wallace's post-election comment was: "As a result of this election the Democratic party will either become more progressive or it will die. I do not expect it to die."

Baldwin, Marcantonio and others who participated in that campaign insist that there was no "plot" involved in bringing Wallace and Pepper into the New York area independent of the Tammany machine. Pragmatically, there was a campaign on, an immediate victory to be won. Both Mead and Lehman had excellent New Deal records, and Marc, as always, was faced with a tough fight in his own bailiwick. With victory lost, Beanie publicly stated, "We independent progressives have got to start devoting all our energies now to make sure that in 1948 the people in this country have a chance to vote for a Presidential candidate who is really a progressive candidate." He saw no hope of liberalizing the Republican party and the Democrats, he opined, "Unless the administration changes its course, swings back onto the road of progress and stops dallying at the crossroads; unless the Democratic leadership stops coyly holding hands with spokesmen of privilege and bigotry; unless it ends this clandestine honeymoon with reaction and takes a firm, aggressive fighting role in the struggle for a liberal America; then we will challenge that [progressive] claim."

In a page one "Open Letter to the President of the United States," in the Nov. 17, 1946 issue of the *Chicago Sun,* Marshall Field, publisher and editor, told Harry S. Truman, "In our respectful opinion the hour has come for you to create a notable precedent in American history." It was that he appoint a Republican Secretary of State, after conferring with GOP leaders, and then resign his office so that the Republican could become president. Simultaneously, the same suggestion was made by a leading Democrat, Sen. William Fulbright of Arkansas.

But Harry Truman would hear nothing of it. Instead, on Nov. 11, 1946, he issued his first statement since the election, calling for "wisdom and restraint" by both parties and a continuation of bipartisanship in support of his foreign policy. Carroll Reece, chairman of the Republican National Committee, was particularly pleased by that portion of the President's statement denouncing "persons in either party who may seek in the field of foreign affairs an opportunity to achieve personal notoriety or partisan advantage by exploitation of the sensational by the mere creation of controversy." That he took to mean Wallace and Pepper, and there seems no reason to doubt that he was correct in his judgment.

# ¶ 6 THE LIBERALS SPLIT. *Whether or not to work with Communists becomes an irreconcilable issue and causes Popular Front organizations to splinter.*

That Henry A. Wallace's dismissal from the cabinet should be the signal for an increased amount of third party talk was, of course, natural. Wrote James Reston, in the *New York Times,* for Sept. 21 1946:

"There is every expectation that dissatisfied 'liberal' elements in both the major parties may make another attempt to start a third party with Mr. Wallace and Sen. Claude Pepper of Florida as the leaders."

In several statements, Rep. Vito Marcantonio heralded the Wallace firing as the beginning of the disintegration of the Democratic party and "creative of the historical conditions necessary for creation of a new political party." On Dec. 20, 1946, he told an American Youth for Democracy rally that the Republicans were "the party of the National Association of Manufacturers and domestic fascism" and that the Democrats had forfeited their right to represent progressives.

Grant Oakes, president of the United Farm Equipment and Metal Workers of America, CIO, declared: "Harry Truman has ousted the only Roosevelt man in his administration. He has chosen the path to war. He leaves the people no alternative but to organize a third party of their own in 1948." In that year Oakes was to become the Progressive party's candidate for Governor of Illinois.

102

Leo Krzycki of Milwaukee, vice chairman of the Amalgamated Clothing Workers, received tremendous applause as he opened the third American Slav Congress, on Sept. 20, 1946, in New York, by saying, "Wallace received a raw deal. We are ready to accept the challenge. He s nominated for President right now." At the Political Action School, n late June, George Prinsky of the American Slav Congress had roundly denounced Truman for "using food as a political weapon" and had declared that what really goes on behind the so-called Iron Curtain is 'a great upswing on the part of the people to make sure the old reactionaries do not come back."

At the 11th international convention of the United Rubber Workers of America, on Sept. 16, 1946, at San Francisco, Paul Schnur, secretary of the San Francisco CIO council, drew prolonged applause when he uggested, "We'd better start thinking in terms of an independent political party based upon labor." In separate resolutions, the convention deplored he firing of Wallace, who "has consistently fought for the rights of abor and for a lasting peace for all peoples," and called for "eventual establishment of a political party which will more truly represent the nterests of the American people."

At Miami Beach, Fla., on Sept. 20, 1946, the Brotherhood of Railway Trainmen, at its 28th national convention, denounced Truman or removing Wallace from office, resolving, "President Truman has emoved from the cabinet every progressive appointed by the late Franklin Roosevelt." The convention extended an invitation to Wallace to address it, but he was unable to do so.

On Sept. 28, 1946, the Oregon State Industrial Council, CIO, in convention at Portland, unanimously resolved to favor formation of a new political party of "workers, farmers, veterans, women, Negroes and other liberal sections of the population, with labor playing the major and leading role," immediately after the Nov. 5 election.

After Truman's sweeping decontrol order, on Nov. 10, 1946, Louis Hollander, New York State CIO president, predicted increasing pressure rom within the ranks of organized labor for third party activity unless he leadership of the Democratic party "returned to the policies and principles of the New Deal."

On Dec. 7, 1946, the American Institute of Public Opinion (the Gallup organization) conducted a national poll on the question, "If a hird party is formed in this country by Henry Wallace, Claude Pepper, he CIO and other labor groups, do you think you would vote for hat party?" The answer was: yes—10 per cent; no—78 per cent; no opinion—12 per cent. A week later, on Dec. 14, 1946, it asked: "Regardless of how you yourself feel, which party do you think will win the presidential election in 1948?" The results were: Republican—79 per cent; Democratic—9 per cent; no opinion—12 per cent. In between, on Dec. 11, 1946, the AIPO asked Democratic voters only, "If you had to decide today, who would be your choice for President in 1948?" The results were: Truman—48 per cent; Wallace—24 per cent; Byrnes— 0 per cent; Eisenhower—8 per cent; and the rest scattered, with nobody receiving more than 1 per cent.

Henry Wallace wasn't jobless long. Dante M. Pierce, publisher of *Wallace's Farmer and Iowa Homestead,* was unsuccessful in his attempts to persuade his editor-on-leave to return to active duty. In its Oct. 21, 1946 issue, the *New Republic* confirmed rumors that with the Dec. 16 issue Wallace would become its editor. "As editor of the *New Republic* I shall do everything I can to rouse the American people, the British people, the French people, the Russian people and in fact the liberally-minded people of the whole world, to the need of stopping this dangerous armament race," Wallace wrote as part of the announcement. On Nov. 12, the first day he actually took over his new magazine office, Wallace was introduced to a small group of newspaper and magazine executives by Michael Straight, son of the late Willard T. Straight, a Morgan partner and one of the magazine's founders in 1914. Michael, 29, had recently become publisher of the magazine. At the Waldorf-Astoria lunch, Wallace predicted that reactionary Republicans would remain in office until another depression. He said the so-called bipartisan foreign policy was really a Republican policy and "violently anti-Russian." He said that James Reston of the *New York Times* had been responsible for influencing Senator Vandenberg to adopt his new form of internationalism.

Wallace's first magazine editorial was entitled "Jobs, Peace, Freedom" and began: "My job as editor of the *New Republic* is to help organize a progressive America." He explained, "The American people have rejected, as they will always reject, a Democratic party that is not militantly progressive. Americans have called for a new leadership. They will not find it in the present Republican hierarchy; until they find it, they will not rest." Wallace called FDR "a progressive first and a Democrat second" and recalled, "Only in Roosevelt's first term did the progressives really have a majority in Congress." After that, the passage of progressive measures was largely due to Roosevelt's own skill. "The drift toward war," he wrote, "has gone so far that all governments act as if they had a mandate from their people to prepare to win the next war. . . . Our present search for security leads to insecurity and war. We are searching in the wrong ways, and the search itself is vain." And he suggested, "Of course, we need organization. The primary effort of progressives may be to rebuild the Democratic party as a liberal party. But we are the captives of no party. If the Democratic party is incapable of change, we shall strike out along other lines."

The "striking out" that had been going on throughout 1946 was both toward unity and away from it, however. On April 5-7, 1946, there had been held a "Win the Peace" conference in the Department of Commerce auditorium in Washington, with 23 members of Congress and 200 others listed as speakers and sponsors, and 712 delegates from 28 states in attendance. Rep. Adolph Sabath (Dem., Ill.) lambasted Rep. John Rankin, and Sen. Claude Pepper pointed out that the League of Nations had failed because it had been too addicted to maintenance of the status quo. Some progressive resolutions were passed: opposing universal military training; extension of the draft; Herbert Hoover's appointment as director of European food relief; recognition of Franco

Spain; and calling upon the United States to assume the leadership in working for freedom for colonial peoples. Nothing much, however, came of the attempt to form an organization.

Before Wallace's Madison Square Garden speech, a call had gone out for a Conference of Progressives, to be held on Sept. 28 and 29, 1946, at the Hotel Continental in Chicago. Its signers were C. B. Baldwin, Elmer Benson, Frank Kingdon and Clark Foreman for the NC-PAC; Harold Ickes and Jo Davidson for the ICC-ASP; Philip Murray and Jack Kroll for the CIO-PAC; James Patton of the National Farmers Union and Walter White of the National Association for the Advancement of Colored People. The idea for it had occurred after the tremendous success of the Roosevelt Memorial Dinner, in April, which had impressed Murray and Hillman enough to obtain their consent to go along. Unfortunately, Hillman died before the Conference convened.

The approximately 300 delegates from 35 states adopted a plan to ring doorbells, so as to get 50 million to vote on Nov. 5, and named a Continuations Committee of 50 to plan another conference, in mid-January in Washington. The preamble of the program which it adopted charged that "The Congress has let the people down" and included a long spelling-out of that indictment. It endorsed: a workable price and rent control law; passage of the Wagner-Ellender-Taft Long-Range Housing Bill; abolition of the poll tax; a permanent fair employment practices act; abolition of the House Committee on Un-American Activities; passage of the Murray-Wagner-Dingell Bill for Federal Health Insurance; a 65-75 cent minimum wage amendment; more liberal loans to veterans; greater benefits for disabled veterans; withholding of funds under the GI Bill of Rights from institutions practicing discrimination; federal aid to education; expansion of the Ever-Normal Granary Program to all crops to insure minimum farm income, control surpluses and insure food supplies; a Federal fine arts bill; creation of a Missouri Valley Authority; enforcement of the anti-trust laws; and a national fiscal policy based on progressive taxation of large incomes, the reduction of taxes on low incomes and exemptions of all incomes below the level required for a minimum standard of decent living.

The foreign policy section, authored by J. Raymond Walsh, called for "a swift return to the progressive global thinking of Franklin Roosevelt. We must base our foreign policies once more on that world good-neighborliness which was his legacy to us." The first step, the statement went on to say, is recovery of the "mutual trust among the great powers." Specifically, the foreign policy resolution called for: German decartelization and eradication of the social and economic basis of Japanese militarism and imperialism; reparations for American allies who had suffered badly; quarantines of Spain and Argentina; an end to colonialism and imperialism; a free, united and independent China, an end to foreign intervention there, and continuation of pressure to oblige the Chiang Kai-shek government to build "a democratic coalition of all elements in China's political life"; admission of 100,000 European Jews to Palestine; an international relief agency, such as UNRRA; American leadership in disarmament, including an end to the United States' attempt to obtain

105

military bases around the world; an end to plans to invigorate the military establishments of Latin American nations; rejection of "the evolving pattern of close military alliance with Britain"; cessation of American manufacture of atomic bombs and destruction of existing stockpiles of the bomb, simultaneous with agreement by other nations to outlaw atomic weapons; criticism of the Baruch plan because of its "easy stages" provisions, as pointed out by Wallace in his July 23 letter to President Truman; and American assistance in the industrial development of undeveloped areas of the world.

When printed, this provided cheerful reading for Roosevelt idolators; but I vividly recall the late Prof. Louis Wirth, University of Chicago sociologist, characterizing the conference as "mostly a lot of talk," because "it never came to grips with the real issue: are you going to support the bipartisan get-tough policy against Russia or aren't you?"

What Wirth, and the rest of us who attended the conference as mere delegates, didn't realize was that it was really remarkable that anything at all resembling unity came out of it. Behind the bold facade, the ranks of liberal and/or progressive leadership were disintegrating. At the opening session, Henry Morgenthau Jr., chairman, warned against any third party talk as merely "a trap set by reactionaries," and his views were almost immediately seconded by Walter White, who quoted Wendell Willkie as saying it would take six years to get a new political party on the ballot in enough states to make it worthwhile.

At a session on the first day, Harold Ickes caustically remarked that maybe the firing of Wallace would turn out to be a good thing, since at last Truman might have some idea of what American foreign policy was supposed to be.

A discordant note was provided by Philip Murray, who vehemently declared that organized labor "wants no damn Communists meddling in our affairs." This was consistent with a statement which Murray had persuaded the United Steelworkers of America, of which he was president, to adopt unanimously on May 14, 1946, at its Atlantic City convention. The "guts" of that statement had been: "This union will not tolerate efforts by outsiders—individuals, organizations or groups—whether they be Communist, Socialist or any other group to infiltrate, dictate or meddle in our affairs." And it was consistent with the declaration Murray persuaded the 8th constitutional convention of the CIO to adopt on Nov. 18, 1946: "We . . . resent and reject efforts of the Communist party or other political parties and their adherents to interfere in the affairs of the CIO. This convention serves notice that we will not tolerate such interference."

Earlier, Murray had "jumped all over" the original version of J. Raymond Walsh's foreign policy statement, but Baldwin and John Abt had intervened, to win Murray's consent after a little "toning down." The full committee responsible for submitting the statement met at lunch, following Murray's speech at the morning session. Louis Adamic, the Yugoslav-American author, expressed grave concern over the effect Murray's blast might have in inciting promiscuous red-baiting. Florence Eldridge (Mrs. Fredric March, wife of the stage and film actor) agreed with Adamic that all popular front forces were needed to fight the growing American forces of reaction.

"Maybe you misunderstand me," said Murray, after Elmer Benson had also added his criticism.

In order to clear up "misunderstandings," if that was what was wrong, a small group met with Murray for breakfast the next morning, at the Stevens hotel. Morgenthau and Pepper were there and a feeling of harmony seemed to prevail. Then Benson went into a bedroom alone with Murray, to express alarm at rumors he had heard that Murray might resign as president of the CIO.

"You can't do that, Phil," eBnson declared. "Workers all over the world, and progressive people, look to you for leadership."

The response from Murray was one of the most surprising experiences of Benson's life.

Beating his breast and actually tearing at his clothing, Murray wailed, "You don't know what I've gone through! My soul has just been torn apart!" And he kept repeating the same words, so that there was no use in continuing the conversation.

What was the matter with Philip Murray? An overwhelming amount of evidence that I have encountered leaves no doubt that it was this: when Murray talked about interference in union affairs by outsiders, he meant all but one group of outsiders, mention of which he omitted. And that group, whose pressure he had successfully resisted for years, had finally broken down his resistance. This was the Roman Catholic Church, operating chiefly through the Association of Catholic Trade Unionists. As a matter of fact, Murray had begun his address to the conference by declaring that only three things were important to him: (1) his church; (2) his union; (3) his family.

Except for the popular media of communication, which have a hush-hush policy as regards almost anything that might aggravate religious controversy, there was no secret about the program of ACTU (organized in 1937; became nationwide in 1940) to promulgate the labor-management views of the church, based on two papal encyclicals: Leo XII's "Rerum Novarum" in 1891 and Pius XI's "Quadragessimo Anno" in 1931. John L. Lewis would have nothing whatever to do with ACTU and, although his successor's door was open to everyone, Philip Murray held out against any divisive movements throughout the war years. Then, however, two of his leading lieutenants—David McDonald, who succeeded him upon his death as president of the Steelworkers, and James Carey, CIO's secretary-treasurer—became converted to the Church's strong anti-Communist campaign. It was still not easy, however, for Murray to undertake any purge of left-wingers in the CIO, although his task became easier after Walter Reuther defeated R. J. Thomas for president of the United Automobile Workers in March, 1946, largely with ACTU help.

Saul Alinsky, in *John L. Lewis* (Putnam, 1949), quoted Lewis as remarking, after observing Murray with four priestly advisors following him everywhere at a CIO convention, "I began to feel here for the first time, a great power from the outside was being exerted into the organization of the CIO and that Philip Murray was the subject of its intentions . . ." Several Catholic labor leaders have told me that the presence of Father Charles Owen Rice of Pittsburgh, author of *How to De-Control Your Union of Communists,* and many other priests at CIO affairs got to be embarrassing for them as Catholics. "At the 1947 convention in Boston," one of these Catholics told me, "you couldn't get through the door without tripping over eight priests."

The capture of Philip Murray as a supporter was a great victory for the Association of Catholic Trade Unionists. Murray's change of heart as regards the importance of a popular front of all anti-fascist forces, including Communists and other strong liberals, made impossible the achievement of any united action, such as that contemplated by the resolution-makers at the Chicago Conference of Progressives.

Although Henry Wallace resisted urgent invitations to attend, his spirit, as several reporters noted, seemed to hover over the meeting. Representing him was Harold Young, his first assistant who, after the firing, with NC-PAC financing, set up a political office for Wallace in Washington and maintained it until October, 1947, when it was moved to New York's Hotel McAlpin. Young refused a place at the speakers' table, but said he would deliver a message from the floor at the proper time. He was given a tremendous buildup as the emissary of "the man whom, etc."; when he staggered to his feet to say not much more than "Glad to be with you," it was a terrific anti-climax.

Nevertheless the conference unanimously adopted a resolution addressed to Henry A. Wallace:

> Carry on in your fight for the fullest, freest discussion of that basic problem of our day—international cooperation.
>
> Carry on with confidence that you have the support of the millions upon millions of Americans who believe in the program of Franklin Delano Roosevelt.
>
> We urge you to speak frequently and as you have always done, forthrightly . . .
>
> The Roosevelt coalition organized here will build thoroughly and constructively the corps of volunteer citizens who will help carry the fight for peace to every doorstep in the nation.

As already indicated, the foreign policy statement included the same criticism of the Baruch atomic control plan that Wallace had made in his July 23 letter to President Truman, even though Baruch had been condemning Wallace in the press for his refusal to admit that he was wrong in his comments, and had been attempting to bring pressure to bear on Wallace through Pepper, Mrs. Eleanor Roosevelt and others. This action was taken on the second day of the conference, after Harold Ickes had spoken and departed.

On Oct. 8, 1946, it was revealed that Ickes was, as he put it, "pretty damn sore" over the Baruch plan criticism, for which he blamed Harold Young, who was guiltless. Ickes also let it be known that he didn't like the decision of the ICC-ASP executive committee to write to Truman, protesting Wallace's dimissal. In *Age of Suspicion* (Random House, 1953), James Wechsler repeats a canard which was current at the time: that Ickes became disillusioned because copies of his comparatively conservative speech had not been mimeographed early enough for release to the press. He did not give credence to the explanation given him that the mimeograph machine had broken down. I have unquestioning confidence in the honesty of the man who was in charge of that mimeograph machine, and he has volunteered the information to me in personal conversation that "the damn thing *was* overworked and it *did* break down, and it was just bad luck that it happened to be Ickes' speech which was coming up next." I don't know whether this will convince Mr. Wechsler, but it does me.

Furthermore, I disbelieve the reasons Ickes gave for his resignation, on Nov. 12, 1946, as executive chairman of the ICC-ASP. He said it was because the Continuations Committee of the Conference of Progressives, meeting on Oct. 15, 1946, in New York, had in general reaffirmed its stand that the United States should cease manufacture of atomic bombs; although it accepted Baruch's explanation that he intended to present the "easy stages" proposal as a single package, specifying at what stages American authority and information would be released. I believe Ickes' resignation was because his salary, since he assumed the position the preceding March, had been mostly unpaid. The organization just couldn't raise the monthly payments on his $25,000 annual honorarium for the use of his name.

At a press conference before he left Chicago in September, Philip Murray partly offset the effect of his earlier speech, when he denied that he expected to engage in any purges in either liberal or labor organizations. "I'm not a very good hunter," he said, in reply to a question as to whether there was to be a hunt for Reds in the CIO. Also, after the Oct. 15, 1946 Continuations Committee meeting, in New York, Murray fairly purred, for the benefit of the press: "We expect this movement to expand and become in due course the most powerful liberal and progressive organization brought together in the history of the country." Unquestionably, he said, there would be political activity, but there had been no discussion of a third party. Among those attending the three-hour closed session were: Abt; Baldwin; Kroll; Benson; Morgenthau; Davidson; Kingdon; Hannah Dorner; Robert Kenny, then president of the National Lawyers Guild; Foreman; Eugene Johnson, representing A. F. Whitney; Nisselson; Pepper; Chester Bowles; J. Raymond Walsh; Walter White; and Jacob Potofsky, president of the Amalgamated Clothing Workers.

Meeting in Washington on Nov. 8, 1946, the Continuations Committee interpreted the election results as an expression of dissatisfaction with the 79th Congress, "dominated by a reactionary coalition," and not as "an affirmative vote in support of reaction." Morgenthau presided at that meeting, which was to plan the mid-January rally. This was a well-attended meeting, with Murray; Kroll; Baldwin; Benson; Davidson; Foreman; Kenny; Walter White; George Addes of the UAW; William Pollock; Hannah Dorner; Mrs. Mary McLeod Bethune; Hyman Blumberg of the Amalgamated; Morris Cooke; Mrs. Gifford Pinchot; Paul Fishman; Jerome Udell; and others.

However, there never was another meeting, and no January conference, despite repeated attempts on the part of Beanie Baldwin to persuade Philip Murray to call one. According to one who was in attendance, stony silence had greeted the suggestion by Addes that the only way to make political action effective was by ward and precinct organization. "Murray torpedoed it," Albert J. Fitzgerald told me. "Murray said that these people don't represent anybody. Only he (Murray) had a following; the others were star gazing. Right then, he predicted that things were going to get pretty tough, that relations between the United States and the Soviet Union were worsening and people in the labor movement were going to have to get solidly behind the Truman administration. While Lee Pressman sat there saying nothing, Phil was pretty vague about what he was driving at. Then he said that others were going to have to mend their ways and stop following the Communist party line. That was after the meeting itself; he never went that far in the meeting, where he just hinted around."

"Murray killed it for fear the Commies would take over," James Patton, president of the National Farmers Union, told me.

Others blame James Carey for having been the "evil influence" behind Murray.

Everyone agrees that Murray had no intention of working to keep the Conference of Progressives alive before the Washington meeting, but that he either lacked the courage or had other reasons for not saying so frankly at that time.

October 23, 1946 was publication date for a 200-page *Manual of Practical Political Action,* put out by the NC-PAC as an outgrowth of the June Political Action School. In eight loose-leaf sections, replete with photographs, graphs, charts and other illustrative material, the Manual today is a virtual collector's item. It is a textbook of what an amateur wanting to become a professional politician should know about organization, personnel, finance, research, publicity, advertising, literature and issues. Referring to the third party question, the editorial introduction said: "There is little question that with a few exceptions all truly liberal Americans would prefer to have a party of their own, taking clear-cut stands on all major issues and rallying ever-new forces to their banner." But "realistic analysis," the editors continued, "reveals obstacles to the establishment of an immediately effective third party. . . . The need for a third party will be determined by the future ability of independent organizations to make impressions on the candidates and platforms, and on the office-holders and voting records of the major parties. This manual is intended as a guide to the establishment and operation of effective independent political organization" which, the editors concluded, could "greatly reduce the obstacles to building and operating a political party." Perhaps the most valuable feature of the Manual was the case histories of successful political action by non-party groups and individuals.

As early as May 12, 1946, a merger of the ICC-ASP and the NC-PAC had been discussed, primarily to solve money problems.

The ICC-ASP came into existence during the 1944 campaign and was the brainchild of Hannah Dorner, a Broadway public relations counsel. During its two years' existence, she was executive director; Jo Davidson, the famous sculptor, whose bust of FDR provided the image on dimes now in current use, was chairman. As other "big names" were added to the payroll, mostly for their public relations effect, fancy titles were concocted for them. James Roosevelt, for instance, was called "national director" when he joined in February, 1946, and Harold L. Ickes was "executive chairman" from March to October of that year.

This semantic adeptness is a clue to how the ICC-ASP operated in general. It went in for large, money-raising spectacles and eschewed anything resembling ward and precinct political activity.

The ICC-ASP enrolled a tremendous amount of talent. Among its 10,000 members by the end of 1945 were a large number of America's leading artists, musicians, composers, actors, authors and scientists. Others, who were not formally affiliated, often were obtained as performers or speakers at functions. Here are some of the names of those listed, as either initiating sponsors or members of the board of directors:

> Louis Adamic, Franklin P. Adams, William Rose Benét, Mary McLeod Bethune, Ernst P. Boas, Louis Bouche, Van Wyck Brooks, James Cagney, Louis Calhern, Henry Seidel Canby, Eddie Cantor, Mady Christians, Rufus F. Clement, Marc Connelly, Morris Llewellyn Cooke, Aaron Copland, Norman Corwin, Thomas Craven, John Cromwell, Russell Crouse, Bartley Crum, Marcia Davenport, Bette Davis, Olivia De Havilland, Agnes De Mille, Moses Diamond, Olin Downes, Guy Pene duBois, Donald Du Shane, Albert Einstein, Florence Eldridge, Philip Evergood, Henry Pratt Fairchild, Edna Ferber, William S. Gailmor, Rudolph Ganz, Ben Grauer, Oscar Hammerstein, Moss Hart, Lillian Hellman, Miriam Hopkins, Langston Hughes, Howard Koch, Leon Kroll, John Howard Lawson, Canada Lee, Max Lerner, Peter Lyon, Fritz Mahler, Thomas Mann, John T. McManus, Fredric March, Dorothy Maynor, Lowell Mellett, Yehudi Menuhin, Alfred E. Mirsky, William Morris, Alonzo F. Myers, John T. Peters, Martin Popper, Nelson Poynter, Walter Rautenstrauch, Fritz Reiner, Paul Robeson, Boardman Robinson, Edward G. Robinson, Robert Rossen, Arthur Schnabel, M. Lincoln Schuster, Harlow Shapley, Herman Shumlin, John Sloan, Raphael Soyer, Vilhjalmur Stefansson, Alfred Strelsin, Carl Van Doren, Mark Van Doren, Max Weber, Orson Welles and William Zorach.

The ICC-ASP's first public event was a banquet, honoring Archibald MacLeish upon his appointment as an assistant secretary of state. Speakers included Senators Wayne Morse and Claude Pepper, and Rep. Helen Gahagan Douglas. It was at a Businessmen for Wallace reception, in which the ICC-ASP collaborated, on Feb. 26, 1945, that Henry Wallace heard the news that the Senate committee had voted against his confirmation as Secretary of Commerce. Wallace thereafter spoke at a midnight standing-room-only rally in a Broadway theater, at which Orson Welles, Elliott Nugent, Norman Corwin and others appeared to support his nomination to the cabinet. Bette Davis, Edward G. Robinson and Walter Huston appeared on a 15-minute radio network program to support Wallace.

At an early ICC-ASP luncheon, Mrs. Wendell Willkie introduced a Woman's Pledge for Peace, which was signed by women all over the country. Morris Cooke represented the committee before the Senate Foreign Affairs Committee, in support of the United Nations charter; Dr. Harlow Shapley, eminent Harvard astronomer, did the same in support of the Full Employment Bill, before the Senate Banking and Currency Committee.

The ICC-ASP acted as a talent agency to provide glamorous motion picture stars and other headline figures for all sorts of occasions all over the country. Never before, and certainly at no time during the red-baiting days, has there been anything like this participation in public affairs of outstanding persons in the arts. It sent a delegation to Washington to lobby for the FEPC bill. In New York, Norman Corwin headed a movement to oppose continuation of the House Committee on Un-American Activities. For the committee, Dr. Alonzo Myers called a meeting of educators, to resist the recommendation of a committee of the American Dental Society that racial quota systems be maintained in dental schools. That was done through the group's Educational Division. The Science and Technology Division sponsored conferences of leading scientists and representatives of government to discuss the formation of a national science and research foundation; it also sponsored many public meetings, at which some of America's leading scientists pleaded for control of the atomic bomb, and the peacetime development of atomic energy research under international control. Dr. Reuben Gustavsen, then vice president of the University of Chicago, and Dr. Harold Urey, atomic scientist of the same school, were among those who spoke frequently under ICC-ASP auspices. The ICC-ASP maintained a Washington office.

Early in 1946, it became apparent that the ICC-ASP and the NC-PAC were working for very much the same program, and that they were competing with each other for financial contributions from the same potential donors. At a dinner honoring Jo Davidson, on Oct. 28, 1945, the ICC-ASP raised $22,000 from about 1,000 persons, who listened to Oscar Hammerstein, Olin Downes, Harlow Shapley, Bill Mauldin, Frank Sinatra and a number of others. On April 25, 1946, it presented a galaxy of talent to discuss the United Nations. Then it became thoroughly obvious that the competition for support between the NC-PAC and the ICC-ASP was wasteful, as the April 25 affair was obviously an attempt to "stay in business" after the huge success of the NC-PAC's Roosevelt Memorial Meeting of April 12.

Shortly thereafter, it was agreed that the two organizations would conduct their fund raising jointly, and a separate office for that purpose was set up in the Forrest Hotel. Then, however, there developed the inevitable arguments over how the budgets for the two recipients of liberal largesse were to be prepared. The Sept. 12, 1946 Madison Square Garden rally, which ended in Wallace's dismissal from the Cabinet, was the largest joint undertaking of the NC-PAC and the ICC-ASP, but even at that time the rivalry between the two groups was evident. Before the rally, the NC-PAC honored Wallace at a private dinner for about 75 of its own members; about midnight, after the rally, the ICC-ASP sponsored a reception at the Astor House.

The decision to merge the two organizations was made by their respective leaders on Nov. 13, 1946. At the time, the NC-PAC was between $25,000 and $30,000 in debt, due largely to the failure of Sidney Hillman to follow through on his promise to persuade the Amalgamated Clothing Workers to wipe out the 1944 deficit. Only $5,000 was ever received of that pledge. By this time Hillman, of course, was dead. He was always considered cool to the idea of merger, and several who were close to him in his last days have told me he definitely warned that it might lead to control by Communists. The NC-PAC had been Hillman's "baby" and, although he had been unceremoniously ousted from its leadership, he still worried about it. He was not pleased by its increasing blasts at President Truman, believing that it was necessary to "stand in" with the administration no matter what the provocation. His remonstrances to Beanie Baldwin, the operating head, however, were not strong or peremptory.

Hillman, all hands seem to agree, was not an easy man to work for. He came to be too much of a prima donna, and Baldwin in particular was the object of his wrath whenever anything went wrong. Lew Frank relates a rather humorous anecdote, which occurred in 1944 or shortly thereafter, when "Clear it with Sidney" was still a watchword. There was to be a dinner honoring Ferdinand Smith, National Maritime Union official, and newspaper accounts had included the fact that Baldwin had reserved a table. (Smith was known as a left-winger, and in 1949 was deported, after 37 years in the United States.) When he read the news story, Hillman stormed into the office and, while Beanie was on the telephone, threw himself onto a sofa and complained, "The trouble around here is that nobody ever clears anything with me." J. Raymond Walsh had a long interview with Hillman just a few days before he died, at which time Hillman expected to be placed in charge of CIO's international activities and wanted Walsh to be his assistant. Walsh confirms the fact that Hillman was "uneasy" about Beanie Baldwin, but his distrust never took any concrete form or expression. I think there is no doubt that, because of his long experience in working closely and effectively with the White House, Hillman would not have favored the merger of the ICC-ASP and the NC-PAC, and that he would not have gone along with the Progressive party in 1948. His reasons were different from those of his rival, Philip Murray, but they added up to the same thing: squeamishness over too close an alignment with left-wingers, and fear of breaking ties with the White House, whoever the occupant might be.

By comparison with the ICC-ASP, the deficit carrying NC-PAC was financially flush. The ICC-ASP intellectuals were over $100,000 in the hole by the end of 1946 and, although they said they would be able to pay this off before the merger occurred, they didn't do so. The debt became the burden of the successor organization, the Progressive Citizens of America.

After that occurred Hannah Dorner and Beanie Baldwin both became executive vice presidents of the PCA—with the understanding, however, that the latter would have charge of all finances. This was a "face saving" arrangement, which was supposed to last until May 15, 1947 only, when Miss Dorner was to resign. When that date arrived, she didn't want to quit but Baldwin felt, undoubtedly correctly, that there couldn't be two bosses, so he forced compliance with the agreement. Hannah Dorner continued as a member of the PCA board of directors, and was on the first executive committee of the Progressive party in early 1948.

Henry A. Wallace did not boycott the founding convention of the Progressive Citizens of America, as he had the Conference of Progressives. Rather, he was one of the featured speakers, along with Mayor Fiorello La Guardia of New York. Whereas the latter specifically warned against attempts to form a third party, Wallace "teased the convention with his offhand reference to third party possibilities," to quote John K. Weiss, in the Dec. 31, 1946 *PM*.

"It was a good speech. I wrote it myself," Henry Wallace has told me.

Because it was short and because, after he broke with the Progressive party in 1950, Wallace insisted that his attitude at the time was that the United States should work for an agreement with the Soviet Union before the latter became strong enough to constitute a threat, it is here reproduced in full:

> I am glad to attend this meeting of independent citizens who believe in progressive political action. You have invested your time and money to try to elect progressive Democrats in many a hard campaign. You have shared in many victories for good government. You failed in some of the fights which you put on last fall, and most of you knew in advance that you would fail. But you went through with the fights because we had to keep the progressive torch burning. Battles have been lost, but there is a war to win. To keep the progressive faith alive is, with us, not a matter of political expediency but of profound American conviction.
>
> The fundamental progressive faith is so broad that we should not allow ourselves to be divided on any minor issues. The essence of the progressive faith, as I see it, is belief in the goal of peace, prosperity and freedom in one world. Those who put hatred of Russia first in all

114

their feelings and actions do not believe in peace. Those who hold up Russian standards as a guide for us in the United States do not believe in freedom. As American progressives we are not interested in any fight between the Russia-haters and the Russophiles. We believe that such fighting is engineered by the enemy. We shall not allow the attacks of the enemy to stampede us into foolish red-baiting. Nor shall we allow those who owe their primary allegiance to some foreign power to determine our course.

Belief in freedom is the first article in our credo and we shall fight for all freedoms which are in accord with a peaceful world and a fully employed, prosperous America. I still believe in a free American press, even though it lies continually about Russia and labor—and thus endangers both world peace and industrial peace. The cure for such lies is more freedom, more education, more knowledge and more decent self-restraint. We do not believe in the freedom of monopoly, whether of the press or of cartels, to interfere with the free, private initiative of small businessmen. But neither do we believe in that excess of anarchic freedom which produces the chaotic extremes of the business cycle and leads to recurring periods of bankruptcy and unemployment. We believe that labor, business and government can act together through the President's Economic Advisory Council to prevent the business cycle from going to such dangerous extremes as it did from 1925 to 1933.

Belief in freedom does not mean that we stand for turning the country over to the "laissez-faire" big-business interests and their special pleaders in the journalistic and political world. It does not mean repeating the planless, selfish mistakes of the twenties all over again. The "laissez-faire" freedom of selfish big business inevitably leads to depression, higher tariffs, political confusion in many nations, revolution in some nations, and eventually —war. To prevent this we must have a certain amount of both international and national planning. Eventually the United Nations must become a World Federation, but we cannot expect Russia to become part of such a federation until the United States has demonstrated its ability to eliminate the excesses of the postwar business cycle.

We progressives believe that the United States can eliminate the excesses of the business cycle without danger to peace or to the essential freedoms. To do the job we must live in the future, not in the past. The Republican leadership in Congress is in serious danger of repeating its mistakes of the twenties as it deals with tariffs, taxation and fiscal policies. To prevent the Republican Congress and the "laissez-faire" big businessmen from leading us down the high road of boom, bust and war is the immediate justification for our progressive existence. The ultimate justification of the progressive cause is a positive program of world peace, world prosperity and world freedom.

We progressive, independent citizens believing in political action are not defeatists. Roosevelt is gone, but in the true Roosevelt spirit we are looking ahead to a better organized movement. We believe that three-fourths of the American people will believe in our message provided we go all out to get it over to them. American labor, whether AFL, CIO, Railway Brotherhood or independent, is with us once they understand the issues. So also are the majority of the artists, scientists and professional people. They all believe in the fundamental Americanism of our approach. The American doctrine is a revolutionary approach. It is as revolutionary as the Declaration of Independence or the Gettysburg Address. It affirms the equality of man, the freedom of man and the pursuit of happiness as the goal of man.

More and more the American people will question a program of imperialism and heavy armament as the true road to peace, prosperity and freedom. Your job as a progressive organization is to reach that majority of the population which is potentially progressive, but which, due to lack of information, is in the hands of the conservatives at the present time. If you succeed, the pattern of Postwar II will be different from that of Postwar I. In your hands rests the responsibility for leadership. You should pass up no opportunity to advance the progressive cause. Continually, you should work with the President's Economic Advisory Council. If you have any channels through which to work, you should do everything you can to make President Truman's message to Congress this January as forward-looking as his message of September, 1945. We must continually make it clear to the Administration that we, as progressives, would prefer the election of an out-and-out reactionary like Taft in 1948 to a lukewarm liberal. We want this to be a genuine two-party country, and not a country operated by a fake one-party system under the guise of a bipartisan bloc.

We have less use for a conservative, high-tariff Democratic party than we have for a reactionary, high-tariff

116

Republican party. If need be, we shall first fight one and then the other. At the moment our objective is to make the Democratic party out-and-out progressive. If the new Independent Citizens for Political Action (now the Progressive Citizens of America) is to be effective as an organization, its members will move into every precinct in the country to educate the people and control the political machinery.

We must also uphold the good right arms of all progressives who are in Congress, as well as those who were defeated last November. Kopplemann, Hook, Mac-Murray, Outland, Mrs. Woodhouse and others who were faithful public servants can be useful during the next two years. They should be busy writing articles, making speeches and taking part in your councils. We shall see them in Congress again.

As we work we must fight off the enemy, as his stooges try to stir up jealousies and get us fighting among ourselves. We shall never be against anything simply because Russia is for it. Neither shall we ever be for anything simply because Russia is for it. We shall hold firmly to the American theme of peace, prosperity and freedom, and shall repel all the attacks of the plutocrats and monopolists who will try to brand us as Reds. If it is traitorous to believe in peace—we are traitors. If it is communistic to believe in prosperity for all—we are Communists. If it is red-baiting to fight for free speech and real freedom of the press—we are red-baiters. If it is un-American to believe in freedom from monopolistic dictation—we are un-American. I say that we are more American than the neo-Fascists who attack us. The more we are attacked the more likely we are to succeed, provided we are ready and willing to counter-attack. On with the fight!

The only strong opposition during the months of negotiations which led up to the two-day meeting, on Dec. 28-29, 1946, at the New York Hotel Commodore, had come from the Communists within the NC-PAC and the ICC-ASP. They evidently did not believe any effective independent political action could grow out of any organization which was mainly middle-class. Nevertheless, only three floor fights developed at the convention, which was attended by approximately 300 from 21 states. And only one of them related to a political issue—peace-time military training. The Young Citizens' PAC wanted a plank condemning it, but were talked out of their proposal by Midwestern delegates, who said its inclusion would weaken the chances of obtaining mass support in their part of the country.

There was considerable discussion of how the $3 annual dues were

117

to be apportioned between the national office and the state and local organizations. The by-laws as adopted provided for a 50-50 split. The third dispute was over the name of the new organization. At first, "Independent Citizens for Political Action" was proposed and adopted. The question was reopened, however, by a California delegate, who said "political action" wouldn't go over well on the West Coast, and suggested the inspiration that had just come to him: "Progressive Citizens of America." Almost without debate, this name was adopted, the only serious competitor being "National Congress of Progressives."

There was no left-right quibbling. Those for whom the united front idea was anathema weren't present to start it. The claim that the PCA was a Communist "first step" toward a new party just isn't so. Article II, Section a, of the by-laws set forth the objectives of the PCA as follows:

> *Objects.* With faith in the common sense of the American people and conscious of the necessity for their full and effective participation in the processes of democracy by which our common purposes must be transmitted into constructive national policy, we have formed this organization of progressive citizens for political action.
>
> This organization bases itself on the principles on which the United States was founded. We are confident that every needed reform in our national life can be achieved through the United States Constitution and the orderly use of the ballot. It is our purpose, by encouraging the full and intelligent use of the ballot, to strive for a secure, abundant, democratic America, with equal freedom for all.
>
> The objects of this organization shall be:
>
> To propose and support legislation which will serve the economic and social needs of the people.
>
> To promote and cultivate the continuance and extension of democracy through the full and free use of the franchise.
>
> To strive for a just and enduring peace throughout the world.
>
> To promote a program in which the resources of the nation are organized to provide full employment and a high standard of living for all.
>
> To promote the cultural life of the people, protect their health and provide equal educational opportunities and facilities for all.
>
> To promote social, economic and political education for

118

all the people through the use of every available means of communication.

To safeguard the national economy against exploitation in any form by monopolistic groups.

To eliminate from our national life all discrimination based on race, color, creed or national origin.

To protect and promote the civil rights of all Americans, including the unrestricted right of labor to organize and bargain collectively.

To work for the realization of the Four Freedoms.

To work for the election of progressive men and women pledged to support a legislative program for the achievement of the foregoing objects.

To these ends we seek to unite all progressive men and women in our nation, regardless of race, creed, color, national origin or political affiliation, in an organization which is independent of all political parties and dedicated to the objectives enumerated herein.

Article VI, Section a, read: "Membership shall be open to all persons who support the objects of the organization as set forth in Article II."

Membership was to be through local chapters, which state chapters would charter. There was also provision for memberships-at-large, for persons not residing in areas where the minimum of 50, required to form a local chapter, had been obtained. The national annual convention was declared to be the highest governing body. Delegates would be assigned on the basis of one for every 100 members in a local affiliate or major fraction thereof, as determined by membership rolls 60 days before the convention. A 30 per cent representation was to constitute a quorum.

The by-laws established a board of directors of 200, with each affiliate permitted one member and others to be elected by the convention as a whole. The board was to meet every three months, with 25 per cent attendance constituting a quorum. It was to elect a national executive committee of 30 to meet monthly, with one-third attendance constituting a quorum. There was to be a chairman, 30 vice chairmen, a secretary and a treasurer; and the board was authorized to designate, from among its vice chairmen, one or more to be executive vice chairmen and salaried executive officers. The board was empowered to establish national divisions, and divisions of the various arts, sciences and professions were to establish a National Council of the Arts, Sciences and Professions, to have a consultative relationship with the board and executive committee. There was also provision for a young people's division. On all questions upon which a vote was to be taken, with nobody at any time possessing more than one vote, a majority would decide.

The following extracts from the Program for Political Action which was adopted indicate the long-range objectives:

> Our government has fallen to men whose world vision is caught within a new isolationism. They view the world not as a brotherhood of peoples but as an economic pie to be divided among cartels. This is a recipe for international anarchy.
>
> These convictions have led us to form this organization for political action. Our aims can be simply stated. We seek unity among progressives. We seek to combat political apathy, which is reaction's weapon. We seek to enlist millions of people in year-round action on national, state and local issues.
>
> As this organization is firmly built, it will determine in real democratic fashion the course it will take. It is apparent that the Republican party has long since lost any possible claim as a liberal party. The Democratic party has repeatedly served the progressive cause. Under the administration of Franklin D. Roosevelt our nation made significant democratic advances, and charted a program for peace and security, embodied in the Economic Bill of Rights and in the principle of international friendship and collaboration. The Democratic Administration has now abandoned this program. The Democratic party is notoriously tainted by jim-crow reaction and machine greed. It is not clear now whether this party will recover its progressive tradition or surrender to its own brand of ignorance and bigotry. We want to be clear on one thing. If the Democratic party woos privilege and betrays the people, it will die and deserve to die. We cannot, therefore, rule out the possibility of a new political party, whose fidelity to our goals can be relied upon. We, the people, will not wait forever—we will not wait long for the Democratic party to make its choice.

There followed a long list of specific endorsements of legislative and administrative actions. Jo Davidson, former ICC-ASP chairman, and Frank Kingdon, former chairman of the NC-PAC, were elected co-chairmen. Herman Shumlin, theatrical producer and director, became secretary; and Michael Nisselson, president of the Amalgamated Bank of New York, became treasurer.

In his syndicated column for Jan. 4, 1947, Harold Ickes interpreted Wallace's speech as an indication that he abandoned the hopeless idea that progressives could work through the corrupt Democratic party. However, Ickes predicted failure for the PCA, because it lacked a grass-roots base. He said that the 200 directors and 30-man executive

120

committee setup of "big names" were a sign of weakness rather than strength.

Actually, the real weakness was not the names that were there, but those that were absent. As the PCA was forming, another meeting, of people who also called themselves liberal and who had been in the vanguard of New Deal supporters, was in the making. It was an invitational affair, sponsored by the Union for Democratic Action, and was attended by about 150 persons, on Jan. 4, 1947, in Washington. It resulted in the formation of a committee of 25, with Wilson Wyatt, former housing expediter, and Leon Henderson, former OPA administrator, as co-chairmen, to proceed with the nationwide organization of the Americans for Democratic Action.

"We reject any association with Communists or sympathizers with communism in the United States as completely as we reject any association with Fascists or their sympathizers," read a laconic statement, issued at the end of the one-day closed session. According to Barry Bingham, editor of the *Louisville Courier-Journal,* the "keynote" was sounded by Mrs. Eleanor Roosevelt, who advised the group it needed "not a negative approach against any country or ideology," but a "positive program of promoting democracy everywhere."

That program, as set forth in a six-point statement, was initially as follows:

1. The New Deal program must be expanded to insure decent levels of health, nutrition, shelter and education.

2. Civil liberties must be protected from concentrated wealth and overcentralized government. They must be extended to all Americans regardless of race, color, creed or sex.

3. Any sound foreign policy requires a healthy and prosperous domestic economy.

4. The United States must continue to give full support to the United Nations. The conference endorses the American plan for international control of atomic energy.

5. Because the interests of the United States are the interests of free men everywhere, America must furnish political and economic support to democratic and freedom-loving peoples the world over.

6. Within the general framework of present American foreign policy, steps must be taken to raise standards of living and support civil and political freedoms everywhere. These policies are in the great democratic tradition of Jefferson, Jackson, Lincoln, Wilson and Franklin D. Roosevelt. We reject any association with Communists or sympathizers with communism in the United States as completely as we reject any association with

Fascists or their sympathizers. Both are hostile to the principles of freedom and democracy on which this Republic has grown great.

The committee of 25 was comprised as follows:

Charles G. Bolte, New York City, chairman, American Veterans Committee; Elmer Davis, Washington; George Edwards, Detroit, president, Detroit Common Council; Ethel S. Epstein, New York City; Leon Henderson, Washington; Hubert Humphrey, mayor of Minneapolis; Mrs. Clyde Johnson, Cincinnati; Reinhold Niebuhr, New York City; Edward Prichard, Jr., Paris, Ky.; Franklin D. Roosevelt, Jr., New York City; Frank W. McCulloch, Chicago; Mrs. Gifford Pinchot, Washington; Bishop William Scarlett, St. Louis; Walter White, New York City, president, Nat. Ass'n for Advancement of Colored People; Wilson W. Wyatt, Louisville, Ky.; Harvey Brown, president, International Association of Machinists, independent; David Dubinsky, president, International Ladies Garment Workers, A. F. of L.; Hugo Ernst, Cincinnati, president, Hotel and Restaurant Workers, A. F. of L.; B. F. McLaurin, international representative, Brotherhood of Sleeping Car Porters, A. F. of L.; James Killen, Washington, vice president, International Brotherhood of Pulp, Sulphite and Paper Workers; John Green, Camden, N. J., president, Shipbuilding Workers, CIO; Walter P. Reuther, president, United Automobile Workers, CIO; Willard Townsend, president, United Transport Service, CIO; Samuel Wolchok, president, Retail, Wholesale and Department Store Workers, CIO; James Loeb, Jr., Washington, secretary of Union for Democratic Action.

On the committee of the whole there also appeared the names of the following: Stewart Alsop, Chester Bowles, James B. Carey, Marquis Childs, Kenneth Crawford, Elmer Davis, Morris Ernst, Lester Granger, Allen Haywood, Daniel Hoan, Rep. Chet Holifield, Joseph P. Lash, Alfred Baker Lewis, Edouard Lindeman, Edgar A. Mowrer, Mrs. Eleanor Roosevelt, Paul A. Porter, Bishop G. Bromley Oxnam, Nelson Poynter, Sidney Hook, Gardner Jackson, Emil Rieve, Arthur M. Schlesinger Jr., Jerry Voorhis and many others, to a total of well over 100.

There was nothing sudden or surprising about this split, which turned out to be irrevocable, within the ranks of liberals. The cleavage, centering around the issue of the popular front, was of long standing and had come to a minor head in 1939, when the spiritual predecessors of the PCA, then organized under Franz Boas as the Committee for Democracy and Intellectual Freedom, clashed publicly with the Committee for Cultural Freedom spearheaded by John Dewey and Sidney Hook, potential ADAers. I shall relate more of this background in a later chapter, devoted to the role of liberals in the 1948 campaign and thereafter.

The split—ideological, tactical, or of whatever type—was also fundamental when the Liberal party broke away from the American Labor party in 1944, in New York. It got its first postwar public airing after a letter from James Loeb Jr., national director of the Union for Democratic Action, was published in the May 13, 1946 *New Republic*. In it, Loeb argued strongly against what he interpreted to be the substance of resolutions passed at the Win-the-Peace conference a month earlier, "that the present critical tension in internal affairs is due *exclusively* to the imperialistic, capitalistic, power-mad warmongering of the Western democracies aimed at the destruction of the peace-loving workers' democracy of the Soviet Union." He wrote:

> Liberals must decide whether it is their conviction that the *sole* objective of the progressive movement is economic security, or whether human freedom, which has historically been a co-equal dynamic of progressivism, is still a commendable objective. . . .

> No united-front organization will long remain united; it will become only a "front." This is sometimes, but not always, due to the fact the Communists are more active, more consecrated, more zealous than their liberal associates. More pertinent is the fact that independent liberals, whether we like it or not, simply will not group themselves into a disciplined, semi-conspiratorial caucus whose aim is to retain or obtain control of the organization. Thus they are handicapped in their competition with even a small number of disciplined Communists who automatically follow their own leadership and make use of any legitimate differences of opinion to further their own strategic advantage.

First to reply, in the May 20, 1946 *New Republic,* was Stanley M. Isaacs of New York, whose letter said in part:

> I disagree wholly with his thesis that Communists must be excluded from organizations supporting a progressive cause and that when they succeed in infiltrating such an organization, the liberals should abandon it — and incidentally the cause it advocates. I grant the difficulty of dealing with well-organized Communists who want to dominate. But I am not afraid of Communist infiltration and certainly will not abandon a just cause because I object to some who have joined in its support. Nor will I secede and help to organize a new group with the same objective — a move that invariably ends in the two organi-

123

zations attacking each other instead of the common enemy. Witness the AFL and the CIO.

To do what Mr. Loeb suggests is to fall for the strategy which Fascists and their predecessors have used since time immemorial to divide and conquer — to destroy their opponents piecemeal. They proceed to attack an organization as a Communist front and the liberals who are active in it as fellow travelers, if not Communists. Some liberals thereupon are intimidated into public repudiation. Those who persist are now handicapped because the fascist critics point to those who are left as evidence that all who remain *must* be Communists. When they succeed in blackening the reputation of those who have stuck grimly to the anti-fascist cause, they then turn against those who resigned and label them Communists or "fellow travelers," because at one time they were connected with the organization. The end result is demoralizing — the cause is weakened and leaders courageous and important in the fight for liberty and justice are discredited. This is the actual process that is taking place in ruinous fashion in many a field where weak-kneed or tired liberals succumb to fascist maneuvers.

Roger Baldwin, longtime director of the American Civil Liberties Union, contributed the following in the June 17, 1946 issue:

I commend to others a policy resulting from a long personal experience with Communist operations. (1) Cooperate with admitted Communists in those public movements where partisan participation appears desirable. (2) Contribute to agencies under their control, even when not so admitted, when they are doing a useful public service not inconsistent with liberal objectives. (3) Defend the rights, whether of admitted or concealed Communists, but reserve the right in so doing to characterize accurately their loyalties. This is not red-baiting. (4) But resist being a party to public deception by joining or sponsoring the committees, meetings, petitions and protests of agencies known or suspected to be under Communist control while professing a disinterested public service.

If there was one of those liberal organizations which was not affected by the "drive the Reds out" campaign, which began almost with the war's end and which the Loeb letter brought into the open, I do not know which one it was. The drive invariably was initiated by the right, and resulted from fear that the left would try to gain control, rather than from any actual activity. In other words, the purges were in the nature of "preventive warfare."

One of the first organizations to be hard hit was the American Veterans Committee, which still was struggling to get started. With the slogan "Citizens First, Veterans Second," the AVC was born abroad before war's end; it promised to be unique among veterans' organizations, in that it would not primarily be a bonus-seeking, super-patriotic group, useful to headline-conscious young lawyers with political ambitions.

Nevertheless, the latter was about all it ever amounted to, the chief beneficiaries being Gilbert Harrison and Michael Straight of the *New Republic*, Franklin D. Roosevelt Jr., Chat Patterson and Oren Root Jr. In 1946, the AVC claimed 100,000 members; in 1947, it had 45,000; and on June 1, 1948, its paid-up membership was 27,343. In November, 1946, it adopted its own loyalty oath and in the next two years devoted a considerable amount of time to the trials and expulsions of several of its left wing leaders. In the meantime, the purposes for which the overwhelming majority of its members had joined — to work for progressive social legislation — were ignored. By the time AVC got through cleansing itself, its rank-and-file had become bored, and had quit in such numbers that there wasn't enough strength left for the organization to pull any weight with anyone.

In April, 1947, a number of persons were defeated for re-election to the board of directors of the Independent Voters of Illinois, soon to become an affiliate of the Americans for Democratic Action; whereupon Frank W. McCulloch (after 1948, Sen. Paul Douglas' administrative assistant, and President Kennedy's appointee as chairman of the National Labor Relations Board) went to Milburn P. Akers, of the *Chicago Sun,* with an interpretation of the election. "Pete" used this for his "Strictly Political" column, under the heading, "I.V.I. Vote Hits So-Called Left-Wingers." The account charged that "The I.V.I. left-wing element had sought to unseat a number of directors who had opposed their policies during the past year," and explained, "In several past elections the I.V.I. has been under fire for allegedly having extreme left-wingers on its board."

Two days later, Akers gave me space for a reply which, in large part, read as follows:

> Your article creates the impression that the election represented the views of the entire membership of IVI. You must know that the framework of IVI permits no such expression. IVI is run by a Board of Directors of 23 which is elected by a Board of Governors of 108. Who elects the Board of Governors? The Board of Directors does. It is a vicious closed circle with the IVI membership being completely disenfranchised.
>
> The so-called "left-wingers" protested this organizational setup as undemocratic and detrimental to IVI's best interests. If there were any ideological differences—related to foreign or domestic policies involved—I do not know what they were. The "left winger" issue was raised as a smokescreen to frighten the unknowing. It was a complete phony.
>
> More important, the election outcome was obtained by

125

methods which by no stretch of the imagination can be condoned by any believer in the democratic process. The tellers were three rival candidates—"right wingers," you would call them erroneously. Contrary to precedent, in violation of the Constitution of IVI and unknown to the voters as a whole, these tellers permitted the casting of votes by proxy; and they permitted cumulative voting. That is, a ballot on which only one name was marked was counted as 23 votes for that person. That is the only way in which there was a spread of about 20 votes between the 23rd and 24th candidates. If the votes had been counted one for a candidate, the results would have been entirely different. In other words, many declared victors did not really win.

Among the background details that were never told were: the fact that, as a result of its undemocratic setup, the IVI had lost all but about 800 of its former 6,000 members; that the "rule from the top down" had virtually killed organizational activity for more than two years; that the leadership did not want a broad mass-membership, largely because of its hopes to line up, in 1947, with the Republicans, to help name a fusion candidate for Mayor of Chicago (a dream which ended with the GOP successes in November, 1946); that many resolutions by the board of directors, instructing different committees to work for constitutional revision, were sabotaged, as were innumerable other board actions; and especially, that the "left wing purge" claim was made in an attempt to offset open red-baiting charges that had been made by Russell Root, the Republican mayoralty candidate, after the IVI had endorsed his Democratic opponent, Martin H. Kennelly. Root had mentioned names, and they were *not* those of anyone who was defeated for re-election to the board of directors; quite the contrary, they were those of the purgers.

The charge that there was any leftist plot, or even movement, to take over the IVI was completely without foundation. The "revolt" was entirely from the right, not the left. Its leader explained to me his reason for opposing the "one member-one vote" proposal of the so-called "left" as due to his belief that control of the IVI must be kept in the hands of "the right people." He said, "The rank-and-file should realize that some of us have had much more political experience than they, and are better able to make decisions." Furthermore, the tactics used by McCulloch and his supporters in the IVI emulated and outdid those which are usually supposed to be the prerogatives of the "boring from within" Communists. McCulloch even cast a cumulative voting proxy for Willard Townsend, president of the United Transport Service Employees, who was in Japan at the time, explaining it was authorized by his wife. His "packed" committee of tellers accepted the proxy.

The vacillation of these so-called Chicago liberals was shown in their attitude toward Henry Wallace. On Dec. 4, 1944, a banquet was attended by over 1,200, in Chicago's Palmer House, to honor Marshall Field on the third anniversary of the founding of the *Chicago Sun*.

126

This paper had called for a fourth term for FDR in a front page editorial, on May 12, 1944, and had implored the Democratic convention to renominate Wallace. Speaker of the evening was Vice President Henry A. Wallace, who criticized the press of the nation for its conservativism and political bias, with special reference to its twenty years' handling of Russian news. There was considerable rivalry among the political amateurs, or independents, or non-machine Democrats—the IVI leaders, or "eggheads," as they came to be called in 1952—as to who would meet Mr. Wallace when he arrived, who would escort him to and fro, who would sit at the speakers' table and have any part in the festivities. Everyone wanted to get close to the man who was the symbol of vanishing New-Dealism, and the major prophet of the postwar world.

A month later, these same liberals were diligently at work to drum up support for senatorial confirmation of the nomination of Henry A. Wallace as Secretary of Commerce. On Jan. 26, 1945, Loeb stated publicly, "The 14 members of the Senate committee who voted against Henry Wallace stand condemned before the American electorate for having betrayed the people's will."

On Jan. 29, 1945, the Union for Democratic Action, in collaboration with the *New Republic,* sponsored a testimonial dinner, in Wallace's honor, at the Hotel Commodore, in New York. In its monthly newsletter, announcing the affair, appeared this eulogy:

> Henry Wallace held tenaciously to the course of domestic liberalism which had provided the major reforms and basic social legislation of the New Deal, even after the economic royalists began to move in on Washington as dollar-a-year men. As the President became increasingly preoccupied with the military conduct of the war and the international politics of the Grand Alliance, Wallace became the chief spokesman of the New Deal, the liberal conscience of the Administration, the living symbol of its enduring values. Wallace became more and more the eloquent champion of the people. With simple courage, he stated the revolutionary implications of democracy, formulating its timeliness and wisdom in terms of current economic reality . . . American progressives look to Henry Wallace for leadership in the days ahead.

Later, in connection with the literature which ADA put out during the 1948 campaign, I shall recommend that the reader of this book turn back to this page, to go over the foregoing again.

In October, 1946, when Henry Wallace came to Chicago for a political speech, once again Frank McCulloch and a few other IVI leaders hung on to his coattails. I know, because I was there. A year and a half later, I was on the platform debating with these same fellows, who were talking about what a great president Harry Truman was. And as for Wallace? They had literature from which to quote—*not* that Wallace had changed; *not* that he had *failed* to change with the times, but that he *never* had been any good.

# ¶ 7 WALLACE GOES TO EUROPE.

*Enraged Congressmen interrupted their debate on the Truman Doctrine to lambast Wallace for his platform attacks on that doctrine in five West European countries.*

The difference between the Progressive Citizens of America and Americans for Democratic Action was not long to remain one of abstract principle only. On March 12, 1947, President Harry S. Truman appeared before a joint session of both houses of Congress, to enunciate what became known as the Truman Doctrine. Specifically, it was a request for an immediate appropriation of $40 million, for military and economic aid to Greece and Turkey and the sending of American civilian and military personnel to those countries, as a bulwark against internal communism and external threats, presumably from the Soviet Union.

The PCA immediately denounced the proposal as heading the country toward war, announcing "the end of an American policy based on one world" and substituting one which "divides the world into two camps." It added: "A world divided into two camps will eventually move to an atomic arms race and total atomic destruction."

The ADA, on the other hand, at its March 30 organizational conference in Washington, "overwhelmingly" approved the Truman plan by a voice vote, after "thorough discussion" of the issues, according to the statement made public by Wilson Wyatt, chairman of the ADA national board, at the end of the day's deliberation by approximately 250 delegates.

That was the day before the PCA packed Madison Square Garden for a "Crisis Meeting," with Henry A. Wallace and a number of other speakers. Wallace, however, had not waited until then to speak out. On March 13, the day after Truman spoke, he broke a public silence of two and a half months by going on the raido to assert: "March 12, 1947 marked a turning point in American history. It is not a Greek crisis that we face, it is an American crisis. It is a crisis in the American spirit. That which I feared when I wrote President Truman last July has come upon us."

The most memorable line in this Wallace speech was, "When Truman offers unconditional aid to King George of Greece he is acting as the best salesman communism ever had." To this conclusion he led up by agreeing that Greece needed economic aid, as did the people of many other countries devastated by war. But, he asked, "If aid to the people of the world is our objective, why did the President and Congress allow the United Nations Relief and Reconstruction Administration to die?" He particularly scored the $150 million earmarked for Turkey, no ally of the United States in either war, which, he said, would be used for military purposes only. Truman, he said, proposed "in effect that America police Russia's every border. There is no country too

128

reactionary for us provided it stands in Russia's expansionist path. There is no country too remote to serve as the scene of a contest which may widen until it becomes a world war."

By sanctioning Winston Churchill's Fulton, Mo. speech a year earlier, according to Wallace's interpretation, "Truman committed us to a policy of combating Russia with British resources . . .

"I say that this policy is utterly futile . . . The world is hungry and insecure, and the people of all lands demand change. American loans for military purposes won't stop them. President Truman cannot prevent change in the world any more than he can prevent the tide from coming in or the sun from rising. But once America stands for opposition to change we are lost. America will become the most hated nation in the world."

Wallace pointed out that at the time Truman spoke, a United Nations commission was in Greece investigating the threat to that nation's security. "If Greece is in danger let the United Nations tell us the facts and recommend action. America will do what the United Nations recommends. Why should President Truman undercut its action? . . . "

Because of the poor press coverage that this speech obtained, the PCA bought full-page advertisements in newspapers throughout the country, to reprint it in full.

The day Truman spoke, the administrative committee of the PCA was holding a luncheon meeting, at which it listened to the broadcast. At its end Dr. Frank Kingdon, chairman, broke a water glass as he pounded the table and shouted, "That man has just set us on the road to war!" From Hannah Dorner came the suggestion, "Don't you think you could run a Garden meeting around this?" After three days of negotiation, Madison Square Garden was obtained for March 31. Wallace, who had been diligently devoting himself to his duties as *New Republic* editor, had refused several invitations, during January and February, to speak under PCA or any other auspices. He immediately agreed to Beanie Baldwin's suggestion, however, that he deliver the radio broadcast the next day and headline the program at the Garden rally. The "house" was sold out three days in advance: a phenomenal occurrence for a political meeting at which admission was charged; instead of ward-heelers being handed out passes with the admonition to see that they were used—or else. Likewise, it was the March 31 Crisis Meeting at which a new show-style technique was used. Instead of a formal chairman, there was an unseen narrator with a script. Before each speaker mounted the rostrum the platform was darkened and when the spotlight finally played on the person, he announced his own name and then launched into his address.

The most quoted lines from that meeting were those of Dr. Harlow Shapley, Harvard University astronomer, who demanded, "Why not frankly say what you mean, Mr. President? If you mean oil, why say Greece; why say Turkey, when you mean gravy? When we mean commercial gravy for a few, at the potential expense of the blood of the many. Greece, oil, Turkey, gravy—it's hash—and I don't like what they are cooking up. I don't like the way they cook it." Shapley rapped the

129

alleged interests of American oil companies in the Truman proposals; he also lambasted the House Committee on Un-American Activities, especially for its attacks on Dr. Edward U. Condon, director of the Bureau of Standards.

Elliott Roosevelt spoke forcefully, charging that the Truman Doctrine completely vitiated the plans for a lasting peace which his father had formulated. "Today," he said, "our government leaders, by their actions, have undermined the future of the United Nations . . . They have committed us to a two-world program . . . I believe that the future of our country depends upon our revitalizing the Democratic party before the 1948 elections . . . the people must have a *real* choice at the polls . . . Unless the Democratic party recognizes this challenge . . . it will be defeated in 1948."

Jo Davidson, Harold Russell, the no-armed veteran who starred in *The Best Years of Our Lives;* Norman Corwin, Frank Kingdon and Zero Mostel also preceded Henry Wallace on the program. Wallace spoke on "Back to the United Nations" and also charged that oil interests were important in influencing Truman. He pointed out that many war-torn countries, not only Greece, needed aid and called for it through a United Nations organization. He said that if the UN is weak, Senators Vandenberg and Connally were largely responsible for refusal to appropriate more money for it. "If the United Nations is untested," he declared, "let us test it. If the United Nations lacks support, let us support it. If the United Nations is weak, let us strengthen it."

Between the time the meeting was announced and its occurrence, what became known as the "domestic" Truman Doctrine had also been announced, on March 23, 1947. It was Executive Order 9835, calling for the first loyalty investigation of Federal employees. Wallace took a swat at it on March 31, when he said, "The Truman program must turn Americans against each other. It will threaten everything in America that is worth fighting for. Intolerance is aroused. Suspicion is engendered. Men of the highest integrity in public life are besmirched. The President's executive order creates a master index of public servants. From the janitor in the village post office to the Cabinet member, they are to be sifted and tested and watched and appraised. Their past and present, the tattle and prattle of their neighbors, are all to be recorded."

The day before, in an open letter to the President, Jo Davidson and Frank Kingdon had urged immediate revocation of the order. The PCA objected particularly to the sections of the order which specified that the employing department or agency would be able to exercise discretion regarding the extent to which the employee should be made acquainted with the charges against him, and its right to refuse to disclose the names of confidential informants. This, the PCA argued, went counter to the centuries-old basic principle of Anglo-Saxon law: that an accused person was presumed to be innocent until proven guilty, and had a right to know exactly the charges against him, meet his accusers in open court, and have the right to cross-examine them. The order also gave complete power to the Attorney General to prepare a list of "totalitarian, Fascist, Communist or subversive" organizations, without prior hearings. "There is not a sentence, not a word in the order," PCA charged, "which limits the power of the Attorney General to single out organizations for blacklisting. There is no standard by which he is to judge what is subversive or totalitarian. There is no way of reviewing his action, no appeal from the finality of his determination."

By contrast ADA, the day before, had endorsed Truman's program "to exclude from Government employment people who adhere to foreign governments or totalitarian political philosophies in any case where such adherence may endanger the best interests of the United States." In San Francisco, on April 15, 1947, Henderson, ADA leader, said of Henry Wallace, "We are moving at about 180 degrees from him."

It is interesting to note that Truman's action had been anticipated a long time in certain quarters. Before Franklin D. Roosevelt was buried, Willard Edwards wrote for the April 14, 1945, *Chicago Daily Tribune*:

> Foes of subversive trends in this nation today expressed belief that President Truman will lend the weight of his office to congressional efforts aimed at elimination of Communistic-minded bureaucrats from the Government structure.
>
> A prominent member of the House Committee on Un-American Activities said he expected this policy of obstruction to change under Mr. Truman. Several other members agreed that new life had been injected into the committee's inquiry because of the expectation that the White House would give it firm support."

Henry Wallace had been one of those New Dealers who refused to cooperate with the Red hunters. When Martin Dies, original chairman of the House Committee on Un-American Activities, wrote him, on March 29, 1942, to say that 35 employes of the Board of Economic Warfare had been affiliated with so-called "front" groups and that one was a nudist, Wallace's comment was that the letter read as though it were from Paul Joseph Goebbels, the Nazi propaganda chief.

*     *     *     *

Once back in the limelight, Henry Wallace did not abandon it for a long time to come. In January, he had received an unsolicited invitation from Kingsley Martin, editor of the British *New Statesman and Nation*, to visit England for a series of lectures in April. This was announced in the press on Jan. 13, 1947, two months before Truman expounded his doctrine, thus indicating the untruth of later charges that Wallace's trip was improvised to coincide with congressional debate of the Greek-Turkish aid proposal. Jo Davidson, Beanie Baldwin, Hannah Dorner and other PCA leaders had gone to see Michael Straight in January, to inform him that he had monopolized Wallace too long, and that the *New Republic* editor had to take a greater part in public affairs than merely writing a weekly editorial for the magazine.

131

Of Wallace's days as magazine editor, his personal secretary, Mrs. Viola Scott, whom Wallace personally hired in December, 1946, tells me: "He wrote most of his own copy. Often he did it weekends, at South Salem, and gave me penciled copies to type for him. He worked hard at his job, but by the end of the week he always became restless, wanting to get back to the farm for the weekend. On Mondays he would return, dirt under his finger nails, all pepped up, with plenty of orders to keep everyone busy. We learned to expect the weekly cycle of activity." Mrs. Scott said that many of Wallace's editorials came from "off his head." She thought the one he wrote on the death of Fiorello La Guardia was especially eloquent.

In the rush to pack to get off for Europe, Henry Wallace missed the annual Jefferson Day dinner in Washington, on April 5. However, he gave his $100 ticket to his son-in-law, Leslie Douglas, who heard President Truman reaffirm faith in the United Nations and declare that, by assisting free nations to maintain their freedom, the United States was aiding the UN. Before his plane left La Guardia Airport, at 3:04 p.m. on Monday, April 7, 1947, Wallace was unable to comment on the President's speech, because he had not yet read it. He did recall, however, that the preceding August, at a Cabinet meeting, he had favored aid for Greece when most of the other Cabinet members were against it.

Pushed for an answer as to whether he was a candidate for the Presidency, he replied, "What do you think?" Then his bearded friend, Jo Davidson, stepped forward and placed his own $35 beaver fedora on Wallace's head, saying, "If I can throw any hat in the ring it will be one made out of beaver."

On the eve of Wallace's departure there was made public a "Message of Greeting and Friendship to the Progressives of Great Britain from the Progressives of America," signed by 132 persons. Gotten up in the form of a scroll, the message included the following: "The success of the United Nations depends on the continued cooperation of Great Britain, Russia and the United States. We believe that this peace must be based upon economic cooperation, removal of barriers that block international trade, cooperation with all countries of the world to build up backward areas, the use of atomic energy for peaceful purposes and tireless struggle for a strong United Nations, with progressive universal disarmament."

Among the signers were the following: Robert Kenny, Sen. Claude Pepper, R. G. Tugwell, J. Raymond Walsh, Louis Adamic, Elmer Benson, Howard Mumford Jones, James Patton, Vilhjalmur Stefansson, Sen. Glen Taylor, Dr. Gregory Zilboorg, Carl Van Doren, Rep. J. A. Carroll, Bartley Crum, Clark Foreman, Jack Kroll, Rep. Adoph Sabath, Elliott and Faye Emerson Roosevelt, Lee Pressman, R. J. Thomas, Norman Corwin, Rep. Helen Gahagan Douglas, Sen. Matthias M. Neely, Freda Kirchwey, Donald Ogden Stewart, John Cromwell, Van Wyck Brooks, Rep. W. R. Granger, Fredric March, Sen. Elbert D. Thomas, Thomas Emerson, Martha Dodd, Olin Downes, Aaron Copland, Dashiell Hammett, Mrs. Elinor Gimbel, Lowell Mellett, Thomas Mann, Charles A. Graham, Sen. H. M. Kilgore, Sen. James T. Murray, Harlow Shapley, Arthur Miller, John T. Tunis,

Rep. Charles R. Savage, Carey McWilliams, Gene Kelly, Paul O'Dwyer, Helen Keller, Frank Kingdon and C. B. Baldwin.

Actually the signatures that appeared on the scroll were the work of a handwriting expert who put them all on a single document; he copied the signatures, however, from letters in which their use had been authorized.

The purpose of the scroll was to offset the effect of a cable which 70 Americans calling themselves liberals had sent on Jan. 23, 1947, to Ernest Bevin, British Foreign Minister. Drafted by the editor of *The New Leader*, it stated: "You should understand that American support for Wallace's position on foreign policy comes from a small minority of Communists, fellow-travelers and what we call here totalitarian liberals." Bevin was told that "The policy of the Labor government cannot be considered imperialistic by any stretch of the imagination," and a call was made for strong American-British unity. It compared these American Wallace supporters with a group of dissident members in the British Labor party, led by Crossman and Zilliacus. The full text appeared in *The New Leader* for Jan. 25, 1947. On its appearance, Wallace called it "as curious a misinterpretation of my views as the collection of signers who refer to themselves as 'American liberals'." By this he meant among others: Henry Luce, publisher of *Time;* Stanley High, a *Reader's Digest* editor; Malcolm Muir, publisher of *Newsweek;* the Very Rev. Robert I. Gannon, president of Fordham University; Matthew Woll, an AFL vice president; Dorothy Thompson, A. A. Berle, H. V. Kaltenborn, Harry D. Gideonse, John Chamberlain, Eugene Lyons, of the *American Mercury;* Clare Boothe Luce, Lawrence E. Spivak, *American Mercury* editor; Philip Burnham, editor, and Harry Lorin Binsse, managing editor of *Commonweal*. Among those who for years had been generally considered deserving of the liberal appellation, however, were Oswald Garrison Villard, Roger Baldwin, A. Philip Randolph, Arthur Garfield Hays and Sidney Hook.

Ernest Bevin, to whom the cable was addressed, had become Foreign Secretary in August, 1945, when the British Labor party surprised the world by a substantial victory over Winston Churchill's Conservative party, as the Potsdam conference was being held. His first speech had been delivered on Aug. 20, 1945, in support of Secretary of State Byrnes' communiqué stating that the United States would not recognize the Georgieff provisional government of Bulgaria. This speech, Herbert Matthews reported in the *New York Times* for Aug. 21, 1945, "solidly and completely lined up the Labor Government with the former Churchill coalition Government on the question of foreign policy. There is no better way of summing up his speech than to say that if Winston Churchill had made it there would have been no surprise."

Wallace arrived on Tuesday, April 8, 1947, in London, with ten dozen hatching eggs to present to experimental agricultural stations in England. In a prepared statement, he explained that he had "come to England and western Europe to discover those forces that must be united in behalf of peace." The next day, in a press conference, he called for an "understanding" with the Soviet Union as the only preservative of peace and warned that all three nations—the United States, the Soviet Union and Great Britain—were continuing to be imperialistic. He denounced the Truman Doctrine and recommended destruction of atomic bombs.

Within a few days British newspapers had responded to Wallace's presence strictly according to their known political biases. In the *New Statesman and Nation* for April 12, 1947, Kingsley Martin, editor and Wallace's host, welcomed the former Vice President with a laudatory review of his entire political career, and praise for his present opposition to the Truman foreign policy. On the other hand, the London *Mail* and *Observer* and the *Manchester Guardian* soon were to suggest that Wallace might better do his talking at home.

And that, it is not surprising, was what a great many Americans were saying too. Forrestal recorded that, at a Cabinet meeting on April 4, 1947, even before Wallace departed, he had suggested revocation of the former Cabinet member's passport, but President Truman thought such action would cause severe criticism the world over. Before Wallace really got started abroad Truman, furthermore, extended what was journalistically labeled an "olive branch" to both him and Claude Pepper. At his April 10, 1947, press conference, the President said he had no desire to read either rebel out of the Democratic party; that, in fact, he expected both men to support the Democratic ticket in 1948.

The very day of Truman's conciliatory statement, April 10, in a nationwide broadcast over the Mutual Broadcasting network, sponsored by the PCA, Sen. Claude Pepper charged that the Truman Doctrine would "sabotage the United Nations . . . destroy any hope of reconciliation with Russia, launch the United States upon an unprecedented policy of intervention in remote nations and areas of the world unilaterally, ally us with reactionary and corrupt regimes, subject this nation to the serious accusations of aspiring to become the new Rome or the old Britain and risk for the American people a war which may destroy civilization."

On the same program, James Patton charged that "The Truman Doctrine is a military venture outside the United States—and therein lies the danger"; Robert Kenny called it "scarcely a genuine relief program, but rather a political and military policy"; Eugene I. Johnson, speaking for A. F. Whitney, asked, "Need we support governments in Greece and Turkey which forbid working people to organize in free and independent unions, where elections are one-party or military affairs?"

Nevertheless, in comment on Truman's conciliatory statement, Pepper told the press, "The President certainly was right. I have been in the Democratic party directly and ancestrally for a long time and I have no idea of getting out of it. We Democrats differ with each other sometimes in primaries, but we don't leave the ancestral home." Pepper, as Truman had pointed out, attended the April 5 Jefferson Day dinner.

In London on April 11, Wallace's comment on Truman's statement was: "I shall be campaigning in 1948 with all my power, but I will be campaigning for the ideals of the free world and the men who best express these ideals. I hope, but I cannot guarantee, that they will be on the Democratic ticket." When, the next day, at Stoke-on-Trent, he was asked if he intended to found a third American political party, he replied that such a party might be a possibility and suggested that perhaps Pepper, "a fine sincere liberal," might head such a movement. Reached by phone in Miami, Fla., Pepper called this "kind and complimentary of Mr. Wallace," but repeated, "I have insistently advocated to all liberals that it would be a grave mistake to make any effort to organize a third party. I expect to support and work for the Democratic nominees in the general election."

This attitude did not prevent Pepper from being Wallace's chief defender in the Senate, when the reports of the itinerant ex-Vice President's statements abroad caused Senators Eastland of Mississippi, Vandenberg of Michigan and several others to erupt into violent denunciations of Wallace. "No American citizen has the moral right to conspire with foreign peoples in order to undermine and to weaken the hand of his country," Eastland declared on April 11. He then made a point of the fact that Jacques Duclos, secretary of the French Communist party, had been among those who had invited Wallace to visit France before returning home. At this juncture Pepper clarified the record to show that other signers of the invitation had been Edouard Herriot, president of the National Assembly and chairman of the Radical Socialist party (which is neither radical nor socialist); Leon Blum, ex-premier and leader of the Socialist party; and Maurice Schumann, leader of the Popular Republican party. Eastland's rejoinder was, "I want to leave the impression that the policies of Mr. Wallace are the policies advocated by the Communist party in France."

At a packed Central Hall auditorium in London, Wallace declared that a great opportunity for world leadership lay in British hands, if Britain opposed the current American foreign policy. He got thunderous applause when he declared, "The world is devastated and hungry; the world is crying out, not for American guns and tanks to spread more hunger, but for American plows and machines to fulfill the promise of peace." Wallace advocated expenditure of $50 billion over ten years, through the International Bank on World Reconstruction, administered by United Nations agencies.

At Stoke-on-Trent, on April 12, Wallace blamed the failure of the League of Nations on its use by groups of nations "to gang up on Soviet Russia" and asked, "Are we to allow the same situation to develop in the United Nations?" He hit at both American and British imperialists, and called any plan to "buy off" communism with $400 million "futile." As for Senator Eastland, Wallace said, "If it is a crime to work for peace in Britain, I stand convicted."

At Manchester, he declared that since the death of Roosevelt the American government had fallen into the hands of men who believed the United Nations was "doomed to insignificance." He denied that Russia, which lost 20 million people fighting Fascism, was warminded and deplored American witch hunts, evidently meaning Truman's loyalty program. Wallace said, "I believe that this witch hunt is part of a larger drive to destroy the belief, which I share, that capitalism and communism can resolve their conflicts without resort to war."

135

By now, both houses of Congress were in an uproar. In the Senate, where debate on the Greek-Turkish aid proposal had been going on for a week, Sen. Edwin C. Johnson of Colorado, a leading opponent of the Truman Doctrine, said he wished Henry Wallace would do his talking at home instead of abroad. Newspaper commentators began to say that Wallace was improving, rather than hurting, the chances for the bill's passage. Vandenberg was described as "seething with indignation" because Truman refused to make a public statement regarding Wallace. Claude Pepper and Glen Taylor were about the only members of the Senate who did not speak up in criticism of Henry Wallace, in what the *New York Times,* for April 13, 1947, said was "probably the most vehement congressional reaction in years to the pronouncements of a public figure."

In Liverpool the next day, April 13, Wallace called Vandenberg great but hysterical. "There is only one circumstance under which phrases like 'treasonable utterances' could be used to describe my speeches. That would be when we were at war. If we were at war I could not, as a patriotic American citizen, use the phrases that I have used in England in discussing American foreign policy. The fact that such words as 'treason' have been used in describing my trip indicates that, in the minds of the men who use these phrases, we actually are at war. It is to overcome that state of mind that I am in Britain and am making this foreign tour."

Over the British Broadcasting Company that night, Wallace became stronger than ever in criticism when he said, "The immense power and wealth of America is being used for strategic and military purposes rather than to raise the standard of living in countries which could become a great market for American exports . . . A great national awakening has occurred in Asia and in other parts of the world which we used to think of only as colonies. This new nationalism will turn into communism and look to the Soviet Union as their only ally, if the United States declares that this is the American century of power politics rather than the Century of the Common Man."

In response to a question as to why he didn't go to Russia, on April 13, at Liverpool, Wallace said he did not consider the time ripe for such a visit, and that he would be handicapped by lack of knowledge of the Russian language. But, he declared, "I have a hunch that if I could speak Russian, Mr. Stalin would let me speak to the common people there just as I am speaking to you today. When I get back to America, however, my government may not want to let me have a passport to get out of the country again. And if I did go to Russia, I know the Republicans would make every effort on the floor of the Senate to make the people believe I was revealing every American secret, including the atomic bomb."

The trans-Atlantic debate between Henry Wallace and members of Congress entered a new phase when Rep. J. Parnell Thomas, chairman of the House Committee on Un-American Activities, and Rep. John Rankin announced that the Logan act of 1799 "covers Wallace like a cloak." That act, which appears today in revised form in the United

136

States Code as Section 5 of Title 18, grew out of the activities of a Dr. James Logan of Philadelphia, later a United States Senator, who went to France on a self-appointed mission to see Talleyrand and others, at a time when it was rumored that the French fleet might attack the American coast. Although his interposition helped restore good feeling between the two countries, Secretary of State Pickering resented his interference and persuaded Congress to pass the act, which provided as follows:

> Every citizen of the United States, whether actually resident or abiding within the same, or in any place subject to the jurisdiction thereof, or in any foreign country, who, without the permission or authority of the government, directly or indirectly, commences or carries on any verbal or written correspondence or intercourse with any foreign government or any officer or agent thereof, with an intent to influence the measures or conduct of any foreign government or of any officer or agent thereof, in relation to any disputes or controversies with the United States, or to defeat the measures of the government of the United States; and every person, being a citizen of or resident within the United States or in any place subject to the jurisdiction thereof, and not duly authorized, who counsels, advises, or assists in any such correspondence with such intent, shall be fined not more than $5,000 and imprisoned not more than three years.

In a special statement, issued on April 14 in London, Wallace reiterated that he could be accused of "giving aid and comfort to an enemy" only if a state of war existed, and asserted that "those who propose to take action against me betray their present state of mind." Regarding the congressional suggestions that he might be more effective at home fighting adoption of the Greek-Turkish aid proposal, he declared, "I *did* campaign against these proposed military loans in the United States, and the British people, through the medium of the press, knew my attitude very well before I came here." The next day, after reading up on the Logan act, he declared that it in no way applied to him, since there was no pending dispute between Great Britain and the United States that he was attempting to ameliorate. He compared himself to Winston Churchill, who spoke at Fulton, Mo., as a private citizen.

At home, the voice of Rep. Walter K. Granger of Utah was the only one raised in defense of Wallace in the House of Representatives. He expressed the hope that "this unholy issue" of the Greek-Turkish program would not be submerged by attacks on "a great, good Christian American citizen, such as Henry Wallace." Others began clamoring for revocation of Wallace's passport. A resolution introduced by Rep. L. Mendel Rivers, S. C., to brand Wallace's speeches and activities "a grave disservice" to his country was referred to the Foreign Affairs Committee. Rep. Charles A. Eaton, chairman of that committee, remarked, "If Mr. Wallace doesn't make a more profound impression on the British public than he has on this committee, he might as well come home. Mr. Wallace's effect on the committee is, as it ought to be, a complete zero." In the Senate, John L. McClellan, Ark., introduced a similar resolution.

Through its national commander, Louis E. Starr, the Veterans of Foreign Wars, on April 15, recommended to President Truman that Wallace's passport be recalled. The President maintained public silence, but Attorney General Tom Clark, at a Philadelphia dinner, on April 15, said anyone "who tells the people of Europe that the United States is committed to a ruthless imperialism and war with the Soviet Union tells a lie." The next day Vandenberg descended from the rostrum, where he was serving as acting president of the Senate, to reply to criticisms that members of Congress did not feel free to oppose the bipartisan foreign policy, especially the Greek-Turkish proposals. In what included an unmistakable reference to Wallace he said, "I have never challenged the fact that every Senator has a complete right and duty to face the facts in this situation. I have no challenge to the exercise of that right whatsoever, so long as it is exercised in this country. I might add I am not interested in itinerant saboteurs."

At a meeting that day of Democratic national committeemen from New York, Rhode Island, New Jersey and Connecticut in Washington, Edward J. Flynn of the Bronx described Wallace as one of the "lunatic fringe that every party has had to contend with," and Sen. Theodore F. Green of Rhode Island declared that Wallace was "not a matter for the courts, nor a matter for Congress, but a matter for Miss Emily Post." The next day, at a Jefferson Day dinner in New York, W. Averell Harriman and Sen. Thomas Connally of Texas praised Truman, virtually nominating him for election in 1948. Connally interpolated in his prepared eulogy the statement that "slanders scattered in Europe by an American, that Mr. Truman is an imperialist, fall harmless at his feet; domestic detractions rebound upon their authors."

On Thursday, April 17, 1947, Henry Wallace left England for Stockholm. He took with him a letter signed by 111 members of both houses of the English Parliament, expressing "sincere thanks and warm appreciation" for his speeches and statements, which had recaptured "something of the high ideals and purposes" of Franklin Delano Roosevelt. Wallace was described in the letter as "the foremost advocate of achievement through the United Nations of one world in which the common man everywhere might find security and peace." The letter expressed general agreement with Wallace's world views.

That Wallace had not made the same impression on all British leaders, however, was apparent the very next day when, at a Conservative party meeting in London, Winston Churchill was reported to have alluded to Wallace as "one of that happily small minority of crypto-Communists," and then defined a crypto-Communist as "one who has not the moral courage to explain the destination for which he is making." Churchill also declared, "When I am abroad I always make it a rule never to criticize or attack the government of my own country. I make up for lost time when I get home." After this version of his remarks appeared, Churchill issued a correction to indicate that what he actually said was, "We have had here lately a visitor from the United States who has foregathered with that happily small minority of crypto-Communists who are making a dead set against the foreign policy which Mr. Bevin, our Foreign Secretary, has patiently and steadfastly pursued with the support of nine-tenths of the House of Commons." A week later, at the largest convention in 30 years of the Labor party, held at Bournemouth, the 1,300 delegates endorsed the Truman Doctrine and repudiated Wallace's ideas on foreign policy.

In the meantime, at Stockholm University, Wallace had taken cognizance of the original version of Churchill's remarks as follows: "I understand today a great British leader to whom we owe a debt of gratitude honored me with the name of crypto-Communist. It suggests I am maneuvering for world peace. I refuse to be disturbed by name-calling or hatred, no matter how distinguished the source from which the name-calling comes. You cannot conquer hate by fighting it. Love creates a greater circle than hate."

At a lunch the same day, Wallace declared, "I am not a Communist. I am not a Socialist. I am not only an American capitalist—or, as I told the House of Parliament in London—I am a progressive Tory who believes it is absolutely essential to have peace and understanding with Russia." The next day, at Oslo, Wallace charged that Churchill "dare not confess publicly the private conviction that war is inevitable." That evoked a formal statement from Churchill, "My view is as follows: war isn't inevitable, but it would be inevitable if Britain and the United States were to follow the policy of appeasement and one-sided disarmament which brought about the last war."

Regarding Churchill's correction of his crypto-Communist reference, Wallace said, "I now see from a news dispatch received this morning that Mr. Churchill was misquoted about calling me a crypto-Communist. It was only that my parliamentary friends were crypto-Communists. I only had a cup of tea in the House of Commons in company with Mr. [Konni] Zilliacus who is half Finn and half American. We had tea in the full view of everybody. Is Mr. Zilliacus a crypto-Communist? It's news to me, but I would doubt it. Now that this tempest in a teapot has blown over, the world may breathe easier once more."

Wallace's appearances in Scandinavia were sponsored by various trade unions, and the crowds were tremendous. Wallace appealed to them, because of their geographical position, to act as a bridge between East and West. "It is time," he said at Stockholm, "to build up the middle path of international feeling, not against Russian communism nor American capitalism but for a practical, common man's democracy."

Although he lunched with the mayor of Stockholm and dined with the minister of social affairs, Wallace was not received by the Regent Crown Prince Gustav Adolf, nor did any one of the American legation attend any function, with the exception of one attaché. In London, Ambassador Lewis W. Douglas had dined privately with Wallace and Prime Minister Clement Attlee, but boycotted all public meetings at which

Wallace appeared. Wallace had reached Paris by April 22, the occasion of Douglas' speech at a Pilgrims' dinner. This was a traditional affair—the maiden speech of a new American ambassador to the Court of St. James's. Although Douglas did not mention Wallace by name, his address was generally considered a reply to the former Vice President. He defended the Greek-Turkish aid plan and declared that American isolationism properly was dead.

Another American snub Wallace received while on this trip came from Harold Stassen, former Minnesota Governor. He denied that his failure to reply to a note Wallace sent him when they were in Stockholm at the same time was meant as a deliberate evasion, but he told newsmen, "It is not proper to discuss the foreign policy of the United States in a foreign country."

In one of his three Oslo speeches, Wallace indicated that, despite the drubbings he had been getting on both sides of the ocean, he thought he had accomplished something. "Americans," he declared, "are denied the fifth freedom—access to full information. While the American press is the finest in the world and doesn't tell deliberate lies, it engages in selective use of the truth. That is the latest word in propaganda. Americans are not nearly as hysterical about Russia as would appear from American newspapers. When I return to the United States, I presume a blanket of silence will descend on me again. I broke through that silken curtain by coming to Europe. It was worth the trip."

Whereas in Oslo Wallace was the luncheon guest of a coalition committee of local political parties, from left to right, before he reached France most of his intended hosts there had gotten cold feet. According to Michael Straight, who accompanied Wallace on this trip and did a great deal of his speech-writing, this was due partly to the fact that Pierre Cot, without authorization, posed as Wallace's agent there. It was largely due, of course, to fear of incurring the displeasure of the American government, and there may have been pressure applied by the United States Embassy in Paris. Anyway, as early as April 18, Leon Blum declined to say whether he still was a sponsor of Wallace's impending Parisian visit, and the office of the Popular Republican Movement, headed by Foreign Minister Bidault, told reporters they would have to see Cot, left wing member of the National Assembly, for any news of arrangements. On the eve of Wallace's arrival four days later, the Popular Republican party leaders all announced they had backed out as sponsors of Wallace's proposed speech at the Sorbonne. When Wallace appeared in Paris, most of the important leaders found it convenient to be out of town.

In the meantime, 70 American supporters of Wallace had addressed another message to all French leaders, saying Wallace's proposed visit to France would set a "pattern of . . . one world and the free interchange of opinions between the leaders of the people of all nations of good will." The signers included Van Wyck Brooks, Norman Corwin, Bartley Crum, Jo Davidson, Lillian Hellman, Robert Kenny, Frank Kingdon, Carey McWilliams, Arthur Miller, Elliott Roosevelt, Vilhjalmur Stefansson, Sen. Glen Taylor, R. G. Tugwell, J. Raymond Walsh and Aubrey Williams.

Before going to Paris, the Wallace party stopped at Copenhagen. There, the death of King Christian caused cancellation of a large public meeting, but in press interviews Wallace took another swat at Churchill, saying he disagreed with the Britisher's explanation that World War II had been caused by failure of the Western nations, including the United States, to build armaments. Rather, Wallace said, a strong contributing cause of World War II was the failure of the United States to act as a creditor nation after World War I. He said, "When the United States required foreign nations to pay war debts, it was inevitable these debtor nations, in despair, should engage in activities endangering the road to peace."

Just a few hours before the United States Senate in Washington voted, 67 to 23, in favor of the Greek-Turkish aid bill, Wallace, in a broadcast from Paris, on April 22, advocated a nonpolitical American loan to Russia, through the United Nations, to repair war damage, and opposed Russian demands for reparations out of current German production. The next day Rep. Joseph Martin declared that Russia was not eligible for a loan through the World Bank, since she was not a member of it. Pepper again supported Wallace, saying, "Prosperity, like world peace, is indivisible. I have always favored loans upon a fair and impartial basis to any nation that applies, be it Yugoslavia, Russia or somebody else we don't like." Pepper was one of seven Democrats to vote against the Greek-Turkish aid bill, the others being Byrd, Johnson (Colo.), McKellar, Murray, O'Daniel and Taylor.

Wallace made three important speeches in Paris. At the Sorbonne, with only the Communists, of the four original sponsoring parties, represented on the platform, he pleaded with France to remain democratic and to act as a "link between the United States and Russia." At an Anglo-American association lunch, he showed his concern over the desertion of all but left-wing sponsorship by revealing that a group of members of the Popular Republican movement had called on him privately, and said, "I want to try to avoid being monopolized by the extreme left who have been so friendly to me in Paris." He also declared that, during their last conversation, President Truman had favored a nonpolitical loan to the Soviet Union, but added, "I do not know whether he still does."

Wallace's most important Parisian speech was delivered on April 23, 1947, at a dinner sponsored by the American Veterans Committee. In it, he repeated much that he had said in other places about the part American isolation and economic policies played in causing World War II, and the necessity for a worldwide relief and reconstruction program through the United Nations. As he had in Oslo, he argued that the success of the Russian experiment was necessary for the best interests of the world. A few extracts from his speech follow:

> I believe that communism grows rapidly in significance in all areas where there is scarcity or racial discrimination. I believe that communism, like early Christianity, will thrive under the martyrdom of persecution.

To the only two American Communists whom I absolutely knew were Communists, I said, "You believe in materialism as the sole explanation of history. I believe in idealism . . ."

I also said that, just as capitalism in the United States must change with the changing times, so also must communism in Russia. Both communism and capitalism must take more account of the nature of man himself and learn to serve his desires with more goods and more freedom, or neither can survive.

I mention all this because of the tremendous drive in the United States today toward policies which might easily lead to World War III.

I believe that toughness breeds toughness and that both the United States and Russia, by their actions, have already undermined the solemn cause for which their young men died.

I recognize the conflicts that exist between capitalist, Socialist and Communist societies. I assert that they are not irreconcilable. I answer that these conflicts can be resolved without resort to war . . .

Wallace laid the traditional wreath on the Tomb of the Unknown Soldier, with the American Veterans Committee providing a color guard. Then a group of women, Les Femmes de France, presented him with a red-lettered box containing "our most precious possessions"—the last letters written to them by their sweethearts or husbands before they were executed by the Germans for their activities in the wartime resistance movement.

In a final interview in Europe, Wallace declared that, although he opposed "political strings" to foreign loans, he agreed that any loan to the Soviet Union probably should be made conditional upon an understanding as regards Germany "and perhaps other points." He suggested again that priorities for nations needing loans be fixed by a UN committee. Wallace also said in Paris that "While I deplore terrorism Jewish resistance in Palestine was necessary to arouse the conscience of the world," since 11 million Jews are entitled to be heard in the United Nations.

Wallace left Paris on Saturday, April 26, and reached LaGuardia airport at 3:35 a.m. on Sunday, April 27, 1947.

While he was in the air, Sen. Walter George (Dem., Ga.) was demanding to know "whether the right hand of our State Department knows what its left hand is doing," because the Voice of America had broadcast a review of Russell Lord's new book, *The Wallaces of Iowa*, a few days earlier. George said he didn't know the nature of the review but objected to its bad timing.

Actually, as Burton Paulu pointed out, in an article, "The Smith-Mundt Act: A Legislative History," in the Summer, 1953 *Journalism Quarterly,* the review, prepared several weeks earlier, was broadcast only once and then in German, not "to Russia, glorifying Henry Wallace," as Rep. John Taber of New York charged. Also, Paulu wrote, "If examined objectively, it should have offended only the Wallaces—and not their critics." Nevertheless, "Congressional response in general was almost violent, although most of the critics made no attempt then or later to find out just what the program had said."

Because of the emphasis which has been given, in this and preceding chapters, to the activities of Henry A. Wallace, the roles of some others, who were fighting at the same time for virtually the same things, have been underplayed.

Right beside Claude Pepper in his defense of Wallace, and in his attacks on the bipartisan foreign policy, was Sen. Glen Taylor of Idaho. Well do I remember when Leo Lerner returned from attending the opening session of Congress, on Jan. 3, 1947, and told a group of us, attending an executive committee of the Independent Voters of Illinois (later to affiliate with Americans for Democratic Action), that the man to whom to look for leadership in the fight for liberalism in Washington was not Pepper but Taylor.

What provoked this was Taylor's first-day successful fight to refuse a seat to Theodore G. Bilbo, just re-elected senator from Mississippi after a campaign in which Negro voters had been terrorized to stay away from the polls. The Republicans had planned to challenge Bilbo, but Taylor feared the GOP might seat him "without prejudice" pending an investigation, after which a two-thirds vote would be necessary to remove him. In fact, Democratic Sen. Alben Barkley attempted to do just that, but Republican Sen. Robert A. Taft came to Taylor's rescue, and Taylor's Resolution No. 1 of the 80th Congress passed. Taylor had jumped to his feet, when Bilbo's name was reached by the reading clerk, before Republican Sen. Homer Ferguson of Michigan was able to do so. His resolution, on which he spoke for an hour, charged "conspiracy to prevent citizens of the United States from exercising their constitutional rights to participate in elections." Bilbo was reported to see some humor in what happened when he explained, "This nincompoop Taylor stole the Republicans' show. The greatest joke of the 80th Congress is that a cowboy named Taylor stole the whole show."

There was no doubt about Taylor's being a cowboy. The son of the Rev. and Mrs. Pleasant John Taylor, he was born on April 12, 1904, on a farm near Kooskia, Idaho. He left school at 15 and became an actor. In 1927, while playing in musical comedy in Montana, he met Dora Pike. They married and formed the Glendora Players, an itinerant stock theatrical company, which continued until the depression of 1929 wiped it out. Then Taylor became a factory worker in several Western states and began to study on his own what he had not had the opportunity to learn in the classroom: what was wrong with the economic and political system. The New Deal solution attracted him and, while not relinquishing his membership in the Sheet Metal Workers, AFL, he established residence in Pocatello and, in 1938, ran for Congress. Neither then nor at any subsequent time did he have Democratic organization support. Nevertheless, in 1940, he successfully defied the machine and won the Democratic primary for United States Senator, to replace William E. Borah. He lost the general election that November, lost the primary again in 1942, but in 1944 won both the primary and the general election, to be able to go to Washington in January, 1945, as Idaho's junior Senator.

To attract audiences, Taylor played his banjo and sang, along with his wife and, when they became old enough, his sons: Glen Arod, born in 1936; Paul Jon (always called PJ), born in 1942, and Gregory Alan, born in 1946. Thus, it has been correctly said of Glen Taylor that he was not only *for* the people, but *of* the people as well. He was truly from the grassroots and never tired of saying that his senatorship was the best job he ever had. Len DeCaux, longtime editor of the *CIO News,* has told me how, shortly after arriving in Washington, Taylor naively phoned him to say he was sympathetic to labor and would like to be placed on the CIO's mailing list. "He sounded like a nice simple boy from the country, very sincere and modest," DeCaux recalls.

Taylor first obtained widespread attention for his resolution, introduced Oct. 24, 1945, calling upon the President to urge American delegates to the UN to propose, at the first meeting of the General Assembly, a commission to draft a plan for a world republic. As previously noted (see page 30), on March 6, 1946, he joined veteran Senators Pepper and Kilgore in condemning Winston Churchill's Fulton, Mo. speech. Despite his newness on the national scene, he was one of the principal speakers on March 15, 1946, when the ICC-ASP honored Harold L. Ickes (see page 31). He was reported to have declared that Churchill had joined the "tough talk boys" and that his proposal "would in effect serve notice on Russia that the two English speaking peoples had banded together to perpetuate the age-old game of European power politics which has started the two world wars of our time."

With Republican Sen. George D. Aiken of Vermont and Democratic Rep. Charles R. Savage of Washington, he appeared on July 6, 1946, on an NBC network broadcast, on which he agreed with his colleagues that "our foreign policy has been definitely pro-British. . . . Instead of one world we're moving toward a two world system: the Soviet Union against Great Britain and the United States." After the Republican victory in November, 1946, and before the new Congress convened in January, 1947, Taylor publicly urged President Truman to ignore "the enormous amount of pressure" to "persuade him to deliver a state of the union message to the 80th Congress which would embody a Republican point of view." Taylor said Truman's mandate "is to support and preserve the gains made by the people under three Roosevelt administrations."

After his successful move against Bilbo, on Jan. 28, 1947, Taylor joined with Pepper and Morse to try to break the Senate filibuster against a Federal law to outlaw the poll tax. On Feb. 18, 1947, he told the

New York chapter of the American Jewish Congress that the fight to prevent David E. Lilienthal from becoming chairman of the Atomic Energy Commission was the greatest lobbying campaign in history. On March 13, 1947, he joined with Pepper in an unsuccessful fight on the proposal to submit the 22nd Amendment, limiting the Presidency to two terms, to the states. He and Sen. William Langer (Rep., N. D.) lost, by a 66 to 14 vote, an attempt to amend the motion to abolish the Electoral College also. With Rep. Helen Gahagan Douglas of California, on March 20, 1947, he sponsored a bill for temporary housing assistance for veterans in the $30 to $50 rental range.

Glen Taylor really "came of age" with his fight against the Truman Doctrine. On March 25, 1947, he and Pepper co-sponsored a resolution to force the entire Mediterranean problem into the United Nations. Specifically, they wanted the Reconstruction Finance Corporation to be authorized to make available at once $100 million for economic aid to Greece, to be administered by the UN. Within 45 days, the General Assembly of the UN would be convened to create an international relief fund. Over the radio on April 4, 1947, Taylor called the Truman proposals "an oil grab in the Middle East." He said: "It becomes unmistakably clear that the objective is not so much food for the Greek people as oil for the American monopolies—the oil that lies in the great underground resources in the lands just east of Greece and Turkey." He said the Truman Doctrine involved "a new imperialism," based on "dollars and atom bombs."

As the main speaker, on April 10, 1947, at a Jefferson Day dinner at Syracuse, Taylor declared: "If we eliminate the suffering and hardship of periodic depressions we need never fear communism or Communists . . . I do have a mighty big bone to pick with the Republicans, on their responsibility for the depression which is inevitable if they follow their present policies. That depression can create more Communists overnight than the Republican witch hunters could track down in a month of Sundays."

As the Senate debate on the Greek-Turkish aid proposal developed, Taylor held the floor for almost the entire day of April 15, 1947. He supported the substitute bill, which he and Pepper had introduced, to restrict any aid to Greece to eliminate its military features. Pepper was in Florida at the time and Taylor defeated an attempt by Majority Leader Scott Lucas to obtain agreement for a vote at 1 p.m. the following day on a pending amendment.

In his lengthy speech, Taylor compared the Truman program to Japan's invasion of Manchuria in 1931, as a first step in the direction of disaster. "Japan's action wrecked the League of Nations," he said. "Our action will just as surely wreck the United Nations. The world started on the long one-way street to World War II when Japan was allowed to take unilateral action in its invasion of Manchuria. Are each and every one of us willing to examine the proposal and deny that it will place us on a similar one-way street to World War III?"

On the two following days, April 16 and 17, Claude Pepper spoke— for four hours on the 17th. He accused the United States of trying to pick

145

a fight with Russia in her front yard and complained that nobody was seeking to comprehend the Russian viewpoint on anything. "The Russians," he said, "have as much right in there (meaning the Dardanelles) as we have to be in Panama, to be perfectly frank. Now, if we are to get down to the morality of these issues, I do not think we can wrap the cloak of holiness around ourselves and protect our strategic interests and say 'God-ordained' without saying that these other people have got something on their side when they make the same demands."

When Senator Hatch suggested that the Soviet Union should present the matter to the United Nations, Pepper agreed, but added that he had not heard of the British referring the matters of the Suez Canal or Gibraltar to the UN.

And those were about the last fighting words by any national leaders who shared Henry Wallace's views, before Wallace himself returned from abroad and met the press at the Georgetown apartment of his assistant, Harold Young. Fresh from France, he spoke mostly of that nation which, he said, was being compelled to choose between the extreme right and the extreme left, with possible civil war as the ultimate result. He touched on almost all the issues he had discussed abroad; called Henry Luce an imperialist; declared that the Democratic party must stay liberal to survive; advocated a $50 billion loan to restore devastated areas; declared there was widespread fear of the effect of the Truman Doctrine in Europe, the only group defending it being "the extreme right-wingers led by Winston Churchill," and declared that the United States was "on the road to ruthless imperialism, but it's not that yet." These ideas he repeated on a CBS broadcast, on April 30, 1947.

Commenting on a reporter's statement that his wife had expressed the wish that he would quit public life and return to the farm to live, Wallace said Mrs. Wallace had made no such statement to him. Asked if he expected to be a candidate in 1948 for the presidency, he replied, "You can't tell what I'll do next year."

# ¶ 8 WALLACE TOURS AMERICA.

*Professional politicians were dumfounded and alarmed as 200,000 persons paid admission to pack auditoriums from coast to coast and to contribute to the PCA's treasury.*

When Henry Wallace intimated at the end of April, 1947, that he did not know what he would be doing in 1948, I am positive he meant it.

There are some who were close to him at the time, both on the *New Republic* and through Progressive Citizens of America activities, who believe Wallace returned from his European trip "raring to go," eager to announce himself soon as a candidate for the Presidency, either on the Democratic or a third party ticket. Others who were equally close deny this, and I accept Wallace's own statement to me that, until September, 1947 at least, he continued to hope that his attacks upon the Truman administration would have a strong enough effect within the Democratic party to cause drastic changes in policy.

Wallace's actual decision to run as an independent candidate was made less than a month before he publicly announced his intention, on Dec. 29, 1947. Long before that, however, there were many who predicted that such was the only possible consequence of his actions, and there was never any doubt in his own mind after September, 1946 that he would be prominent in the 1948 campaign.

From Oakland, Calif., on May 22, 1947, for instance, Edwin A. Lahey wrote in the *Chicago Daily News:* "At this stage of the Pilgrim's Progress it appears inevitable that Henry A. Wallace will lead a third party in 1948."

In their syndicated column for May 29, 1947, the Alsop brothers wrote, "The formation of a third political party in the next 18 months is now a positive probability."

On June 5, 1947, in a roundup story from Washington, the Associated Press quoted Republican Senators Owen Brewster, of Maine, and H. Styles Bridges, of New Hampshire, as believing Wallace would start a new party in 1948, in the hope of winning in 1952.

By that time, those who were promoting Wallace as an individual, and the ideas which he expressed, were as highly encouraged as some segments of the Democratic party high command were worried. At a meeting of the national board of directors of the Progressive Citizens of America on June 28, 1947, at Chicago's Hotel Knickerbocker, C. B. Baldwin reported on the PCA's first six months.

At that time, paid-up membership was estimated as about 25,000, with chapters in 19 states, 15 of which had paid personnel. The debt of $113,000 inherited from the ICC-ASP and the NC-PAC, mostly the former, had been reduced to $70,000 and the PCA was $15,000 ahead on its own activities.

> We have discovered in these last six months, Baldwin reported, that, where we have been able to break through and be heard, we have met with tremendous enthusiasm and support from great numbers of people.

> We are able to affirm, after six months of operation, that there are millions of Americans who believe in our program, but who are not yet organized to fight with us.

> That is the promise for PCA. It is a mighty challenge and, depending on how we meet this challenge, may well rest the future prosperity of the United States and the peace of the world.

> We have every reason—and need—to hope and to aim high.

With virtually the same personnel who had worked in the NC-PAC national office, the PCA nationally continued to issue statements regarding current political issues. As the grass roots organization began to develop, there were more small meetings, often devoted to local problems, more distribution of literature by hand rather than by mail, and more letter writing and delegations to public officials.

Nationally, the PCA sponsored National Rent Control and Housing Week, Feb. 17-23, 1947, to work for continuation of Federal control beyond its scheduled June 30 expiration date. On Feb. 7, Dr. J. Raymond Walsh, a national PCA vice chairman and, since February, New York State chairman, appeared before the Senate Banking & Currency Committee in Washington to oppose any "across-the-board increase" in rents, as bound to "reduce the consumer's purchasing power, create grave hardships for families living on sub-standard incomes in sub-standard dwellings, and have disastrous consequences on the nation's economy." For the PCA, Dr. Walsh endorsed the Wagner-Ellender-Taft Federal Housing Bill. The same day, Baldwin wired an appeal to Sen. Charles W. Tobey, the committee's chairman, "to appoint a special subcommittee to make a cross-country tour of cities and towns to hold public meetings on rent control." A fortnight later, on Feb. 20, 1947, Jo Davidson and Frank Kingdon wired Tobey, to protest the previous day's action of the House of Representatives in denying additional funds to the Office of Price Administration for enforcement and also directing the agency to return $9 million of previously appropriated funds. This, the PCA co-chairmen said, was an attempt to destroy the OPA and eliminate rent and sugar controls; they asked Tobey and his committee to oppose Senate concurrence in the action.

During National Rent Control and Housing week, throughout the country, PCAers distributed 100,000 "eviction notices," which were pamphlets gotten up in legal format, with "eviction notice" on the cover

148

to present arguments in favor of the continuation of the OPA. When a delegation of about 150 New Yorkers, headed by Alfred K. Stern, attempted to see the Governor and legislators in Albany on Feb. 18, however, Gov. Thomas E. Dewey summoned state troopers to prevent them from getting into the legislative galleries. On a strictly party vote, the House upheld Speaker Oswald D. Heck, 102 to 40, in ordering the gallery doors locked. He and Sen. Benjamin F. Feinberg, who persuaded Governor Dewey to send the troops, said the delegation was "Communist-led" and had planned a "stay in" demonstration. At a protest meeting on Feb. 23, 1947, at the Hotel Commodore, New York City, Ira Hirschmann denounced this action on the basis of his background in Europe, where he had been a special representative of the State Department and also served as inspector general for UNRRA.

"Any Europeans who may have looked to leadership in this country to destroy fascism would look with great horror on the action that occurred in Albany last week," Hirschmann declared. "Governor Dewey has shown his hand and he has also done us a service. We have seen symptoms that he wanted to be the man on horseback and now we have proof."

At the same meeting, Frank Kingdon declared, "Here is a preview of 1948. Here is an announcement, by one of the leading candidates for the Presidential nomination, that he chooses to call out the police to prevent peaceful citizens from approaching their own legislature."

On March 10, 1947, Fiorello La Guardia became chairman of a newly formed National Fair Rent Committee, "to combat the real estate lobby's drive to break rent ceilings." To provide tenants an opportunity to present new evidence in favor of the continuation of rent control, the Banking and Currency Committee was asked to reopen its hearings. Chester Bowles and Henry A. Wallace were prominent members of the La Guardia committee.

When Congress passed a bill continuing rent control but permitting a 15 per cent "voluntary" rent increase, on June 14, 1947, the PCA protested and called for a Presidential veto. The PCA called the bill "janus-faced hypocrisy," because it turned enforcement over to a housing expediter without adequate funds, and because it removed new construction from its jurisdiction.

As originally planned, National PCA Lobby Day, March 21, 1947, was to have been the occasion for approximately 200 PCA leaders to descend on Washington, to visit congressmen in the interest of continuing rent control; to urge passage of the Wagner-Ellender-Taft Housing Bill; to oppose anti-labor measures; and to advocate tax law reforms. After President Truman enunciated his doctrine on March 12, however, the emphasis in the interviews that day was shifted to consideration of the newest turn in American foreign policy. Meeting in Washington the next day, the PCA's board of directors set as its minimum program: (1) defeat of the anti-labor legislation; (2) defense of the civil rights and liberties of all political and racial minorities; (3) holding the rent line and providing housing for the homeless; (4) tax relief for the needy, but not for the greedy; (5) no budget cuts for essential services; adequate appropriations for the administration and enforcement of all social legislation.

"In helping mobilize the people for immediate legislative action on the vital issues of 1947," the PCA board declared, "PCA will play its part in setting the political stage for 1948. The kind of struggle waged on these issues, and its outcome, will determine the kind of platforms and candidates presented to the electorate next year. Only in the course of such a struggle can the problems confronting political independents find a political solution. Only such a struggle can guarantee that the American people will have a progressive alternative, under whatever party label, in the 1948 national elections."

On March 26, 1947, three days after President Truman had called for a loyalty check of Federal employees, the PCA's Executive Committee issued a strongly critical analysis of it. On Feb. 19, Davidson and Kingdon had protested to the Senate members of the Joint Committee on Atomic Energy because of the attacks, led by Sen. Kenneth McKellar (Dem., Tenn.), against David E. Lilienthal's appointment as chairman of the Atomic Energy Commission. They defined the issue as "whether men who hold to the Roosevelt philosophy of enlightened government are to be driven from public life through the use of undemocratic techniques of slander and innuendo." The next day, the PCA directed attention to another "dangerous threat" to civil liberties, this time to "the principle of freedom of the airways." The occasion was the decision of the Columbia Broadcasting Company to cancel the Sunday afternoon news commentary of William L. Shirer, "a major step toward a complete blackout of the liberal viewpoint in radio." On Dec. 23, 1946, the CIO-PAC had protested the dropping of Frank Kingdon's daily news programs by station WOR. In its letter to the Federal Communications Commission, it cited "the dismissal of many commentators associated with the progressive viewpoint," specifically mentioning John Vandercook, Robert St. John, Don Hollenbeck and Don Goddard. At the same time, an "array of reactionary commentators like Fulton Lewis Jr., Henry J. Taylor and Upton Close" continued on the air.

A "Crisis-in-Radio Conference," at which Shirer and Clifford Durr, Federal Communications Commissioner, were the main speakers, was held on April 19, under the auspices of the Radio Division of the New York State PCA. A similar rally, at which Kingdon and other PCA leaders spoke, was held on May 8, under the sponsorship of the Voice of Freedom Committee.

After President Truman requested Congress to appropriate $24,000,000 to administer his loyalty program, on May 16 the PCA urged the House Appropriations Committee to "not appropriate one cent of the taxpayer's money for the purpose of undermining civil liberties." On May 27, 1947 the PCA called for passage of the Case Federal Anti-lynching Law, "to end the fiction that poll tax states and local governments can or will enforce justice against lynch mobs." On June 11, the lawyers division of PCA sponsored a "Crisis Meeting on Civil Liberties" at the Hotel Commodore, with Abraham L. Pomerantz, former deputy chief counsel at the Nuremberg trials of ex-Nazi leaders, acting as chairman. J. Raymond Walsh and Martin Popper, secretary of the National Lawyers Guild, also spoke.

By now, as might be inferred from the sponsorships of some of the affairs cited, the PCA was operating more and more through committees and divisions. The membership of some of them was pretty high-powered. On Feb. 5, 1947, for instance, in anticipation of the March 10 meeting of the Council of Foreign Ministers in Moscow, a special Committee on Germany was named by Davidson and Kingdon. On it were such authorities as William L. Shirer, Van Wyck Brooks, Elmer A. Benson, Saul K. Padover, Mrs. J. Borden Harriman and Ira A. Hirschmann. In its initial statement, this committee expressed grave concern "with the evident drift away from the policies agreed upon at Potsdam for the complete denazification of Germany and the destruction and removal of its war potential. We are equally concerned with the recent declaration of John Foster Dulles, made with the avowed approval of Senator Vandenberg and Governor Dewey, negating the principle of four-power control of the German war potential and advocating the economic reconstruction of the Ruhr and the Rhineland as the industrial base of a Western bloc."

On Feb. 26, 1947, Jo Davidson announced that a number of American writers, artists and musicians had signed a manifesto, originally prepared by a group of French intellectuals, calling upon the Big Four ministers "to hold the essential and primary effective measures to disarm Germany." The statement declared: "Any peace not founded on disarmament would be precarious and illusory, and those who would conclude it would carry in the eyes of the world the terrible responsibility of future catastrophes which it would engender."

Among the American signers were: Eugene O'Neill, John P. Marquand, Thornton Wilder, Katherine Anne Porter, Edna Ferber, Van Wyck Brooks, Robert Hillyer, John Erskine, Louis Untermeyer, Walter Damrosch, George S. Kaufman, Frank Kingdon, Lewis Mumford, Franklin P. Adams, Henry Seidel Canby, Mark Van Doren, Carl Van Doren, Julian Street, Hugo Ballin, Guy Pène DuBois, William McFee, Sidney Waugh, William Rose Benet, Leon Kroll and Struthers Burt.

The three major PCA divisions were Youth, Women's and Arts, Sciences and Professions (A.S.P). The A.S.P., in turn, was split into 11 divisions: art, science, music, film, literature, advertising and publicity, law, radio, theater, medicine, social service and building industries. The medical division set up a permanent committee to provide free medical care to strikers; the advertising and publicity division aided in the preparation of advertisements; the film division prepared a catalogue of films available for use in community chapters and organized a class in the use of projectors; the lawyers division analyzed state election laws; to cite only a few typical activities.

Headed by José Ferrer and Lillian Hellman, the theater division of the PCA was formed on Feb. 28. This meeting discussed discrimination in the theater, the taxation of theater tickets and theater workers, and the Federal Fine Arts Bill and the Committee on UNESCO. The artists division sponsored a mass meeting to protest the State Department's cancellation of its touring American art exhibit, which was done after Harry Truman said of some of the paintings, "If that's art, I'm a Hottentot." The music division sponsored "young artist recitals" in Philadelphia. The literature division auctioned valuable manuscripts to raise money to finance its activities, which included testifying before the New York school superintendents in protesting against the banning of Howard Fast's *Citizen Tom Paine*.

About 50 leading scientists from all over the country attended a National Science Conference, on April 12, 1947, at Chicago's Hotel Continental, under the leadership of Dr. Harlow Shapley, director of the Harvard Observatory. Among other things, they resolved that, as a first step toward international control of atomic energy, the United States should cease production of atomic bombs and that all pure material presently stockpiled should be denatured and made available for peaceful purposes only. They also said that "complete freedom of scientific research and expression, including publication and international communication, must be restored and maintained in this country and everywhere," and favored establishment of a national science foundation.

Throughout March, 1947, the women's division, organized in February, conducted a month-long political workshop in New York with 200 registrants, participated in lobbies to Washington and sent delegations to visit senators and congressmen at their homes. A "Fashion is Politics" show, on April 25, attracted 800 women, with 400 more unable to get in. The affair was held on the second anniversary of the United Nations. Faye Emerson Roosevelt was guest speaker and six Broadway actresses modeled clothes. They were: Uta Hagen, Lois Wheeler, Nina Foch, Edith Atwater, Ruth Ford and Fredi Washington.

On June 15-16 the youth division, of which the dancer Gene Kelly was honorary chairman, sponsored a National Youth Lobby in Washington, which 449 youths from 16 states attended. They saw congressmen in the interests of rent control, Federal aid to education, the vote for 18-year-olds, the FEPC, opposition to peacetime military training and similar issues. By mid-1947, there were youth divisions in 16 states, with a total membership of over 1,000.

\* \* \* \*

Whereas all of these and similar activities were valuable in building the organization, the headlines continued to go primarily to Henry Wallace's activities. He had decidedly not received a favorable press as a result of his European trip. A typical comment was that of the *Saturday Evening Post*, in an editorial, "We'd Hate to See Wallace in a Martyr's Role," in its May 1, 1947 issue. "Now that the show is over," the *Post* said, "it looks as if Anglo-Saxon solidarity may have been cemented on at least one thing: heartfelt gratitude to the late FDR for giving Henry the business in the Democratic national convention of 1944."

Before Wallace went abroad, it had been decided that a cross-country American speaking tour would be a natural follow-up on his return. It was to be a joint venture of the Progressive Citizens of America and *The New Republic,* which hoped thereby to increase its circulation, to meet the heavy costs it had incurred by an increase in size and more expensive makeup, a venture which fell about $800,000 short of costs. While Wallace was away, Beanie Baldwin and Helen Fuller of the magazine worked on the itinerary, and on May 2, 1947, Wallace made his first public platform appearance in the Public Music Hall at Cleveland.

The journalistic greetings he got were among the best he was to receive anywhere for the next three years. Editorialized the *Cleveland Press:*

> This newspaper does not need to tell Henry Wallace, the city's guest today, or any one else, for that matter, that we do not agree with him.
>
> Yet we welcome him to Cleveland and we beseech for him—although we think that is unnecessary in this city of the open mind—a respectful hearing.
>
> We welcome Henry Wallace as a spokesman for an important viewpoint in America. It is the viewpoint of dissent and protest against the Truman policy toward Greece and Turkey. It is the viewpoint of the so-called "soft" policy toward Russia.
>
> It would be a mistake to dismiss Wallace's influence as being only with the ragtag of opinion, of the leftists, the Communists and fellow travelers, and the neurotic fringe of ulcerated dissidents we have always with us.
>
> Henry Wallace also represents the honest doubts of a considerable body of Americans of moderate and thoughtful political conviction. They are apprehensive lest America, wittingly or unwittingly, walk down another "road to war." We think they are mistaken in their quest for principle and leadership, but we do not discount their honesty or the importance to them of their estimate of Henry Wallace's viewpoint . . ."

The same day, the *Cleveland News* more typically addressed itself "To Henry Wallace, Here Today," as follows:

> Dear Mr. Wallace:
>
> This is no welcoming greeting, on occasion of your speech in Cleveland tonight, since the *News* disagrees with you thoroughly about public issues and will oppose the projects and policies you propose; that is, whenever we can fully comprehend what it is that you propose.

153

With (we believe) the majority of clear-thinking Cleve-
landers, we felt shocked that you would take your disagreement with our national foreign policy to the platforms
of foreign countries at a dangerous time like the present.
We estimate you as irresponsible for having done so.

This is merely to tell you that we have free speech and
a free press in Cleveland; that, no matter how your words
may seem to strain freedom, they can be said and heard
in this city; that, despite our antipathy, this newspaper
felt obliged to report your statements abroad, so that
our readers might be informed about them; and that,
since your words here are news, we will report them
fairly in our news columns—whatever we may advise
about you and them in our editorial statements.

The News.

What they had to report primarily was Wallace's summary of his
European impressions: "Any attempt to force Europe to join an Amer-
ican armed camp—and that is the logical next step of the Truman
Doctrine—will result in catastrophe, violence and bloodshed in Europe."
Whatever chance the recent conference of foreign ministers at Moscow
might have had for success, he said, was shattered by President Truman's
Greek-Turkish aid program.

Across the continent and back, Wallace's speeches were mostly repetition of what he had said abroad. At a luncheon on May 12, 1947,
in Minneapolis, sponsored by the Independent Voters of Minnesota,
he said, "Communists should be treated as human beings rather than
people who should be put in jail." He declared that, in his opinion,
99 per cent of those who were being called Communists actually were
not that; after World War I, he recalled, he had been called a Bolshevik,
and since World War II he had been called a Communist more than
once. At a news conference, he said the Presidency "holds no glamor
for me" but added "If it would help the liberal cause I would be willing
to run for it." He said Soviet fear of America was based partly on
expectation of an economic depression here. The alternative to the
"Truman policy of loaning money for military purposes abroad" was
"to use American money through the United Nations for plows and
tractors, rather than for guns and fighter planes." Wallace's evening
rally was sponsored by the Democratic-Farmer-Labor party and the *New
Republic*.

What was dumfounding to professional politicians and the press,
regarding Wallace's tour, was not what he said but the overflow crowds
that he attracted. The jamming of the largest public meeting places in
most of the leading metropolitan centers had been achieved, furthermore,
by methods without precedent since the La Follette Progressives of
1924 used similar ones. That is, admissions were charged, usually rang-
ing from 60 cents to $2.40 or $3.60; whereas the usual way to fill a

154

hall for a political meeting is to distribute passes to recipients of party patronage, with orders that all of them be used. In the case of the Wallace meetings, not only did the estimated 100,000, who came to hear him during the month of May, 1947, pay an average of over $1.50 to get in, but they usually dropped about the same amount in the collection baskets, after a strong appeal for funds by J. Raymond Walsh or some other spellbinder.

The Chicago Stadium rally, of May 14, 1947, was the first time admission had been charged in the city for a political rally in modern times, and 22,000 people packed the Stadium, with an estimated 5,000-10,000 more listening to the program by loudspeaker in the streets outside. Said Edwin A. Lahey, of the *Chicago Daily News,* to members of the Wallace troupe. "I'm here, I've seen it, and I still don't believe it." Then he received permission from his newspaper to accompany Wallace to the West Coast, during which trip he spent perhaps more off-hours chatting and taking fast walks with the former Vice President than did anyone else.

The attitude of the Democratic machine was amusing to us in the PCA. Before the rally, there hadn't been a peep out of anyone from that camp. The morning following the unprecedented triumph, there were a number of phone calls to say that this or that high-up party man would like to have a few minutes with Mr. Wallace. It is understandable, but undoubtedly rotten politics, that such feelers were answered somewhat in this manner: "The next time Mr. Wallace comes to town, why don't you try to get in touch with him before his speech? He always has more time then. Today, he's too busy to see you."

The Chicago Stadium rally was staged by utilizing the same techniques that had proved so successful March 31, 1947 at Madison Square Garden. There was, in other words, no chairman. Instead, Louis "Studs" Terkel, widely known radio commentator and actor, served as master of ceremonies, using a script which he read over the loud speaker system. Before each speaker ascended the platform in the center of the arena, the lights were dimmed and then spotlights suddenly were played on the central figure. Because this was the first time they had seen such a show, nobody seemed to mind that the preliminaries consumed more than two hours before the man they had come to hear was introduced. When, after 11 p.m., Henry A. Wallace finally was presented, the ovation—all the newspapers agreed—lasted six minutes. Studs helped it along by intermittent cries of "Wallace in '48," but the crowd, which interrupted Wallace at least 20 times, also enjoyed chanting, "We want Wallace."

Once he had quieted his enthusiastic supporters Wallace improvised, "And I say, we want peace." Then he launched into his orthodox denunciation of American foreign policy, especially the Truman Doctrine, which he defined as "a curious mixture of power politics and international carpet bagging" and "a doctrine of unlimited aid to anti-Soviet governments. The administration," he said, "is playing politics with the misery of Europe."

At the rally, Wallace "brought down the house" when he said, "I say that if the Democratic party betrays its responsibility to the people, the people will have to find other means of political expression."

As usual, the fairest newspaper account of the Stadium rally was by Lahey, in the *Chicago Daily News*. Editorially, the same newspaper, under the title, "Reckless Demagogy," declared that Wallace proposed only "an utterly reckless, wasteful, indiscriminate outpouring of American money everywhere, especially in Russia," and added, "Wallace's tour is a definite threat of third-party revolt against Truman in 1948."

The *Herald-American* gave very brief inside-page coverage to the rally, under the headline, "Claque 'Nominates' Wallace President." The *Tribune,* also on an inside page, called the demonstration "carefully planned, dominated by Left Wing elements." As a prelude, it ran a brief Associated Press article, from New York, that William Z. Foster, Communist party chairman, had told a Madison Square Garden rally, "The main danger to European democracy comes from American imperialism." In the *Sun,* Milburn P. Akers gave full coverage, with numerous snide remarks thrown in. He said the "Wallace in '48" chants reminded him of the "voice of the sewer" which had called "We want Roosevelt," at the 1940 Democratic convention in the same place. He identified Paul Robeson, who both sang and spoke before Wallace appeared, as the "Negro baritone recently described by Pravda as one of the Soviet Union's 'sincere friends' in America"; and Zero Mostel, comedian who entertained, as "listed by the House Un-American Activities Committee as an entertainer who frequently appears in behalf of so-called 'front' organizations." The story in the *Times,* by Richard Rendell, was "straight," without innuendo, but its entire editorial space was devoted to answering Wallace's argument that there could be an understanding with the Soviet Union. It pointed to the Kremlin's failure to become a member of most United Nations agencies, so that it must be considered "the real culprit in today's muddled world picture."

R. J. Thomas, vice president of the United Automobile Workers who had been deposed as president a year earlier by Walter Reuther, concluded his Stadium talk with, "If anti-labor bills are passed by a Republican Congress and signed by a Democratic President, labor will have to consider very seriously its position with regard to both major parties in 1948."

The night after the Chicago meeting, May 15, 1947, Wallace spoke to a sell-out crowd in Detroit, mostly automobile workers, according to the press. For their benefit, he recalled the depression days and lambasted Congress for pushing anti-labor bills. "The Truman Doctrine," he said, "is the strongest weapon that communism was ever given." He repeated that Europeans, living in fear of war, want food and fuel rather than guns and tanks from the United States. Two nights later, on May 17, Wallace encountered one of the first attempts to incite a crowd demonstration against him. At the airport when he arrived in Austin, Texas, was a group of University of Texas students, with a sound truck playing *The Internationale* and displaying the hammer and sickle. Students supporting Wallace chased them away and, despite protests from two American Legion posts, the Catholic War Veterans and the Disabled American

Veterans, the Wallace meeting was held in the university gymnasium, and there was an interracial reception for him. In his address, Wallace accused John Foster Dulles of being the real author of the Truman Doctrine, by "conjuring up an aggressive hatred of Russia," which has "conjured up also a new isolationism."

From then on, interferences of one sort or another with Wallace's attempts to speak were almost daily occurrences. A month earlier, the directors of the Hollywood Bowl had refused its use for a Wallace rally on May 19, saying, "The Hollywood Bowl is dedicated to the cultural interests of the community, and the association does not believe that those interests are served by making the Bowl a forum for the dissemination of propaganda or a sounding board for controversial issues."

It didn't do any good to point out that Wallace had spoken there on Sept. 29, 1940, while a candidate for Vice President; that Franklin Roosevelt had done the same during the 1932 campaign, as had many others, including Eugene V. Debs, Wendell Willkie and Thomas E. Dewey.

The Wallace rally was held in Gilmore stadium and, according to informants who were at both affairs, made the Chicago Stadium meeting seem like a Quaker picnic by comparison. About 30,000 occupied every seat, and stood and sat in every available inch of space. When California's Attorney General Robert W. Kenny said, "I'm going to give you Henry Wallace—the man for '48," pandemonium broke loose.

Shortly before Wallace appeared in Los Angeles, the House Committee on Un-American Activities had been there, for the first series of hearings regarding alleged Red influence in the motion picture industry. So, although he repeated the main points he had been making in other places in regard to America's foreign policy, Wallace concentrated on the subject of civil liberties and domestic witch hunting.

"I say those who fear communism lack faith in democracy," he declared. And he reviewed many "infamous instances" in American history, including the Salem witchcraft trials, Negro lynchings, the Tom Mooney and Sacco-Vanzetti cases, the hysterical evacuation of 100,000 Japanese-Americans from the West Coast during World War II. "I speak of only one source of shame to decent Americans who want their country to be admired by the world," Wallace declared. "I mean the group of bigots first known as the Dies committee, then the Rankin committee, now the Thomas committee—three names for Fascists the world over to roll on their tongues with pride." Wallace especially scored a recent statement by J. Parnell Thomas that the movie star Robert Taylor had told him that Lowell Mellett, one-time chairman of the National Emergency Council and wartime OWI official, had forced him to accept the leading role in a wartime film, *Song of Russia*. Said Wallace:

"The committee's present smear of patriots who served so well in wartime, under the guise of an investigation of communism in Hollywood, is the most outrageous and shameful abuse of all. . . . There was no more loyal and devoted servant of Franklin Roosevelt than Lowell Mellett." And then he gave his own credo:

"I am not afraid of communism. If I fail to cry out that I am anti-Communist, it is not because I am friendly to communism but be-

157

cause at this time of growing intolerance I refuse to join even the outer circle of that band of men who stir the steaming cauldron of hatred and fear."

Appearing with Wallace and Kenny also were Dr. Linus Pauling, chemistry director and atomic energy expert of the California Institute of Technology, who warned against atomic warfare and condemned the Truman foreign policy as "aggressive unilateral action"; and Dr. Claude Hudson and Earl Robinson. Almost "stealing the show" from Wallace himself, however, was Katharine Hepburn, whose address was made into pamphlet form several times, and distributed for years. The glamorous film star reviewed the attacks on writers, actors, scientists and educators, by citing specific examples including: the demand by the Thomas committee that Norman Corwin, previous year's winner of the Wendell Willkie Foundation's "One World" award, submit his scripts to it; the banning of William L. Shirer and Frank Kingdon as radio commentators; a warning to a Los Angeles commercial announcer that, because he had made recordings for labor groups, he would be identified by his voice and lose his value to his sponsor; the Thomas committee's investigation of the script of "Deep Are the Roots," a stage play dealing with the problems of Negroes in the South; the banning of Paul Robeson meetings in Peoria, Ill. and Albany, N. Y.; the banning by New York and Detroit high schools of Howard Fast's *Citizen Tom Paine;* the introduction, by California State Senator Tenny, into the state legislature of 11 bills which, if passed, would "set California education back 50 years"; the banning by the State Department of the traveling exhibit of American paintings; the refusal of the Hollywood Bowl for the Wallace rally; and a number of other similar cases.

Earlier in the day, Wallace had appeared at a conference of the Los Angeles County Democratic Central Committee, at which he declared, "If the Democratic party departs from the ideals of Franklin D. Roosevelt I shall desert altogether from that party." The meeting was boycotted by James Roosevelt, chairman of the Democratic State Central Committee, although he came to the Gilmore stadium that night as a "paid guest." There is no record as to whether he contributed to the $31,625 collection, which was started with a $1,000 gift from Mrs. Elliott Dexter, widow of a silent screen writer. In later versions, the amounts contributed by some of Hollywood's stars were exaggerated. First accounts were more accurate: Charles Chaplin and his wife, Oona O'Neill, gave $500; Edward G. Robinson gave $200; and John Garfield, Hedy Lamarr, Cornelius Vanderbilt, Jr., Director Frank Tuttle, Budd Schulberg, David Draper and Paul Henreid were among the $100 donors.

So successful was the Gilmore Stadium meeting that the reactionary press had to go "all out" in an attempt to counteract it. It was not so, as originally reported, that the local radio stations cut Wallace off the air. The fact was that his backers had purchased only 15 minutes of time, which they later regretted. One 6-column headline, in the *Los Angeles Herald-Express* for May 20, 1947, read, "L. A. Left Wingers Boom Wallace as the Man for 1948." Another—a caption over a series of eight pictures—was, "Some Well Known Folks Inhale Pink Vapors as Henry ('the Yogi') Wallace Orates." It was above individual pictures of Vanderbilt, the Chaplins, Hepburn and Kenny, Robinson, Mr. and Mrs. John Garfield and Lamarr, with captions telling of their contributions. The caption for a 2-column picture was: "Henry 'The Yogi' Wallace is shown arriving at the platform for his speech. Wallace is escorted to the flag-bedecked platform, including the flag of the Soviet Union. It is only fair to say the American flag was there too." It probably would have been still fairer to say the flags of all members of the United Nations were there.

To some extent, attempts to prevent Wallace from speaking rebounded in his favor. That certainly happened when authorities of the University of California at Berkeley refused to permit Wallace to appear on the campus. Douglas Dowd, chairman of the campus Young Progressive Citizens of America, reported:

> The history in brief is that applications to the university were made several times through all sorts of respectable channels for the use of any one of the numerous campus facilities for a large meeting, but each time the university turned us down with the weakest type of excuse. So a Students' Committee to Hear Wallace was formed with the sympathy of the college newspaper, so that we received plenty of favorable publicity. We arranged for a permit for the use of one of the sidewalks bordering the campus, checked with Wallace, got a P.A. system and were all set. It worked out fine, for without all the publicity and the stupid attempt at suppression on the part of the university, a meeting probably wouldn't have pulled over 5,000; but, as things turned out, out of an enrollment of 22,000 we pulled between 15,000-20,000, Newsreels, *Life,* all the newspapers. The university, suffice it to say, feels rather embarrassed about their 18th-century stand.

Several newsmen and others who traveled with Wallace in both 1947 and 1948 have declared that he was at his best when speaking extemporaneously to college students and other youth groups. On this occasion, he certainly measured up. He began by thanking Mayor Lawrence Cross for "the use of the sidewalk" and commented that it is necessary for a university president to "get the maximum appropriation possible." Then he summarized his foreign policy views, with emphasis upon the necessity for government planning to avoid depression. He said Harold Stassen seemed to be the Republican with views closest to his own.

Wallace spoke on May 20 in San Francisco and on May 21 in Oakland, to enthusiastic overflow audiences. In the former speech, he recalled the founding, in the hall where he spoke, of the United Nations as the realization of the dream of Franklin D. Roosevelt, many of whose words, including some of his last ones after he returned from Yalta, Wallace quoted.

Some people say that we are failing because of the inadequacy of the administrative machinery of the United Nations, Wallace said. I say that UN cannot have failed because it has never been tried.

Some people say that UNRRA demonstrated the futility of world cooperation. I say that it demonstrated that world cooperation is our only hope.

UNRRA did not perish because it had failed. It perished because it was successful. UNRRA was administered most efficiently in the Ukraine, White Russia, Poland, Yugoslavia and Czechoslovakia. It was because these countries were due for continued assistance from UNRRA that UNRRA was destroyed.

Wallace scored Truman for killing both UNRRA and lend-lease, and said that the Truman Doctrine would breed rather than stamp out communism among poverty-stricken people.

In his Oakland speech, he dwelt upon the terrible destruction that the war had caused in many European countries, especially the Soviet Union, whose dead numbered 30 times that of American dead. He advocated a 10 per cent cost-of-living rollback and other social legislation, blamed the Republican Congress for making no progress toward achievement of FDR's economic bill of rights, and charged Dulles and Vandenberg with being the originators of the Truman Administration's foreign policy. "If communism is a menace," he said, "then give the people proof in terms that they understand, instead of a rousing hatred and hysteria. . . . Today, in blind fear of communism, we are turning aside from progress and aside from the United Nations. We are approaching a century of fear."

In Vancouver, on May 25, 1947, before a crowded high school auditorium audience, Wallace answered a question regarding that city's 8,000 unemployed by saying that capitalism must learn to plan if it is to survive. "The only way we can make the capitalistic system work is by the election of progressive Democrats," he said. "The Republicans have lost their perspective. I know. My father was a Republican and they broke his heart. I know them as utterly fine people but they always vote wrong. They have an outworn state of mind and they cannot meet the future." He also declared that two-thirds of the American people were opposed to the Truman Doctrine. Asked the next day, in a press conference in Portland, how he arrived at the figure, he said, "I got it from a newspaper man," and then laughingly added, "I must not betray the source of my information."

In Portland, Wallace spoke to 1,200 Jefferson High School students, to whom he criticized American aid to Chiang Kai-shek. He also addressed an outdoor meeting of 2,500 at Vanport College, which had only 1,400 students, 90 per cent of them veterans. He commented, "If I am not permitted to speak on a university campus, I will speak off of it

160

and draw a bigger crowd, which is all right with me." He also spoke at Reed College and, of course, at evening mass meetings. Much impressed, Lahey wrote, in the May 28, 1947 edition of his paper:

> If fate and a fickle electorate combined to make Henry A. Wallace President of the United States (an honor he would be reluctant to reject), we would have a John the Baptist in the White House.
>
> After ten intimate days of life with Henry, the writer feels that John the Baptist is the only appropriate figure to evoke in describing the unbridgeable gulf that stretches between Wallace and the world, the flesh and the devil. Wallace is an incurably simple soul. His belief in God and Christian doctrine is as real as his devotion to simple fare. His reputation as a Bolshevik probably comes from overdoing his ethical beliefs. His greatest thrill on the present trip was the temporary breakdown of racial segregation that occurred during his visit in Austin, Tex. He has talked about it fervently time and time again since he was in Texas.
>
> Henry's insistence that we get along with the Russians looks like sheer Communist appeasement to his critics, and plain mawkishness to liberals who support the Truman doctrine, but it is strictly "brotherhood of man" stuff to Henry, who believes that God loves even the Russians.

Lahey has told me other anecdotes of that trip, in addition to the many he used in his well-written articles. Especially he recalls Wallace's unguarded comments during the fast walks the two men took together, usually punctuated by long periods of silence. "You could have crucified the man by printing his off-the-record remarks," Lahey said, and he told me several of them. One incident, which it does no harm to mention now, was Wallace's use, in a speech on the state capitol steps in Olympia, Wash., of remarks made to him a day earlier by Federal Judge Mack, regarding the machinations of the private utilities to sabotage the public power program in the Northwest. Afterwards, Wallace confessed to Lahey that he probably should not have used what Judge Mack told him. "Forget it," Ed said. "Mack may be impeached Monday morning, but forget it, it's over now." And it was.

Lahey left Wallace at Denver, to which place they flew from the West Coast for a May 28, 1947 mass meeting. His paper, the *Chicago Daily News,* had assigned him to cover a bank robbery in Kansas City. It happened that President Truman was there at the same time, and Lahey made a personal report to some of his leading aides—Charles Ross and Matt Connelly—regarding his impressions of the Wallace crusade. In essence, he told them that Harry Truman was "a dead pigeon" politically because of Wallace, and the gloom in the Hotel Muhlenberg was dense when Lahey left. Ed also is known to have written a similar opinion to Philip Murray, CIO head, and to others at the time.

"There weren't any Communists along on that trip," Lahey told me, "except one fellow who was tagging along trying to get material for a magazine article." From Seattle, Lahey had written: "The Henry A. Wallace evangelistic road show is a four-man act." In addition to Wallace himself there were Harold Young, former Dallas lawyer and politician who had been with Wallace since 1940; Beanie Baldwin; and Michael Straight of the *New Republic*, principal speech writer.

While Wallace was meeting with ministerial, labor, youth and other groups in every city visited, Young and Baldwin—especially the latter, since the former was needed at Wallace's door—made contacts with professional politicians. Straight has told me that Baldwin confided in him that he had lined up approximately 110 votes for Wallace at the 1948 Democratic national convention. Baldwin doesn't recall having ever mentioned so definite a number, but thinks he might have been that optimistic regarding the West, as a result of the barnstorming trip.

Wallace arrived in Denver simultaneously with the publication of a journalistic scoop by Robert S. Allen, syndicated by the North American Newspaper Alliance and printed in the *Denver Post*. It pertained to a personal letter that President Truman had allegedly written to Lewis E. Starr, national commander of the Veterans of Foreign Wars, in response to Starr's recommendation, over a month earlier, that Wallace's passport be revoked. Because it was a personal letter, Starr supposedly refused to reveal its contents, although he said he wished he might do so. To the best of my knowledge, the contents of the letter have never been revealed, except for Allen's revelation that "it is reliably understood that in the letter the President bitterly characterizes Wallace as a 'publicity hound' and charges him with making 'wild statements' concerning the Administration's foreign policy; also that the President brands as 'not worthy of cognizance' Wallace's charges that the Administration has embarked the country on an imperialistic course." Unconfirmed, according to Allen, was the report that the letter also said, "Only one man in America compares with Henry Wallace. That man is Aaron Burr." In the light of Harry Truman's record as a letter writer, it is not too difficult to believe he might have written such sentences.

Wallace declared Starr's comment "not worth answering because Starr is so irresponsible in his statements. Starr is the same man who criticized Gen. Evans Carlson, marine raider commander who died Tuesday in Portland, Ore. and called him a Communist. Carlson was the finest, most courageous man I ever knew."

In Denver, the main Wallace speech at Mammoth Garden was sponsored by the Rocky Mountain Council, an independent political group, which had grown out of an independent effort in 1944 to assist the election of Franklin Roosevelt, and an unsuccessful attempt to elect Charles A. Graham to Congress. It was given credit for the victory of John A. Carroll as a candidate for Congress in 1946, one of four Democrats in the country to unseat Republican incumbents that year. Wallace spoke off the record at a Council sponsored lunch, where he was seated next to the widow of former Sen. Edward P. Costigan, conferred with Colorado church, labor, political and community leaders, and had a press conference with college and high school students during the day. At night, with the hall filled to its 5,000 capacity, he criticized Congress for reducing appropriations for the U.S. Forestry Service, Soil Conservation Department and Department of Agriculture. He said there should be a Tigris, Euphrates and Jordan River Authority, to provide public power plants similar to those on the Big Thompson and Blue rivers in the state of Colorado, "without which the West would stagnate."

Wallace wrote a guest editorial for the *Denver Post*, in which he declared that the paper's use of its editorial column to disparage him "to the utmost" indicated it was "worried and badly worried." He chided Palmer Hoyt, publisher and national ADA leader, for having called him Public Enemy No. 1 and for advocating a preventive war against Russia. Answering under the title "Peddler of Shopworn Dreams," Hoyt said he had called Wallace the "Number 1 Enemy of the Republic," not "Public Enemy No. 1." In an interview, Wallace said he did not blame President Robert Stearns, of the University of Colorado, for having banned the American Youth for Democracy from the campus, because public sentiment "had been whipped up" to a point where Stearns had to act or face loss of an appropriation. Despite this evidence of pressure, Wallace was allowed to speak on Thursday, May 29, 1947, at a University of Colorado convocation in the university park chapel. He had lunch with the Boulder Social Action Council, and spoke at a public meeting in Mackey Hall on the campus, in the afternoon. Then he flew to Bismarck, N. D.

There, on May 30, 1947, he said that the farm program, "which Roosevelt and I built with the farmers' help, is being systematically destroyed at the moment when the need is going to be the greatest. The blood of the dead AAA is on the hands of the Republicans." Wallace's appearance was sponsored by the North Dakota Farmers Union, whose national president, James Patton, Wallace had praised in his Denver speech. Again Wallace said, "If the Democratic party becomes the war party and the party of reaction by 1948, I shall take a Democratic vacation. If the cause of peace can be helped, I shall do more than take a vacation. The day is coming when labor will agree on a real labor party in cooperation with forward-looking farmers, businessmen, professional men and scientists."

Wallace's tremendous crowds, *The Christian Century* declared editorially on June 4, 1947, meant that large hosts of Americans were resentful at the Truman Administration's failure to turn victory into peace, had no confidence in the Greek-Turkish aid program and were open to appeals for new leadership. *Collier's* for May 31, 1947, on the other hand, declared it had stopped taking "Hollering Henry" seriously, because he had proved himself irresponsible by criticizing American foreign policy abroad. "Never again," the magazine editorialized, "will we let our blood pressure go up on account of anything he may do. He is a child politically, a man who doesn't know his friends from his foes, a liability to any organization with which he teams up, and a ham actor who dearly loves the sound of his own voice."

As regards the last charge there was some validity, but who was there at the time who could fail to be impressed by the tremendous response Wallace had evoked? Wallace was stimulated and encouraged by the receptions he had received, and so were all his followers. It would have been impossible to have felt otherwise.

The same day, June 5, 1947, that Secretary of State George C. Marshall spoke to the alumni of Harvard University at Cambridge, Mass., to enunciate what became known as the Marshall Plan for European relief, Henry A. Wallace was in Raleigh, N. C., to address an unsegregated meeting, sponsored by the Southern Conference for Human Welfare. There he was entertained by Josephus Daniels, Secretary of the Navy in Woodrow Wilson's cabinet, at whose home he was interviewed by the press. Jonathan Daniels, son of Josephus and a presidential secretary, did not appear. He has told me he absented himself because of the unflattering description he wrote of Wallace in *Frontiers on the Potomac.* According to a letter which Lew Frank, Jr., HAW's amanuensis at the *New Republic,* wrote to his wife at the time, the Associated Press "shorthanded" a statement by Wallace to make it seem he would under no circumstances support Harry S. Truman in 1948. This Wallace himself corrected four days later, in another press interview in Newark, by pointing out that he always qualified his comments on 1948 by declaring that his decision would depend on whether the Democratic party became "the party of war and depression." At Raleigh he was quoted as saying, "I'm doing everything I can to make the Democratic party a liberal party. If the Democratic party becomes a war party, a party of reaction and depression, then I'll no longer be a Democrat." Anyone who interpreted that as meaning he wouldn't support Truman in 1948 had pretty definite ideas as to what Wallace's chances of liberalizing the Democratic party were.

In the afternoon Wallace drove to Chapel Hill, where President Frank Graham introduced him to a University of North Carolina audience.

Introducing Henry Wallace on June 7, 1947 at Montgomery, Gov. James Folsom of Alabama declared, "If I had half the guts and everyone here had half the guts of the man I am about to introduce to you, this would be a better world in which to live." Then Wallace told of the great urge for peace among the common people of Europe, pleaded for trade and general understanding with the Soviet Union, and said of his introducer: "They tell me here in Alabama that your Governor has the greatest ability of any man in the state's history to speak the thoughts of the common man, and he made this same thought very clear last night when he said to me: 'If we were trading with those people, there wouldn't be any talk of war.' I think Jim Folsom is right and so do most of the 200,000 people I have spoken to—face-to-face— at home and abroad, during the past two months."

"Russia is aggressive," Wallace admitted, "but her aggressiveness is the kind we would have if half of the oil of the world were in Cuba and

Russia had the inside track in developing it, protected by aircraft car-
riers patrolling the Gulf of Mexico and a 700,000-man army in Mexico
armed by Russian guns and planes. We would feel fearful and insecure
and would inevitably take countermeasures in various Latin American
countries. Russia does not want war and cannot wage war unless our
policy of antagonizing the progressive mass of people in every country
in the world throws them all—*against their real wishes*—into the Communists' camp."

Wallace also tackled a local problem. "I notice that there is a
proposal before your legislature that all school teachers be required
to take an oath that they are not Communists. I doubt if you have any
Communist school teachers in Alabama, but you will have, unless the
teachers are assured the decent livelihoods and security to which they
are entitled. School teachers, as people in all walks of life, will only
look to communism as an alternative when they lack basic security.
Investigations and intimidation and solemn oaths can't suppress communism in Alabama or anywhere else in the world. The chance for good
wages and good working conditions is the only defense against communism."

In that press conference, on June 9, 1947, in Newark, at which
he set the record straight as to his voting intentions in 1948, Wallace
denied he and Fiorello La Guardia were planning a ticket, expressed faith
in the good sense of Secretary of State George Marshall and "spelled out"
the "outward signs" of a drift toward war as "plans to spend between
$1,750,000,000 and $2,000,000,000 for military training for our youth,
the export of arms to Latin American countries and the blessing of Peron."
Wallace was asked to comment on a statement by President Truman,
calling the coup in Hungary an outrage. He did: "It was the same as if
Stalin had called the action of the United States in Turkey and Greece
an outrage. The United States and England have their Greece and
Turkey, and Russia has her Hungary and Bulgaria."

Wallace put in a gruelling 14 hours that day. After the morning
press conference, he drove to Elizabeth, where 5,000 workers of the
Singer Sewing Machine Works, mostly members of Local 401, United
Electrical Workers, sacrificed their lunch hour to hear him denounce
the pending Taft-Hartley bill and urge them to work at the precinct
level, to "take over the Democratic party in order that you may have
a bigger say in its policies."

Back in Newark, he attended a closed luncheon meeting with civic
and labor leaders, and in the afternoon conferred with a group of ministers. Then there was a public reception, followed by a closed dinner
for 535 leaders of the New Jersey Independent Citizens League, a PCA
affiliate and the day's co-sponsor, at Essex house. The first evening
appearance was at an open air rally in Lincoln park, where he pos-
tulated, "Why do people come to hear me? They come to hear me
merely because I am the one man who is not afraid to stick his neck
out." This didn't exactly jibe with the editorial opinion, the day before,
of the *Newark Star-Ledger* which, among other things, said:

"But Wallace has now shrewdly chosen to become the voice of the
opposition on foreign policy. The two great parties are for the moment

united on foreign policy. The disgruntled elements—the Communists, the fellow-travelers, the isolationists, the extreme pacifists, the confused, the despairing, the heart-broken, the hysterical and the skeptical—have no banner to which to rally effectively, except the banner of Wallace."

Whoever the people were, there were an awful lot of them that night, in both Lincoln park and the Mosque. Wallace himself summed up the day's reception, according to *The Trentonian* for June 10, 1947: "I'm simply overwhelmed. It was tremendous."

In his own bailiwick, Dr. Frank Kingdon assumed the job of fund raiser, which he was to continue to perform for the next six months. He left no doubt of his hopes when he said:

"Liberals must organize before 1948, and the voters will select the delegates to the 1948 convention. They should pick the man of their own choice as the Presidential nominee. There isn't a better man available than Henry A. Wallace." He called for a fall campaign "to win the Democratic Presidential nomination or to make him the people's nominee."

Canada Lee and Josh White, entertainers, appeared with Wallace, as did James Imbrie, state chairman of the New Jersey Independent Citizens League. Wallace's attacks on the Truman Doctrine were the same as he had made in several other places. He answered a heckler, who wanted evidence that Russia did not want war: "If we had suffered such devastation, would we want war?" He added: "It is not communism which alarms reactionaries of the United States and the world; it is that we shall make democracy really work from top to bottom." He warned that America was getting a world-wide reputation as a center of reaction, and that at the present rate of change, within a decade we might be praising Hitler and Mussolini as heroes who paved the way for us to fight the Soviet Union.

Thousands were unable to get into the packed Mosque for what the *Newark Evening News* for June 10, 1947, said revived "memories of old-fashioned revival meetings yipping with delight." Two nights later, on June 11, 1947, Wallace debated Thomas K. Finletter, at a Norwalk, Conn. Town Hall meeting, on the merits of the Truman Doctrine. With Norman Cousins of the *Saturday Review of Literature* acting as moderator, Finletter spent more time advancing the ideas of the World Federalists, with which he was connected, than he did arguing for the Greek-Turkish aid program. Wallace used all his usual arguments against it and predicted that its first extension was already being planned, in the form of a $500 million loan to the Kuomintang government of China. Wallace admitted that in the '20s Soviet leaders, including Lenin and Stalin, had made inflammatory statements, but said Franklin Delano Roosevelt and Harry Hopkins had convinced him that under Stalin the Soviet Union had abandoned any ideas of world revolution and was willing to coexist peacefully with the capitalistic world. Wallace again identified himself as "one of those who hope that Russia will make a grand glorious success of communism—in Russia. I think we are more likely to have peace if it does so."

All that Henry A. Wallace had done so far in 1947 was prologue

166

to the prodigal's return—his first public appearance in Washington since his dismissal from the cabinet, nine months earlier. Sponsored by the Southern Conference for Human Welfare, the meeting was an open-air one on June 16, 1947, at the Watergate Amphitheater and, despite prodigious efforts, first to prevent its being held and then to discourage attendance, over 10,000 persons, including the author and one of his sons, lined the Potomac for what was to be Wallace's last major speech before Labor day.

The effort to stop the Watergate meeting began a week earlier. On June 10, 1947, Rep. Herbert A. Meyer (Rep., Kan.) called Henry A. Wallace "the evil tool of those who would destroy America" and demanded, "When will the Attorney General of the United States do his duty and indict this renegade?" Recalled Meyer, "Let it not be forgotten that this Henry Wallace is one of the heritages left us by the late Franklin Delano Roosevelt," which was a preview of things to come, after the Republicans returned to power in 1953 and undertook to convince the American public that it had survived "20 years of treason" under the Democrats.

On Friday, June 13, 1947, a group headed by Rep. Alvin E. O'Konski (Rep., Wis.) went into U. S. District Court in Washington, to apply for an injunction to restrain Secretary of the Interior Krug from permitting the National Capital Parks, a unit of the National Park Services within the Department of the Interior, to issue a permit for the Wallace gathering. O'Konski argued that the Southern Conference was "a group sympathetic with those who advocate overthrow of our government by force," and in his petition maintained that Henry A. Wallace "found it impossible to subordinate his political philosophies and beliefs to those of the Administration of President Truman and it was therefore necessary for the President of the United States to summarily discharge him or request his resignation."

This frank appeal for punishment for political heresy was refused and so on Saturday, June 14, 1947, the House Committee on Un-American Activities carried out the threat it had been making for almost a fortnight and published a blast at the Southern Conference for Human Welfare, after refusing Clark Foreman's request to appear before it. In the October, 1947 *Harvard Law Review*, Prof. Walter Gellhorn, of the Columbia University Law School, wrote "Report on a Report of the House Committee on Un-American Activities" which, after painstaking analysis, left virtually nothing of the Rankin-Thomas report worth believing. "The report demonstrates," Gellhorn wrote, "not that the Southern Conference is a corrupt organization but that the Committee has been either intolerably incompetent or designedly intent upon publicizing misinformation."

Actually, the Southern Conference, which existed until 1948, was founded in 1938 by a group of 1500 Southerners, largely under the impetus of the report of the National Emergency Council on the South which caused President Roosevelt to say "The South presents right now the nation's No. 1 economic problem." It worked to eliminate the poll tax, and favored anti-lynching legislation, the ending of all racial discrimination, and better health and educational opportunities for everyone.

There was never any follow-up of the House committee report. Its purpose was almost unashamedly to injure the Watergate meeting, which was under the sponsorship of what it called a "most deviously camouflaged Communist-front organization," although in its text it flatly stated that neither Dr. Clark Foreman, president, nor Dr. Frank Graham, president of the University of North Carolina and honorary president of the conference, was a Communist. Nevertheless, it mentioned organizations to which persons whose names appeared on the conference letterhead had belonged, or petitions sponsoring liberal causes which they had signed. Among those whose connections the committee didn't like were Harold L. Ickes, Mrs. Marshall Field, Dorothy Parker, Mrs. Gifford Pinchot, Melvyn Douglas, Paul Robeson and Joseph E. Davies.

In the House of Representatives the day of the Watergate meeting, Rep. Chet Holifield (Dem., Calif.) read a telegram from Foreman, denouncing the committee report as "one of lies and half truths." Upon motion of Rankin, the telegram was stricken from the *Congressional Record* by a 146 to 7 vote. A motion, by Rep. Vito Marcantonio, to set aside Rankin's motion failed 147 to 10. Rep. John H. Folger (Dem., S. C.) scoffed at the insinuation that Frank Graham was Un-American, and Rep. Helen Gahagan Douglas (Dem., Calif.) bravely announced that she intended to attend the Watergate meeting. A chorus of boos greeted this announcement.

" 'Unjustified' is a justified though mild term in the circumstances," editorialized the *Birmingham* (Ala.) *News-Age-Herald* in denouncing the Rankin-Thomas smear of the Southern Conference, and its comment typified widespread press reaction.

Foreman opened the meeting with, "Friends, Americans and observers" and several speakers who preceded Wallace on the Watergate program mentioned the fact that the Un-American Activities committee had announced it would have observers at the meeting. Wallace himself commented, "I hope you will not be purged because of your presence here tonight." For the first time at a Wallace meeting photographers were active taking flashbulb pictures of sections of the audience.

At the meeting, Sen. Claude Pepper introduced Wallace, saying, "If an election could be held in the world today as to who was the world's foremost private citizen, as a spokesman of peace and democracy; if there were to be chosen one man in private life who speaks to the world in the spirit of Franklin D. Roosevelt, it would be the American citizen I now proudly present to you."

Wallace's speech was mostly about Soviet-American relations. He called upon President Truman and Secretary of State Marshall to invite Premier Stalin and Foreign Minister Molotov, of the Soviet Union, to meet with them in Berlin, to draw up "an agreement which will cover all the points at issue between the United States and the Soviet Union." He recalled that in preceding months, in three interviews —with Alexander Werth, a British journalist; Elliott Roosevelt and Harold Stassen—Stalin had indicated cooperation between the two powers to be possible. "I can see no legitimate reason," Wallace declared, "for believing Stalin's statements a quarter of a century ago and doubting his statements in the past six months. Stalin can change his mind in 25 years. Most of us have. Twenty-five years ago I was a Republican."

He referred to a third party in two places in the speech:

> It will be important—if the Democratic party succumbs to Wall Street domination—to have a new party to let the people of the world know that those who believe in peace and understanding still have some means of expression.

> It will be important as evidence that this is still a democracy.

> It would provide the evidence that the United States has not gone completely imperialistic and psychopathic.

> And like third parties in other periods of American history it would have a long-term influence on American life.

Later, he said:

> I have mentioned the possibility of a third party. Let me add a few words on that subject:

> I am convinced by a careful study of the American political scene that a truly liberal party—whether it be the Democratic party or a new party—can elect a useful number of congressmen in 1948.

> Such a liberal bloc in the Congress will help halt the present reactionary trend.

> I would prefer to see a genuine two-party system.

> I would rather congratulate the administration on a reversal of present trends and on assuming some dynamic, positive, liberal leadership. The trend of the past year has been the other way.

At his Washington press conference earlier that day, Wallace asserted that, in his opinion, Great Britain and the United States would fight if the Soviet Union attempted to expand into central Turkey and thus threatened Saudi Arabian oil. He added that he hoped his words would "get back to Russia" and said, "I'm no warmonger; far from it. But it is important for Russia to know there is a point beyond which she shouldn't go without awakening resistance. I'm confident our Navy would fight if she got into Turkey because our Navy is determined to get Saudi Arabian oil." In his opinion this oil should be made available to all nations, including the Soviet Union, under Article IV of the Atlantic Charter, but he believed in being realistic.

169

Gross receipts of the Watergate meeting were $20,000 of which $12,000 came from admissions and the rest from contributions.

Before he left Washington, Wallace spoke to the 449 delegates to the National Youth Lobby. He epitomized his six months' activities when he said: "You may be right in demanding that there be a third party in 1948, but I'm playing it different. The progressive Democrats in Congress are playing it still differently." He warned of the difficulties which would be encountered, if a third party attempted to get on the ballot in the 48 states, and left the subject wide open by declaring that, as of that time, nobody could tell what the wise procedure would be in 1948.

Then he returned to his *New Republic* office on weekdays, and his South Salem farm on weekends, with almost no public appearances of any kind until Labor day, Sept. 1, 1947. His most important public statement during that period was a 15-minute CBS broadcast on June 22, when he called Secretary of State Marshall's proposals on June 5 at Harvard "a great advance" over the Truman Doctrine. "The Marshall doctrine," he said, "looks toward an overall program which is what I have been advocating all along . . . Marshall recognizes that the fundamental problem is one of economics, that Europe must share in the effort and that she must be aided as a whole and not country by country. He left the door open for Russia to participate in the plan." In the *New Republic* for July 14, Wallace regretted Russia's refusal to join the first Marshall Plan conference in Paris but blamed Soviet suspicions on the Truman Doctrine.

On June 18, 1947, Norman Thomas, perennial Presidential candidate of the Socialist party, heckled Wallace in an open letter, in which he asked the latter if he rejected the theory that Communist totalitarianism, using the Russian army and its "other army—the international Communist movement," was "relentlessly, patiently and boldly seeking world power." If Wallace rejected that theory, Thomas demanded, "on what grounds do you explain the Russian tactics in Korea, Manchuria, the Balkans, Hungary, Austria and Germany or the Communist party policies throughout the world?" Thomas asked how Wallace distinguished "except in racism between the tactics of Fascist and Communist totalitarianism."

On July 2, 1947, Wallace answered Thomas, though he refused to engage him in public debate. Wallace wrote, "I don't doubt that the Communists everywhere want eventually a Communist world, but I believe they are essentially interested—at the moment—in strengthening the Soviet Union as an example of the type of socialism they have in mind. I seriously question whether the Russians are interested in world domination at a time when they are struggling to rehabilitate themselves from the devastation of war."

As regards Russian tactics in Korea and other places, Wallace wrote Thomas, "I have little first hand knowledge of these tactics, but I would hazard the guess that they don't differ greatly from the tactics of others . . . Basically, I believe that Russian tactics are directed to providing the security she needs to rebuild, and I think we can do a great deal to end any abuses on her part by contributing to that sense of security through economic assistance and sincere pledges of friendship with the Russian people." To Thomas' question regarding the differences between communism and fascism, Wallace wrote, "that 'except in racism' tells a great deal of the story," and added his belief that Communists were sincerely interested in getting a better world and, while he didn't accept their world plans, he did not doubt their sincerity. "The Marxists," he wrote, "seem to agree that it is possible to have a society of abundance for all peoples while the Fascists believe that they are superior people who alone are entitled to the fruits of production."

Thomas wasn't satisfied with Wallace's replies because Wallace didn't comment on concentration camps, police states, lack of civil liberties, systematic destruction of Baltic peoples and similar matters.

The day after the Watergate meeting, Adolph A. Berle, Jr., onetime assistant secretary of state and chairman of the New York Liberal party, also took a crack at Wallace. At the annual convention of the International Ladies Garment Workers Union in Cleveland, Berle predicted that war with the Soviet Union was imminent and called on Wallace to sever his ties with the PCA and support the Truman Doctrine. The PCA, according to Berle, was "an appeasement party," whose guiding geniuses were "American Communists and fellow travelers, acting in accord with their Moscow correspondents," definitely determined to establish a third party in 1948 so as to guarantee a Republican victory.

In Brussels, on June 26, 1947, Eric Johnston, former president of the United States Chamber of Commerce and then so-called motion picture czar, said that Wallace had created misconceptions regarding the United States in Europe, where he had been traveling. Johnston denied the United States was imperialistic, the center of world reaction and/or heading toward economic collapse.

In August, 1952, Henry Wallace asked me to write down—and then read back to him for checking—the following "statement of faith," to indicate what his thinking was in 1947 and 1948:

> Fundamental has been my approval of a steadily strong United Nations, looking toward full employment in one world of peace; expanded world trade; progressive capitalism in the United States—all three being realized to a considerable extent by the investment of surplus United States capital through the United Nations in so-called backward nations and using United States technical experts in backward nations of the world. Through that, expanded world trade to make progressive capitalism work in the United States and give the United Nations real meaning. Search for understanding between the United States and the Soviet Union so as to make it possible for the United Nations police force to be stronger than the combined forces of the US and the SU.

> As the USSR became stronger and more recalcitrant, and Korea occurred, I took a definite stand. I always made it

clear that I am for progressive capitalism, never a Socialist. I am for a mixed economy of the Scandinavian type and always made it clear whenever extremists were in conversation with me that I believe in God. There never has been any change on that. I think the Communists always have known what my views are. I don't know which are Communists but they certainly knew how I felt. They adopted a number of my statements and phraseology and I didn't adopt theirs. They followed my ideas.

I have tried that out on a number who were close to Wallace at the time, and they agree that it is a pretty good summing up of what made Wallace "tick" in those days. For detailed "spelling out" of how he felt on specific issues during June, July and August, 1947, one has only to consult the files of the *New Republic* for those months.

# ¶ 9 LABOR BECOMES AROUSED.

*Wallace appealed to the rank-and-file after labor leaders, though infuriated by the passage of the Taft-Hartley act, generally remained loyal to the Democratic party.*

If he had not vetoed the Taft-Hartley Labor Act on June 20, 1947, Harry S. Truman would never have been elected President of the United States on Nov. 2, 1948. He might not even have won the Democratic party nomination in July, 1948.

As it was, the CIO and some other labor groups joined with ADA at the Democratic convention to promote a "draft Eisenhower" movement, despite the general's public disavowal of any desire to be a candidate. In addition to Truman's earlier weak record on legislation of interest to organized labor, there was the strong suspicion that he had not exercised sufficient energy in persuading members of his own party to vote to sustain his Taft-Hartley veto.

In the House of Representatives, there was never the slightest chance of defeating the bill or of sustaining the veto. The June 5 vote there for the bill was 320 to 79, and the June 20 vote to override the veto was 331 to 83. In the Senate, however, there was a closer margin. On May 14, the first vote had been 68 to 24 for the bill, and on June 6 it was 54 to 17 on the final version, as worked out by conferees of both houses. At that time 17 Democrats joined with 37 Republicans in favor of the bill, while 15 Democrats and two Republicans were opposed.

When the Senate, on June 23, overrode Truman's veto, 68 to 25, only two Democrats who had voted for the bill's passage changed their votes to sustain the president. They were Scott Lucas of Illinois and

John J. Sparkman of Alabama. There were 20 Democrats and 48 Republicans for overriding, and 22 Democrats and 3 Republicans for sustaining the veto.

The three days between the veto message and the vote to override were hectic ones. For 28 hours 32 minutes, the Senate remained in session: the longest continuous period since 1927. During that time Senators Pepper, Taylor, Murray, Kilgore and Morse filibustered in the attempt to gain time for public sentiment to crystallize. The filibuster collapsed for lack of support. While it was progressing, Majority Leader Alben Barkley took no part at all and was quoted as saying to Morse that "sometimes pressures do more harm than good." Truman himself took his family and some White House staff members to a professional baseball game, between the Washington Senators and St. Louis Browns, at which he unveiled a plaque to Walter Johnson, one of baseball's "immortals."

After Morse sank to his seat, exhausted, the Senate agreed to vote on the veto message at 3 p.m. on Monday, June 23. Labor lobbyists did what they could, in the capital and throughout the country. William Green, AFL president, declared, "The nation's workers hail President Truman's veto message as a masterpiece of statesmanship," and Philip Murray, CIO president, praised the "penetrating analysis," which fully exposed "the devastating effect on our national economy if the bill becomes law." Sen. Robert A. Taft, one of the bill's co-sponsors, charged that Truman's message was merely a paraphrase of a memorandum by Lee Pressman, CIO general counsel, which Sen. James Murray had put in the *Congressional Record*. This charge Pepper denounced as "an unworthy insinuation."

Those who overrode the Taft-Hartley veto had six votes to spare, but for several days it had been held possible that the margin would be closer. The papers were filled with reports of plans to bring Sen. Robert Wagner, seriously ill in New York, to Washington by special train to vote with the minority; and of a four-motored Constellation that was kept warmed up for four hours, at a Paris airfield, for possible use by Sen. Elbert Thomas of Utah, who was in Geneva attending an international labor conference. Although, before the vote was taken on Monday, President Truman addressed a letter to Barkley, expressing the hope that Democrats would vote to sustain his veto, and although it later was announced that the Democratic National Committee would pay for the unused railroad car and French airplane, high CIO officials were still skeptical. So Philip Murray called Senator Thomas by transoceanic telephone and learned from him that, rather than being urged by Democratic leaders to return, he had been told by them that it would be unnecessary for him to do so.

"We were hellishly mad at the time," Lee Pressman has told me. However, Pressman and several others who knew him agree that Philip Murray never held a grudge long against anyone, with the sole exception of John L. Lewis, his predecessor as chairman of the CIO. I never knew Murray, but I've talked to at least ten of his intimates. To such questions as, "What was Murray's attitude on that?" I got an identical reaction;

without exception I was informed: "You never got definite answers from Murray." Throughout the war years, they all agreed, Murray was the "great compromiser." It was he who kept together the widely diverse elements which went to make up the CIO. Although a devout Catholic, until 1946 he withstood pressures, from the Association of Catholic Trade Unionists and other church groups, to attempt a purge of Communists and other Left Wing elements in the CIO. He leaned heavily on Pressman, whose Left Wing tendencies were no secret, to help keep the Left Wingers "in line."

As regards the proper function of the organized labor movement, Murray was conservative. He believed in collective bargaining and in economic pressure, and he never favored direct political action to the point where it threatened to overshadow orthodox union activities in importance. In November, 1946, he caused the CIO-PAC headquarters to be moved to Washington from New York, so as to be "under his wing" more closely. The kiss of death he administered to the Conference of Progressives was described in Chapter 6. He declined election to a vice presidency of the Progressive Citizens of America and, on Feb. 19, 1947, recommended to a meeting of CIO vice presidents that all CIO leaders dissociate themselves officially from both the PCA and ADA. That resulted in the withdrawing from ADA of Walter Reuther, president of the United Automobile Workers, and John Green, president of the Marine & Shipbuilding Workers. Despite Mrs. Eleanor Roosevelt's protest on March 7, 1947, the Murray edict against ADA remained in force until February, 1948.

All CIO leaders felt a great debt of gratitude to Franklin Delano Roosevelt for Section 7-A in NRA and the subsequent National Labor Relations (Wagner) Act. With Philip Murray, this feeling was deeper than with most of the others. More than once, at CIO executive board meetings, when funds were needed for the Southern organizing drive or for some other cause, he would point to FDR's picture on the wall of his plush office and declare, "My friends, I want you to know that we would not be here if it were not for that great American. The CIO was born under his friendly interest. We're only here because of the New Deal, 7A, and the Wagner act, which restored the balance. This great American has made possible underlying economic gains. From time to time, as we talked of events, I made FDR a promise which, under God, I hope to keep, that the CIO will not stop until it has organized the South, till we have removed the chains from the victims, colored and white. So help me God, I won't stop as long as God gives me breath." And then he would call the roll, asking, "How much will you give for FDR?"

This attitude meant that the CIO, under Philip Murray, considered itself closely linked with the Democratic party, come what may. In 1947, FDR had not been dead long enough for this attitude to be altered to any appreciable extent. In addition, some of his critics have contended, Murray had become dependent upon government agencies to fight his battles with management for him. "He never negotiated himself," one told me. "Rather, he let the White House or someone else do it." As a result, some Left Wing CIO leaders felt, Murray made a "bad deal" in 1946, when he consented to the smashing of OPA and permission for the steel industry to raise the price of steel $5 per ton, in exchange for an 18½ cents per hour wage increase for steelworkers. Murray's critics say it would have been better for him to have settled for a 16¢ wage increase and no lifting of price controls, which many charge started the post war inflationary cycle.

Throughout 1946 and 1947, Murray kept reiterating what, as far as I am able to determine, he first said publicly at the CIO convention on Nov. 1-5, 1943: "It is definitely not the policy of the CIO to organize a third party, but rather to abstain from and discourage any move in that direction. For, even apart from the insurmountable technical problems of placing such a party on the ballot in 1944, a third party would only serve to divide labor and the progressive forces, resulting in the election of political enemies. The primary political task today is to weld the unity of all workers, farmers and other progressives behind candidates, regardless of party affiliations, who support the war program of our Commander in Chief and enlightened domestic and foreign policies."

He repeated the same viewpoint in his *New York Times* article of April 11, 1946; on June 27, 1947, after a CIO executive board meeting to discuss the effects Taft-Hartley would have; on Aug. 11, 1947, at the United Steelworkers of America convention in Pittsburgh and on several other occasions. In other words, there was never the slightest doubt how Murray felt about a potential third political party, and there was never any possibility that those who started the Progressive party of 1948 did not know how Murray stood. Much was later made of the fact that little or no attempt was made, by Progressive party leaders, to try to solicit the cooperation of Murray. Although no official approaches were made, I know of some labor leaders who did try to persuade Murray privately that he should go along.

I also know that Henry A. Wallace in mid-July, 1947, tried in vain to arrange a meeting with Murray. This Wallace did entirely on his own initiative, phoning Murray at a New York hotel. Wallace does not recall the incident, but Kermit Eby was in the room alone with Murray while the 15-minute conversation took place. It was rather one-sided, with Wallace attempting to convince Murray that he should be sympathetic to what he was doing and Murray stalling Wallace with evasive statements, such as that he'd have to wait and see, no decision had been reached as yet, etc. When, on Jan. 23, 1948, at the CIO executive board meeting at which Wallace's candidacy was denounced, Murray stated that Wallace had never made any attempt to get in touch with him, Eby was crestfallen. At a snack bar with another CIO official after the meeting, he confessed to no appetite because he had lost faith in someone for whom he previously had had respect. To the best of my knowledge, the July attempt had no follow-up, and there are some who believe that Wallace was discouraged from trying again by Pressman, John Abt, Baldwin and others. There are a few who think these evangelists for a new party were fearful that, if the two men met, Murray might have been able to dissuade Wallace from the path he was taking. This I doubt. I don't think anything could have kept Henry Wallace from running for President in 1948. By the fall of 1947, he had become convinced it would be impossible for him to capture the Democratic party nomination, and so an independent candidacy was the only alternative for him. He has confirmed what his close associates recall, that all summer long he kept saying he would run if he foresaw the possibility of obtaining 3 million votes. The tremendous crowds that turned out to hear him, the letters he received and the delegations which visited him late in the year led him to his final decision to announce.

Of Wallace's popularity with the rank and file of labor, there was no doubt. Hundreds of thousands, if not millions, of workers believed what Philip Murray had said, when he introduced Wallace at the national CIO convention in 1944: "Henry Wallace, to the workers of America, symbolizes the aspirations of the common man. We love him because he is one of us, a common man. The principles which he has enumerated are the ones to which the CIO adheres."

On April 13, 1947, an emergency rally of CIO officials from all over the nation was held in New York, to organize the campaign against the Taft-Hartley and other pending laws. At it, Murray accused Big Business of attempting to force strikes in leading industries, by withholding overdue wage increases, despite a 20 per cent rise in living costs. He called the pending anti-labor laws "the first real step toward the development of fascism in the United States," and his views were echoed by many another present. This and similar talk is what labor leaders, who went along with the Progressive party in 1948, had in mind when they told me, "We were just trying to do what Murray and all our other leaders had been saying."

The emergency rally was thrown into a tizzy by Irving Potash, vice president of the Fur and Leather Workers Union and a member of the Communist party National Committee, when he spoke up against the unmistakable anti-Red sentiment which had been developing for over a year in the CIO. Said Potash, "I speak to you as a Communist. Not a one of you will buy peace for yourselves by joining a witch hunt. Not a one of you will escape the same hounding, the same hunting." Before he was able to proceed much further Emil Rieve, president of the Textile Workers, angrily interrupted. He and several others roasted Potash royally for his comments.

Five days later, the PCA issued a broadside against the Taft-Hartley bill as "the greatest sneak blow since Pearl Harbor at the civil liberties and standard of living of the American people." Its analysis of the bill concluded, "The Taft and Hartley bills would have their place in Nazi Germany but not in democratic America." In an open letter to President Truman on May 4, 1947, the PCA urged him to veto the portal-to-portal bill which, it said, would nullify the Fair Labor Standards Act and "would expose our lowest paid workers to merciless wage cuts and sweatshop conditions." Four days later, Murray also called for a veto of the bill to eliminate Federal court jurisdiction over so-called portal-to-portal pay suits. The National Lawyers Guild came out against the bill, as did Secretary of Labor Schwellenbach. Nevertheless, Truman signed the bill, which barred nearly $6 billion worth of claims for past wages.

Both the AFL and the CIO held huge Madison Square Garden rallies against the Taft-Hartley bills. At the AFL rally on June 4, 1947, attended by 35,000, William Green declared that the AFL would oppose every member of Congress who voted to override President Truman's veto. Mayor William O'Dwyer and Senators Wagner (Dem., N. Y.), Langer (Rep., N. D.) and Magnuson (Dem., Wash.) also spoke against what they agreed was a measure authored by the National Association of Manufacturers.

The CIO's rally, on June 10, 1947, was a much larger affair, with 60,000 present to hear Philip Murray assail what he called "a dangerously provocative bill." The biggest applause of the evening, however, was for a man who was not present—Henry A. Wallace—whose message to the rally set off two minutes of shouting, "We want Wallace," and "Wallace in '48."

On June 12, 1947, the PCA called upon Congress to enact legislation to roll back prices approximately 10 per cent at the retail level. On June 24, 1947, the PCA declared, "The Taft-Hartley slave labor bill became law today because President Truman failed not only to command the necessary two-thirds vote to sustain his veto but also . . . to command the votes of more than half of the members of his own party in Congress . . . The failure of the Democratic party to defeat the Taft-Hartley bill may well mark a turning point, not only in the history of American labor, but in the history of American political parties as well."

While the congressional debate regarding the Taft-Hartley veto was raging in Washington, the International Ladies Garment Workers, AFL, was holding its 26th convention in Cleveland. That the ILGWU wanted nothing to do with Henry Wallace was made very plain in the board statement, which categorically rejected "the pro-Russian appeasement sentiment advocated by Henry A. Wallace and his followers," and accused the PCA of having "swallowed in toto the Communist party 'line' on international affairs." The report excoriated Communists within the labor movement and declared that the "expansionist policies" of the Soviet Union constituted the principal menace to the peace and security of the world. This was the gathering at which Adolph A. Berle called the PCA an appeasement party (see page 171). As regards the rival ADA, the board advised ILGWU members to take a "keen and close interest." The New York Liberal party was also preferred over the American Labor party, which was termed "a political front" for the Communists.

A resolution adopted ten days later recommended that the AFL work for a Congress in 1948 "on which the people of this country can rely." Independent candidacies in localities where neither the Republicans nor Democrats named progressives were approved, but an amendment to endorse a new national political party was overwhelmingly voted down as tending to isolate it politically and strengthen its enemies.

The ILGWU's stand was no surprise to anyone, because David Dubinsky had long been recognized as the leading American labor leader opposed to Communists and all other Left-wingers. One of the original group of eight which formed the Committee for Industrial Organization on Nov. 10, 1935, which became the Congress of Industrial Organizations a year later, he had persuaded his union to return to the AFL in November, 1938. He also (see page 49) had been a leading figure in causing the Liberal party to break away from the American Labor party in 1944.

Quite different was the background of A. F. Whitney, president of the Brotherhood of Railroad Trainmen. It was he who, on May 27, 1946, said that his brotherhood would use its entire $47 million treasury, if necessary, to defeat Harry Truman in 1948 (see page 42). On June 30, 1946, he had praised Truman's veto of a "gutted" OPA bill, at the School for Political Action; however, he had assailed both Congress and Truman on Sept. 3, 1946, at a Labor Day picnic in Highland, Ind., and in a radio address from Chicago, in which he said something about "goose-stepping with Wall Street." On Sept. 18, 1948, at the Miami convention of his union, he called the 79th Congress the worst of all times, denounced Truman again for his handling of labor matters, and joined Claude Pepper in praising Henry A. Wallace (see page 97).

Whitney's hands shook and his voice quavered, according to press accounts, when he appeared before the House Labor Committee on Feb. 25, 1947, to denounce the pending anti-labor bills as worse than anything he could recall during his entire 57 years in the labor movement. He characterized labor as "fighting in almost its last ditch before Congress to save democracy."

On March 21, 1947, at Cleveland, Whitney had said, "We advocate dispatching food and clothing for the suffering people of Greece, with the provision that distribution should be supervised by United States personnel," but denounced any military aid for either Greece or Turkey.

This was the same A. F. Whitney who, on July 20, 1947, at Pittsburgh, declared that Truman's veto of the Taft-Hartley bill had "vindicated him in the eyes of labor." He declared that there was no potential liberal Republican candidate for the Presidency and that a third party was "out of the question." Whitney's public relations man, Walter J. Munro, issued a statement praising Gael Sullivan, acting chairman of the Democratic National Committee, for his fight against the Taft-Hartley act, which led Edwin A. Lahey to comment, in the *Chicago Daily News* for July 24, 1947:

> This is indeed a feather in the cap of Sullivan, who has worked hard to rebuild the defenses of the Democratic party.
>
> But all the deal proves about Whitney is that he is a hypocritical old goat.

Nevertheless, Whitney's about-face provided the answer, to a considerable extent, to the poser Clayton Knowles had presented in the *New York Times* of June 21, 1947: "There also was a division of opinion on whether the President's action [the veto] would be sufficient to forestall a third party movement led by Henry A. Wallace with whom he broke on foreign policy issues."

Henry A. Wallace went ahead with his third party anyway, but he did so knowing that he lacked the support of virtually every important labor leader in the United States.

Not long after he abandoned his effort to defeat Truman, Whitney began actively campaigning for the Democrats. On Jan. 20, 1948, while most other labor leaders were still toying with the idea of trying to force Eisenhower on the Democrats, Whitney visited the White House with Harold McGrath, National Democratic chairman, and emerged to say that he was for Truman's re-election. Two days earlier, he had resigned by letter from the PCA, of which he was a vice chairman. In an interview, he said he had tried to talk Henry A. Wallace out of starting a new party, but Wallace tells me he has no recollection of any such activity on Whitney's part. In July, 1948, Whitney was the only American labor leader who accepted an invitation to address the Democratic national convention. Len DeCaux, who worked with the railroad brotherhoods from 1927 to 1934, before he became editor of the *CIO News,* thinks Whitney was conditioned by the experience the brotherhoods had in 1924, when they endorsed Robert M. La Follette Sr. in his third party attempt, went down to defeat, and suffered long political isolation thereafter as a result. When Whitney decided, in mid-1947, to bet on Truman in 1948, he took a long shot, but he turned out to be smarter than most other political forecasters.

Another who became silent in mid-1947, after a year and a half of expressing views similar to those of Henry Wallace, was Elliott Roosevelt. In the spring of the year, he had told a meeting of about 1,500, at a PCA organizing meeting on the Samuel Rosen estate in Westchester County, that followers of his late father should plan to storm the Democratic national convention in 1948, to make Henry A. Wallace the party's nominee for President. Elliott's remarks at the March 31, 1947, crisis meeting have been reported (see page 130). On the second anniversary of his father's death, at a memorial service sponsored by the PCA, he lambasted Truman's domestic policies as leading to a depression "that is almost upon us," and criticized the Truman foreign policies as making the threat of war "a menacing possibility." He joined Fiorello La Guardia, J. Raymond Walsh and Bartley Crum in declaring that Wallace was correct in insisting that aid to Greece and Turkey should be handled through the United Nations. Elliott Roosevelt said at that meeting:

> The leaders of our country are convinced that we must prepare for conflict. They believe that they have failed to reach an understanding with other world powers. They believe that our former allies are planning our downfall. They are paying lip service to the United Nations on the one hand and sounding the drums of war at the same time. We are told that we are faced with an expanding militarism fostered by the Soviet Union. I believe that

179

understanding can be reached with the Soviet Union. I believe that the democracy of Jefferson and of Franklin Delano Roosevelt can be made the dominant political force of the world and without appeasement or the sacrifice of national honor.

That was Elliott Roosevelt's last public statement favoring Wallace's policies. On March 27, 1948, he and Franklin Delano Roosevelt Jr. both issued public statements endorsing Gen. Dwight D. Eisenhower as the Democratic nominee for President. Stated Elliott:

My position is a very simple one. I am a Democrat. I believe that the Democratic party has failed to provide the leadership that was needed in the winning of peace. That peace can still be won.

The best way to win it is through the election of a candidate of one of the two major parties who will unite both liberals and conservatives in this country on a program of American world leadership to sell democracy throughout the world.

The Democrats have the opportunity. Eisenhower should be their candidate. I have always supported him and shall continue to do so.

To reporters, he denounced Henry A. Wallace's third party movement, but FDR Jr. was even more outspoken, saying: "The third party candidate in no conceivable way reflects or inherits the liberal objectives and principles of my late father. In a moment of world crisis he is confusing and dividing the country. Nor have the men suggested for the Republican nomination demonstrated any marked ability to unite the American people."

These views were consistent with those FDR Jr. had been expressing for two preceding years. He had been an original ADAer and was a frequent speaker at ADA functions. On March 22, 1947, at Newark, he called communism the immediate danger and fascism the long-range danger in the United States. The "Commies," he told the New Jersey chapter of ADA, are "mere squatters on the American liberal tradition."

Henry A. Wallace once told Lew Frank Jr., his principal speech writer in 1948, that he considered FDR Jr. a dangerous young man, and asked Lew to promise always to oppose him. This Frank had been doing in the American Veterans Committee, in which he was a rightist leader of the left and Michael Straight, *New Republic* publisher, was a leftist leader of the right. In an attempt to smear Lew Frank, whom Straight hired for the magazine in May, 1947, FDR Jr. prepared an unfavorable "dossier" on Frank, mostly easily disproved statements.

Three persons independently have related to me an anecdote of the PCA organizational meeting at the Rosen estate. Frank had expressed regret to Elliott because the latter had been absent from a recent national

180

AVC convention, at which Elliott's name had been suggested by the left wing for national commander. Also suggested, by the right wing, had been the name of Franklin D. Jr., which had caused Straight so much embarrassment that he phoned Mrs. Eleanor Roosevelt to make an elaborate apology for appearing to cause a family split. "What Mike doesn't realize," Elliott is reported to have said, "is that I hate Frank and Frank hates me."

What caused Elliott Roosevelt to "fold" so suddenly and completely, after such a brave start through his books and speeches? Generally it is believed that it was economic pressure from his mother. Whatever virtues Elliott may have, business acumen has never been listed among them. Nor was he always possessed of political sense, as when he was prepared to make a speech seconding the nomination of Jesse Jones to be vice president, at the 1940 Democratic convention. He, at one time or another, was associated in a business way both with Jones, whom his father distrusted sincerely, and with William Randolph Hearst, one of his father's leading newspaper critics.

Since we're started on the Roosevelt family, we might as well continue by examining the question, which naturally arises at this time, as to why Mrs. Roosevelt, in 1947, sided with son Franklin and against son Elliott and—if she did—successfully shut up the latter in his attacks on the Truman administration.

The explanation for Mrs. Roosevelt's position, in my opinion, is two-fold:

1. As a result of her experience as a leading sponsor of the American Youth Congress in the late '30s and early '40s, she was thoroughly allergic to any organizations in which there was a trace of Communist influence.

2. Despite widespread belief, she was not her husband's confidante in political matters, and consequently was incapable of judging whether Truman's foreign policy was what FDR would have supported.

In 1944, Mrs. Eleanor Roosevelt was among the most disappointed of American liberals at the failure of the Democratic party to renominate Henry Wallace for Vice President. She vehemently blamed "that evil Jimmy Byrnes" for his part in the defeat of Wallace. In the July 7, 1944 *New Republic,* she reviewed Henry Wallace's book, *Democracy Reborn,* a collection of his speeches during the preceding ten years, giving it high praise.

Commenting in one of her syndicated columns, in late January, 1945, regarding the testimony of Jesse Jones and Henry A. Wallace before the Senate Commerce Committee, she wrote, "What stands out, as you read—at least to me—is that one man is looking backward and the other man is looking forward."

Wallace, meanwhile, pleaded for unity among progressives. In his *New Republic* column in late January, 1947, he declared that although he spoke to the founding convention of the PCA, he was not a member, and he did not believe Mrs. Roosevelt belonged to ADA. During the 1948 campaign, ADA attempted to make quite a bit out of this, as an indication of lack of integrity on Wallace's part. On Jan. 22, 1947, James Loeb, ADA secretary, issued a statement: "It is unfortunate that Mr. Wallace, without consultation with either Mrs. Roosevelt or with responsible officers of the ADA, should have sought to give the impression that Mrs. Roosevelt has severed her connection with the organization.

"Mrs. Roosevelt has authorized me to state that she has consented formally to continue to serve as a member of the committee of the whole. Mrs. Roosevelt served as chairman of the nominating committee at the Jan. 4 organizing conference. At that time she made it clear that because of other duties, particularly with the United Nations, and also because of her conviction that the leadership should be taken by younger people, she could not accept office in the ADA."

On March 7, 1947, Mrs. Roosevelt implored Philip Murray to lift his ban on participation by CIO officials in ADA, as well as in the PCA. When the statements of her sons endorsing Eisenhower were made public a year later, she commented, "I always let my children do what they think is right." As for herself, because she was serving on the United Nations Commission on Human Rights, she felt that she should take no part in partisan politics. Nevertheless, in the June 12, 1948, issue of the *Christian Register,* a Unitarian publication, she wrote, "I think Henry Wallace is being fooled. I have always been fond of Henry, but he never has had to work with the Russians as I have." This may or may not be considered inconsistent with what she had told the American Academy of Political and Social Sciences on April 3, 1946, in Philadelphia:

"Russia has been closed off from the rest of the world. Because she knows the world is opposed to her economic and social policies she is suspicious and antagonistic. We should think back to the early days of our republic, when a great many people of the world disapproved of the experiment we were trying. We were suspicious of them and we were antagonistic. We had a chip on our shoulder then, but we are very different now. Our standards have changed, but we must realize those things take time."

While many labor leaders were lambasting Wallace, or warning against any third party attempt in 1948, others were talking quite a different language. On April 11, 1947, in San Francisco, at its seventh biennial convention, the International Longshoremen's and Warehousemen's Union, whose president was Harry Bridges, condemned Truman's record in vigorous language as a "betrayal" of the American people and the Roosevelt program. It pledged itself to "work in every way for his defeat as a candidate for the President of the United States in 1948, and for the selection of a candidate who will truly think, talk and act in the best traditions of the late Franklin D. Roosevelt."

At its fourth constitutional convention, May 4-8, 1947, at Cleveland, the United Packinghouse Workers of America, CIO, passed a resolution which slapped the reactionary post-war attitude of representatives of both major parties in Congress; claimed that the November

946 elections demonstrated that the old two-party system merely "presents us with a choice between Tweedledum and Tweedledee"; and called or "an independent political party so as to give the voters an opportunity or representatives that will act in their interests." There were several ervent speeches favoring the resolution and none against it. Henry Walace's name was mentioned more than once.

At the national convention, on June 29, 1947, of the Townsend Plan, its originator and leader, Dr. Francis E. Townsend, declared that he oldsters, who had been battling for more than a decade for higher pensions, should start thinking of the advisability of a third party. In 948, Townsend endorsed Wallace.

Slightly more cautious was Daniel J. Tobin, president of the International Brotherhood of Teamsters convention at San Francisco, on Aug. 1, 1947. Tobin, who had been chairman of the labor division of the Democratic party in all Roosevelt campaigns, declared that for 41 years he had opposed formation of a third party, but the new anti-labor legislation might "drive toilers and their friends into a third party." He was not optimistic of the chances for success of such a venture, until organized labor was united.

After condemning the record of the 80th Congress, the International Woodworkers of America, CIO, at its eleventh annual convention, Aug. 6-29, 1947, in St. Louis, concluded that the kind of program it desired cannot be expected from either of the two major parties but can only be projected and effectuated by the formation of a people's party under the leadership of the united labor movement and rallying to its banner all sections of the labor movement . . . the AFL, the CIO, the railroad brotherhood and independent unions, working farmers, professional workers, consumers; members of minority, racial and religious groups; and all people advocating a progressive and liberal program."

At St. Paul, on Sept. 6, the Mine, Mill and Smelter Workers heard Vito Marcantonio say, "If the Democratic party does not cease me-tooing the Republican party, if it does not carry on a fight to repeal the Taft-Hartley act, if it continues to be a war party, there will spring from the masses of the people a new political party." The union unanimously went on record as favoring "a truly people's independent party."

In the late spring of 1947 the board of directors of the PCA was augmented by the addition of Aubrey Williams, publisher of *Southern Farmer* and former director of the National Youth Administration, and of Carey McWilliams, widely known author and sociologist. At the PCA board of directors meeting, on June 28, 1947, in Chicago, Jo Davidson, then in France, was made honorary chairman and Frank Kingdon and Robert W. Kenny became co-chairman. The vice chairmen were: C. B. Baldwin, Elmer A. Benson, Van Wyck Brooks, Norman Corwin, John Cromwell, Bartley Crum, Marshall Dimock, Hannah Dorner, Clark Foreman, Lillian Hellman, John P. Peters, Paul Robeson, Harlow Shapley, Paul Tishman, J. Raymond Walsh, A. F. Whitney and Bishop R. R. Wright. Honorary chairman of the young people's division was Gene Kelly.

The board reaffirmed its adherence to the nine-point program adopted at the Dec. 29, 1946 founding convention (see page 120), and passed a number of resolutions intended to "expand and deepen" it. It called for public ownership of coal mines, railroads and electric power; lambasted the House Committee on Un-American Activities; called the rent control act, passed by the 80th Congress, a fraud, largely because of its "voluntary" 15 per cent rent increase clause; called the Taft-Hartley act "the most vicious attack in the history of our country upon the fundamental rights of American workers"; and gave support to the Marshall Plan to the extent that it was "consistent with the principles of the United Nations and the unity of the Great Powers." It declared that the plan, however, "cannot be isolated from total policy of which it is one element, for its character will inevitably be determined by the politics which gives it direction." Therefore, the PCA declared, "we must continue to advocate and work for the complete reversal of the Truman Doctrine," which it called a plan to extend "military aid to despotic governments and military dictatorship," and which thus was "the path to war."

The PCA's statement on political policy included the following:

> The independent forces, of which we are a part, support the Roosevelt Democrats in and out of Congress who continue their courageous fight for the building of peace through a strong United Nations and a liberal domestic policy. We shall encourage every effort of these Democrats to change the present policies of their party and to nominate progressive candidates for all offices in 1948.

> At the same time the independent forces must further organize in wards and precincts to make certain that in 1948 the voters of the United States shall be guaranteed the opportunity, by a new party if necessary, to have a clear choice between progressive and reactionary candidates for President.

> The PCA will do everything within its power for the attainment of this objective. We will cooperate with every group moving in this direction.

One such group with which PCAers cooperated was that backing former Rep. Charles R. Savage, in the May 18, 1947 special primary in the 3rd Congressional District in Washington. Running as an avowed "progressive," Savage defeated an avowed Truman supporter, Smith Troy by 16,536 to 11,555. At the June 7 runoff election, however, Russell V Mack, a Republican who supported the Truman foreign policy, won over Savage by about 1,000 votes, out of a total of nearly 65,000.

Organizationally, throughout the summer of 1947, the PCA operated much as in the preceding six months. At the local level, community groups were organized as much as possible on a ward and precinct basis. Nationally, the PCA continued to issue statements regarding current problems. One of the most successful PCA activities during this period was the conference on the subject of thought control, July 9-13, 1947, in Hollywood. The 432-page proceedings, published in the form of six pamphlets, is a masterful summary of the first post-World War II attacks on civil liberties, with statements from scores of the nation's leading intellectuals.

As he had announced he would, Henry Wallace restricted himself, during July and August, 1947, mostly to *New Republic* work. In the July 3 issue of the magazine, he called on all elements of the labor movement and small farmers to fight the feudal leadership of the Democratic party in the South. He pointed out that 17 of the 20 Democrats who had voted for Taft-Hartley in the Senate were Southerners and declared that the Southern Democrats wanted to restore the two-thirds rule at Democratic national conventions, so as to control the party again. He wrote:

> If the feudalists succeed in this the Democratic party will be dead and a new party will take its place. A decade hence it is all too possible that we shall say: "the third party was conceived on the day the Southern Democrats voted to override the Taft-Hartley veto. It was born on the day the Southern Democrats took over control of the party machinery at the national Democratic convention in July of 1948."

What a great many of those Southern Democrats actually did at that time, of course, was to walk out of the Democratic party and form the States' Rights or Dixiecrat party of 1948.

American newspapers of July 20, 1947 carried an account of an interview, which Wallace had given the New York representative of Tanyug, official Yugoslavia news agency, and which had appeared in Yugoslav newspapers. Wallace was quoted as believing that the Marshall Plan had delayed an economic depression in the United States. Contrary to his earlier qualified support, he now questioned the plan's advisability, "if it divided the world in two parts and if the primary aim is to revive Germany for the purpose of waging a struggle against Russia." He was noncommittal on his 1948 plans. He said, "No other country is so misunderstood in the United States as Yugoslavia."

By this time all of the Russian satellite countries had rejected invitations to the Paris conference, which 16 nations attended, beginning July 12, to draw up an inventory of needs, in accordance with the suggestion that Secretary Marshall had made a month earlier in his Harvard speech. In dropping out, after having first accepted, Czechoslovakia explained that it believed its participation in the conference might be construed as an anti-Soviet Union action.

On July 26, 1947, Wallace spoke at a Nassau Independent Voters Association meeting, at the Old Westbury, L. I. home of Michael Straight. Among other things, he said, "How much happier it would be if President

Truman would take all those things which he believes we want from Russia, and if Stalin would take all those things which he believes Russia wants from us, and at a meeting of the two heads of government each item was canceled against each other."

Americans for Democratic Action continued to follow the dictum Chester Bowles had expressed at its Jan. 4, 1947 founding conference: work for a liberal progressive front without Communists and through the Democratic party, "with all its faults," and without "any illusions about a third party." On July 19, 1947, Wilson Wyatt warned from Chicago that a third party in 1948 would be a "catastrophe" for American "democratic liberalism." Wyatt was one signer of a statement that day, declaring ADA support for the Marshall Plan as "a conclusive answer to those who decried the 'negativism of the United States foreign-aid program.'" Other signers included Leon Henderson, Paul Porter, Robert Sherwood, David Dubinsky, Barry Bingham, George Edwards, Arthur Schlesinger Jr., Emil Rieve, Willard Townsend and John Green.

After the garbled account of Wallace's statement of intention regarding Truman in 1948, growing out of his June 5, 1947 press conference, Sen. Claude Pepper publicly upheld Wallace's demand that the Democratic party become the "liberal" party, but reiterated that he never would follow Wallace, or anyone else, into a third party. In the press for Aug. 15, he was reported to have endorsed Truman for reelection in 1948. After a visit to the White House, Pepper said the President had proved himself "sincere, honest and human," and that "he is the salt of the earth to this country. I don't think there is any question but that the President should and will be nominated, should be and will be elected." A month later, on Sept. 14, 1947, President Truman was reported to have rebuked Gael Sullivan, executive director of the Democratic National Committee, for saying during a radio forum that neither Wallace nor Pepper would be asked to speak for the Democratic party in 1948. Almost immediately thereafter, Pepper began speaking under Democratic party auspices.

As for Glen Taylor, on May 24, 1947, at a New York state CIO council meeting in Albany, he denounced Taft-Hartley as "the first step toward depression," based on "the time-honored Republican theory that what is good for the rich is eventually good for everybody." On July 1, 1947, he asked the Senate to investigate the real estate lobby, which Truman had denounced as "selfish and short-sighted." Truman had suggested such an investigation when he signed the emasculated rent control bill. Taylor's resolution called for $50,000, to enable the Senate Banking Committee, headed by Sen. Charles W. Tobey, to do this before Jan. 1, 1948.

Taylor went to Minneapolis Aug. 1, 1947, to speak at a luncheon sponsored by the Democratic-Farmer-Labor party. He deplored disunity among liberals, saying, "Republicans always get together after an interparty fight. Liberals don't. They go home and pout like kids if the man they want is not nominated to run for office." Taylor said he had been asked why he didn't repudiate Communist support. "I'm not repudiating

186

any support," he replied. "Anyone who is going my way can come along as far as I'm going." He related that during three campaigns in Idaho he issued vigorous denials whenever he was called a Communist, and he lost every time. The fourth time he just ignored the charges and he won.

In a rousing Labor Day editorial, "Come Out Fighting!" in the Sept. 1, 1947 *New Republic,* Henry Wallace made his most forthright appeal up to that time, to rank and file workers and liberals, to join him in "a new pattern for political action," despite the "opportunism" of many of their leaders. Written after consultation with a number of Wallace's close associates, the editorial proclaimed that reaction was growing in the United States because of the absence of such action. Wallace deplored timidity and compromise. A few extracts from the editorial will indicate its tone as a whole:

> Progressives cannot win by playing an unprincipled game. When we practice cleverness at the expense of honesty, we inevitably lose. Try as we may, we can be neither as cunning nor as dishonest as the opposition. There is no reason to try. Progressives have both the principles and the majority of the people. The job is one of mobilizing that majority by exposing unprincipled actions and providing direction through principles.

> It is a never-ceasing wonder to me that some experienced leaders of labor remain vulnerable to adjectives hurled by the opposition—"idealistic," "impractical," "communistic" and the dozens of others used by reactionaries . . . We can't let the enemy call the signals.

> No labor official interested in political progress will proclaim support of the present administration at this time. . . . On this Labor Day, 1947, we should not be discussing which is the lesser of evils. We should be planning to avoid the necessity of such a choice by winning control of the Democratic convention. We should be planning to get the best possible candidates for Congress in every congressional district . . .

> The summer is over. Labor Day is here. It is the time to "come out fighting."

Wallace's Labor Day speech, on Sept. 1, 1947 in Detroit, delivered after he had walked two miles at the head of a parade, in which estimates say 50,000 to 65,000 participated, was an extension of his editorial comments.

"Your influence in combating depression and war will be in direct proportion to the amount of organization you build," he told the cheering mob in Cadillac Square. "If we don't make the Democratic party into a party of peace and prosperity, we shall build a new party," he asserted, as thousands roared approval.

If, after that reception, Henry Wallace had not thought he was very much in the running for the Presidency in 1948, he would have been much less than human. And he would have been about the only person who paid attention to what was going on who failed to believe it.

# ¶10 POLITICAL ORGANIZING BEGINS. *Not waiting for Wallace to decide whether his appeals to the Democrats to reverse their policies would succeed, efforts to provide third party machinery got under way.*

Resolutions by labor unions, university professors, PCA units, or others asking Henry A. Wallace to establish a new political party did not provide the machinery by which it could be done.

All over the United States, in 1947, there were old-time Socialists, of about half a dozen varieties; oldsters who had campaigned with Old Bob La Follette in 1924, or with Teddy Roosevelt's Bull Moosers in 1912; there even were some septuagenarian and octogenarian Populists and Non-Partisans, in whom the flame of agrarian revolt had not been extinguished.

Organizationally, however, third partyism was at about its lowest historical ebb. During the 12 years of the New Deal, most of the agrarians, anti-monopolists and other dissenters had found it possible to unite behind Franklin Delano Roosevelt. The only incipient revolt had come from Philip La Follette who, on April 28, 1938, had called 3,500 Midwest liberals together, to establish a National Progressive party. Partly because the symbol adopted—supposedly an X mark in a ballot circle—was widely called a "castrated swastika," but mostly because, in November, 1938, Phil was defeated for a fourth term as Governor of Wisconsin, the movement died aborning.

On March 16, 1946, at Portage, Wis., 500 delegates heard a message from Henry A. Wallace urging the Progressives of Wisconsin, "with their great tradition of liberal action," to "come home to the party of Roosevelt rather than return to the party of Hoover." It was greeted with mingled cheers and boos, and did not succeed in swaying the vote which resulted: 284 to return to the Republican party; 51 to join the Democratic party; 77 to continue as the Progressive party of Wisconsin; and three to join the Socialist party.

So Sen. Robert M. La Follette Jr. entered the primary of the

Republican party, which he had left in 1934, and was defeated by Circuit Judge Joseph R. McCarthy of Appleton.

Whereas the Wisconsin Progressives became Republicans, the Minnesota Farmer-Laborites, who had run the state throughout the '30s, combined with the Democrats in 1944 to help re-elect FDR. Then Elmer A. Benson—successor to Floyd Olson, three times F-L Governor, who died in 1933—lost control of the party to Hjalmar Peterson, who led the farmers back into the Republican party, which then elected Harold Stassen Governor in 1938.

No branch of the Socialist party had amounted to much since Eugene V. Debs polled 919,199 votes in 1920, while a Federal prisoner because of his opposition to American involvement in World War I. In 1932, Norman Thomas got 882,000 votes; in 1936, he got 188,000; in 1940, he got 99,000; and in 1944, he got 80,000. Thomas has led the remnant of the party in the direction of pacifism and vigorous anti-communism and anti-Russianism. When Wallace was bounced from the Cabinet in September, 1946, Norman Thomas and Harry Fleischmann, national secretary, called him "the heir of the policy of appeasement which was disastrously followed, first by Neville Chamberlain at Munich and later by Roosevelt and Truman at Cairo, Teheran, Yalta and Potsdam."

In 1947, only in New York State was there a functioning third party of any importance. It was the American Labor party, founded in 1936 with the blessing—if not at the suggestion—of Franklin Roosevelt, to battle harder for New Dealism than the traditional Tammany Democratic organization gave signs of doing. And the ALP had been weakened, in 1944, by the defection of its right wing to form the Liberal party.

By the end of 1947, indigenous third party movements were well under way in two other states with large electoral college votes. They were California and Illinois.

The first move toward what became the Independent Progressive Party of California was taken at the second biennial convention of the Marine Cooks and Stewards Union, CIO, May 5-9, 1947, in San Francisco. Under the leadership of its president, Hugh Bryson, three resolutions calling for third party action were consolidated into one and passed unanimously. They instructed the national officers and general council to "immediately seek the broadest support toward this goal [to which] we have here dedicated ourselves," which was to build "a new political party based on the trade union movement and composed of farmers, white collar workers, professional people, veterans and minority groups."

So instructed, Bryson addressed himself by letter to every national and international CIO, AFL, railroad or independent union in the United States, to solicit support in establishing the grass roots for a new third party. He also communicated with every union local in California and, on Aug. 1, 1947, called a meeting of labor sympathizers with his idea in San Francisco. It then was decided to hold a meeting on Aug. 24, the day after the two-day session of the California Legislative Conference at Los Angeles. Approximately half of the 1,236 delegates to that conference—a traditional meeting of unionists to decide on a state legislative program—stayed over for Bryson's meeting. At the conference, Bryson explained his two-fold motive as follows:

"First, a more prosperous and democratic America, which means jobs without discrimination at decent wages, housing, education, security for our aged, sick and unemployed.

"Second, we want peace. We want an end to imperialism, adventure and suppression of colonial peoples and dollar diplomacy which is already leading us to a third world war which can only mean total destruction."

The Independent Progressive Party of California was launched under the auspices of the Joint Trade Union Committee for a Third Party. Under California law, two methods were open to the new partyites. One was to obtain the signatures of 275,970 (10 per cent of the total vote for the Governorship in 1946) on petitions, to be filed 95 days before the June primary, or March 27, 1948. The other was to persuade 1 per cent of the governor's vote, or 27,597, to change their party registration. The IPP chose the former course because it did not want to discourage registered Democrats from voting for candidates favorable to Wallace in the Democratic primary.

Mrs. Elinor Kahn, who became executive secretary of the IPP, and other leaders have told me that even if the Wallace movement had not developed nationally, there would have been a third party attempt in California and that, as it turned out, tying up with the national Progressive party hurt rather than helped the state movement. The reason for this belief is that the cross-filing system in California made it inevitable. By this system, any candidate could file in the primaries of both the Democratic and Republican parties. If he won both primaries, in November he would be running only against himself, unless there was an independent candidate on the ballot.

Just this sort of situation had occurred in 1946, when Earl Warren won both major party primaries in June, as candidate for Governor. The primaries had been held just a few weeks after Truman seized the coal mines and was threatening to break a railroad strike by drafting strikers into the armed services (see page 42). Consequently, thousands of workers who usually voted in the Democratic primary stayed home. This fact, plus the mobility of former war workers, which temporarily disenfranchised them, led to a particularly low total vote in 1946. Thus in 1948, comparatively fewer signatures were needed on petitions to qualify a new party.

Operating against the chances for success of such a movement was the viewpoint held by some other outstanding California liberals that, despite the 1946 fiasco, the Democratic party was "capturable" in 1948. The proper word is doubtless "recapturable" because, from 1934 to that time, the liberal or New Deal wing had been dominant in California Democratic politics. For all practical purposes, the Democratic party did not exist prior to 1934. Instead there were two branches of the Republican party, the liberal one led by Hiram Johnson. Then came the End Poverty in California (EPIC) movement, led by Upton Sinclair, which it took a tremendous amount of money to defeat, after this new grass roots movement had thrown a terrific scare into the magnates of the Union Pacific, the Giannini-controlled Bank of America, the Hollywood money moguls and others, whose political control of the state had never before been seriously challenged.

Ten years later, there were New Economy barber shops and Abundance restaurants to be found in small towns all over California, remnants of the EPIC campaign. The "bloc" of Hollywood liberals, which was the object of so much congressional scrutiny a decade and a half later, got its start in EPIC days, in part as a reaction to the threats of Louis B. Mayer to move out of the state if Sinclair won.

In San Francisco, there was a weak Democratic party machine, led by Bill Malone; but its interests were mostly local patronage. In Los Angeles, there wasn't even the semblance of a traditional big city machine. The liberals controlled the county committee, and the basic setup of the party made continued control easy. Local clubs were affiliated directly with the state organization, rather than through any intermediary hierarchy. Hence there was no Tammany-like setup to buck.

After recalling that the progressives had controlled the Democratic party in 1934, 1938 and 1942, Robert W. Kenny, Attorney General before 1946, when he lost the Democratic gubernatorial primary to Warren, has written me: "We needed a third party here like a hole in the head. We had control of a second party and might have remained in control had it not been for this alien doctrine which came in from the East and dictated that the left wing sever itself from the Democratic party and go into seclusion as a separate Independent Progressive party. Such a move might have been wise in Pennsylvania but it was utter folly in California."

It was Kenny, by then a national co-chairman of the PCA, who tried to head off the formation of the IPP by calling a Democrats-for-Wallace conference on July 19, 1947, at Fresno, which about 350 from all of the state's 23 congressional districts attended. Among them were 53 of the 600 members of the Democratic State Central Committee. To them Kenny said:

> For over two years now, the American people have been traveling through a dark tunnel, stumbling, falling, groping for the way. Henry Wallace is the first pinpoint of light for the American people since the death of Franklin D. Roosevelt . . . Wall Street is counting happily on a race between Dewey and Truman. They would rather have Dewey win, as they expect he will—but the stock exchange would shudder only slightly if a miracle came to pass and Truman were elected . . .
>
> We are not starting a third party. We are here as Democrats, fighting for a live and progressive Democratic party. . . . If we do the job we're setting out to do, the Democratic party has nothing to fear from a third party. There was no third party talk in the days of FDR because the Democratic party, as the party of the people, held out

hope to independent voters. A Democratic party which will unite behind the ideals and policies of Henry Wallace will find a third party not an enemy but an ally. If liberals, fearing a third party, decide to back Truman, they suffer nothing but defeat—win, lose or draw.

It undoubtedly is true that in any state with a cross-filing system a third party is bound to develop sooner or later. If, however, Henry A. Wallace or Beanie Baldwin had urged strongly that the effort be postponed until after 1948, I believe it is equally certain that Bryson, Mrs. Kahn and the others would have acceded to the request, no matter how reluctantly. An outstanding fact regarding the Progressive party, regardless of whatever evaluation anyone wants to put on it, is that Henry Wallace did not participate in the making of such decisions. Furthermore, this was not because others were attempting to "box him in" or "crowd him out." Wallace just wouldn't be bothered with such matters. His concern was with the issues at a high idealistic level. At this stage he trusted Baldwin thoroughly; and, of course, any candidate for important office must have a campaign manager in whom he has confidence, and to whom he leaves organizational details.

So Beanie listened to both sides and, for all practical purposes, told both of them to go ahead in their own way. Kenny wanted Wallace to announce his candidacy about the time that he did—before Truman's State of the Union speech in January, 1948—and to express the hope that he would be supported by the Democratic party as well as by any independent groups already formed, or which might be formed before the 1948 campaign. He wanted Wallace personally to contact Democratic leaders sympathetic to him, to encourage them to fight within the party for pro-Wallace delegates to the 1948 Democratic convention and, in states where any such activity within the Democratic party was impossible, to encourage the formation of indigenous third party movements. Kenny thought then and still thinks that there was an excellent chance to capture the California and possibly the Oregon and Washington delegations, and that their placing Wallace's name in nomination at the 1948 Democratic convention would have been wise. The closest Wallace came to endorsing the Kenny effort was a wire of felicitations which Harold Young sent to the Fresno meeting.

In not discouraging the IPP Baldwin ignored not only Kenny, but also Barney Conal of the Voters' Research Institute, whom he had engaged in September, 1947 to make an impartial scientific survey of the California situation. Conal came to virtually the same conclusions as had Kenny. He reported that there was strong middle class and professional support for Wallace, or—more properly put—opposition to Truman, especially in the Los Angeles area and that what happened when the IPP was formed was "like bloodletting." By his action in inviting Wallace to the state in October, 1946, after he had been dismissed from the Cabinet, James Roosevelt, Democratic state chairman, had demonstrated his own early leanings away from Truman. In mid-1947, he was still *persona non grata* with many conservative Democratic leaders, who boycotted a July 5 Jackson Day dinner, at which he was to speak. By the end of the year, Gael Sullivan and J. Howard McGrath succeeded in getting Jimmy back into the orthodox fold. By then a large number of his potential supporters, had he continued to oppose Truman and support Wallace, were starry-eyed because of their memories of the huge Gilmore Stadium and other large Wallace meetings of that Spring, and there was no stopping them. Once the IPP signature drive got under way, Kenny was left high and dry, without rank-and-file support sufficient to wage any kind of intra-Democratic party fight. He kept his Democrats-for-Wallace committee alive, and did some speaking for Wallace during the 1948 campaign, but his movement lacked political force. Carey McWilliams, who shared Kenny's views, resigned from the PCA, and Reps. Chet Holifield and Helen Gahagan Douglas, who had been Wallace sympathizers throughout most of 1947, even refused to cross-file in the IPP, of which more later.

*     *     *     *

In Illinois, cross-filing has never been legal. By mid-summer, 1947, the PCA in Illinois was involved head-over-heels in a campaign to challenge a long-standing practice of the Democratic and Republican machines: this was to present a single, supposedly non-partisan, slate of candidates for election to the Superior Court of Cook County (Chicago), which shared virtually equal jurisdiction with the Circuit Court. There were 21 judges to be elected in November, 1947, and there was considerable grumbling, especially among Republicans, who were encouraged by their success in November, 1946, to believe that they could do better than get six of their party on the slate beside 15 Democrats.

It would have been impossible to disguise the fact that the PCA also had in mind winning a sufficient proportion of the vote in the judicial election so as to qualify as a new party in 1948, in the event Henry A. Wallace decided to make the attempt. The newspapers at the time duly reported this motive and also criticized the leadership of both the Republican and Democratic parties for their slate-making activities. On Aug. 27, 1947, the Chicago *Daily News* editorialized:

> The political horse trading between Cook County Republicans and Democrats has been concluded. The political bosses have picked the Superior Court judiciary. The voters had no voice in the matter. They will have no voice in November.

> The coalition plan for judicial elections was supported and adopted years ago on the theory it would help to keep the courts out of politics. It has not had that effect. Rather, it has corrupted the courts to the point where judgeships are political plums to reward faithful workers.

> Six of the sitting judges slated for re-election are unqualified by the Chicago Bar Association's standards of fitness

or because of advanced age. They were slated because
they had powerful political backing. . . .

Taking the name "Progressive," in late July the PCA began circulating its petition for a complete slate of 21 candidates. It had not been easy to get up that slate. A number of lawyers sympathetic either to the progressive cause or to the attempt to provide opposition to the coalition slate nevertheless were unwilling to allow their names to go on the ballot. Several who at first consented later backed out, pressure having been "applied" in some cases. Nevertheless, as finally constituted, the Progressive slate included at least half a dozen who were decidedly better qualified than an equal or larger number of those on the Democratic-Republican slate.

During this period, the smugness of the high command of the old parties was complete. Apparently, they thought at first that the task of obtaining the proper number of signatures would be insuperable. On Aug. 18, however, there were deposited with the clerk of Cook county 5,326 pieces of paper, stacked 4½ feet high when tightly packed, containing the signatures of 121,722 registered voters of the county to nominate the slate of 21, whereas only 105,000 were needed. The rumors that the validity of the petitions would be attacked before the election commissioners did not materialize and, in the light of later events, both the Republican and Democratic county chairmen faced heavy criticism from their own people for not having done so.

Heading the Progressive slate was Homer F. Carey, professor in the School of Law of Northwestern University. He was a man of unquestioned ability and unimpeachable reputation. Get almost any old-time "insider" of Cook County politics into a corner, even today, and he'll admit the likelihood that Professor Carey won the 21st place on that list of winning candidates instead of Wilbur F. Crowley, formerly an assistant state's attorney. Because of some offense Crowley had committed against a reporter, the *Chicago Herald-American,* a Hearst newspaper, went all-out in its campaign to defeat Crowley, advocating a vote for Carey, whose name appeared on the ballot just opposite Crowley's. The Chicago Bar Association committee on candidates wound up endorsing Carey, and two others on the Progressive slate. Several of the others refused to appear before the association's committee, after it became known it was asking what were considered "red-baiting" questions. The *Daily News* endorsed Carey and one other Progressive candidate; the *Sun* formally endorsed four of them; while Milburn P. Akers, the political columnist, gave what amounted to an endorsement to seven.

When the official results were announced, Crowley had 334,833 and Carey 313,848. The high man on the coalition slate received 465,655, and the low man on the Progressive slate 139,721. There was no doubt that the Progressives had qualified as a party, unless it could be successfully contended that the judicial election did not constitute a general election as prescribed by law. That issue was not decided favorably for the Progressives until almost a year later.

It was largely because of the success of PCA activities in Illinois,

194

especially in the judicial election, that Henry A. Wallace, when he finally made up his mind to announce his independent candidacy for the Presidency in 1948, selected Chicago as the site for the announcement, on Dec. 29, 1947. Even before that announcement, however, a virtually complete slate of Progressive candidates for Cook County offices in 1948 had been announced. Under the law, the 21 judicial candidates constituted the central committee of the new party, and it went to work immediately, because of a February filing date to be on the ballot for the April primary. Heading the slate again was Homer Carey, as a candidate for state's attorney; he later had to decline the nomination because of poor health, which led to his death a year later. On the slate also were a number of lawyers, who had been unwilling to run for Superior court judge but who were encouraged by the outcome to "stick out their necks."

\* \* \* \*

For a dozen years before 1948, the American Labor party in New York had provided evidence of what several biographers of third party movements of the past have noted: in the beginning, the new party attracts dissenters of many kinds who, because of their diversities, soon begin to splinter into factions, either fighting for party control or quitting to form still-newer parties.

Certainly there had been nothing starry-eyed about most of those who had a hand in the formation and direction of the ALP, from 1936 on. They were mostly cold-blooded political pragmatists, struggling for control and shifting their alignments, within and without the ALP, to suit their own interests. This is not to say that political idealism was nonexistent. That would be as improper to say as a similar statement regarding either the Democratic or Republican party would be inaccurate. There always are overall or fundamental areas of agreement or objectives, but so many possible ways of achieving objectives exist that maintaining unity is a major problem.

The ALP qualified as a legal party its first time out, in 1936, by polling more than 50,000 votes for Governor. Its first real victim was the New York Socialist party, from which pro-Roosevelt members had deserted to form the Social Democratic Federation of the United States, and to join forces with the ALP. After 1936, these Socialists wanted the ALP to attempt immediate expansion into a national labor party, similar to the British Labor party, but Sidney Hillman and David Dubinsky, ALP leaders, preferred to keep the party local, as a balance of power in New York City and state politics. After December, 1948, when they failed to qualify to remain on the ballot, the New York Socialists, by referendum, voted to recommend to their members that they join the ALP as individuals.

Because his support of President Roosevelt had angered some Republicans, Fiorello La Guardia welcomed the ALP. On the other hand, the Democratic party saw it under the control of labor leaders other than those in the AFL who had traditionally headed Democratic labor committees. In 1937, the Democrats tried to destroy the new party, by legislative action to prevent cross-filing. Gov. Herbert Lehman vetoed the bill, however, and his veto could not be overridden. In August, 1937, La Guardia's plurality as a successful candidate for Mayor of New York was 454,465, and his vote on the ALP line was 482,559, more than the margin of victory. In January, 1938, William Green, president of the AFL, had charged Labor's Non-Partisan League, of which the ALP nominally was the New York arm in its beginning, with being only a CIO agency, and recommended that all AFL members withdraw from the ALP. In April, George Meany, then president of the New York State Federation of Labor (president of AFL after Green's death in 1953), urged all state AFL affiliates to quit the ALP. On Aug. 24, 1938, the New York AFL, in a resolution, spoke of "that Communist-infested dual labor organization known as the CIO."

In 1940, the ALP polled 417,407 votes for Franklin D. Roosevelt, who carried the state over Wendell Willkie by 221,725. In 1941, it polled 435,374 votes for La Guardia, whose plurality over William O'Dwyer was 132,283. In 1942, James A. Farley succeeded in winning the Democratic gubernatorial nomination for John J. Bennett, Attorney General, over FDR's objections. Fearful that this might lead to control by Farley of the New York delegation to the Democratic national convention in 1944, the ALP decided to run its own candidate. It tried just about everyone else it could think of—Tugwell, Berle, Willkie, La Guardia, McGoldrick and even Dorothy Thompson—before it persuaded Dean Alfange to make the run. In October, the Amalgamated Clothing Workers, whose representatives had not had a part in this decision, endorsed Bennett, who by this time had also received the blessing of FDR. The ALP vote of 398,466, however, was not what defeated Bennett, who got 1,510,180, to 2,120,454 for Republican Thomas E. Dewey. Possibly a Democratic candidate more suitable to the ALP might have won.

In 1938, Communist participation in the ALP was approximately 12 per cent, according to an analysis of the vote received by the CP's only candidate that year—Israel Amter, running for representative at large. This survey was made by Stephen Beisman Sarasohn, who wrote *The Struggle for Control of the American Labor Party, 1936-1948*, as a master's essay in political science, at Columbia University in 1948. Nevertheless, charges of Communist domination were made by Louis Waldman, head of the Social Democratic Federation and, after the Hitler-Stalin pact of Aug. 23, 1939, the left-right issue became predominant in the ALP, as it did in a great many other organizations. Hillman and Dubinsky called a citywide conference on Sept. 30, 1939 and, by a 605 to 94 vote, a resolution was passed, roundly denouncing and condemning the "brazen conduct" of the Soviet Union. Less than a week later, on Oct. 6, 1939, the left wing outlasted the right at a New York County Committee meeting. It took some court action and another convention, however, before the left wing won control, by a 455 to 314 vote. Eugene Connolly became county chairman, but the real leader was Vito Marcantonio, a former Republican congressman, defeated in 1936,

196

who joined the ALP in 1937 and returned to Congress in 1938 as its candidate. Because of the constitutional setup, whereby each assembly district of the state had five members on the State Central Committee, from then on the state organization continued in the control of the right-wingers while the left-wingers were on top in New York City. In addition to Connolly, at this time Marc's chief lieutenants were Joseph Curran, president of the National Maritime Union, and Michael Quill, president of the Transport Workers of America. The former resigned in 1946 as chairman of the Greater New York CIO Council and as an ALP vice chairman, and became a leader in the purge of left-wingers in the CIO, which Philip Murray was getting under way. Quill stuck with the ALP until March, 1948, of which more later.

In June, 1940, the left-controlled New York County Committee of the ALP denounced FDR for allegedly abandoning the New Deal, and in September left-wingers walked out of the New York State CIO convention, when it endorsed Roosevelt. The April 2, 1940 ALP primary was a right-left struggle for control of the state committee, which would select the Presidential electors. At the state convention, on Sept. 14 at Utica, the vote was 442 to endorse FDR and Henry Wallace, as against 234 for "no candidate" and 11 for Norman Thomas. In November, FDR's plurality in New York State was 211,725; he got 417,409 ALP votes.

In 1941, the New York City ALP was getting ready to run Marcantonio for Mayor on a peace ticket against La Guardia, because of the latter's support of FDR's program of aid to the allies. And then, on June 22, 1941, the Nazis invaded the Soviet Union and, bingo, everything changed overnight! On Jan. 23, 1941, the Greater New York CIO Council, of which Curran was chairman, had attacked the lend-lease program as engendering "a blackout of civil liberties and suppression of organized labor and other free American institutions." On July 17, it urged "complete aid to all countries which fight fascism to the end that fascism or the threat of fascism be wiped off the earth."

On May 19, 1944, the right wing, led by Dubinsky and the ILGWU, quit the ALP and formed the Liberal party. It also endorsed FDR, and in November the President received 2,479,677 Democratic votes in New York; 584,594 ALP votes; and 320,331 Liberal votes.

In June, 1945, William O'Dwyer accepted ALP endorsement for Mayor; but Edward J. Flynn, Democratic leader in the Bronx, ordered all Democratic candidates in his bailiwick to decline such endorsements, presumably because of the ALP's left-wingishness. Flynn opposed O'Dwyer's nomination as the Democratic candidate. O'Dwyer got 1,119,225 votes, of which 259,368 were American Labor party.

With the Dubinsky group gone, the Amalgamated group soon became the right wing of the ALP, in control of the upstate committeemen, whereas the left wing of Marcantonio and Quill was stronger in New York City. And that is the way it was when the executive board of the New York State CIO met on Sept. 3, 1947, in Albany, amid rumors that the Amalgamated was about to fight continued endorsement of the ALP. The vote, however, was to continue endorsement by a 4 to 1 mar-

197

gin, with Amalgamated voting with the majority. More basic was the long wrangle over American foreign policy. The right wanted a resolution to endorse the Marshall Plan, condemn all forms of totalitarianism and abolish the veto in the United Nations Security Council. The left wanted to condemn the Truman Doctrine, but receded to a willingness to stand on the foreign policy resolution adopted by the national CIO convention in 1946 at Atlantic City, which called on the United States to stop stockpiling atom bombs, renew Big Three meetings, sever diplomatic relations with Franco Spain and withhold financial aid to Chiang Kai-shek.

Two days later, the fight shifted to Saratoga Springs, where the state CIO convention began. The vote to continue support of the ALP was overwhelming and, after three days of wrangling, a compromise resolution on United States foreign policy condemned "excessive use of the veto power" in the UN Security Council and urged that a veto be subject to overriding by three-fourths of a General Assembly vote. The United States was urged to assume the leadership in seeking world peace.

That the Amalgamated would quit the ALP if the ALP decided to go along with any national third party movement in 1948 was well known to Wallace, Baldwin and other future Progressive party leaders at the time. In October, 1947, two ALP leaders in the Bronx and one in Queens resigned, charging undue Communist influence. One of them, Charles Rubinstein, president of the United Civic Association of the Bronx, said:

"There is a group within the party that applauds a Henry Wallace when he attacks the policies of the Democratic Administration and applauds a Senator Morse when he criticizes the Republicans, but will not tolerate criticism of their leader. Who are these people? I have a right to believe that they are misguided Communist sympathizers. They must learn to hear the truth about themselves. I believe they should function solely within the Communist party. They have no more moral right to intrude into any other political party than they would have to intrude into our private homes."

On Nov. 3, 1947, Alex Rose, Liberal party, jubilantly announced that both Earl Browder and William Z. Foster were enrolled members of the ALP, which was then cooperating with the Republicans in support of a judicial candidate.

If all of this proves nothing else, it certainly demonstrates the validity of the old saw about politics making strange bedfellows. When I became a Democratic candidate for Congress in 1944, an old party leader gave me this advice: "In politics there are sons-of-bitches and sons-of-bitches, but as long as they're *your* sons-of-bitches, they're all right." Asked why he didn't repudiate Communist support in 1936, Joseph R. McCarthy remarked, "They can vote, can't they?"

By August, 1947, there began to be circulated all over the United States "A Message of Greeting and Support to Henry A. Wallace." It began, "We salute you for your leadership in the cause of America's peace and economic well being. You are the true spokesman for the millions of liberals who are now uniting to demand a return to the program of the late Franklin D. Roosevelt," and concluded, "you are the logical leader for the new grouping of liberals which is now taking place spontaneously, whatever its eventual form may be. We pledge our support to you in the effort to restore liberalism to the domestic and foreign policy of the United States." I have no idea how many hundreds of thousands of these statements were signed, or whether or how they were delivered to Mr. Wallace. Gathering signatures, however, helped the PCA to build organizationally and to create a valuable mailing list.

As he was leaving the Mutual Broadcasting Company studios on Sept. 10, 1947, following an informal interview by Leland Stowe under United Electrical Workers auspices, Henry Wallace was asked if his program remarks should be interpreted to mean he intended to stay in the Democratic party and try to reform it. He replied, "Yes, that is exactly what it does mean." On the air he had said he did not necessarily favor a third party.

The next night, Sept. 11, 1947, the day before the first anniversary of the speech which had led to his dismissal from the Cabinet, Henry Wallace returned to the Madison Square Garden scene of that speech. He told 19,000 persons inside and 6,000 more, who listened in the streets to loudspeakers, at a PCA-sponsored "Progressive Counter-Attack" rally: "I wish that what I said a year ago could be out-of-date by this time. But unfortunately we have made no progress in coming to an understanding with Russia. We now have a clearly defined policy for the Near East, but it is a policy for war, not peace. We have accepted the bankrupt and bankrupting British policies in Greece and Turkey."

In this speech Wallace charged that Herbert Hoover had been influential in formulating the Truman Administration foreign policy. "Forty-six days after the death of Franklin Roosevelt," he said, "Herbert Hoover was welcomed to the White House. Two years later, it is Hoover's thinking which guides our foreign policy. In February of this year, Mr. Hoover went to Germany as a special investigator for President Truman. Today his report, urging the rebuilding of German industry, is the very core of our entire program for European reconstruction. It is a program which is a direct contradiction of the Potsdam agreement."

Wallace assailed "a psychosis about communism, which has been carefully nurtured by men whose great fear is not communism but democracy." He made two points about communism:

First—we can't suppress ideas with force or legislation. If we try, we automatically express a lack of confidence in the give-and-take of the democratic process. We show that we lack faith in our ability to make *our* system produce abundantly.

Secondly—if we believe it is impossible to live in the world with communism, we are accepting the inevitability of suicidal war.

The closest he came to announcing his own intentions was, "Today I say that if the Democratic party is a war party, if my party continues to attack civil liberties, if both parties stand for high prices and depression—then the people must have a new party of liberty and peace. The people must have a choice."

Fiorello La Guardia was prevented, by the illness which caused his death ten days later, from introducing Wallace. Instead, he sent a message, read by Ira Hirschmann, highly laudatory of Wallace. La Guardia also wrote:

> The American people have been caught unaware. They have lost control of their government. We are back in the old days of trusts, big money and predatory wealth. The New Deal initiated by Franklin D. Roosevelt is for the moment dead. . . . A two party system with one platform is just about as bad as a one party system with no platform. This does not mean that there must necessarily be a third party. It does mean that a third party must be ever ready in reserve.

And those were just about La Guardia's last public words.

Frank Kingdon, now firmly established as the No. 2 man on every Wallace program, called for a "second party, a people's party." Aubrey Williams lamented the prosecution of Carl Marzani, former State Department employee; the House Committee on Un-American Activities' probe of the Joint Anti-Fascist Refugee Committee; and the Truman loyalty order. He called for the defense of the civil liberties of Communists, saying, "Collaboration with reactionaries anywhere is the shortest road to fascism." Lena Horne deplored Jim-Crowism in Washington; Canada Lee read a eulogy of the late Brig. Gen. Evans Carlson, by Michael Blankfort; Paul Robeson gave the first public reading of Langston Hughes' ballad "Freedom Train"; J. Raymond Walsh spoke; and the audience passed resolutions urging repeal of the Taft-Hartley act, admission of Jewish refugees into Palestine and a price rollback. John Randolph was the narrator.

Wallace's Madison Square Garden speech was a preview of a series to follow, along the Eastern Seaboard, until Oct. 17, when he departed for his second foreign trip of the year; this time he went to Palestine, with a stop in Rome on the return trip, which brought him back to New York on Nov. 4. The principal speeches were delivered as follows: Sept. 19—Philadelphia; Sept. 20—Camden and Trenton; Sept. 22—Boston, to the United Electrical Workers convention; Sept. 30—Boston area; Oct. 1—Soldiers Field, Cambridge; Oct. 2—Pittsfield, Mass.; Oct. 3—Springfield, Mass.; Oct. 8—New Haven; Oct. 10—Providence; Oct. 15—Baltimore.

Everywhere he went, the reception was the same as it had been in the spring. The largest available auditoriums were sold out in advance and overflow crowds listened to loud speakers in the street, and besieged Wallace at luncheons, receptions and on the street. With Dr. Frank Kingdon acting as fund raiser, those who paid their way to get in emptied their pockets before they got out. W. E. Mullins summarized the Boston Arena and other Boston area speeches in his "As I See It" column, in the Republican *Boston Herald,* for Oct. 2, 1947: "The damage being done President Truman by Henry Wallace's political circus must be devastating."

Mullins commented on the nature of the support Wallace was obtaining:

> The Wallace gatherings are certainly cosmopolitan. The first impression is that they are composed of overalled workmen, minority groups whose lineages are easily recognizable and confused college boys. This is not the fact. There are these readily recognizable groups and there are also professors, well-dressed men and women of cultured and refined backgrounds and persons obviously in the professional fields. If they continue they surely will destroy Truman and they make no secret of their intention to accomplish this objective.

Appearing with Wallace, at different times during this fall series of speeches, were Paul Robeson, Paul Draper, Canada Lee and Zero Mostel. Wherever he went, local celebrities appeared on the platform for him. J. W. Gitt, publisher of the *York* (*Pa.*) *Gazette & Daily,* for instance, "brought down the house" in Philadelphia with a one-sentence introduction of Wallace, "I'm sure nobody came here to hear me make a speech." Between his Camden and Trenton speeches the next day, Wallace spoke to several hundred at Applebrook Farm: the Deal, N. J. country estate of Mrs. Elinor Gimbel. At Cambridge, Prof. Harlow Shapley arranged a dinner meeting at the Harvard Faculty Club. At Lowell, Mass., Albert J. Fitzgerald, national UE president, was on the program.

At Philadelphia, Wallace took cognizance of increasing ADA and similar support for Truman when he said, "Every day now, 'headline names' announce their support for the Administration. But 'headline names' won't determine the results at the polls in November, 1948." In that speech Wallace upbraided Truman for having sent orders Sept. 16 from the battleship *Missouri,* on which he was returning from Brazil where he had addressed the closing session of the Inter-American Conference for the Maintaining of Continental Peace and Security, directing that James V. Forrestal be sworn in immediately as national defense secretary because of "an international emergency." Wallace stated: "The President refused to discuss the emergency. I insist that if there is a genuine emergency this action rates as the very lowest method of breeding fear. It is not a technique which will melt Russian stubbornness. It will certainly not endear us to peace-loving people anywhere in the world."

At Trenton, Wallace defended the right of Communists "to express their beliefs unless they seek to overthrow this nation." At Mrs. Gimbel's place, he said, "You don't get peace planning for war." At Camden, he meant Sen. Ralph Flanders (Rep., Vt.) when he said, "When the men who would fight communism talk about necessary unemployment, they are not fighting communism, they are breeding it," and he called a recent suggestion by Sen. Robert A. Taft that Americans eat less "not American." He summarized: "The right to starve isn't something to be defended and the right to a job isn't something that is interference with the rights of an individual."

About one-fifth of the 1,000 delegates to the United Electrical Workers convention did not applaud, when Wallace criticized the minority's leader James Carey, former UE president and then CIO secretary-treasurer, for having charged the union with being Communist-led. Wallace told the convention that the real world crisis was "not on the Greek border but in American grocery stores." He advocated a special session of Congress to restore rationing and price controls.

The ammunition he was allegedly giving communism, Wallace said at Cambridge, on Oct. 1, 1947, was "not in the criticism but in the policies and conditions which I criticize." In speech after speech, Wallace lamented what he called a fictitious anti-Soviet fear campaign and pleaded against infringements of civil liberties at home. He talked of his own strong Christian upbringing and pleaded for tolerance and brotherhood. He said his original hopes, that the so-called Marshall Plan indicated a reversal of American foreign policy, had been diminished as the Truman Doctrine remained "the basis of our foreign policy." He regretted, however, that the Soviet Union had not chosen to participate in the plan.

Robert Kenny, who had just flown in from the West Coast, told the Boston press that Wallace definitely was a candidate in Oregon, Washington and California.

"If it's a choice between Tweedledum and Tweedle Dewey," Kenny said, "the Democrats would stay home and not vote."

"Did you say Tweedle Tru and Tweedle Dewey?" a reporter asked.

"I said very carefully Tweedledum," Kenny replied, while Wallace grinned.

When he arrived in Boston, about 10 p.m. on Monday, Sept. 29, Wallace was greeted by so many hundred supporters that he temporarily became lost from his followers. A PCA luncheon the following noon—an invitational affair—had to be moved to a larger hotel room than originally planned; instead of the original 100 expected, 500 came. Angus Cameron, editor at Little, Brown & Co., was in charge, with Professors Alan M. Butler and Howard Mumford Jones of Harvard at the speakers' table. Wrote Mrs. Marjorie Lansing, executive secretary of the Massachusetts PCA, in an informal report at the time:

> Mr. Wallace received a beautiful ovation as he walked up
> to the speakers' dais. The guests at this luncheon were
> primarily old Boston families, known as "Brahmins": in-
> tellectuals drawn from Harvard, MIT, Boston University,
> publishing houses, writers and business people. They were
> not rank and file PCA people—canvassers—who were
> to come to the Arena that evening . . . I was happy
> chuckling over a contribution of $50 from a woman who
> had telephoned before the luncheon that she wanted to

hear Mr. Wallace, but she was sure she wouldn't like him. This Beacon Hill grand dame struck me as a test case for Mr. Wallace's appeal.

Frank Kingdon raised $5,200 that noon.

At the University of Massachusetts—an all-GI school of 1800— the next day, "the scene in Greylock gymnasium was a typical campus post-war note. All the GIs were packed in this gym, plus their wives, babies and dogs. Students were literally hanging from the rafters, listening to the words of the former Vice President." During the day of Oct. 1, 1947, Mr. Wallace was chauffeured by a representative of the mayor of Lowell, who insisted on a detour past his own home, so that Mr. Wallace could have his picture taken with him and his family, while the neighbors, mostly of Greek descent, jammed the streets to watch. The night before, Wallace had had a rapid conversation in Spanish with a night club entertainer at his hotel.

During the AVC-sponsored Cambridge meeting a weird looking character dressed in a long coat decorated with hammer and sickle and carrying a bear's head mask which had fallen off suddenly jumped over the fence into the field. He was promptly chased away by police but not until Wallace wondered why his sober remarks seemed to be causing amusement.

A hard-working PCAer from Brookline took two days off to drive Wallace across the state and back, explaining, when Wallace asked how he could be away from work, that "because of the serious state of the world today" he couldn't afford not to do so. About halfway to Pittsfield, on Oct. 2, the car was stopped by state police, who thought it was going too fast. It turned out that these police were supposed to be escorting the Wallace party, which from then on they did.

In Pittsfield occurred one of the few instances when his close associates believed they saw Henry Wallace on the verge of tears. It was occasioned by the third installment of "The Morgenthau Diaries," by Henry Morgenthau Jr., which appeared that day in the Oct. 11, 1947 issue of *Collier's*. In it, the former New Deal Secretary of the Treasury told of the circumstances under which Franklin D. Roosevelt had recognized the Soviet Union diplomatically in 1933. One paragraph of the magazine story read:

> Opposition came, also, strangely enough, from Henry Wallace who called on the President late in October in order to express his fears about the "religious effect" recognition would have on the country. That conversation left the President thoroughly puzzled. Wallace, he told me later the same day, "is a kind of mystic."

In an earlier installment, in the Sept. 27, 1947, issue of *Collier's*, Morgenthau had written: "Wallace's whole theory of spending in order to reduce agricultural production always seemed nonsense to me." In an installment to come, in the Oct. 24, 1947 issue of the magazine, he was to quote FDR as saying he never could understand what Wallace was talking about when he spoke on economic matters, and to reveal that it was Wallace who persuaded him, as Secretary of the Treasury, to put on the dollar bill a seal showing the Great Pyramid with a Latin motto, "Nocus Ordo Seclorum," which might be freely translated as "New Deal." Morgenthau added: "It was not till later I learned that the pyramid—taken from the obverse side of the Great Seal of the United States—had some cabalistic significance for members of a small religious sect." Morgenthau called Wallace "a puzzling figure," and "not in those days one of the militant liberals of the Administration."

On Jan. 27, 1945, when Wallace's confirmation as Secretary of Commerce was in the balance, Morgenthau had issued a public statement saying, "He is in the truest American tradition a Yankee businessman, with the horse sense to recognize that we are living in a world of change. I know that Henry Wallace made a genuine contribution to good government and free enterprise as Secretary of Agriculture. I believe he can make an even greater contribution as Secretary of Commerce."

This statement, however, Morgenthau neglected to include in his *Collier's* articles. Neither did he quote from his speech of Feb. 22, 1945, when he addressed a dinner meeting of the National Council of American-Soviet Friendship at the Waldorf-Astoria Hotel, on an occasion celebrating the 27th anniversary of the Russian Red Army. At that time, Morgenthau didn't sound too different from Henry Wallace when he said: "The true secret weapon of this war has been the development between us and our allies of a great and enduring coalition. Hitler must be demented indeed if he still hopes to disrupt the coalition we have forged against him . . . The death knell for any such hope was tolled resoundingly at Yalta in the Crimea. There the leading statesmen of the world's three greatest powers demonstrated again that the unity created by the war is to endure even beyond it and us to serve as the bulwark of the future peace."

In Pittsfield, Henry Wallace sat dejectedly on the edge of his bed, obviously grieved at what his former New Deal partner had written about him. He said he had never been close to Morgenthau personally, but he didn't believe Morgenthau would do something like that to him. He described Morgenthau as possessed of a one-track mind, with no great grasp of ideas.

To an audience of 1,500 at Pittsfield, a tremendous turnout for a place of that size, Wallace advocated precinct political action to fight for world peace, and urged patience and tolerance upon the nation's policy makers. He also spoke at the General Electric shop gate and was the house guest of Leon Mohill, prominent businessman.

The next day, enroute to Springfield for an evening meeting, Wallace spoke to 2,500 Smith College students at Northampton and a full house of Mt. Holyoke College students at South Hadley. In several of his New England speeches, Wallace quoted Thomas Jefferson as saying, "The man who never looks into a newspaper is better informed than he who reads them; inasmuch as he who knows nothing is nearer to truth than he whose mind is filled with falsehoods and errors." He also frequently quoted James Stewart Martin, former American decartelization chief in Germany, that "within a period of two years U.S. policies for the treatment of Germany have changed their course by 180 degrees. Now in all important respects they coincide with what the German financiers, industrialists and politico-militarists have wanted us to do, ever since they surrendered."

And he ended most of his speeches:

We can have peace.

We must have peace.

We shall have peace.

Henry Wallace spent the weekend with Paul Sweezy at Manchester, Vt., and on Tuesday, Oct. 8, 1947, spoke at New Haven. According to the next day's *New Haven Register:* "It was a mixed crowd and unusual for a political gathering in many respects. Young people, including many Yale students, middle class New-Haveners and a generous sprinkling of intellectuals from many parts of the state made up the audience in proportion as listed. Industrial workers were a small minority."

The description of the money-raising part of the program was typical of what amazed but unconverted reporters in other places had written:

> Dr. Kingdon, using the money-raising technique of the revivalist rostrum, exhorted contributions "to organize Connecticut for Wallace." He started out with a plea for one thousand dollars. In less time than it takes to write a check, an usher hurried to the platform and handed one to one of the four girls stationed there. Reporters asked the name and address of the $1,000 donor but were denied the information.

> It was like an auction in reverse. Instead of building up the figure, it was lowered. No other $1,000 contributions were announced. Nothing came in at $500, or $400. David Fishman gave $300. When the figure reached $250 the dam broke. For half an hour the money actually poured in, with Dr. Kingdon who had previously exhorted the audience to "Fight! Fight! Fight!" now imploring them to "Give! Give! Give!"

> Then Kingdon asked 3,000 to stand with each person holding $1 over his or her head. Two photographers, unknown to New Haven newsmen, were called to the platform. It was announced that they would take pictures which, according to Kingdon, would "appear in all the New Haven papers." Such pictures, of course, would show those who were giving the extra $1, and also those who were seated. This psychology brought additional scores to their feet. Flashlight bulbs exploded.

That looked like the end of the collection drive, which was now getting boresome to those who came solely to hear Wallace. But it wasn't. Ushers passed containers to scoop up any small change available.

About $11,800 was raised that night, in addition to the approximately $6,000 from the sale of tickets.

Wallace began his New Haven speech by reminding the audience that he lived only a few miles from the Connecticut border and often shopped in the state; the newly enacted Connecticut 3 per cent sales tax had caused his wife to lose her enthusiasm to do so, he said. Then Wallace praised Connecticut's Chester Bowles, saying he had been proved right as OPA head in opposing the lifting of Government controls after V-J Day. Fiorello La Guardia was also right in advocating international relief, with no strings attached because of political reasons, either through UNRRA, which he headed, or some similar UN agency. Wallace deplored wheat conservation in this country while Europeans lacked bread. He advocated shipping abroad 100 million bushels of wheat, chiefly to France and Italy.

Wallace commented on "the big news of the week": the announcement that the Communist parties of nine European nations were going to have a clearing house for the exchange of information at Belgrade. He said he did not know whether, as charged by some, this meant a restoration of the Comintern. "The significant thing," he said, "is that the new organization tells us which way the wind is blowing. Trygve Lie said that the great discussions on the veto question were symptoms, not a cause. So it is also with this new international Communist organization. This is the most unmistakable symptom we have had yet of the split between the United States and Russia, which has become a worldwide disease . . . As long as the disease continues, the symptoms will get worse and worse. The internal life of both countries will be poisoned."

He made virtually the same statement at a testimonial dinner to Sen. Claude Pepper on Oct. 12, sponsored by the American Slav Congress, at the Hotel Pennsylvania. Pepper himself called for a year's moratorium in the United States on "all name calling and all irreconcilable issues." He advocated total disarmament and an American advance of $50 billion in five years to the U.N.

Two days earlier, ADA had publicly declared, regarding the establishment of the new Communist agency in Belgrade, "The Communist declaration is a challenge to Henry A. Wallace, to open-minded members of the PCA and to every American liberal to speak out on this vital issue." The statement was signed by Wilson Wyatt, Leon Henderson, Franklin D. Roosevelt Jr. and Hubert Humphrey.

The same day, also, the report of a special Congressional Committee on Foreign Aid, headed by Rep. Christian Herter (Rep., Mass.), was made public. After six weeks of study in 18 European countries, the 19-member committee reported general agreement that the need for economic relief was great in France, Italy, Germany and Austria, but that it had differences within its ranks as to whether stop-gap emergency assistance or a long range program, such as proposed by Secretary Marshall, was better. Most of the committee minimized the danger of a totalitarian sweep of Western Europe.

During his press conference on Oct. 10, 1947 at Providence, Wallace was asked to comment on the Morgenthau revelation that Wallace had opposed diplomatic recognition of the Soviet Union in 1933. He replied that he had been "shocked" by the ruthless manner in which the Soviets had achieved their collectivization program. "But," he added, "looking back on the whole situation, if Russia had not done it, the United States would probably be a German dependency today." Replying to a question regarding Russia's current intentions, he said, "I don't hold either with the reactionary capitalists who want world government in their name or with the Communists who want world government in their names"; a statement which crept into more than one of his speeches.

Near the end of his address on Oct. 15, 1947, to a packed Fifth Regiment Armory in Baltimore, Wallace interpolated a comment to retract a statement he had made at his press conference that morning, regarding *Speaking Frankly,* James F. Byrnes' book, which had been published the day before by Harper. His original statement had been to the effect that he was impressed by the peaceful tone of the former Secretary of State's comments.

> Since then, Wallace told his audience of 8,000, I have read certain parts of the book in which he (Byrnes) said, if other methods fail, he is in favor of building bigger and better atom bombs to drive the Russians from Germany.
>
> It is this point which is the heart of the bipartisan bloc which accounted for my being fired from the Cabinet.
>
> I want to make it clear that is still the point with which I disagree.

In his address he rapped business interests that were supporting the get-tough policy, while they were also profiting handsomely from it. "The very interests who are today supporting a foreign policy which has been backed with appropriations of $25 billion for armaments helped kill subsidies which kept food prices down during the war. Those subsidies cost $2 billion a year. Since June, 1946 when price control ended, American families have seen $10 billion—an average of five dollars a week for each family—added to the grocery bill."

He rapped Wall Streeters, the "eat less" program, the killing of UNRRA and the influence of Herbert Hoover.

In the morning Wallace had spoken to 200, under the auspices of the Citizens Committee for Justice, in the Enon Baptist Church. He made a ringing denunciation of racial segregation and announced he had canceled a speaking engagement scheduled for Nov. 15 in Little Rock, Ark., because local authorities there insisted that the meeting be Jim-Crow.

207

At noon Wallace spoke to an outdoor meeting of Johns Hopkins students, saying, among other things, that General Eisenhower might make a good President, under certain conditions. His opinion seemed to stem mostly from his high regard for the general's brother Milton, president of Kansas State college, whom he described as "one of the smartest cookies you ever saw." Evidently referring to the fact Johns Hopkins authorities had refused the suggestion that Wallace be invited to be an assembly speaker, he said, "Considering the nature of their financial foundations, I never blame the president of a great educational institution. He's got to be true to his bread." This was a favorite Wallace expression.

Simultaneously with Wallace's appearance on the campus, there appeared a statement by him in the undergraduate newspaper, the *Newsletter,* commenting upon the welcoming speech which Dr. Isaiah Bowman, president, had made on Sept. 29 to incoming students. Dr. Bowman had declared that the Soviet Union was a worse dictatorship than Hitler's Germany had been and little different from Czarist Russia. According to Wallace, the president was "either exhibiting ignorance or deliberately contributing" to the perpetuation of misconceptions. "One need not accept socialism or condone dictatorship to make honest appraisals of Russia," he said. "It is frightening to hear an educator advance the theory that you can contain ideas by force. . . . The greatest danger in the world today is not conflicting ideologies but the perpetuation of ignorance. Dr. Bowman has made a distinguished contribution to that end."

The *Baltimore Sun,* whose reporter, Howard Norton, covered more Wallace meetings in 1947 and 1948 than any other newspaperman in America, started its story of Wallace's day in Baltimore on page 36 and continued it on page 10, a "jump" practice not common with newspapers but characteristic of the *Sun.*

Two days later, accompanied by Michael Straight, publisher of the *New Republic;* Lewis Frank, Jr., member of the magazine's staff and Wallace's principal speech writer; and Gerold Frank, Zionist authority, Henry Wallace departed from La Guardia airport for Palestine, "to see whether in any way my knowledge of agriculture and industry would tend to facilitate the cause of peace in the Near East." At the airport, he told reporters:

"If the bipartisan policy is being followed by both parties then they are clearly parties of war. There will be a party of peace and I will cooperate and support it to the fullest of my ability. I look upon the bipartisan approach as laying the foundation for potential war."

The *New Republic* was the sole sponsor of the trip.

# ¶11 TRIPS TO PALESTINE AND THE AMERICAN SOUTH. *After a peaceful fortnight abroad, Henry Wallace attempted to promote the cause of civil liberties, then under serious many-pronged attack, by defying Jim Crow in Dixie.*

The idea for Henry A. Wallace's trip to Palestine in October, 1947 originated with Michael Straight, publisher of the *New Republic,* of which the former Vice President was editor.

In view of the international debate that was being waged at the time, concerning the political future of the Holy Land, the trip was a legitimate journalistic enterprise. On Sept. 3, 1947, a special United Nations commission had recommended a plan of partition to create independent Jewish and Arab states. On Oct. 11, 1947, in the UN Political Committee, the United States had accepted partition in principle, but with reservations. During the preceding year, there had been considerable wrangling over alleged sabotage of the report of an Anglo-American Commission of Inquiry which recommended admittance of 100,000 European Jewish refugees into Palestine "as rapidly as conditions permit." Bartley Crum, an American member of the commission, in his *Behind the Silken Curtain* (Simon & Schuster, 1947), bitterly criticized both the British and certain elements in the American State Department for delay in carrying out the commission's recommendations.

Straight's motive, however, was not merely to cover journalistically one of the world's most important news stories. He thought getting his illustrious editor physically out of the country would "slow things up, provide a cooling-off period, help get Wallace back to a consideration of basic principles and off domestic issues, including political ones." At first he had encountered opposition from PCA leaders, who had been stage-managing most of Wallace's activities during the preceding six months, in what was apparent to everyone was an attempt to build him up as a candidate for the Presidency in 1948. It was the anticipation of the financial donations which Wallace probably would be able to obtain from American Jewish sources upon his return from Palestine that led the PCA leaders to acquiesce to the plan for the trip.

The whirlwind barnstorming in which Wallace had engaged, in both the spring and early fall, had not been exactly what Straight anticipated when he agreed, early in the year, that Wallace should become active on the platform as well as in the editor's cubicle. He had approved the European trip on which he accompanied Wallace as a speech writer, but when the American tour which followed it became such an unprecedented personal political success, he began to be alarmed. Today, Straight frankly admits he didn't know what to think at the time. When Wallace was dismissed from the Cabinet, Straight had flown to Washington immediately, to persuade him to become editor of the *New Republic*. Wallace's acceptance of this offer was a great triumph for Straight, as Wallace rejected numerous other offers and refused to take more than his Cabinet salary of $15,000, although Straight was prepared to offer more.

Subscriptions to the *New Republic* increased, but never anywhere near enough to defray extra expenses. The "plugs" which the magazine obtained from the platform at Wallace rallies often were perfunctory or forgotten, and the press frequently overlooked the co-sponsorship that the *New Republic* provided. Young Mike almost had to stand at the door and hand out sample copies, to obtain any benefit from the shows.

Some of the mass meetings also frightened Straight, as they did some others, who couldn't help recalling the newsreels they had seen, not many years before, of frenzied crowds at Nuremberg. A timid suggestion to Wallace that, if his crusade in opposition to the Truman Administration was to assume political form, he should pay more attention to organizational problems was ignored. Straight thought that if Wallace was thinking of running for President, he should get himself "a Jim Farley" and control the setting up of local groups dedicated to his cause. "Otherwise," he told HAW, "all kinds of Wallace clubs will spring up and you won't have any control over them."

At the end of the spring, 1947 trip, Wallace asked Straight to tell him what Communists, if any, had been prominent in promoting his meetings. Straight was unable to do so; all he could do was indicate which rallies had had broad and which narrow sponsorship.

In getting Wallace away for a fortnight in October, Straight hoped for the opportunity to talk the entire situation over quietly with him. He looked forward to the long plane ride over the ocean, but when the party of four was aboard he found himself seated next to Gerold Frank, Middle Eastern authority, who had ghosted Crum's book, whereas Wallace sat with Lewis Frank Jr. (no relation). That chance missed, Straight looked for another on the return trip. The best he could do, however, was a few comments to Lew Frank to indicate he was alarmed, as the plane was settling in the bay at Athens. These remarks were so casual that Lew doesn't even remember them. Quite obviously, Straight was too overwhelmed by timidity to be able to talk to his editor, either in the air over the Atlantic, in New York, or anywhere else. Several persons who have known him for years have volunteered psychiatric diagnoses of the young publisher, but I doubt their pertinence here. To explain his timidity, this fact would be enough: here was a 29-year-old, inexperienced employer of a 59-year-old former Vice President of the United States who, he had eyewitness evidence, was considered almost as a savior by hundreds of thousands, if not millions, of persons all over the world.

Furthermore, Mike Straight didn't know his own mind at this time, as he saw the widespread enthusiasm and support for Wallace. Although his personal inclinations might have been toward ADA (Americans for Democratic Action), he also observed that the Progressive Citizens of America was proving itself a much more vigorous outfit. As indicated by the stand he had taken during Wallace's European trip early in the year, he was against the Truman Doctrine and his first reaction to the Marshall Plan was one of skepticism. He had been "catching hell" from a lot of his former friends in the Union for Democratic Action, predecessor to ADA, because of what Wallace was writing in his magazine. Strong anti-Wallace pressures also existed within his own staff. So much so that, at one point, William Harlan Hale, editor in charge of articles, resigned. This was in protest against Straight's continuing Wallace as a contributing editor from the time of his announcement— Dec. 29, 1947—that he would run, until late July, 1948—the time of the Progressive party nominating convention. In an article, "What Makes Wallace Run?" in the March, 1948 *Harper's,* Hale had his uncomplimentary say.

On April 1, 1948, Straight was reported to have told an audience of City College students that if Harry Truman were the Democratic candidate he would be for Wallace. By convention time, 1948, he was for Dwight Eisenhower to be the Democratic nominee. Having invested so heavily in Henry Wallace, however, he was, to state it conservatively, in an extremely awkward position. How could he repudiate Wallace publicly? He never did so, although some of his own magazine pieces, especially on the Marshall Plan, were actually answers to what Wallace was saying.

Henry Wallace's trip to the Mediterranean area did not stir up any furor comparable to that which had resulted from his spring trip to Europe. This was so largely because Wallace made few public appearances or statements. Instead, he spent his time visiting kibbutzim, studying agricultural problems and listening rather than talking. At Tel Aviv, Jerusalem and other places he met with labor leaders, politicians and others, but confined himself to such remarks as "I have long believed that there would never be peace in the world until there was peace here in Palestine," a quotation from a talk to the Jewish press association in Jerusalem.

Wallace arose early and worked in the fields with Jewish farmers. He joined in folk dancing in the villages. Thomas F. Reynolds wrote from Gaza, in an article which the *Chicago Sun* used in its Oct. 30, 1947 issue: "When you see a former Vice President of the United States in battered tennis shoes and dusty gray slack suit sampling the soil of the Palestine desert, you've seen everything." Reynolds said Wallace had come "back to the soil this week and was completely at home. . . . If he had been running for office in the Palestine desert he couldn't have looked more a country boy from Iowa or acted more completely the genuine role of world-famous agronomist and expert on Iowa corn and New Salem white leghorn pullets and hybrid strawberries. . . . The welcome being extended Wallace in this most tortured political spot in the Middle East is a strange phenomenon, indicating that while he is a prophet without a party following at home, his pleas in the United States for understanding Russia have captured the imagination of little people here."

When he left for home, Wallace pleaded with Jews and Arabs both to "abide faithfully by the ultimate decision of the United Nations."

In Jerusalem, he was treated courteously by the American consulate and at Rome was entertained at lunch by Ambassador James Dunn. Wallace had an audience with Pope Pius XII, but received no answer from the Pontiff to a pointed question, "What are you going to do for Palestine?" He did, however, obtain two rosaries blessed by the Pope. When he hesitated, upon being asked to choose between a black and white one, the Holy Father suggested that he take one of each.

Upon his arrival home, on Nov. 4, 1947, Wallace's first comment, at La Guardia field, was regarding the suicide the day before of John G. Winant, former Republican Governor of New Hampshire and more recently American Ambassador to Great Britain; his book, *Letter From Grosvenor Square* (Houghton Mifflin, 1947), had come off the press the same day. Farvue, the farm which Wallace owns near South Salem, N. Y., formerly was the Winant home. Said Wallace, "First of all I want to say that I was inexpressibly shocked by the death of John Winant. I counted him a close personal friend and a first class type of public servant."

Although Wallace's trip had been entirely a *New Republic* journalistic junket, the Progressive Citizens of America began capitalizing upon it immediately. On Nov. 5, 1947, the day after Wallace's return, it staged a dinner for 1,000 at the Hotel Astor, at which Wallace spoke on "World Peace and the Crisis in Palestine." He reported that his trip had convinced him that rank and file Arabs and Jews wanted to and could co-exist peacefully, "unless outside interests stir them up." He declared that a Jordan Valley authority, to provide cheap electric power, was badly needed and urged American help to establish it.

Henry Wallace's only important message to the United States while in the Middle East was a telegram to the two-day Conference on Cultural Freedom and Civil Liberties; this was held on Oct. 25-26, 1947 at New York's Hotel Commodore, under the auspices of the National Arts, Sciences and Professions Council of the PCA, with Dr. Harlow Shapley, Harvard University astronomer, as conference chairman. It read:

> From here where Elijah fought the prophets of Baal and close to the mount of Jesus' famous sermon, people without fear ask, "Has America really gone crazy?" Is the un-American committee evidence that America is traveling the road to fascism? On behalf of millions everywhere you must answer no so loudly the people of the world can hear. You must destroy the un-American committee at the polls and in the courts, or it will destroy many of the foundations of democracy and Christianity.

The conference, which attracted about 1,000 intellectuals, operated mostly by means of panels, at which the Truman loyalty program, Taft-Hartley, atomic secrecy, and, especially, the House Committee on Un-American Activities, were condemned by a number of nationally prominent speakers and in resolutions. The conference was timed to coincide with the Washington hearings of the Thomas-Rankin committee into communistic influences in the motion picture industry; these opened on Oct. 20, 1947, and ultimately led to the serving of prison sentences for contempt by ten Hollywood writers and directors, who refused to answer questions related to their political beliefs and affiliations.

"Make no mistake about it, ladies and gentlemen," O. John Rogge, former assistant United States attorney general, told the opening session, "what we have in our midst today is incipient fascism. . . . Sen. Claude Pepper did not go far enough when he advised Hollywood artists and writers to appear but to answer no questions pertaining to their private political beliefs or ideas. My advice to our Hollywood friends and to all others is not to appear at all." He explained his advice by declaring the un-American Activities Committee was operating unconstitutionally.

Rogge had been fired from his Department of Justice position when he was dramatically taken off an airplane at Spokane, Oct. 25, 1946, after he presumably "leaked" information that Nazi documents he had discovered in Germany in April-June, 1946 revealed that 24 members of Congress had collaborated with or been used by George Sylvester Viereck, German agent in the United States, for propaganda purposes. After strong complaints, especially by Sen. Burton Wheeler (Dem., Mo.), Attorney General Tom Clark, with President Truman's acquiescence, suppressed Rogge's report and discharged Rogge after he had made a few public speeches revealing some of the contents.

On Nov. 7, 1947, Rogge was to make news when he publicly charged that Attorney General Tom Clark's office had intentionally leaked to newspapers reports about the special federal grand jury then investigating subversive activities in southern New York. This, Rogge contended, was part of a scheme to build up the grand jury investigation into an "anti-Soviet witch hunt" which would culminate within ten days in a latter-day version of the Reichstag fire (which the Nazis set to win the 1934 election that brought them to power after they successfully blamed the fire on the Communists). Rogge revealed that there was planned a "dramatic round-up of dozens of Communist leaders and alleged fellow-travelers" to coincide with the beginning of the special session of Congress which President Truman had called to begin Nov. 17. This Rogge compared to the A. Mitchell Palmer raids following World War I. Rogge's reference to Pepper had been inspired by the Florida senator's public statement Oct. 21, 1947, that the Hollywood investigation might be "the Stalingrad in the attack on civil liberties in this country . . . I would advise witnesses to stand up and say, 'I am an American and it's none of your business what I think and what I write.'" At the same time Glen Taylor had called the committee "fascist minded" and said its activities "parallel those of pre-war leaders in Germany, Italy and Japan."

At the New York conference Robert W. Kenny, attorney for some of the Hollywood Ten, at that time 19, agreed with Rogge as to the Thomas-Rankin committee's unconstitutionality. He said its probe represented a "first step toward complete blackout of freedom of expression in this country."

It was at the Thomas-Rankin committee hearings that Adolphe Menjou testified subversive meanings can be put into a scene by "a glance, a voice inflection or a grimace" and defined a Communist as anyone who applauds the singing of Paul Robeson. Also it was there that Mrs. Lela Rogers, mother of the famous Ginger and a longtime red-chaser on the West Coast, said, "When my daughter was making 'Tender Comrade,' an RKO picture, she was given a line to read. Here's as close as I can recall it: 'Share and share alike—that's democracy.' I think that's definitely Communist propaganda."

For a day or two it was believed the Motion Picture Association, headed by Eric Johnston, was going to "stand up" to the committee and defend those who opposed its inquisition. Official Hollywood quickly capitulated, however, and fired the ten recalcitrant witnesses who pleaded no constitutional privilege but refused to answer questions which they said were outside the committee's authority to ask. They were cited for contempt Nov. 24, 1947, by a 346 to 37 vote of the House of Representatives and attempted through the courts for more than two years to win a reversal. May 29, 1950, the United States Supreme Court for the second and last time refused to review their cases, as well as those of several officers of the Joint Anti-Fascist Refugee Committee who had refused to submit their records for committee inspection mainly on the ground that to do so would jeopardize the safety of many former Spanish Loyalists and their families which the committee, an officially approved wartime relief agency, had aided. Ultimately Dr. Edward Barsky, president, Howard Fast, the novelist, Prof. Lyman R. Bradley of New York University and some others served penitentiary terms of from six months to one year. So did the Hollywood Ten, all of them men with brilliant records of achievement in their field.

When the motion picture producers decided not to defend the ten, a number of other Hollywood actors and officials were left "high and dry" in their attempt to be of assistance. At their own expense a group of 27 movie stars had flown to Washington to be observers at the hearings. They belonged to the recently-organized Committee for the First Amendment and they put on a dramatic hour radio program to relate their observations. Among the features was an imitation by Groucho Marx of Rep J. Parnell Thomas as he questioned friendly and unfriendly witnesses, and a statement by Thomas Mann, the Nobel prize winning author who had fled Hitler Germany, to the effect: "I have seen this happen before. This is the way Hitler started." Almost immediately thereafter the original group issued a public statement condemning the hearings and pressure began to be exerted. Humphrey Bogart and his wife, Lauren Bacall, were among the first to backslide, allegedly after being shown a copy of the *Daily Worker* in which they were praised. Almost simultaneously Danny Kaye canceled an Indiana University lecture sponsored by the American Veterans Committee. Most of the handful who held out against the pressure to retract their original stand suffered oblivion as far as their professional careers were concerned or further harassment by the same committee or other investigating groups. Or else they learned to recant, sometimes to grovel, or to act as informers.

The Hollywood blacklist soon reached about 300 and the capitulation was not entirely unexpected. When Johnston assumed his position, there had been received warning from a high official close to the White House that he could be expected to take orders from a certain group of bankers. The Warners, formerly considered personally liberal, had become embittered because of a long strike on their set the preceding year.

The PCA and the Committee for the First Amendment were not alone in condemning the Hollywood investigation. The New York chapter of ADA issued a statement, signed by 65 notable figures of the stage, screen and literature, charging, "Witch hunts are the methods of hysteria." Philip Murray wrote to Sen. Arthur Vandenberg and others to advocate the committee's abolition. The *New York Herald Tribune* editorialized, on Oct. 22, 1947: ". . . the beliefs of any ordinary men and women who write for the screen are, like the beliefs of any ordinary men and women, nobody's business but their own, as the Bill of Rights mentions." Many another newspaper commented similarly.

J. Parnell Thomas' answer, on Nov. 7, 1947, at Allendale, N. J., was to say his committee tactics were fair. He estimated that there were 100,000 dues-paying Communists in the United States, another 100,000 who followed the party line, and 2,000 or 3,000 more "bleeding hearts, the chief of whom is Henry Wallace." Two years later, Thomas was convicted of having defrauded the government in the operation of his office, through collection of salaries from payrollers who did nothing to earn them. He was sentenced to from six to 18 months and fined $10,000. He had served a little more than half of the maximum when he was pardoned by President Truman and was released, on June 8, 1950, contrary to the ruling of Federal Judge Alexander Holtzoff, without having paid the fine. In 1954 Thomas was overwhelmingly defeated in the Republican primary when he attempted to return to Congress. The vote was 32,405 for Rep. William B. Widnall, who pledged support to President Eisenhower, to 4,216 for Thomas, who supported Sen. Joseph McCarthy of Wisconsin.

The PCA started a nationwide petition campaign, to bring pressure on Congress to abolish the Committee on Un-American Activities—by passage of a resolution which Rep. Adolph Sabath (Dem., Ill.) had introduced on Jan. 10, 1947—and to vote against citing the "Hollywood 10" for contempt. Then its attention was diverted by a number of instances of interferences with the right to peaceful assembly, guaranteed in the First Amendment to the Constitution of the United States.

In the Spring, 1948 issue of *Public Opinion Quarterly* appeared an excellent eyewitness report, by Robert C. Myers of the Educational Testing Service; it described the mob action which prevented Gerhard Eisler, German Communist, from addressing a meeting on Oct. 26, 1947, in Contemporary Auditorium, Trenton, N. J. under the sponsorship of the Communist party of Mercer County. The meeting was to be held under a court injunction which countermanded a City Council order that it be stopped. Led by members of the Veterans Alliance, a mob of several hundred beat up a Newark couple representing the Civil Rights Congress, rushed the entrances and prevented anyone from speaking from the platform. Concluded Myers:

> The events of Oct. 26 were neither bizarre nor unique, but followed closely the patterns of mob behavior which have been outlined by psychologists and sociologists. They cannot, however, be called unimportant. Mounting international tensions, combined with the instability of certain social norms at home, provide a fertile soil for similar phenomena in other cities, and several such disturbances have occurred since the affair at Trenton.

The very next night, the Independent Citizens of New Jersey, a PCA affiliate, had scheduled a rally in the auditorium of the New Jersey State Teachers College in Jersey City. A week earlier, the local Catholic War Veterans had announced it would conduct a mass picketing demonstration against the rally; whereupon James Imbrie, chairman of the committee, appealed to Gov. Alfred Driscoll for state trooper protection. This aid was refused, but the veterans' group voluntarily called off a mass demonstration and only about 75 pickets showed up that night.

In a packed auditorium, 2,000 persons heard Dr. Frank Kingdon formally announce his candidacy for the Democratic nomination for United States Senator from New Jersey; this had previously been prophesied at more than one PCA rally, the first time being Sept. 20, 1947, at Camden. With Kingdon on the program was Paul Robeson. The turnout, Imbrie told the audience, was "the answer to Trenton," meaning that it showed Americans could not be deprived of their right to peaceful assembly.

One of the other disturbances which Myers undoubtedly had in mind was the near-riot which occurred on Saturday, Nov. 1, 1947, in Independence Square, Philadelphia. Although the 100 policemen on hand made only one arrest—of a Temple University student who threw some used flashlight bulbs—the stench bombs, noise from a siren on a Voiture No. 1 Forty and Eight engine and boxcar, and heckling by about one third of the approximately 1,200 present prevented virtually all speech-making. One of the intended speakers, Francis Fisher Kane, 81-year-old former U.S. attorney and winner a few years earlier of the Bok award as Philadelphia's outstanding citizen, was showered with missiles but not seriously injured.

In an open letter to Attorney General Clark, PCA Co-Chairmen Robert W. Kenny and Frank Kingdon declared:

> For many months we have warned that the witch hunt hysteria instigated by the Thomas Committee in Washington would lead to just such reverberations on the local level as occurred in Philadelphia and other cities in recent weeks. Until the Thomas Committee is abolished, its very existence will continue to be interpreted as the go-ahead sign for defamation of civil liberties throughout the nation.

A smaller-scale incident had occurred Oct. 13, 1947, in New York when military police raided a PCA party in a private apartment on a tip, presumably by an ADAer, that some soldiers in attendance were likely to become involved in a riot or disorder. In 1948 such occurrences were not infrequent.

On Friday evening, Nov. 7, 1947, there was a rousing housewarming in Princeton, N. J., where Frank Kingdon was establishing residence in order to be eligible to run for public office. The rent was being paid by the Independent Citizens of New Jersey. The next day, Henry Wallace and Beanie Baldwin left New York by train for St. Louis where, on Nov. 9, another speaking tour was to begin. Kingdon was to join them at Trenton and, when the train failed to stop at that station, it was feared he would be left behind. However, he was at the North Philadelphia station and in fine fettle for meetings: Nov. 9 in St. Louis, Nov. 10 in Pittsburgh, Nov. 12 in Cleveland and Nov. 13 in Cincinnati. Conflicting appointments then compelled him to return to New York, and he was replaced as money-raiser on Nov. 14 at Dayton by William S. Gailmor, former radio commentator.

In St. Louis' Kiel auditorium and Pittsburgh's Syria Mosque, Wallace gave the same speech, the only time of which I am aware that he followed that practice. His theme was the same as before, but the approach was fresh and the anecdotal material up to date. "I assert that we shall not get peace until the major powers prepare for peace," he said, and then charged the Wall-Streeters and military men in charge of the American government with promoting a foreign policy bound to lead to disaster. "Roosevelt had Wall Street men and military men working in government," he explained, *"but—*under Roosevelt, he ran the Wall Street men; they didn't run him."

Wallace took cognizance of the recent outbreaks of violence and the refusal of a hall in Newark for a lecture by Kingdon:

> The veterans and others who have taken part in these recent outbreaks are not so much the culprits as the victims. They are the people who have been poisoned by screaming headlines and the senseless repetition of fear words. They are the victims of an evil conspiracy directed by men who remain safely aloof from the mob violence they instigate. The pattern is not unfamiliar to those who witnessed the rise of fascism in Germany and Italy. I charge that the current anti-Communist and anti-Russian hysteria is being deliberately nurtured by men who fear democratic solutions of fundamental social and economic problems. They don't fear communism. They fear democracy!

Wallace scored Truman for having told a press conference, on Oct. 17, 1947, that rationing and price control are "police state methods," and added, "I insist that controls, democratically legislated, are a necessity and that the President's repetition of the NAM line is the most

217

damaging evidence of the extent to which the Administration has capitulated to Wall Street at home as well as abroad." Finally, Wallace reported on his Mediterranean trip: "I have visited foreign countries many times. Never before have I found such widespread suspicion of the purposes of the United States. Always I have come back to the United States feeling 'what a blessed land we have.' This time when I came back I took one look at the papers, and suddenly realized that the forces of black reaction had carried the United States perilously close to the Germany of 1932."

At a press conference in Pittsburgh, on Tuesday, Nov. 11, 1947, Wallace was asked the usual questions and gave the usual answers. He said he had not heard Dr. Kingdon the night before call him a "people's candidate for President" but gave his stock reply to questions regarding his relations with the Democratic party: "If it is clear that the Democratic party is a war party, there will have to be a peace party in the United States. If I can help that party in any way, I will." As to why he didn't criticize the Soviet Union more often he said:

> I have criticized it many times. Do you want me to engage in any special brand of Red-baiting? I believe that Red-baiting should be dampened down.
>
> I think both the United States and Russia have been out grabbing. They have been consolidating their positions. For that reason they haven't cared to talk final settlement [of the war]. But both have now grabbed as much as they can.

At least, that is what the *Pittsburgh Sun-Telegraph* quoted Wallace as saying. The next day, under the title, "Communists, Henry Wallace and 'Progressives'," the same newspaper editorialized:

"It does not follow that because a man may occasionally agree with a Communist he is a Communist . . . But when a man, or any group, consistently follows all of the party line, it is reasonable to suspect that there is more in it than mere coincidence."

The same day, the *Pittsburgh Post-Gazette* began its editorial on "Doc Wallace's Elixir":

"The Henry Wallace Medicine Show was literally a howling success. Before it left town, a surprising number of Pittsburghers had bought a bottle of old Doc Wallace's elixir, a strong dose compounded of indirection, political vitriol, theatrics and just plain woolly-mindedness." A few other extracts from this column-length piece follow:

> There is no denying that Mr. Wallace has a large and enthusiastic following. He is packing people in at rallies all over the country. It is a phenomenon we cannot explain except to the extent it reflects fear of an economic crisis (fed by soaring prices) and the mistaken notion that Mr. Wallace inherited the mantle of Franklin Roosevelt. . . .

218

Unquestionably there are in Mr. Wallace's audiences many sincere liberal and progressive citizens, along with a lot of Pinks and chronic malcontents. It remains to be seen if the Wallace elixir is potent enough to blend dissenting groups into a cohesive third party . . . Meanwhile we must look upon the effort with concern. There is in it the seeds of a dangerous class conflict we would like to see this country spared.

That noon, Wallace spoke at the East Pittsburgh gates of the Westinghouse Electric Corporation and, in the afternoon, to college students at Carnegie Music Hall in Oakland. On Thursday, Nov. 13, 1947, he spoke in Cincinnati's Music Hall, to which the meeting was shifted after the University of Cincinnati decided that it "cannot get into politics and feels it unwise to permit any one group to do so," thus canceling the use of its auditorium.

"Yesterday," said Wallace, "we had another official plea from the Administration to support the utterly corrupt dictatorship of Chiang Kai-shek." (The White House report related to the operation of the Greek-Turkish aid program through Sept. 30, 1947. New aid for China, totaling $300 million, was recommended by Secretary of State Marshall before the Senate Foreign Relations Committee.)

On Wednesday, Nov. 12, 1947, Wallace addressed 2,000 rubber workers in Akron in the afternoon, and an evening rally in Music Hall of the public auditorium in Cleveland. He called Akron "a progressive oasis in the desert," and praised the United Rubber Workers for helping to re-elect Rep. Walter B. Huber. He had a good word for John L. Collyer, president of B. F. Goodrich Co., who had served on a businessmen's advisory committee when Wallace was Secretary of Commerce.

"No Gag Here" was the title of the following editorial, in the *Cincinnati Times-Star* for Nov. 14, 1947:

Henry Wallace either does not know or does not want to know why the University of Cincinnati refused permission for him to make a speech on the campus under the sponsorship of a student organization.

The University of Cincinnati is not a private institution. It is municipally owned, the property of the City of Cincinnati. For that very reason it must remain non-partisan. It cannot appear to take sides or sponsor one political idea as against another. . . . It denied its facilities to both sides in the recent councilmanic election. . . . The University, simply, cannot be a forum for politics. . . .

Nobody in Cincinnati is trying to gag Mr. Wallace. As a matter of fact this city is interested in his views, representing, as they do, ideas which are pretty foreign to the beliefs of most of the citizens. Mr. Wallace had the opportunity to express those views at Music Hall last night, and nobody at the University attempted to prevent students from going to hear him talk. That is not enforcing political purity, by a long shot.

In the *Dayton Herald* for Nov. 15, 1947, Alvin Rosensweet marveled at Wallace's ability to endure his strenuous schedule. The day before, he had spoken to students of Antioch College at Yellow Springs; during the afternoon in Dayton, he had recorded a radio speech, addressed 100 CIO leaders and another group interested in Palestine, attended a reception in his honor, and conferred with numerous individuals and small groups; in the evening, he spoke to 500 at the Biltmore Hotel, under PCA auspices.

Wallace's evening address consisted of a two-pronged attack on the Truman administration: for a foreign policy which, he warned, would lead to war, and for a domestic policy of Red-baiting which endangered American civil liberties.

From Dayton, Henry Wallace went south, under the sponsorship of the Southern Conference for Human Welfare. Only a fortnight earlier, on Oct. 29, President Truman's Committee on Civil Rights had made public its 178-page report, *To Secure These Rights;* this, after the President endorsed it in a special message to Congress on Feb. 2, 1948, started the Dixiecrat revolt.

As a consequence, before Wallace appeared, large segments of the South were seething. That the journalistic welcome the former Vice President received was far from enthusiastic is putting it mildly. This was especially so after it was announced that all Wallace meetings would be non-segregated; scheduled appearances in Nashville, Little Rock, Memphis, Asheville, Greenville, Knoxville, Chattanooga and Columbia were canceled because public places where such meetings could be held were unobtainable.

According to Frank Kingdon, in his Nov. 12, 1947 *New York Post* column, this was "the first time in our history that a figure of importance has entered the South on this condition." Kingdon said that on his trip Wallace would be the Freedom Man, corresponding to the Freedom Train. "I suppose," he wrote, "a lot of people will say that Wallace is right in principle but that they doubt the wisdom of his tactics. They will say that this kind of direct action is premature, that the South has to be educated out of its present prejudices. The answer to this is that action is education."

Quite differently, Georgia's former liberal Governor, Ellis Arnall, who had supported Wallace in 1944, was quoted on Oct. 29, 1947 by the Associated Press as saying, "I can see nothing to be gained from Wallace's visit to Georgia at this time."

The most bitter blast, in anticipation of Wallace's tour, came from another with a reputation as a Southern liberal: Ralph McGill, editor of the *Atlanta Constitution.* In his signed column for Nov. 15, 1947, he said Wallace's trip had made a great many people "angry to the point of being violent." Wrote McGill:

220

In Atlanta, one of the cities where Mr. Wallace will speak, his sponsors, the Communist-infiltrated Southern Conference for Human Welfare (with its officials apparently getting most of the "welfare"), will be grievously disappointed if someone does not create a disorder so as to give them the publicity they seek.

Since there is a great deal of similarity between the mental mechanisms of the Ku Kluxers and the officers of the Southern Conference for Human Welfare, we are likely to see a Klan picket line or some other form of protest. Indeed, if there is one I trust someone will look under the robes to see if they be the hired pickets of the SCHW or the real McCoy of the Klaverns.

Under threat of a libel suit, in his column for Jan. 30, 1948, McGill made partial amends for the foregoing blast. "I am glad to say for the editor and owners of *The Constitution* that nothing in that column was meant to reflect upon the honesty, integrity or patriotism of the officers of the Southern Conference for Human Welfare."

Before he reached Atlanta, Wallace spoke on Sunday, Nov. 16, 1947, in Baton Rouge; on Nov. 17 in New Orleans; on Nov. 19 in Macon. Huge turnouts of students greeted him at Louisiana State, Tulane, Dillard and Southern universities, and at a mass meeting in the New Orleans Colonial Hall under the auspices of the Committee for Louisiana of the Southern Conference for Human Welfare. For his Louisiana audiences, he recalled Huey Long's prophecy that "when fascism comes to this country it will come cloaked in the language of Americanism" and added, "Huey Long's prophecy is coming true." Other potent Wallace quotations were: "It really calls for sacrifice to join the resistance movement against American fascism"; "Discrimination and segregation must go"; and "Our most precious freedoms are being undermined by the cry of 'Red! Red!'"

Although he did not diminish his attacks on Truman's foreign policy and proposals for universal military training, throughout the south he concentrated on civil rights issues, especially as they affected the area. At Macon he spoke to the student bodies of both Mercer University and Wesleyan College, to a Negro audience in Washington Avenue Presbyterian church and a mixed audience in the Municipal Auditorium. Although Clark Foreman, president of the Southern Conference, informed the evening meeting that there would be no segregation, Police Chief Ben T. Wilkins told the Negroes present to sit on one side of the auditorium, which they did. Several white people, however, defied the police and ostentatiously sat with the colored people, where they were unmolested by the police.

Wallace attacked red-baiting, particularly as practiced by the House Committee on un-American Activities, and the "get tough" foreign policy and praised the report of the Civil Rights Committee.

Although Grand Dragon Samuel Green, of the Georgia Ku Klux

Klan, had importuned city officials of both Macon and Atlanta to enforce the segregation laws, there were no demonstrations in either place, and the Atlanta evening meeting at the Wheat Street Baptist Church was unsegregated. It was not, however, until it was over and the audience had departed safely that the sponsors were able to relax. They knew that it had been made possible only because of the bulldog tenacity of the church's pastor, the Rev. William Holmes Borders, in the face of severe threats.

Mr. Borders had been approached by Miss Branson Price, of the Southern Conference, to permit use of his church for the rally.

"Do you mean Mr. Henry Wallace, who was Secretary of Agriculture?" the preacher asked. The reply, of course, was affirmative.

"Do you mean Mr. Henry Wallace, who was Vice President?" he then inquired and received the same reply.

"Do you mean Mr. Henry Wallace, who was Secretary of Commerce?" Mr. Borders continued, and when Miss Price nodded with a smile, he gave his reply:

"Miss Price, we'd be very happy to have Mr. Wallace in our church."

There were plenty of others, however, who were not so happy at the prospect. Writes the Rev. Mr. Borders:

> I received threatening telephone calls, at one and two o'clock in the morning, from persons who represented themselves as members of the Klan. I received letters, some typed, some poorly written, suggesting that I leave town immediately, that I was very unwanted and that I would be harmed physically.
>
> I answered on the phone on one occasion that, "I live at [address] and I have no protection in my home other than a fingernail file. You may come any time you choose. I have only one plea and that is that you take me to Five Points at high noon and do me bodily injury there." [Five Points is the busiest spot in Atlanta.]
>
> Again the telephone rang—Br-r-r-r. "Hello." "Is this the preacher?" "This is Rev. Borders." "I represent the Klan. Will that meeting be held in your church tomorrow night?" "Yes." "There is a law of segregation in Atlanta. Will there be segregation in the church?" "The Lord runs my church. See Him. Whatever arrangement you make with Him will be all right with me."

When a threat to burn down the church was received, Mr. Borders called together his deacons and informed them, "Looks as though we're going to have to take out a little extra fire insurance." They did: $100,000 worth.

With plainclothesmen in the audience and uniformed police outside, the meeting was held. There was no violence or the slightest sign of

222

friction. The audience of 3,000 was about equally divided between Negroes and whites, including many Morehouse College students, to whom Wallace had spoken earlier in the day. Among other things the Associated Press reported him as saying was that Stalin "set out to prove that the Soviet Union could develop from a dictatorship . . . into a democratic and then a pure Communist state. He has made a lot of progress but the Russians have a long way to go."

While in Atlanta, Wallace was photographed through the bars at Fulton Tower, local prison, when he visited Horace P. White. White had been sentenced there in April, 1946, for from five to ten years, for cutting the throat of a textile worker who had attempted to pass through a picket line at Whittier Mills during a strike. The CIO, for which White was an organizer, charged that his trial had been unfair, and Wallace in a public statement called the case "one of the most extraordinary reflections on democracy that I have ever heard about." Press reports that the Wallace prison visit was prompted by the CIO were corrected by William V. George, chairman of the Atlanta Civil Liberties Committee, who wrote to the *Atlanta Journal* on Nov. 28, 1947, that it was he who had persuaded Wallace to make it.

Before a mixed audience of 4,000, on Nov. 21, 1947 in the Armory at Louisville, Wallace admitted, "The lot of a liberal is not always a happy one," and then launched into a historical résumé of the fight for civil liberties, from the Alien and Sedition laws of 1800 to recent incidences of violence in Trenton, Philadelphia, Los Angeles and other places. He quoted the resolution passed by a recent conference of Episcopal bishops which contained the following:

> The surest way to fight communism is to work unceasingly at home and abroad for a society in which justice and the dignity of free men are in truth guaranteed to men of every race and condition. An inquisitorial investigation of man's personal beliefs is a threat to freedom of conscience.

He argued that the "first line of defense" is the health of the American people and pleaded particularly for better health facilities for Negro babies.

It was at Norfolk, Va., final stop on the tour, that Wallace and the Southern Conference for Human Welfare scored their biggest victory over Jim Crow. On the wall of the New York office of the Emergency Civil Liberties Committee, of which he is director, Dr. Clark Foreman has a framed copy of the article Glenn Kittler wrote for the Norfolk, Virginia, *Pilot,* for Nov. 24, 1947. It began:

> Dr. Clark Foreman, president of the Southern Conference for Human Welfare, called Virginia's hand yesterday afternoon and won.

> Standing before the 3,000 audience which in the Audi-

torium Arena gathered to hear an address by Henry A. Wallace, Foreman declared tensely:

"There appears to be a state law which prohibits people from meeting publicly. It is the inalienable right of American people to meet together. The memory of Jefferson, Madison and Henry is defiled by such a law.

"If the officers of the law will not allow us to continue our meeting here, we will walk into the streets and hold our meeting there . . ."

Before the meeting, the article related, E. M. French, acting director of the Arena, had told reporters that the meeting would not begin until segregation was observed and a score of uniformed police blocked the wings of the stage. French barred Mrs. Clifford Durr, chairman of the Committee of Virginia, from the platform when he observed the audience was not segregated. When Foreman climbed over the orchestra pit to the platform and said, "We will not accept segregation; if anyone feels uncomfortable he may leave," there was a moment of silence. Nobody, including the police, moved. So Foreman called Mrs. Durr to follow him to the stage, and after her speech announced, "Mr. Wallace is now entering the auditorium and will make his way to the stage."

Henry Wallace followed Foreman over the orchestra pit, while the police stayed ineffectually in the wings. Then Wallace spoke: against the Truman Doctrine, the House un-American Activities Committee and UMT, and for price control. "I am not a radical, although my enemies frequently accuse me of that," he said. "I'm tired of all the good people being called Communists. Communism doesn't deserve that much credit."

Then he retired to Farvue, to ponder what to do in 1948.

# ¶ 12 THE DECISION TO RUN. *In December, 1947 Henry Wallace spoke in upstate New York and received PCA and other delegations urging him to do what he had already made up his mind to do anyway.*

Henry A. Wallace definitely made up his mind to run for the Presidency on a third party ticket at a conference which began at 3 p.m., Tuesday, Dec. 2, 1947, in the studio of the sculptor Jo Davidson, at 60 W. 40th Street, New York.

Present were Wallace; Davidson; C. B. Baldwin, executive vice president of the Progressive Citizens of America; Lewis Frank Jr. of the *New Republic;* and Hannah Dorner, former executive director of the Independent Citizens Committee of the Arts, Sciences and Professions and at the time a member of the board of directors of the PCA. To guide the discussion, Baldwin had prepared a memorandum which, because of its importance to this history of the occasion, is reproduced here in full:

Public announcement of candidacy should be made on January 1 over a national hookup. Full page advertisements should appear in a number of large newspapers on January 2, giving the text of the radio speech announcing the candidacy. Such an early date is important for the following reasons:

(1) Necessity for meeting requirements of state election laws to qualify as independent candidate or 3rd party candidate. In some states this is relatively simple but in most states petitions requiring signatures of from 1 to 10% of the voters are required.

(2) It should precede Truman's message on the state of the union which will be delivered to Congress on January 5. It is important that our forces take the initiative and not be placed in the position of answering what is likely to be a very demagogic speech by Truman, particularly as it will relate to domestic issues.

In order to maintain maximum unity of the Wallace forces it is suggested that the announcement not be in terms of organizing an immediate 3rd party. The purpose sought is a new alignment of American political forces. For instance, in California and in Oregon most of the effort of the progressives has been exerted within the Democratic party. A statement at this time that an immediate 3rd party is to be formed in those states would discourage many people who have put great effort into intraparty activities and who might be lost to an eventual independent candidacy or 3rd party movement. If the announcement is made on January 1, we will then have time to make the decision on a state by state basis. However, it should be understood that in most states an independent candidacy or 3rd party is the only logical instrument for bringing about the realignment of political forces.

A study of the election laws in the various states indicates that a 3rd party or independent candidacy is possible in all but 2 or 3 states. In 4 or 5 small states it will be difficult to qualify. However, in approximately 40 states it appears that it will be possible to get on the ballot. (This is not based on a mere study of the election laws but on the opinions of the 28 PCA state directors, representing 23 states, who met in Chicago last week.)

PCA has already initiated Wallace for President or Draft Wallace movements in a number of states. Many of these meetings have been off the record but public meetings are planned for the month of December and will be greatly stimulated by an actual announcement of candidacy. Student movements for Wallace are already under way on many campuses.

Between now and January 1, in the speech to be delivered at the Brooklyn ALP dinner on December 4 and in the speeches to be delivered in Buffalo, Syracuse, Albany and Rochester, ht efact that the Democratic party has become the party of war and monopoly should be made clear.

Two suggestions are being considered for a meeting of leaders throughout the country supporting Mr. Wallace. The first is that a meeting of approximately 200 leaders from the arts, sciences and professions, labor, religious, minority, nationality groups, and others meet with Mr. Wallace in Chicago on December 29 to pledge their support and establish a temporary organization, to be followed by a much larger meeting early in the spring. The second proposal is that this meeting be delayed until after the announcement and be held some time in January. Under the latter method, a greater and broader attendance would be probable, but because of the delay it might be more advantageous to hold the meeting prior to the public announcement.

Lew Frank has already given much thought and time to the preparation of a publicity campaign, including leaflets, pamphlets, and other media. Considerable of this material can be produced and ready for distribution prior to the announcement.

PCA with its national office and field organization has spearheaded this move up to the present time and will probably have to continue to bear a large part of the responsibility for the campaign. However, it is extremely important that a national Wallace for President Committee be created as soon as possible and that all the organizational mechanisms be set in motion within the next 60 days.

Although the financing of any independent political movement is difficult, we feel that since PCA has been able to raise considerable funds without the benefit of an avowed candidate, this additional stimulation will make possible the obtaining of the necessary resources to do the job.

Time is our most precious asset. An early decision is imperative.

*    *    *    *

For Beanie Baldwin and most other PCA leaders throughout the country, Wallace's decision was almost anti-climactic. Nobody ever doubted the man's intention to keep on fighting the United States' bipartisan foreign policy throughout the 1948 campaign, but until he said "yes," Wallace had given third party advocates some anxious moments, as he was still to do before he spoke on Dec. 29 over the air from Chicago.

At Philadelphia on Oct. 4, the national board of directors of the PCA had issued a political statement which amplified its first sentence, "We are moving ever closer to the disasters of war and depression," and concluded:

> Only if the Roosevelt Democrats unite their ranks around a progressive policy and leadership can they hope to win the support of the independent voters of the nation which is essential for a Democratic victory.
>
> Under the circumstances the independent forces, by a new party if necessary, will insist upon the opportunity in 1948 to vote for a progressive candidate for President . . .
>
> Henry Wallace has pointed the way to organizing the unity of the Roosevelt Democrats and independent forces. We salute his patriotism and support his efforts on behalf of the national welfare.

The PCA's membership, Baldwin reported at the Oct. 4 meeting, had risen from 17,000 dues-payers in May to 47,000 in September, with one-third of them west of Chicago. Many state or part-state PCA organizations then existed, as follows: Northern California, Southern California, Delaware, Illinois, Maryland, Massachusetts, Missouri, Montana, New Hampshire, New Jersey, New York, Ohio, Oregon, Eastern Pennsylvania, Western Pennsylvania, Rhode Island, Utah, Washington and Wisconsin; with organizing committees at work in Arizona, Indiana, West Virginia, Maine and Kansas.

The meeting of PCA state directors, to which Baldwin referred in his memorandum to Henry Wallace, had been held on Nov. 21, 1947 in Chicago, at the same time as a civil rights conference of 250 delegates, mostly to support Truman's Civil Rights Committee's program; the conference numbered among its speakers Robert Kenny, Gerhard Eisler, Carl Marzani, Robert Morss Lovett, Harry Ward and Harold Christoffel. The purposes of the PCA directors' meeting were: (1) to explore the possibilities of influencing state Democratic delegations to the Democratic national convention in 1948 in favor of Wallace; (2) to review the possibilities of getting a new party on the ballot in each of the states. Mrs. Anita McCormick Blaine entertained about 60 delegates at a lavish Drake Hotel lunch.

The day after Wallace gave Baldwin the green light to proceed with arrangements for his announcement speech, Bob Kenny wrote Beanie from Los Angeles to urge that Wallace do so "before Mr. Truman makes another progressive message to Congress," so that "Mr. Wallace will get the credit for forcing any progressive gestures which Mr. Truman makes." His reference was to Truman's address of Nov. 17, 1947, to the opening meeting of a special session of Congress, which he had called on Oct. 23. In it, the President called for a 10-point legislative program as follows: (1) restore consumer credit controls, which expired Nov. 1; (2) regulate speculative trading on the commodity exchanges; (3) extend and strengthen export controls; (4) extend the authority to allocate transportation facilities; (5) authorize measures to induce marketing livestock and poultry at weights and grades that represent the most efficient use of grain; (6) expand the program of encouraging conservation practices, and authorize measures to increase food production abroad; (7) authorize allocation and inventory control of scarce commodities; (8) extend and strengthen rent control; (9) impose consumer rationing on products in short supply; (10) impose price ceilings on products in short supply.

Kenny pointed out that the next Truman message probably would be his State of the Union message in early January, "so there is very little time to lose." He recommended that Henry Wallace "should announce that he will be a candidate for President and express the hope that he will be supported by the Democratic party as well as by any independent groups already formed or which may be formed before the 1948 campaign. Immediately after this announcement Mr. Wallace should make public wires to leaders of the Democrats for Wallace movement in those states where they are now active, i.e., California and Oregon. Such wires should say that he appreciates their efforts in his behalf and that he will make himself available personally to come to their states and speak during the Presidential primary campaigns. The primary election in Oregon is May 8 and in California June 1. Mr. Wallace should give similar assurances of his personal participation to any leaders of third or independent party movements in other states where such leadership and movement have taken definite form. The PCA should encourage the formation of third parties in all of those states where there is no opportunity for possible participation in a Democratic presidential primary."

Although he already had decided to run as an independent, on Thursday, Dec. 4, 1947, Wallace told 1,200 members of the American Labor party of Kings County, at their third annual dinner celebration: "Tonight I speak as a Democrat—as a Democrat who is grateful for the contributions the ALP has made to the victories of my party in times past."

Wallace contrasted Truman's message to Congress, calling for price control, with the President's comment, only a month earlier, that such measures were those of a police state. He criticized Secretary of State Marshall for refusing to make public the report of Gen. Albert C. Wedemeyer on China, saying, "Men who withhold vital information should not talk about Iron Curtains."

The attempts of American military men to create fear of the Soviet

228

Union reminded Wallace of similar charges by Hitler's generals who talked about encirclement. Wallace said:

"I am tired of having them give the Communists credit for every decent proposal. I am tired of their deception. I am no authority on Communist actions and tactics, but I do know what the Communists haven't done. They haven't caused the inflation. They didn't remove price controls. They haven't moved Wall Street and military men into the key government jobs. These things I know and I don't intend to sit by and let red flags in the hands of reactionaries keep me from my small part in stopping the Reactionary Express as it speeds down the tracks toward Yesterday. That train is almost back to the Hoover station now, and the Mussolini and Hitler stations are not far beyond."

*     *     *     *

Perhaps the most dramatic meeting in PCA history occurred Dec. 5, 1947, in Jo Davidson's studio. It was unofficial and informal, instigated chiefly by Hannah Dorner, to bring together approximately 20 persons who had been most active at the top levels throughout the 1947 build-up period. Especially, it was called to persuade Frank Kingdon to go along with Henry Wallace in the decision he had made three days earlier in the same room.

This was the same Kingdon who, Wallace several times has told me and others, was the first person openly to urge him to start a third party. On June 9, 1947, in Newark's Mosque, Kingdon declared his intention to tour the entire United States to make Henry Wallace the Democratic candidate for President in 1948 "and, if not the Democratic nominee, the People's party nominee."

In Madison Square Garden, on Sept. 11, 1947, Kingdon had declared that the vote in Congress on the Taft-Hartley bill had shown that the Democrats and Republicans had formed one party, "a reactionary party," so that it was necessary to form "a second party, the People's party."

On Sept. 19, 1947, Kingdon, Wallace and Baldwin had shared a drawing room on the train from New York to Philadelphia. During the ride, Kingdon had strongly implored Wallace to announce soon that he would be an independent candidate for the Presidency. Wallace had refused to commit himself; instead, he had asked Baldwin if, in his judgment, a third party ticket would receive 5 million votes. Beanie had replied that he did not know, but he referred to an American Institute of Public Opinion (Gallup) poll of June 29, 1947, which revealed that 13 per cent had answered "yes" to the question, "If Henry Wallace starts a new liberal political party, do you think you would vote for the Presidential candidate of that party in the next election?"

That night, in Convention Hall, Kinkdon had told the huge audience, "There is only one man who can take FDR's place and that man is Henry A. Wallace. Philadelphia Citizens Committee wants a new second party because it is tired of a combination of Republicans and Southern Democrats. We want a People's party, for a people's America, in a people's world."

229

The next night, in Camden, Kingdon had been introduced for the first time as a candidate for the Democratic nomination for U.S. Senator from New Jersey. Kingdon himself had described his candidacy as the opening of a national campaign to test whether the people wanted a second party. Paul Robeson had "seconded" the Kingdon nomination, and when Kingdon came off the platform Zero Mostel, the comedian and entertainer, had told him, "Frank, that's the first time I've ever known you to be sincere." Kingdon, witnesses tell me, gave no indication that he recognized this to be an insult, because he had talked so much about the importance of his own candidacy. He was a great admirer of Mostel, who was addicted to cruel "riding" of both Kingdon and his actress wife, Marcella Markham. Long before the Wallace announcement Dec. 29, 1947 and Kingdon's public disavowal of it, Mostel had invited the Kingdons to a New Year's eve party at his apartment. When they appeared, Zero greeted them, "You no good son-of-a-bitch, what makes you think you'd be welcome here?" and slammed the door in their faces. Omitting that part of it Kingdon told me he and Marcella had attended two earlier parties before reaching the Mostel menage where they observed a very hilarious scene. To his wife Kingdon disparagingly remarked, "There's your third party," and the two took their leave.

In his signed column, "To Be Frank," in the *New York Post* for Oct. 4, 1947, Kingdon had commented on the column of W. E. Mullins in the *Boston Herald* (see page 200), which expressed wonderment at the enthusiastic reception Wallace had received on his New England tour in late September. Wrote Kingdon:

> I have an idea that when Mullins or any other observer gets to the bottom of why all sorts of citizens are eager to hear Henry Wallace and contribute to his cause, he will be on the track of something vital and significant coming to life in our politics. These are people daring to rise above the fears, domestic and international, which are plunging us into reaction at home and abroad. They believe that we can overcome our dilemmas and achieve lasting peace and assured prosperity and security here and throughout the world. They rally with enthusiasm to the one outspoken champion of this faith.

In Kingdon's hotel room at Providence, before the evening meeting there on Oct. 10, 1947, Frank and Marcella Kingdon had shocked Beanie Baldwin and others by expressing the belief it might be possible to obtain the support of Frank Hague, notorious Democratic boss of Jersey City, for the Kingdon senatorial candidacy. The argument was that Hague wanted a winner. At the same time, Kingdon was still strong for Wallace's new party candidacy. He was even more so late that night after the meeting. The dollar bill stunt which had proved so successful two nights before at New Haven (see page 205) had been a "flop" at Providence and Kingdon was brokenhearted and full of self reproof. Although ordained a Methodist minister in 1912, the year he came to America from his native England, Kingdon had become a bit of a drinker; in fact, it was frequent practice, when not wanting to mention him by name in confidential letters, for intimates to call him "our drinking friend." Somewhat inebriated on the early morning train back to New York, Kingdon demanded that Henry Wallace start a new political party.

At Pittsburgh, on Nov. 10, 1947, Frank Kingdon had called Wallace "the people's candidate for President." Three days earlier, however, in his *New York Post* column, "To Be Frank," had appeared the first slight indication that Kingdon was beginning to waver. Election results in New York and Kentucky, he had declared, "generally show greater confidence in the Truman administration than existed in 1946. They confirm what public opinion polls have suggested, that Truman hit the low point of approval two years ago and that his stock has been rising steadily over the past 12 months."

Kingdon's column for Nov. 12, 1947 had been extremely laudatory of Henry Wallace's imminent Southern trip, because of Wallace's insistence that none of his meetings be segregated. Then, on Dec. 4, 1947, two days after Wallace had made his decision to run and the day before the second Davidson studio meeting, Kingdon had written in the *Post:*

"I should like to see Harry Truman and Henry Wallace sit down together to talk over 1948."

He had gone on to point out what he considered favorable changes in Administration policies since Wallace left the cabinet, namely: Truman's support of price control and rationing, and the substitution of George Marshall for James F. Byrnes as Secretary of State. Kingdon had deplored a possible Republican victory in 1948. Meaning the Republicans, he had written: "They would proceed to widen every breach and aggravate every difference with Russia. The Marshall Plan for European recovery would become openly and aggressively a program for irrevocably splitting the world in two. As responsible leaders Truman and Wallace should face the consequences of their continued feud. They should ask whether the alternative to their cooperation is not too grave for them to contemplate. The next four years are altogether too uncertain in world affairs for any of us light-heartedly to hand this country bag and baggage to the party of reaction. I think it's at least worth talking over."

In the meantime, Kingdon had solicited the assistance of his close friend, James Imbrie, chairman of the New Jersey Independent Citizens Committee, a PCA affiliate, to help him make a contact with Hague. Imbrie had suggested that an approach might be made through a certain influential Trenton Democrat, to whom he then introduced Kingdon. Not wanting to have anything to do with any such negotiations, Imbrie did not remain for the conference. The next day, Kingdon told him he thought he had made progress and that he was to see someone else close to Hague. Everyone, including Kingdon, agrees that there never was a meeting between the Jersey City boss and the senatorial aspirant.

231

Nevertheless, Kingdon became convinced, fairly early in 1948, that he would be denied the Hague blessing and so, also shorn of PCA support, he withdrew from the race.

* * * *

When Lew Frank arrived at Jo Davidson's, on the evening of Friday, Dec. 5, 1947, he found Jo and Florence, his wife, taking turns copying a statement which Henry Wallace was dictating by long distance from his farm at South Salem. Lew took his turn, and when the informal meeting got under way, the Wallace message was read. It was as follows, with only the first paragraph edited for possible use in the *New Republic*, which never happened.

Dear Frank Kingdon:

You and I in close personal contact in trips to many cities have come to have a deep affection for each other and I am sure, therefore, that you will understand if I write to you in the same public way as you have written to me.

You have been urging in your column that Truman and I as responsible leaders of different viewpoints in the Democratic party should sit down together to heal the breach. Does this mean that you yourself are willing to go along with the Truman-Marshall leadership as it now exists? Does this mean that the possibility of a Republican victory frightens you so greatly that you are willing to accept the reactionary Democratic party leadership as we have it today?

For my part I am not. As a candidate for public office on the Democratic ticket you have reason to ask what are the changes in the Administration policy which would make it acceptable to the progressive groups with which I am associated.

I cannot pretend to speak for all of these progressive groups but I shall do the best I can. First, we can never support the present Administration as long as it represents the Wall Street military point of view. If Harry Truman or Howard McGrath will come out flat-footedly in the next 10 days against Universal Military Training we might be able to sit down to talk things over. I would then suggest some of the things Truman and Stalin should talk about preliminary to finding a basis to an abiding peace. I think Mr. Truman personally would agree with me on many points just as he always did when we sat down to talk things over and especially when we read over together my speech on September 10, 1946. But unfortunately Mr. Truman has many military advisors, many Wall Street advisors and many Republican advisors. One day he has one attitude. Another day he has another depending on the pressures around him and the ebb and flow of the political situation. I am sure you will agree with me that it would be essential to eliminate half the present military-Wall Street personnel in the President's entourage and to replace them with men who are free from the Red phobia and the desire to genuflect to Wall Street and the generals and admirals. I have called many times, as you yourself have heard in many speeches, for a housecleaning in Washington. I have called for freeing our foreign policy from the Vandenberg-Dulles veto. I have called for a genuine Democratic foreign policy that would not back up reactionary regimes all over the world. You say that the Marshall Plan under a Republican regime would openly and aggressively become a program for splitting the world in two. I say that Truman with his present advisors and his present willingness to cooperate with Wall Street and Republican reactionaries inevitably will continue to implement the Truman Doctrine of arming every reactionary government which is willing to fight Russia. Truman is doing the very same thing you fear the Republicans will do. You as a former minister of the gospel undoubtedly believe in the principles which underlie words, and I am therefore certain that you will not embrace a reactionary Republican regime in power rather than a Democratic regime which is equally reactionary but which uses pseudo-progressives to front for it. You say you do not want to hand this country over to the party of reaction. I say we have already handed the country over to the forces of reaction.

The Republicans won the 1946 Congressional elections on the basis of calling every northern Democrat who ran for office a Communist. The Administration in 1947 determined to win the 1948 campaign by out-Red-baiting the Red-baiters. As a result the high command of this Democratic party has become as subversive of civil liberties as was the Federalist party in 1789. Therefore, I say that in order for the progressives to go along with the Truman Administration it will not be enough to come out against Universal Military Training and fire the Wall Street Brass Hats. It must also rescind the loyalty order and give convincing evidence that it is enthusiastically doing everything it can to kill off the Un-American Committee, the poll tax, lynch law and Jim Crow.

Temporarily the Truman Administration has a political stake in trying to control high prices even though Truman himself believes the methods of control are characteristic of a police state. I do not ask for further tangible evidence of the sincerity of purpose of the Democratic high command than their own temporary great political need. This will hold them steady through the greater part of 1948 no matter how much the NAM may roar "police state" as it battles for the soul of Harry Truman.

I understand your situation in New Jersey and I hope you win because I know that you would be battling shoulder to shoulder with Claude Pepper and Glen Taylor. Your speeches would be among the best ever heard in the Senate and I know that if you followed the courage of your convictions the galleries would fill up whenever it was known that you were to talk. You would make a grand Senator. So far as I am concerned my only guide is to do what will best insure understanding with Russia, eliminate all weapons of mass civilian destruction, heal a split world, and bring security to those who fear for their personal liberties, their jobs and their right to say what they think.

I shall be happy to talk to any responsible member of the Democratic high command who thinks he can give assurance that the Democratic party will take decisive action in the next two or three weeks on the following points:

1. The Democratic party will no longer push UMT.

2. President Truman will no longer heed the advice of the Big Brass or Wall Street.

3. The loyalty order will be rescinded and State Department star chamber proceedings will be changed.

4. The Report of the President's Civil Liberties Committee will be backed by the Administration so continuously and enthusiastically as to produce definite legislation.

5. Truman and Stalin will get together to discuss a basis for lasting peace.

There are other points to be discussed but I know that if we progressives had assurances on these five points we could handle the other points satisfactorily and the Democratic party would again be worthy to be known as the party of Jefferson, Jackson, Wilson and Roosevelt.

\* \* \* \*

When the reading was finished Kingdon hardly allowed the customary moment of silence before he shouted at Lew, "You're a liar. You wrote it.

234

Henry Wallace never wrote like that." When I talked to Kingdon almost six years later, however, he admitted that Wallace *did* write it and declared that the statement vitiated his efforts to stop the "mad rush" toward a third party.

It was a bad night for Frank Kingdon. Lew Frank went after him vigorously. Beanie Baldwin assailed him viciously. The most eloquent touch, however, was provided by Harold Young, whose political office for Wallace had been moved on Nov. 15, 1947 from Washington to New York's Hotel McAlpin. Although Young had faithfully traveled with Wallace on many of his trips and had helped with some of his speech writing, his attitude toward a new political party was unknown and he was suspected to be lukewarm if not cold. A huge man, Young was given to dropping cigar ashes on even richly carpeted floors and he was clumsy with furniture. An amusing habit was to shake thoroughly a bottle of bourbon before pouring himself a drink, an action entirely superfluous as an aid to quality imbibing. Several times during the evening of Dec. 5, Young passed his turn to comment on the third party proposition. Finally, however, he indulged in his bottle-shaking act and addressed himself to Frank Kingdon: "Christ had his Judas too."

In January, after having accompanied Wallace to Chicago for his announcement speech, which he helped compose, Young told the people in the PCA office one day that he was going to his Odessa, Texas home for a short vacation but would be back. Nobody in the Wallace movement ever saw him again.

On Feb. 11, 1953, Young wrote me: "Mr. Henry Wallace is one of the country's few great men . . . The Progressive Party venture was a terrible mistake." To an experienced journalist who interviewed him for me, Young said that he never favored the new party venture, primarily because he thought Henry Wallace had a good chance of winning the Democratic Presidential nomination in 1948. Despite all the pressures that developed, Young never believed that Wallace would take the step. He voted the Democratic ticket himself in November, 1948 and denied that his hasty departure from New York was because of disappointment over not being appointed campaign manager by Wallace. He called Beanie Baldwin "a smart and fine man in every way," but said he was "led astray" and that Henry Wallace was politically naive.

Despite these personal feelings, Harold Young could not condone Frank Kingdon's attitude.

Kingdon's argument, which he presented with great vigor, was that Beanie Baldwin had contrived without his knowledge to force a third party decision upon Wallace. He chastised Beanie for having called the Nov. 21, 1947 meeting of PCA state directors in Chicago and especially for not having immediately thereafter asked for a meeting of the national PCA board of directors to have them hear a report on the Chicago meeting. Beanie's reply was that he had acted in accordance with the spirit of the Oct. 4, 1947 resolution, passed at the Philadelphia board meeting (see page 227), and that the Chicago meeting had been private and without publicity.

Without contradicting Harold Young's opinion of Frank Kingdon, this fact seems indisputable: at this stage Beanie Baldwin was working "tooth and nail" to get Henry Wallace to commit himself and was taking no chances on his being exposed to any influences which might delay or distract him in making up his mind. The charge that he acted in a highhanded fashion as regards the PCA was, I believe, justified. Instead of making an attempt to conciliate Kingdon by keeping him informed, he antagonized the man although he certainly knew him, from long association, to be a prima donna. I well recall my first encounter with Kingdon early in 1947, when he described himself as "an egotistical middle-aged man." In addition his recent wife, whom he had married on Nov. 29, 1946, was extremely ambitious for him and violently opposed to his association with Henry Wallace.

The Dec. 5 meeting was not Beanie's idea. Rather it was Hannah Dorner's, and she was another prima donna, who handled the evening very badly. The one man whose sympathy was most desired left it more adamant in opposition. He felt that everyone else in the room was "ganging up" on him, and that he had been the last rather than the first — which he thought should have been his right — to know how fast the political scene was shifting. More than one sympathizer with the third party idea uneasily felt Beanie Baldwin at this stage was highhanded; from Baldwin's standpoint, however, this was a necessary risk.

On Saturday, Dec. 6, 1947, the day following the meeting, Marcella and Frank Kingdon went to South Salem to see Henry Wallace. For six hours they argued with him not to bolt the Democratic party. For part of the time Alfred K. Stern, Martha Dodd, his wife, and Leonard Goldsmith were also there. During the course of his argument Frank Kingdon used Biblical allusions, as he and Wallace often did with one another.

"Why, Henry," declared Kingdon, "you won't have a Gideon's Army to support you."

"That's exactly what we've got," was Wallace's swift reply. Right there was conceived the idea of christening his new party "Gideon's Army," which he did in his Dec. 29, 1947 broadcast.

Kingdon wasn't as firm in his own convictions as he thought he was. The very next day Beanie Baldwin was at Farvue, Henry Wallace's farm (part of the time in the company of Paul Sweezy and Leo Huberman, later co-editors of the *Monthly Review,* who advocated long time research and propaganda work in the tradition of the British Fabian society, which Wallace approved). Beanie overheard one end of a long distance conversation during which Frank Kingdon, calling from Mrs. Katherine Van Orden's home in Verona, N. J., assured Wallace that he had changed his mind after talking to leaders of the New Jersey PCA. Wallace later told Baldwin that Kingdon said to him, "I've made a decision and whatever you decide is all right with me. I'll do anything I can."

Overhearing the other end of the conversation was James Imbrie, "wonderful Jim Imbrie" as so many rightly called him. Before a fund raising dinner, a small group met at the Van Orden home to discuss the situation. While the dinner guests gathered downstairs, in an upstairs bedroom Kingdon was told by a labor lawyer that he had it on good authority that Hague was not going to back him in his Senatorial ambitions. Kingdon then stated without equivocation that he would go along with Wallace and went downstairs to phone South Salem. Imbrie went along and heard the promise of support. Just as the conversation ended with Kingdon telling Wallace he would accompany him on his campaign trips as fund raiser, Marcella Markham Kingdon came in.

"Frank, you haven't committed yourself?" she demanded.

"Yes, I'm afraid I have," was her husband's weak reply.

"You had no right to do it without consulting me. It's a mistake. It's terrible!" This was the theme on which, with variations, she continued to harp all the way to her new home in Princeton, where the Imbries drove her and Frank.

Frank Kingdon told me that the first inkling he received that a third party was imminent was on Nov. 8, 1947, when he was at New Haven and received a long distance telephone call from Mrs. Imbrie; it warned him that Baldwin was lining up PCA leaders to push for it behind his back. Nell (Irish) Imbrie tells me that she never made any such phone call and that she couldn't possibly have conveyed any such information to Kingdon as she possessed no such knowledge at the time. I believe Mrs. Imbrie.

To further understand Kingdon's apostasy a few more facts are pertinent: he had been dropped as a radio commentator by his sponsor, Crawford Clothes, and had just recently landed his job as a columnist for the *New York Post*. For his peregrinating activities on behalf of the PCA he had been getting $1000 a month. This was making him more and more financially dependent upon a crusading outfit which nobody seriously believed could succeed in capturing the country. He needed more economic security than the columnist's job provided. He evidently was serious in thinking he could obtain Frank Hague's support.

Kingdon denies that he ever advocated a new party from the platform. He says when he talked about a second party he meant that the Democratic party should be converted into a people's party. Maybe that is what he meant, but a lot of newspapermen thought he said something quite different.

Not only did Kingdon phone Henry Wallace on Sunday, Dec. 7 and say that he would support him in a third party effort, but a few days later he visited PCA headquarters and said the same thing. This provoked a hugging match between him and the chief "affair stager" of the outfit, who promised bigger and better opportunities for Kingdon to raise funds.

Kingdon resumed his "pitchman" role at Wallace rallies on Dec. 10, 1947, at Cornell University, Ithaca, N. Y. (noon) and Syracuse (evening), and on Dec. 11 at Buffalo. His own newspaper, the *New York Post,* for Dec. 11, 1947, wrote about the Syracuse meeting: "Dr. Frank Kingdon, national PCA co-chairman, shared the platform with Wallace and vehemently demanded a 'second party.' 'We are pretty tired of having one party — one group of which marches under the Republican banner and the other under the Democratic one,' he asserted."

In his upstate New York speeches, Wallace elaborated upon the points he had made in his statement to Kingdon the week before. At Cornell he began, "Cornell University has been noted for many years for the freedom which it accords its faculty. I am not surprised, therefore, that I am allowed to speak on this campus at a time when a few college presidents have permitted their fear to get the best of their belief in civil liberties." This statement was probably provoked at least in part by several "headline cases" during the preceding week, when Howard Fast was prevented from speaking at Columbia University, Brooklyn College and City College, and Arnold Johnson, national legislative director of the Communist party, was banned at City College.

Wallace recalled that it was a lecture at Cornell in August, 1932 which enabled him to pay his first visit to Gov. Franklin D. Roosevelt. If he had not received that invitation to speak, he said, he might never have spent 14 years in Washington. Wallace then went on to compare the times with those 150 years earlier, when Rep. Matthew Lyon of Vermont was jailed for four months under the Alien and Sedition Laws because he had criticized President John Adams in a newspaper. "I have come to Cornell to preach old-fashioned Thomas Jefferson-Matthew Lyon Americanism," Wallace said. Then he charged backers of the bipartisan foreign policy with stifling freedom of expression by fostering unfounded fear of communism.

At Syracuse Wallace said, "America can never be strong morally as long as she appropriates ten times as much for armaments each year as she did before the war." The rest of his speech was a mosaic of those he had been giving since his return from Palestine. A new note was provided when he declared, "The atom bomb should have taught the people of the world that the use of force in human affairs has reached its limit. Those of us who looked on the atom bomb as making 'the rule of reason' essential were drowned out by the militarists who employed the bomb as a weapon of terror against the American people to persuade them of the need for bigger and better armaments. The German militarists employed the same tactics against the German people. Hitler always justified German rearmament by making the Germans believe that they were threatened with encirclement . . . While the masses of people have been diverted into looking for Communist infiltration in movie scripts, the military has really infiltrated our national life as never before. In the past two years the Congress has appropriated 25 billion dollars for military purposes. Our 'get tough' policy has frightened the one nation with which we must have understanding if the world is to have peace. But it hasn't frightened them into humility. It has frightened them into a 'get tougher' policy."

At Buffalo to an overflow crowd of 3,500, Wallace declared, "Certainly the Marshall principle has not been the heart of the American foreign policy since his Harvard speech of June 5. His words and the words 'Marshall Plan' have actually camouflaged other vital foreign affairs developments. Since he spoke at Harvard we have seen developing, as the very core of American policy, the Hoover plan of rebuilding Germany as a bastion of private monopolistic enterprise."

Near the end of the Buffalo speech Wallace came closer than ever before to revealing his 1948 intentions when he said: "The question of whether there will be peace in the Democratic party hangs on whether we are going to have a Democratic party policy for peace in the world. If the record is negative, the Democratic party will die, and there will be a new party — a people's party — a party of workers and farmers, professionals and small businessmen — a truly democratic party."

On his upstate trip it was not Wallace's public speeches but his press conferences that were considered newsworthy. He was questioned at Ithaca about a recent prediction by Sen. Owen Brewster (Rep., Me.) that he would head a third party ticket in 1948 and on a declaration that day by Sen. J. Howard McGrath, newly appointed chairman of the Democratic national committee, that the party would welcome Wallace's support in 1948. Wallace declared: "My attitude today is the same it has been right along. If it is apparent that the Democratic party is a war party, I will do all I can to see there is a third party." ,

From coast to coast, many Wallace fanciers emitted howls of anguish when Wallace was reported to have told reporters at Buffalo that he personally would vote for Sen. Robert A. Taft, if the choice for President were between him and Harry Truman. Referring to Taft's views on domestic policies, Wallace considered him "the most reactionary man in the most reactionary party," with an 18th century mind; nevertheless he said of the Ohio Senator's foreign policy, "It is the most liable to keep peace during the next four years." As for a Dewey-Truman choice, Wallace said, "The people would have no choice of personalities in such an election. Dewey's policies would lead to war. He is out-Trumaning Truman. I really don't know who is a watered-down version of whom." At Albany, Wallace opined that Gen. Dwight D. Eisenhower could be elected President on either major party ticket.

With a large number of laborers in his audience at Albany, Wallace attempted to set the record straight when he said:

In my press conferences these days the newspapermen keep me amused with their hypothetical questions about my preferences in Republican candidates and my preferences between the pre-miracle Truman of today and the different Republicans. I have always answered these hypothetical questions with real pleasure. The game of "make believe" is always great sport, but I find that it is getting just a little too confused. In my press conference yesterday I added Taft to my list of preferences over the Truman-of-the-moment on the basis of Taft's opposition to Universal Military Training. I made it clear that Taft represents the best kind of 19th century thinking and that the voters were entitled to a better choice than that between Taft and Truman.

That point isn't very clear in the morning papers I have seen, so I am going to call a halt to the game of "make believe" because it would take something more than a miracle for me to cast a vote for a Republican candidate for President — something like their nominating Claude Pepper — but it is past the "fun" stage and I don't want anyone to seriously believe that I could vote for Mr. Taft. The people must not be limited to a choice between reactionaries. The people must have a choice between a road to war and a road to peace. The people must have a chance

239

to choose the road to full employment and full production. They shall have such a choice.

I was pleased to have Chairman McGrath say the other day that my party would accept my support in 1948. That was a hopeful sign. I interpret it to mean that there is a chance for a change. I want to assure Senator McGrath that I would certainly support every progressive Democratic candidate for Congress. I shall also hope that there will be valid reasons for me to support the entire Democratic ticket in 1948.

In addition to his mass meetings Wallace met with small groups at luncheons, conferences and receptions in all cities visited. His crowds continued to be large, but Leo Egan wrote in the *New York Times* for Dec. 12, 1947:

"As in Ithaca and Syracuse yesterday his speeches today were received politely but without any marked demonstrations of enthusiasm. In many respects his audiences, both in composition and reaction, resembled those that Norman Thomas used to attract when he was running for public office on the Socialistic ticket.

"There was a marked predominance of young people of both sexes in the audience and the rest appeared to be chiefly white collar or professional people. There was also a noticeable sprinkling of Negroes in the audience."

Typical upstate comment was that of the *Buffalo News* in an editorial, "The Ostrichism of Henry Wallace," Dec. 12, 1947. A few excerpts follow:

"What they [the audience] heard was little other than old-fashioned ostrich isolationism. Father Divine had long since summed up the basic Wallace line in three celebrated words: 'Peace, it's wonderful' . . . Mr. Wallace, in short, is right back where the America Firsters were before Pearl Harbor . . . The curious, the discontented, the confused in mind and the troubled in heart will continue to turn out to hear Henry Wallace talk. But the old-line Americans of liberal conviction — including most of the leading trade unionists of AFL and CIO, and many of the old New Dealers now organized into Americans for Democratic Action — have long since parted company with him on the issue of foreign policy. They see in him a stooge — unwittingly, they hope — for the Communist party line. And they see in that line the antithesis of peace, of prosperity, of freedom and of liberalism."

At Albany, William S. Gailmor replaced Frank Kingdon as fund raiser. After Buffalo on Dec. 11, 1947, Kingdon never spoke (or wrote) for Wallace again. Instead, on Monday, Dec. 15, 1947, he cast the one dissenting vote (there were two abstentions) against 18 affirmative votes at a PCA Executive Committee meeting on the issue of urging Henry Wallace to announce his independent candidacy. Then he resigned his co-chairmanship of the PCA and left the meeting before it was over.

Several persons who attended that meeting, including some of the 18 non-voting board members and three visitors who were there in addition to the 21 executive committeemen, have described it as having been conducted in a quiet atmosphere of deep seriousness. "It was not a 'yes' meeting," Mrs. Elinor Gimbel told me. "The seriousness of it was something unbelievable. It was the most mature meeting I ever attended. Everyone spoke, not to persuade but to inform and to consider. There was no demagogy. Actually the vote could have gone either way, there was so much conscience and concern in that room. Those people were terribly real. It was a great experience."

Stenographic notes taken at the meeting reveal the truth of the statement that there was widespread discussion of possible obstacles to a third party attempt in 1948. A show of hands of all present, however, revealed the sentiment to be 39 to 2 in favor of the resolution, which reviewed the attitude of the PCA's board of directors at its Oct. 4, 1947, Philadelphia meeting (see page 227) and concluded:

"Millions of Americans will stay away from the polls if they are confronted with only a choice between two brands of reaction. These millions of Americans must not be disenfranchised. They must have a choice. Only if Mr. Wallace runs as an independent candidate will they have a choice between progress and reaction."

In opposition to this motion Kingdon, who was presiding, read a previously prepared four page statement in which he raised "three considerations which I believe make an independent ticket not only inadvisable but impractical." They were: (1) Lack of support from the leaders of organized labor most of whom, he said, "will actively, even bitterly, oppose such a ticket"; (2) The impossibility of raising $10 million, which Kingdon figured would be needed for a nationwide campaign; (3) The lack of other organizational support, especially in the American Labor party and the CIO-PAC, which would "fragmentize rather than unite the ranks of progressives." Then Kingdon predicted that, if the motion were passed, the PCA would be split. "So far we have been an opinion-forming body," he said. "This motion would change PCA into a political party. Within an opinion-forming body there can be differences of opinion. Within a political party there has to be party discipline." For that reason, he concluded, if the motion passed he would resign as co-chairman of the PCA.

Present at the Dec. 15, 1947 meeting, but not recorded as having taken much part in the discussion, was James Imbrie, chairman of the New Jersey Independent Citizens League. On Dec. 8, he had written Wallace, "with some hesitation and a deep sense of humility," to advise him not to run on an independent ticket for the following reasons: "Non-labor support, other than unorganized rank and file, insufficient financial support, the unreadiness of the PCA and allied state organizations for the task and the moot question as to whether the third party movement would not materially hurt rather than help liberal Democratic Congressional and Senatorial candidates." However, Imbrie wrote, "I foresee a well-rounded and increasingly powerful independent political machine developing within our organization during the next year or two," and then concluded, "May I reemphasize that, inasmuch as we are united behind your leadership, we will accept as for the best whatever decision you make in this matter. If you decide to move, you can count that every last man and woman in our organization will go all out behind your leadership and

241

that we will stick to the end and accept any eventuality which such action may portend."

And that is exactly what Jim Imbrie, retired Wall Street banker, did. On Dec. 17, 1947, as a member of the PCA committee which notified Henry Wallace officially of the Executive Committee's decision, he restated his stand as he had written it. In 1948 he was the Progressive party's candidate for U.S. Senator from New Jersey and in 1949 he ran on the same ticket for Governor. In 1950 he took an independent stand, between that of Wallace and the PCA, on the Korean war; but he did not follow Wallace out of the party.

Before the eventual Dec. 15, 1947 meeting, Imbrie and Joel Gross, another New Jersey representative on the PCA board, had dinner with Frank Kingdon. When the dessert course was reached Kingdon declared, "Jim, I'm resigning," and for about five minutes refused to listen to argument. When he abruptly arose and started for the elevator, Gross implored Imbrie not to let him go. Jim caught up with him on the floor where the meeting was to be held and pleaded with him again, on the basis of their long personal friendship, but in vain. Seldom have two men of such widely different fundamental traits been such close friends.

About this time Wallace received other letters attempting to discourage him in any third party aspirations. Some of them were inspired by Michael Straight, who urged oldtime liberal associates of Wallace to write them. One such letter, dated Dec. 10, 1947, was from Rep. Helen Gahagan Douglas of California and read in part: "I hope that you won't do so. As you remember, last spring I told you that I felt that a third party could do nothing but elect the worst possible Republican candidates and defeat the few liberal Congressmen we now have in Washington."

On Tuesday, Dec. 16, 1947, Henry Wallace spoke at a PCA rally at Rochester, N. Y., but the closest he came to commenting on the news of the night before was, "I know that if the leadership of the Democratic party does not act to fulfill our pledges of 1944, the party will die and there will be a new party—a people's party—a party of workers and farmers—a truly democratic party worthy of the tradition of Jefferson, Jackson, Lincoln, Wilson and Roosevelt."

The same night that Wallace was talking in Rochester, Dec. 16, 1947, Frank Kingdon addressed a rally of 800 under PCA auspices in Elizabeth, N. J. The crowd yelled for him for Senator and Wallace for President, not having heard of the meeting of the night before. The rally over, Kingdon made public his prepared statement at the PCA meeting and announced his resignation. A hastily called meeting of the board of trustees of the New Jersey group on Wednesday night, Dec. 17, resulted in a 73 to 0 endorsement of Wallace's candidacy and a 48-hour ultimatum to Kingdon to support it also or forfeit the league's endorsement.

For several days, in interviews, on and off the air and in his column, Kingdon was kept busy defending his action. He was quoted as saying, "I sometimes think that I am the only one thinking of the future of Henry Wallace . . . The prevailing consideration is not that it (a third ticket) will elect reaction, but that it will split progressives into fragments and delay any possibility of their coming back in two or four years." In his Dec. 19, 1947 column he called the idea of a third party "a pipe dream . . . The demand for it represents an escape from realities." He answered numerous attacks on himself in his Dec. 20, 1947 column, insisting that he had told Wallace of his opposition to a new party before he decided to run for the Senate himself, and that he had never advocated a third party himself. After Wallace formally announced his candidacy, in his Dec. 31, 1947 column, Kingdon wrote:

"Who asked Henry Wallace to run? The answer is in the record. The Communist party through William Z. Foster and Eugene Dennis were the first . . . The record is clear. The call to Wallace came from the Communist party and the only progressive organization admitting Communists to its membership." That organization, of course, was the PCA, of which Kingdon had been co-chairman.

At Princeton Dec. 30, 1947, Kingdon said Wallace's candidacy was "fostered by the Communists for the direct purpose of dividing and confusing American progressives" and he went on record as spurning the support of the New Jersey Independent Citizens League, which had been paying his rent. At intervals throughout 1948, he wrote further red-baiting columns against the Progressive party; but early in March, after Boss Frank Hague endorsed the CIO-PAC's candidate for the Senatorial nomination, Archibald Stevens Alexander, Kingdon withdrew from the Senatorial contest.

Only one other national PCA officer emulated Kingdon immediately. He was Bartley C. Crum, who resigned, both as national vice chairman and from the PCA, saying he would never support Wallace for President. A fortnight later, after Wallace's formal announcement, New York state chairman and radio commentator J. Raymond Walsh also quit, because he felt a third party movement in 1948 "would kill the chance of progressive politics in America for a long time, possibly for the rest of your life." Neither man, however, joined Kingdon in his "smear" campaign. Newspapers which investigated throughout the country found that most state PCA groups had already gone on record as favoring Wallace's independent candidacy and were engaged in circulating petitions to urge him to accede to the national Executive Committee's request.

On Wednesday, Dec. 17, 1947, a small subcommittee of the PCA Executive Committee formally called on Henry Wallace in his McAlpin Hotel headquarters to inform him of the resolution of two nights before. Among those present were C. B. Baldwin, Harold Young, John Abt, Mrs. Elinor Gimbel, Lillian Hellman, Michael Nisselson, James Imbrie and Josiah Gitt. For several of these, who had not known about the Dec. 2 decision, this meeting represented the first time that Henry Wallace definitely declared his willingness to make the plunge. Everyone present was asked to express his opinion and, except for Imbrie—who repeated the viewpoint expressed in his letter—all strongly urged Wallace to announce before the end of the year. Because of its central location, Chicago was selected as the site of the announcement and it was agreed to select the date on which the most widespread radio coverage could be obtained. When Wallace raised the question of the possible vote he would receive, Gitt replied, "It makes no difference how many votes you get. You are in honor bound to run." In the opinion of many who were "close to the top" at the time—and I know of none who dissents from this view—the insistent urging of Josiah Gitt was a strong factor in causing Wallace to decide to run. It was Gitt whom Wallace asked to walk back to the *New Republic* office with him, at the conclusion of the meeting, for further conversation on the important decision he had made.

Josiah Gitt is a unique example of a man of wealth with strong liberal views; he has held these throughout most of his life, which began on Mar. 28, 1884, at Hanover, Pa. His own explanation is that it was his mother who influenced his thinking. She was the daughter of a Hellertown, Pa. minister who became incensed at the cruel treatment accorded imported Mexican workers in the Lehigh valley. Of Pennsylvania Dutch origin (the name was originally Kidd) and a native of the area, Gitt has been able to "get away" with the espousal of liberal and progressive causes in his newspaper, the *York Gazette & Daily,* and his personal participation in liberal movements. In 1944, he was the Democratic candidate for Congress from his district and polled a heavier vote than Franklin D. Roosevelt. In 1952, after a long hesitancy, his paper supported Adlai Stevenson instead of Vincent Hallinan, the Progressive party nominee; but when Stevenson visited the city, Gitt was snubbed and received no public thanks for his support, although such appreciation was expressed for the nearby Lancaster paper which also supported the Democratic nominee to counterbalance the support given by the other Lancaster paper, under the identical ownership, which went for Eisenhower. Possibly this snub was a factor in the comparatively low vote Stevenson obtained in the district.

When I visited Mr. and Mrs. Gitt at their country estate just south of Hanover, Pa., I remarked that it was a shame he had never been elected President, so that his place could become a national shrine. Not only because of the house, which has more rooms than I could count, or the swimming pool, the garden, the outbuildings, or the telescope, but also because of the marvelous view from atop a hill, which has greater potentialities than Mount Vernon, Monticello, the Hermitage, Hyde Park or any other Presidential shrine I've ever seen.

Inside, one has to compress his shoulders and hips to wend a way between stacks of books, which have long since outgrown the shelves that line the walls of many rooms. Hundreds of books, thousands of books; piled on coffee tables, card tables, boxes and the floor. And if Jess Gitt told me he had read all of them I would believe him. His mother, who died in 1952 at the age of 92, must have certainly been a remarkable woman.

Throughout my research, I have discovered a surprising range of reasons why people joined the Progressive party in 1948, and that statement includes the top leadership as well as the rank and file. In Jess

Gitt's case it was thorough disgust over American foreign policy as it developed during the Truman administration. In other words, he saw just about eye to eye with Henry Wallace from 1946 on. He believed the "get tough" policy was suicidal and that peace could be obtained through friendly negotiations with the Soviet Union.

In 1948, Gitt became chairman of the Pennsylvania Progressive party, which meant he was host when the national PP convention occurred in Philadelphia in July. He resigned from the party in May, 1950, in protest against national policy in regard to the Stockholm and other peace petitions.

\*     \*     \*     \*

Another influential leader in December, 1947, with a background somewhat similar to that of Josiah Gitt was Mrs. Elinor Gimbel. She was the widow of a scion of the famous department store family, who was killed early in World War II while serving in the Air Transport Command. Although she came from a Democratic family and had been for Al Smith in 1928, it was the shock of the depression in 1929 and thereafter that awakened her social consciousness and her desire for activity. One of her vivid recollections is the gray visage of a doctor on Christmas eve, 1932, telling of the wide incidence of illness and the equally wide inability of persons to afford medical care. Mrs. Gimbel became what she facetiously declares some have called her, "a traitor to her class" and embraced New Dealism. It is the only "ism" for which she has ever had any use.

During the war years she was an indefatigable civilian worker. She set up the Committee for Care of Young Children in Wartime and went to Washington to lobby for funds for day camps for the children of working mothers. In 1940, she attended the Democratic national convention and was aghast during the campaign because New York Democratic organizations were not so aggressive in support of the third term as she thought they should be. By 1944, she resolved to do something about the situation. The result was a Non-Partisan Committee in support of the Roosevelt-Truman ticket. It probably contained more independent Republicans than Democrats and was the first of about 20 similar community groups which she inspired and helped to organize. Although these groups affiliated loosely with the National Citizens Political Action Committee, when it was organized in mid-summer, 1944, she was unable to "sell" either Sidney Hillman or Beanie Baldwin on her plan for widespread community organizational activity. So she went ahead and did the job herself. Few of her original supporters deserted when the original Non-Partisan Roosevelt clubs became NC-PAC units and, in early 1947, Progressive Citizens of America units. She and her friend Lillian Hellman would have preferred a quieter approach than the PCA adopted, but they believed that a strong fight was necessary to preserve the gains that had been obtained under Franklin Delano Roosevelt. She never had much use for the Independent Citizens Committee of the Arts, Sciences and Professions and feels that the PCA

245

was a completely democratic organization, for which she gives Beanie Baldwin considerable credit. Of the Dec. 15, 1947 PCA board meeting she says, "Maybe the results pleased the Communists, but that isn't why it happened. Everyone was there and everyone had a chance to talk. These were people of distinction and intelligence."

In 1948, Mrs. Gimbel was national chairman of the women's division of the Progressive party. A woman of few inhibitions, she was able to "tell off" Henry Wallace whenever she so desired, and the same went for anyone else in the organization. She was there because she believed Harry Truman had deserted both the domestic and foreign policies of Franklin Delano Roosevelt, and because she thought Henry A. Wallace still believed in both. She quit the PP in August, 1950, because she felt it had outlived its usefulness, to which decision she had come before the Korean incident. She wanted action, and there wasn't enough doing in the PP to satisfy her. In 1952, she was prominent in the Democratic campaign for Stevenson.

\* \* \* \*

To provide biographical data on everyone who was prominent in urging Henry Wallace to run would be superfluous. Throughout this book, the policy will be to identify as much as seems necessary those persons who, at the time under consideration, were the closest or most influential. According to that criterion one other deserves mention here. He is James Imbrie of Lawrenceville, N. J., who, as mentioned, promised to support Wallace although advising against an independent candidacy.

Imbrie came from old, pious, Scotch-Presbyterian colonial stock. His father, grandfather and great-grandfather had been Princeton trustees and the family also founded and supported the Lawrenceville and other schools. Born in Bayonne, N. J. in 1880, Imbrie entered Wall Street upon his graduation from Princeton and when World War I broke out was one of the leading, if not the leading, munitions manufacturers in the United States. The companies which he owned included Savage Arms and Driggs-Seabury. He also was president of a southern railroad and on numerous corporation boards of directors. His wealth was reputed to be in the millions.

Although a Republican, Imbrie became a believer in Woodrow Wilson's dreams for world peace and spent a reputed $30,000 trying to bring about United States membership in the League of Nations. In 1928, he strongly resented the smear campaign against Alfred E. Smith because of his religion and voted Democratic for the first time. He suffered financially with the depression and subsequently voted four times for Franklin Delano Roosevelt. The turning point of his life occurred in 1937, when he suffered a heart attack and was forced to retire from business and go to Bermuda for his health. There he remained until 1944, when he felt obliged to return to the United States to resume participation in civic affairs. He felt then that Franklin Roosevelt was taking up the fight which Wilson had begun for a world organization.

"When I went to Bermuda," Imbrie says solemnly, out of his deeply religious and idealistic background, "I took a pledge that if I recovered my health, I would devote the rest of my life to the cause of world peace."

Imbrie's practical action was to organize the New Jersey Independent Citizens League, in which Democrats outnumbered Republicans about 60 to 40 per cent. It suppoted FDR in 1944 and was credited with providing the "extra push" which caused him to carry New Jersey by 26,000 votes. In 1945, the league similarly helped elect Gov. Albert Driscoll. It was lobbying by the league which was mainly responsible for passage, in 1945, of New Jersey's Fair Employment Practices Act.

In Jim Imbrie's opinion, the fight for peace that Henry Wallace waged in 1946 and 1947 was in the tradition of his two idols, Wilson and FDR.

Although he already had given his consent to run, at the Dec. 17, 1947 Hotel McAlpin meeting Henry Wallace expressed concern about a new party's potential labor support. He looked around the room and declared that it looked as though the movement would be almost entirely a middle-class one. This was also the concern of Alfred K. Stern, close personal friend of Wallace. So at 11 a.m. the next day—Thursday, Dec. 18, 1947—there was a meeting, at Stern's request, with Wallace, Baldwin, Stern, Straight and a few others. Stern proposed that announcement of Wallace's candidacy be delayed until a nationwide canvass could be made of the sentiment of local labor leaders. He wanted to send Leonard Goldsmith, an experienced labor organizer, quickly on such a trip for that purpose.

Beanie Baldwin not only vetoed the suggestion, but severely chastised Stern for raising it at what he considered too late a time. Anyway, that same day the attempt was made to convince Wallace that he would have adequate rank and file labor support by a delegation of 45 union leaders, headed by State Sen. Kenneth Sherbell, a Brooklyn American Labor party leader and director of the Wholesale & Warehouse Workers Union, CIO; and Irving Potash, of the New York Furriers Joint Council. They represented unions totaling about 263,000 workers in New York City, and presented Wallace with a statement urging him to run and pledging support for his "historic efforts to lead the American people along the course of economic security, civil liberties and peace charted by Franklin Delano Roosevelt." Potash went a step further and told HAW that his union alone would be able to raise $100,000 to contribute to the campaign; a pledge which, however, was never kept.

The same day Wallace was also visited by delegations from the Massachusetts PCA and from Students for Wallace groups at ten New York colleges. The Bay State delegation was headed by Oliver Allen, prominent Boston attorney, who had been a Democratic candidate for Congress in 1946. He was accompanied by Mrs. Marjorie Lansing, PCA executive director for Massachusetts; by Staughton Lynd, of the Harvard University Committee for Wallace; and William Gilbert, New England director of the United Furniture Workers, CIO. These representatives presented Wallace with a resolution which had been adopted, by a 50 to 1 vote, by the Massachusetts PCA, of which Angus Cameron, editor of Little, Brown & Co., publishers, was state chairman. It urged Wallace to run and said, "The enemies of American democracy have secured control over the two old parties in this country. When the last shred of the Roosevelt influence in this country has been torn away, it is time to rally around the man who for millions of Americans has come to mean democracy, security and peace."

The next day, a similar delegation arrived from New Jersey, and within a week others from PCA groups in Eastern Pennsylvania, Maryland and Connecticut. Letters and telegrams poured in from PCA chapters and other supporters all over the country. On the West Coast on Dec. 8, Dr. Francis E. Townsend had advocated a new party in 1948. Rep. Vito Marcantonio, on Dec. 18 at an American Youth for Democracy rally, at St. Nicholas Arena, urged Wallace to run; O. John Rogge did the same thing from a platform in Boston about the same time. Elmer A. Benson, former Governor and United States Senator from Minnesota and a member of the State Executive Committee of the Democratic-Farmer-Labor party, wired from Appleton, Minn.: "I want to join the millions who call on you to lead their fight in November of '48."

On Christmas eve, 1947 from his *New Republic* editor's office, Henry Wallace announced that he would state his own views on the 1948 election over the facilities of the Mutual Broadcasting Company on Monday, Dec. 29, 1947, from Chicago.


# ¶13 THE COMMUNISTS BECOME ACTIVE. *Despite their disappointment that a new party movement developed out of middle-class rather than labor roots, they decided to give it support and thereby incited a propaganda barrage.*

Following the resignations from the PCA of Frank Kingdon and Bartley Crum—to be followed soon by those of J. Raymond Walsh, Albert Deutsch, A. J. Liebling and others—and strong statements by some liberal and labor leaders that they would not follow Henry Wallace, Stewart Alsop wrote in his syndicated column, datelined Washington, Dec. 21, 1947: "The Wallace third party movement has been indecently exposed for what it is: an instrument of Soviet foreign policy. Since the PCA invited him to head a third party, the whole

248

movement has been stripped bare. The bones revealed are communistic bones."

Similar comments came from several other sources. Said Alex Rose, vice chairman of the American Labor party: "Henry Wallace is permitting himself to be used by the American Communists. He has been steadily absorbing the Communist line . . . The third ticket will be the fifth column in action and will have the opposition of the entire labor movement." To Walter Reuther, president of the CIO United Automobile Workers, who spoke on Dec. 18 at a National Press Club luncheon in Washington, Henry Wallace had become "a lost soul." Said Reuther:

"Henry Wallace is a great disappointment to a lot of people in America. It is tragic that he is being used by the Communists the way they have used so many other people. The Communists perform the most complete political valet service of any group in America. They write your speeches, attend your meetings, applaud what you say and inflate your ego. That's what is wrong with Henry Wallace."

Immediately after the PCA Executive Committee resolution of Dec. 15, urging Wallace to run, was made public, the Amalgamated Clothing Workers, through its president, Jacob S. Potofsky, announced it would oppose any third party attempt in 1948; thus indicating that the American Labor party would be split in case Wallace went ahead. Louis Hollander, chairman of the CIO in New York state; Philip Murray, CIO president; Jack Kroll, chairman of the CIO-PAC; and the national officers of the ADA all spoke up publicly in opposition to the idea. Sen. Claude Pepper reiterated his intention of remaining in the Democratic party no matter what happened, and only Sen. Glen Taylor and Rep. Vito Marcantonio in all of Congress spoke words of approval for the PCA's suggestion.

Editorially, from coast to coast, the score was about the same. Even the left wing *New York PM,* in a signed editorial by Max Lerner on Dec. 18, 1947, condemned the proposed Wallace candidacy and did not ignore the Communist angle.

Although many of these first outbursts of adverse comment unequivocally charged that Henry Wallace had become a "tool" or "dupe" of the Communists, there were no specific charges, with names and dates; and there were numerous inconsistencies in the theories advanced by equally reputable and competent observers to explain the alleged motives of the Communists, both American and international.

To the best of my knowledge it was the columnist Dorothy Thompson who made the first specific charge publicly. She did so on April 27, 1948, in a *Town Meeting of the Air* forum which originated in Armory Auditorium at Charlotte, N. C. The topic was "Will the Third Party Bring Us Peace and Prosperity?" and the panelists, in addition to Miss Thompson, were Dwight MacDonald, who supported her in the negative; and Sen. Glen H. Taylor and James Stewart Martin, arguing the affirmative. Here are the pertinent passages from Miss Thompson's accusation:

"The Communist party — let's tell the truth — initiated the movement for Wallace. No other group publicly called for it. It was launched

Nov. 18 by Ben Gold, Communist president of the Fur Workers Union, CIO.

"The second call was made Dec. 9 at a mass meeting in New York by William Z. Foster, Chairman of the Central Committee of the Communist party. This was endorsed eight days later by the Communist-friendly organization Progressive Citizens of America. Leading non-Communist figures immediately resigned.

"Mr. Wallace had not yet spoken himself when the Moscow *Pravda* announced that a third party would enter the 1948 election, and on Dec. 29 Mr. Wallace accepted."

The very next day Philip Murray, CIO national president, gave a slightly different version of the Progressive party's origin. He spoke on April 28, 1948, at the fifth biennial convention of the Textile Workers Union, CIO, at Atlantic City and said, "The Communist party is directly responsible for the organization of a third party in the United States. There is no question about that." And then he declared that the party's inception had been at a Communist meeting in New York in October, 1947.

A fortnight later, on May 10, 1948, at the 16th biennial convention of the Amalgamated Clothing Workers of America, also at Atlantic City, Murray repeated his charge with slight amplification. He had been informed, he declared, that shortly after the national CIO convention, Oct. 13-17, 1947 at Boston, Communist labor leaders were called together in New York and instructed to proceed with formation of a third party.

Whereas Murray disclaimed knowledge of any foreign influence in the founding of the Progressive party, Louis Hollander, chairman of the New York State CIO, who on May 14, 1948 followed the CIO national president on the program at the Amalgamated convention, had no doubt. He flatly declared that the orders had been received from the Communist Information Bureau (Cominform) whose establishment at Belgrade by the Communist parties of nine European nations had been announced on Oct. 5, 1947. Hollander based his conclusion on these circumstances:

A few days before the Labor Day, 1947, weekend convention of the New York State CIO at Saratoga Springs, N. Y. a group of members of the state Executive Board called on him to go over the convention program. "Among the group," Hollander declared, "were three of the most distinguished left wing labor leaders." On the platform Hollander said he did not care to mention names but said, "to the New York delegates they were known. One of them is so distinguished that he is a member of the National Committee of the Communist party." Later in the day Hollander revealed to newspaper reporters that he meant Irving Potash, manager of the New York Furriers Joint Council, and that the other two were Saul Mills, secretary of the Greater New York CIO Council, and Ruth Young, secretary of the New York-New Jersey district of the United Electrical Workers. As Hollander related it at Atlantic City:

These three people, after going over the whole program, asked me, "Will there be any controversial questions at the convention of the state CIO?" I said, "I don't know any, except those that we have discussed here. However, if there is anyone who introduces a resolution on a third party, it will be opposed, and I will be one of those to oppose it." And the gentleman, the gentleman who is a member of the Executive National Committee of the Communist party, said to me, "Why Mr. Hollander, we have no intention of proposing a third party. What for?" So I said, "Well, then, the whole thing will be hunky dory. There will be no trouble." Brother Potofsky addressed the convention; Brother Blumberg addressed the convention. There was no resolution proposed by any of these groups for a third party.

Six weeks later a third party was organized. By whom? The same three people. They sponsored the third party six weeks later. The same three people who had walked into my office, saying that they did not intend to propose any third party!

What happened? Some day it will be revealed by the men and women who were present when this so-called third party was born. A little of it was told to me and I am saying this for the first time. It was born after George Marshall, Secretary of State, addressed the Boston convention of the national CIO. After the convention supported Marshall enthusiastically for his whole recovery program. All this came in from the "international political cartel," from the "brain trust" of those who think for all these page boys all over the world. The page boys were ordered: "You must obstruct CIO now. You must not permit CIO to carry out its European program. It is dangerous because Russia refused to participate in it."

Between the two Atlantic City labor conventions Alfred Friendly had written an article, which the *Washington Post* used on May 2, 1948, under the headline, "Reds Picked Wallace to Run, May Quit Him"; Victor Riesel had used the same material for a column in the *New York Post* for May 7, 1948. A few days after the Hollander blast, on May 17, 1948, the *Chicago Daily News* used a piece from New York by Edwin A. Lahey, headlined "Fight Brewing Over Wallace," which related left wing activities in connection with the Progressive party campaign.

Although charges of Communist sympathy and control increased during the rest of the year, the only specific charges or evidence of Communist origin of the Progressive party during 1948 were those advanced by Thompson, Murray and Hollander, and in the Friendly, Riesel and Lahey articles.

Largely through the auspices of the Americans for Democratic Action, the Alfred Friendly article received widespread circulation. It follows in its entirety:

"The Communist party, as a means of blocking the Marshall Plan, decided last October to back a third party headed by Henry A. Wallace, long before the former Vice President himself announced his candidacy.

"The strategy, adopted in October, 1947, by the party's Central Committee, was to force the CIO to reverse its position, taken the week before, indorsing the European Recovery Program.

"In this way, it was hoped there would be created a large and powerful labor pressure group against the pending foreign aid program.

"Considerations of Russian foreign policy were the almost exclusive reasons moving the Communists to found the third party and pick Wallace as its candidate.

"The two primary goals were defeating the Marshall Plan and winning a Communist victory in the Italian elections.

"The Central Committee of the American Communist party ordered labor's indorsement of Wallace to be secured even if that resulted in 'splitting the CIO right down the middle'.

"The points presented above are the highlights of the carefully planned scheme which culminated in Wallace's formal acceptance of the role of candidate last December 29.

"But there is nothing to suggest that Wallace was a party to, or had direct knowledge of, the Communists' inception and creation of the third party.

"There is now an indication — not firm, but nevertheless of possible significance — that the Communist party having used Wallace and having failed in its objectives — is now thinking of new strategy involving the dumping of Wallace. This indication will be discussed later.

"The Communists' support of the Wallace campaign and their key roles in it have been, of course, obvious for many months. But it was not until last week that a competent authority stated flatly that the Communists were 'directly responsible' for founding the third party movement.

"The speaker was Philip Murray, CIO president, addressing the Textile Workers Union at Atlantic City, N. J., on Wednesday. He said the decision was made at a Communist party meeting in New York City last October. He gave no further details.

"The Washington *Post* is now able to supply a number of those details, with some exactness.

"Its information is mainly from persons who participated directly in the series of meetings where the plans and decisions were made. In addition, there is confirming information from individuals close to the actual participants, who have been told by them what happened.

*"Story Begins With CIO Parley*

"The chronology:

"The CIO national convention was held in Boston last year, beginning on October 13. Two days later it heard a speech by Secretary of

252

State Marshall. The convention concluded its sessions with a vigorous indorsement of the Marshall Plan.

"It refrained from indorsing President Truman for re-election, but it did not lay any foundations, nor even provide an opening for support of a third party movement.

"The ERP resolution and the cold shoulder to a third party were distressing in the extreme to the Communist party.

*"CIO Communists Summoned*

"Accordingly, the CIO convention action was a body blow. Party leaders immediately summoned a meeting of the top Communist members and sympathizers among CIO union officers. The meeting was held within a few days of the convention's close, when union leaders were still in the area.

"There was a long discussion of how to put pressure on the unions and on Congress to defeat passage of the ERP.

"At this meeting, the organization of a third party was not discussed in concrete terms. But delegates from Illinois and California noted that they would move to organize third-party campaigns in their states.

*"Quill Suggests Wallace*

"Wallace was mentioned as a possible candidate by Michael A. Quill, president of the Transport Workers Union, who—only in the last month—has now broken with the Communists.

"In general terms there was a discussion of how to get the CIO to reverse its convention stand and to accept the idea of dumping Mr. Truman and helping a third party get under way.

"Very soon after this meeting — still in October — there was a meeting in New York of the Central Committee of the Communist party. This is the party organ which frames all high policy decisions.

"It consists of William Z. Foster, national chairman of the party; Eugene Dennis, the executive secretary; John Williamson, chief labor official of the party, and several CIO union officials.

*"December 15 Meeting Described*

"The Central Committee decided to create a third party and to obtain Wallace as its candidate.

"The best evidence of what transpired at that meeting are descriptions given to THE WASHINGTON POST of a subsequent gathering at which the official orders were handed out.

"It took place about December 15. Those in attendance were the Communist-minded leaders of unions in the New York area.

"Some 26 persons were present. There were from one to three representatives of every CIO union in New York except the ACW.

"Party Chairman Foster was not present, but Dennis, generally considered the best brains of the organization, was there.

"The most active figure, however, was Robert Thompson, Communist party chairman for New York State.

*"Thompson Announces 3rd Party*

"He opened the meeting with a long speech, saying that it had been decided to create a third party, with Wallace as its head.

"Therefore, he continued, the Communist Party wanted all union leaders to get busy preparing petitions for his candidacy, and literature to be distributed immediately Wallace's formal announcement of acceptance was made. This event was anticipated — correctly, as it turned out —some time during the next couple of weeks.

"CIO unions, Thompson said, should be ready to follow the announcement with an immediate indorsement of Wallace.

"Quill thereupon spoke out in what now seems to have been the beginning of his breakaway from the party.

*"Quill Attacks Decision*

"(Quill has denied he has ever been a card-carrying member of the party, but he has never denied that he was high in its councils.)

" 'Red Mike'—or, more properly, 'Ex-Red Mike'—demanded to know who had made such a decision.

"The Central Committee, said Thompson.

"Quill attacked it bitterly. He said the Central Committee could not tell him or his union that they had to go for Wallace, and that it had no right to do so. He said he would not go along and that the proposed action split the CIO.

*"Planned Squeeze on Murray*

"The Communists in the CIO and those unions which they could influence must pressure for an indorsement of Wallace, Thompson replied, 'even if it splits the CIO right down the middle.'

" 'The hell with you and your Central Committee,' Quill said. He told Thompson to relay his remarks to 'that crackpot' Foster.

"Despite his opposition, the meeting continued on the original line.

"The strategy was made clear: The pressure to be created, it was explained, would be such that Philip Murray could not hold out against it. He would be forced to get a reversal of the convention stand. To save the CIO and his position in it, he would have to indorse Wallace, and denounce the ERP.

*"Must Stop CIO Right Trend*

"Thompson said the Communists and the unions and locals they led should not be wishy-washy about supporting Wallace.

"Already, Thompson continued, the Communist parties in France and Italy were making their decision and there would be revolutions in both countries within two weeks.

*"Wallace's Reliability Questioned*

"The meeting, it may be noted, took place at about the end of the serious Communist strikes in France and Italy.

"At the New York meeting, the talk went on into an hour's discussion on the question of whether Wallace was 'reliable.'

"His meteoric shifts were recalled, as well as an occasion a year or so ago when, at a Madison Square Garden rally, he had made disparaging remarks about the Communists. The question was would he turn against the Communists again, or would he stay in line?

"The Washington *Post* has two accounts, not necessarily inconsistent, on how this question was resolved.

254

"According to one, it was admitted that Wallace was not so adhesively consistent as might be desired, but that he could be held as long as the Communists surrounded him and worked on him. The answer was to the effect that, 'To the extent that we encircle him, to that extent he'll stick.'

*"Communists Fooled by Events*

"According to the second account, it was decided that it did not make much difference if Wallace finally turned against them. The argument was that Wallace was to be used as a tool or lever for Communist foreign policy. The immediate goals were defeat of the Marshall Plan and a Communist victory in the Italian elections.

"The Communist plans fell far short of expectations.

"The CIO reaction was not as hoped. The pressure was less—not enough to bother Murray seriously. The dissent from the CIO convention policy was much less than was anticipated. Only fractions of a few unions fell into the Communist party line."

The Riesel column and Lahey piece were substantially the same, though shorter. Riesel placed the meeting at which Thompson and Quill clashed as a mid-Manhattan apartment of "one of the party's most active women commissars. Right near Bellevue Hospital to be exact." He and Lahey also told of a meeting in the Hays-Adams house in Washington, before the Jan. 22 session of the CIO Executive Board, at which Eugene Dennis allegedly refused to tell Quill who had contacted Wallace.

In response to a letter from me, Dorothy Thompson wrote on Nov. 20, 1953: "I did not pinpoint the start of the Progressive party—at least as far as any *public* record is concerned—without evidence. I referred to a speech by Gold advocating the third party, on the date mentioned. The source was the *Daily Worker* on which I have, however, only my own penciled notes. However, I now think I erred." She then explained that ADA material had convinced her that the Communist origin had been earlier.

The account in the *Daily Worker* for Nov. 19, 1947, of the preceding day's session of the International Executive Board of the CIO Fur and Leather Workers included no mention of any remarks by Ben Gold, president, or anyone else regarding a third party or Henry Wallace. Instead, it stressed Gold's condemnation of the Marshall Plan as "in reality a program of interfering in the economic life of the European countries to dictate the political life of these peoples and also to acquire military bases in Europe." The second paragraph of a story in the *Sunday Worker* for Nov. 23, 1947, however, read as follows: "The board also proposed a united labor campaign to repeal the Taft-Hartley law, the abolition of the House un-American Activities Committee, re-establishment of price controls, formation of a third party and rejection of the Truman-Marshall plan."

Possibly Miss Thompson had access to different editions of the *Worker,* but I checked both the New York and Chicago editions. In any case, endorsement of a third party movement was not new for the Fur & Leather Workers. As related on Page 44, at its 16th biennial convention on May 24, 1946, in Atlantic City—four months before Wallace was ousted from the cabinet—it resolved: "That our incoming international Executive Board and our representatives to CIO give their full support to the establishment of an independent political party of labor and progressive people at the opportune and appropriate time." In the *Fur and Leather Worker* for December, 1947 was reflected the sentiment of the November 18-22, 1947, meeting. A two-page center spread was headed, "Build People's Third Party" and began: "We denounce the unholy alliance of the Republicans and the majority of Democrats." Other extracts were: "President Truman has made common cause with Vandenberg, Hoover, Taft, Dulles and Dewey. In their so-called bi-partisan policy, they have surrendered the interests of the common people to the economic royalists . . . We affirm our convention decision FAVORING THE FORMATION OF A GENUINE PEOPLE'S THIRD PARTY! WE GREET THE SPLENDID BATTLE OF HENRY WALLACE, THE OUTSTANDING CHAMPION OF THE ROOSEVELT PROGRAM. . . The American people must have a candidate through whom and through whose consistent policies they can express their desires and needs for an American program of prosperity, security, democracy and peace."

The Dec. 8, 1947 (not Dec. 9, as she said) occasion involving William Z. Foster, to which Miss Thompson referred, evidently was a rally at Manhattan Center, New York, sponsored by the Jefferson School of Social Science, to commemorate the 100th anniversary of the Communist Manifesto. Once again the *Daily Worker* failed to report any words endorsing or even mentioning Wallace, although it gave voluminous coverage to Foster's criticism of American foreign policy. In its Dec. 11, 1947 issue, however, the *Daily Worker* carried an article under a Syracuse dateline which contained brief mention of a reporter's question to Wallace regarding Foster's endorsement of him earlier in the week. Wallace's reply was reported to be that similar endorsements "didn't seem to prevent Roosevelt from getting elected."

In its Dec. 12, 1947 issue, the *Daily Worker* quoted Wallace as having told 400 General Electric shop stewards at Schenectady, "I'm not a Communist, but I think a Communist is a human being. He has a right to express himself. I think the American Communists should be taken at their face value when they declare in their constitution that they are against the overthrow of the government by force. I'm not following their line. If they want to follow my line, I say God bless 'em. I admire their utter devotion to a cause they think is just." Wallace was also quoted as surmising that the quickest way to bring Communism to the United States would be to permit "reactionary capitalists to continue their drive toward a depression." On the question of a new party he supposedly said, "I have my own reasons for still wanting to keep the boys guessing." Other press accounts that day did not include these quotations.

On Sept. 22, 1947, Foster had been reported by the Associated Press as having told a small Communist group in Portland, Ore. that Wallace was "the man on whom the mantle of Roosevelt has fallen," and the CP's choice among the prospective candidates for the Presidency in

1948. In the *Daily Worker* for Nov. 25, 1947, Foster was reported to have said that a recent trip to western Pennsylvania had convinced him that miners and steelworkers were strong for Wallace, but he warned that considerable hard work would be needed to transform the sentiment into a mass political movement.

On Dec. 8, 1947, William Z. Foster and Eugene Dennis, national secretary of the Communist party, issued a joint blast at the Department of Justice for its preparation of a list of 78 organizations labeled "totalitarian, Fascist, Communist or subversive." This list, prepared by Attorney General Tom Clark in accordance with Truman's loyalty order, was made public by the Civil Service Commission on Dec. 5, 1947. According to Seth W. Richardson, chairman of the commission's loyalty review board, it was "simply one piece of evidence." Since then the list has, of course, been augmented to include well over 200 organizations and has been used widely by government officials, Congressional committees and private employers as the basis for determining the advisability of hiring or retaining employees.

In their statement Foster and Dennis declared: "The purge is aimed at silencing all criticism of the Truman-Marshall Plan. Opposition to this suicidal policy is growing among the American people as well as among the peoples of the world who refuse to barter away their independence for the sake of 'doles' with strings attached.

"The government fears the third party movement for 1948 which is already under way and which is rallying a new coalition to restore the Roosevelt policies. The 'purge' list will inevitably be extended to include all those who favor such a new political alignment. In fact, support for an independent Presidential ticket in 1948 is already viewed as disloyal and subversive."

Possibly this reference was to HR 4482, introduced Nov. 17, 1947 by Rep. C. C. Cole (Rep., Mo.) "to bar un-American parties from the election ballot" if "directly or indirectly affiliated with the Communist party . . . the Communist International or any other foreign agency, political party, organization or government." In March, 1948 the Department of Justice rendered an opinion that the bill was probably unconstitutional. It never got out of committee.

Also on Dec. 8, 1947, in Chicago, at the Illinois convention of the Communist party, state chairman Gilbert Green declared, "There must be a progressive people's alternative to a reactionary Truman and a reactionary Dewey or Taft in 1948," according to the *Daily Worker* for Dec. 9, 1947. The paper quoted Green further:

"We must not make the mistake of believing that this question can or will be decided by the Communists alone. The Communists alone can establish a Communist ticket; they cannot establish a third ticket or a third party. Therefore the key task before us is the job of convincing progressive non-Communist forces of the indispensable need for such a policy for 1948."

I do not know about Miss Thompson's statement that *Pravda* had an early announcement of Wallace's intentions. Under a small one-line head, at the bottom of the back page of its Dec. 22, 1947 issue, however, the *Daily Worker* had a short United Press item from Atlanta; it was to the effect that Gov. M. E. Thompson had told his press conference that he had been advised by Washington sources that Wallace would make his announcement on Dec. 29 at Chicago.

Philip Murray died before I had an opportunity to interview him in connection with this study. I did, however, interview Louis Hollander, who possessed the same or more information, in May, 1948. Hollander fits the stereotype of a hardboiled trade union leader, and it took me almost an hour to pin him down to a statement regarding the evidence in his possession when he and Murray made their charges. Finally he told me, "I'll have to admit I had only circumstantial evidence"—then adding, "—which later proved to be correct." I failed in my attempt to obtain amplification of that remark.

Denials of Murray's charges came immediately from Progressive party leaders. From Des Moines on April 29, 1948, Henry Wallace was quoted as saying: "As the founder of the new party I am amazed to hear Philip Murray use the same tactic in opposing our party that was used so long ago and unsuccessfully against the CIO. Phil knows his statement is nonsense. It always makes me mad to see a man who has performed great progressive service bow to hysteria, but I think the issues will become a lot clearer to Phil as he fights for the wage increase his steel workers need. I hope Phil will find some positive program to offer, and it might be a good idea for him to announce the name of the candidate for whom he is working and the candidate's stand on Taft-Hartley, segregation and wage freeze proposals, and the draft."

Similarly Beanie Baldwin declared:

"Mr. Murray's charge that the new party is a Communist creation is false and nonsensical. The new party grew out of the demand of millions of Americans for a candidate and a program which will back up labor and keep us out of war. The new party has that program and the only candidate who supported the CIO convention policy of wage increases and repeal of the Taft-Hartley act. Who is Mr. Murray's candidate and what is his program?"

In a joint statement regarding Hollander's story of their meeting with him before the Saratoga Springs convention, Ruth Young and Saul Mills said: "The question of a third party in 1948, 1949 or 1952 did not come up in our informal and friendly discussion with Mr. Hollander in August or at any other time. Mr. Hollander apparently has concocted the fable he told in Atlantic City to bolster his own sinking morale." Irving Potash declared, "The statement of Louis Hollander to the Amalgamated convention showed definitely that his memory does not serve him right in this instance."

I have talked with another prominent New York labor leader who recalls having discussed the political situation informally, over some drinks, with Potash at the Saratoga Springs convention. This informant says there was no doubt in his mind that Potash was strongly in favor of a third party at the time. He is certain in his recollection because, although he later supported the Progressive party, at the time he himself was lukewarm to the idea. Others who participated in the convention explain that no attempt at introducing a resolution to favor a new party was made because at that time there was no indication that Henry Wallace would decide to head such a party. The opposition of the Right Wing Amalgamated Clothing Workers to a new party was well known at the time.

Louis Hollander told me that he knew nothing of any of the meetings mentioned in the Friendly and Lahey articles. An interview with Lahey and correspondence with Friendly, furthermore, failed to reveal any further information. I believe both men are being absolutely honest in telling me that they do not recall the sources of their information. I am equally certain that neither man would reveal the source or sources to me if he did remember, as to do so would be in violation of journalistic ethics. Most certain of all am I that the source in each case was either Michael J. Quill, president of the Transport Workers Union, or someone close to Quill.

If the meetings cited—at the apartment of a Bellevue Hospital nurse, the Hays-Adams house in Washington and elsewhere—did not take place as described in these articles, then certainly some similar ones were held about the same time, to stimulate Communists in and out of the labor movement to lend their weight to the attempts to persuade Henry Wallace to become an independent candidate for the Presidency.

If it is accepted that the interest of the Communists in such a candidacy dates from October or November, 1947 only, then the contention that the Communists were the originators of the Progressive party automatically collapses, in view of what has been related so far in this book. Before proceeding to consideration of the possibility that Communist interest developed at an earlier date, however, this must be said of Quill: If he acted as he was reported to have done in the Lahey, Riesel and Friendly pieces, he must have been suffering from severe schizophrenia at the time.

Of "Red Mike," J. Parnell Thomas said, on March 1, 1946, "If there ever was a union that should be cleared at the top by the rank and file at the bottom, it is the one headed by Michael J. Quill, the Red Russian lover." When opening the Transport Workers Union convention, on Sept. 25, 1946, some time after Wallace was booted out of the cabinet, Quill called President Truman "an agent of the bankers and merchants who are working full speed for World War III"; he charged that Byrnes, Connally, Taft, Vandenberg, Dulles and others were trying to "behead men like Pepper and Henry Wallace who really speak for the people." A founder of the American Labor party, Quill was Rep. Vito Marcantonio's chief assistant in the Bronx. He also was a New York City councilman and president of the CIO Council of Greater New York in late 1947.

At the CIO convention in Boston in October, 1947, Quill lambasted the Truman administration and declared, "Today there is one independent voice calling for peace and security and that voice is that of Henry Wallace."

As late as Dec. 30, 1947, *the day after Henry Wallace announced his candidacy, Quill urged union leaders to support Wallace,* although he made it clear that his union had issued no official statement. In January the nationwide Wallace for President committee was organized. *Quill was the first labor leader to join it.* On Jan. 21, 1948, Quill cast one of the 11 votes in favor of Wallace at the meeting of the CIO Executive Board in Washington, which rejected Wallace 22 to 11. In February the Greater New York CIO Council, under his presidency, supported the candidacy of Leo Isacson, who ran for Congress in a special election in the New York 24th district as a Wallace supporter. On March 8, 1948, Quill was one of the sponsors who issued a call for a statewide conference of ALP and PCA leaders to support Wallace, to be held on April 3 under the chairmanship of O. John Rogge.

On March 27, 1948 Quill resigned as president of the New York CIO Council, presumably because he disagreed with its defiance of the order from national CIO headquarters to oppose the Wallace movement. At the same time, Quill was quoted in the press as saying he was still for Wallace personally, but believed in CIO unity as a first requisite. A month later, on April 19, 1948, he blocked an attempt by the Executive Board of the Transport Workers Union to endorse Wallace, again declaring that he was a Wallace supporter personally but believed that the union should settle a current wage difficulty for city subway and bus workers before getting into politics.

It is in the wage negotiations Quill was carrying on with the city that the real clues to his behavior are to be found. These wage increase demands became coupled with proposals by Mayor William O'Dwyer for an upping of the subway fare from 5 to 10 cents. Always, in the past, Quill had vigorously opposed any attempt to link fares and wages. In the *New York Times* for June 18, 1947, Quill was quoted as saying, "One of the things that made New York great was the 5 cent fare. . . We have been opposed to a higher fare and will continue our opposition on the ground that it will be a hardship on the riding public." In the *Transport Voice* for July 12, 1947, Quill wrote, "We refuse to tie our wages to the fare question."

The lead paragraph of a *New York Times* story April 29, 1948, was:
"Mayor O'Dwyer who once barred Michael J. Quill from his city hall office made it plain yesterday that the transit union leader's espousal of a higher fare and his break with Communist elements in the CIO had fully restored Mr. Quill to the mayor's good graces."

Quill settled for a 24 cent per hour wage increase instead of the 30 cent increase that the Left Wingers in his unions wanted. In the City Council he blocked a resolution by Councilmen Davis and Connolly to submit the matter of a fare increase to a public referendum, which O'Dwyer opposed. On July 1, 1948, the 10 cent fare went into effect.

When he resigned, on April 20, 1948, from the American Labor party, Quill charged that it was dominated by "the screwballs and crackpots," who "will continue to carry on as if the Communist party and the American Labor party were the same house with two doors." He specifically mentioned William Z. Foster and Robert Thompson as among those too important in the ALP. By way of answer, Vito Marcantonio, ALP chairman, accused Quill of "associating himself with the real estate and banking interests and devious and double-talking politicians" in support of higher fares. On April 13 the ALP of Bronx County had repudiated Quill, declaring, "he no longer represents the ALP nor the people who elected him."

In late May, 1948, Quill was quoted from Miami as saying that he had changed his mind regarding the Wallace candidacy. After the national CIO Executive Committee endorsed Truman, he was quoted as saying, "Of course I have to be for Truman since I take orders." The Executive Board of his own union, the TWU, however, rejected the Truman endorsement 19 to 5 and left it up to members to vote as they pleased. The vote was a repudiation of Quill, who was chastised for having favored the Truman endorsement at the national CIO committee meeting. Attempting to put the board on record on Sept. 7, Quill himself caused a pro-Wallace resolution to be introduced at the TWU board meeting; it was tabled 17 to 7. The powerful Local 100, however, supported Quill and fired Harry Sacher from his position as chief counsel after 14 years of service. On Oct. 27, 1948 Austin Hogan, president of Local 100, denounced Quill for having made winning a bus strike impossible. "You can't win because of the sellout against you," Hogan told 1,200 strikers at the St. Nicholas arena. The vote to return to work was 1014 to 556.

At the tenth constitutional convention of the CIO, held Nov. 23-26, 1948, at Portland, Ore., Quill explained that his support of Wallace at the preceding year's convention had been because he thought that Wallace would remain in the Democratic party. He said: " . . .When I returned from Boston to New York I was told by some mutual friends on the Hill that things had changed and that Wallace would lead a new political party. Well, I had to make a decision between that kind of politics and saving the Transport Workers and remaining within CIO. I had to decide not only was I a man or a mouse, or was I a man and a louse. I decided not to be a louse. I stuck with CIO."

Quill has never explained his joining the Wallace for President committee, his vote in favor of the new party at the CIO Executive Board meeting, his campaigning for Isacson, or his numerous statements in favor of the Progressive party up to the time he made his deal on wages and fares with Mayor O'Dwyer.

I tried hard to obtain an interview with Michael Quill: in June, 1953 before he went to Europe and in August after he returned. I talked on the telephone to his secretary at least ten times. I talked with his public relations man, Joseph Kutch, who recalled having heard me speak a few months earlier to the Gary, Ind. chapter of the American Newspaper Guild. He was a reporter for the *Gary Post-Tribune* at the time. He told me he had "put in a good word" for me with Quill. Nothing came of it, however. Follow-up letters to both Quill at his office and Kutch at his home went unanswered. I finally sent my letter by registered mail and obtained the return receipt as evidence that I had given Quill the opportunity to present his case here.

To be charitable, this explanation is possible: After Quill made his deal with O'Dwyer in March, 1948, his memory began to play tricks on him. Certainly then, and only then, did he become convinced that he had played a heroic role from the start in opposition to the Wallace movement. Inasmuch as it was Quill's romantic tale that formed the basis for any "evidence" that anyone else ever advanced to prove that the Communists started the Progressive party, I feel his record requires the amount of space I have given it.

At Syracuse, on Sept. 11, 1948, Quill amplified or corrected the story by declaring that the December conference, at which he was told that the CP had decided to support Wallace "even if it split labor right down the middle," was held in the law office of Harry Sacher; and that Eugene Dennis, Robert Thompson and John Williamson, labor director of the CP, were present. The *New York Times* of the next day carried the story. Nobody else has ever publicly declared that he was at any such meetings, thus providing an extremely strong presumption that it was Quill who gave the stories to Friendly and Lahey.

In an article, "Who Runs Wallace," in *Plain Talk* for June, 1948, Victor Lasky cited Quill as authority for the fact that pro-Wallace meetings were held by Communist leaders in New York and Washington. Dwight MacDonald did the same in the summer, 1948 issue of *Politics*. Arthur Schlesinger Jr. tells of the same meetings in *The Vital Center* (Houghton Mifflin, 1949), quoting Quill as saying, "They told me they had decided to form a party and Wallace would head it up."

William Z. Foster denied the Riesel story in the *Daily Worker* for May 18, 1948. "There never was any such meeting and never any things said or done, as Riesel alleges," he categorically stated. Foster chided Riesel for quoting Robert Thompson as calling the Communist National Committee "the Central Committee" and asked, "Who but a fool can believe that the Communist party had or believed it had any such power or decision over Wallace?"

There is no doubt that, by November, 1947, Communists all over the country were loudly advocating a new political party, with Wallace as its Presidential candidate. The generally accepted (Quill) view is that the CP decision was made after the CIO convention, held Oct. 13-17, 1947 at Boston, at which Secretary of State George Marshall spoke and Henry Wallace was positively not invited, as he had often been in the past. It is not true, as sometimes claimed, that the CIO endorsed the so-called Marshall Plan at that convention. Rather, it unanimously adopted a resolution—for which Irving Potash, among others, spoke on the floor—calling for relief, rehabilitation and reconstruction of war-devastated countries.

The resolution also called for progressive universal disarmament and the complete demilitarization and decartelization of Germany and

Japan, and said that "above all, the people of this country demand that there be a fulfillment of the basic policy of our late President Roosevelt for unity of purpose and action among the three great wartime allies—the United States, Great Britain and the Soviet Union—within the United Nations."

The day after the PCA board voted to urge Wallace to run, Alex Rose, vice chairman of the New York Liberal party, termed the action "political extortion"; he said it was the direct result of the breakup of a meeting of the Council of Foreign Ministers in London. He said the Communist fight against Truman and the Marshall Plan was now being transferred to the United States, and that Wallace was being used by the Communists to put pressure on the Truman administration to make concessions to the Soviet Union. The crucial issue, on which the London meeting had dissolved, was the Soviet proposal that it obtain reparations out of current German production, to which the Western powers refused to agree.

Others who took a short-range view of Communist strategy—that the decision to support the effort to establish a third party in 1948 was made comparatively late in 1947—have cited an Associated Press story datelined Moscow, Oct. 22, 1947, which appeared the next day in the *New York Times*. It stated that Col. Gen. Andrei A. Zhdanov, a member of the Politburo and secretary of the Communist party Central Committee, had called upon Communists and sympathizers throughout the world to join in fighting attempts by the United States to achieve "world domination by American imperialism," and stating that the Soviet Union would assume the leadership in attempting to wreck the Marshall Plan and to prevent the United States from converting Europe into a 49th American state.

Still others think the deciding factor was the establishment of the nine-nation Communist Information Bureau at Belgrade, generally called the Cominform, which was decided upon at a meeting held Sept. 21-23, 1947 in Warsaw, and announced on Oct. 5 by the Parisian Communist newspaper *L'Humanité*. Its manifesto condemned American foreign policy as imperialistic and intended to dominate the world and explained, "It is because the Soviet Union and the new democracies have become an obstacle to the imperialists' plans for world domination and for the destruction of democratic movements that a crusade is organized against them." The purpose of the new bureau was announced as the providing of machinery for the interchange of information and voluntary coordinated activities.

Because of the Voorhis act of 1944, requiring the registration of foreign agents, the American Communist party announced on Nov. 2 that it would not become a member. It declared: "The Communist party has concluded that the present political situation in the United States is such that the Communist party should not affiliate. The reactionary and pro-fascist forces now whipping up anti-Communist hysteria and war incitement in our country would undoubtedly seize upon such action by the American Communist party as a pretext for new provocations and repressions against the Communists and all other sections of the American labor and progressive movement." At the same time William Z. Foster branded as a "barefaced lie" the charge that the new bureau was "in any sense directed against the peoples of western Europe and the United States."

The Warsaw manifesto was believed by some to have inspired American Communists to board the Wallace bandwagon but not because of foreign policy. According to Michael Straight, who thinks the manifesto was the deciding factor in that decision, it was rather the statement that the main worldwide danger of the time for the working class was "underestimation of its own forces and overestimation of imperialism's." That, according to Straight, encouraged the American comrades to go ahead. As an indication of that fact he points out that in September there had been a "pulling back" on the part of the Communists, after it became clear to them that the Amalgamated Clothing Workers would withdraw from the American Labor party if it joined a national third party movement. For example, on Sept. 18, 1947, at a Communist rally in Madison Square Garden, Eugene Dennis, after declaring there was no chance for "the people" to win through the Republican or Democratic parties, had said:

> But if the people rely on themselves, organize and act independently; if they utilize the dependence of the Democratic party nationally on labor's vote; and if they take advantage of the struggle in the Democratic party between the pro-Roosevelt and pro-Hoover forces—then the people have some chance to influence the outcome of the Democratic national convention. . .

> There is much speculation these days about what we Communists are going to do—now and in 1948 . . . the Communist party, a most decisive part of the Left, is steering a course with millions of progressive-minded Americans. Our purpose is at all cost to help establish the unity of action of labor and all progressives, to check and defeat pro-fascist reaction and the instigators of World War III. This means that in 1948 we are going to move heaven and earth to help ensure the election of an anti-war President and a progressive congress. Our candidate for the skipper of the Ship of State is a man of the Roosevelt stamp. We will join hands with everyone who is working for the election of that kind of skipper—whether on the Democratic party ticket or on an independent ticket. . .

> Regardless of what party tickets emerge in 1948 we Communists believe that the times require a new political realignment in the United States—the building of the foundations of a strong, independent people's party close-

ly connected with the Pro-Roosevelt-Wallace program and Wallace. Equally, we believe that the times require the forging of a broad, democratic coalition at every level, functioning actively in every Congressional district and precinct.

As an inseparable part of the struggle for victory in 1948, we are helping to develop the third party movement. Together with other progressive forces, we shall promote the trend toward crystallizing a new anti-war and anti-trust people's party in the states and communities.

And there was more of the same, which can unquestionably be interpreted as indicating what the proper nationwide strategy should be in 1948. The third party efforts to which Dennis referred were those on a statewide basis in New York, California and Illinois, especially in California. In the *Daily Worker* for Aug. 14, 1947, Robert Thompson, New York State secretary of the CP, had argued that, regardless of what decision was made nationally, the American Labor party should be strengthened in New York by retaining and increasing the enrollment of those who favored a statewide party but might oppose a national third party.

Further evidence of the fact that the Communists were comparative latecomers to Gideon's Army was provided by Dennis at the Feb. 3-5, 1948 meeting of the Communist party National Committee, at which he said:

"In connection with the development of the Wallace peace campaign and the third party movement, our generally correct political orientation and line was considerably weakened for a time by our failure to wage an adequate and sharp enough struggle against a host of sectarian and opportunist tendencies. We were much too slow in combating the erroneous views of certain party leaders and district organizations, as well as many of our trade union cadres who, up till the announcement of Wallace's candidacy, expressed doubts as to the advisability of an independent Presidential ticket and confused the maneuverings and treacherous position of most of labor's top officials with the position being taken by the rank and file."

In July, 1948 Max Bedacht, former national secretary of the International Workers Order, was unseated as a delegate to the New Jersey Communist party convention when it was learned that he opposed the Foster-Dennis decision to participate in the Progressive party popular front movement. He was reported to have called the PP a "third imperialist party." After he continued to charge that the national CP had "sold out" by collaborating with the PP, which had a non-Socialist domestic program, he was expelled from the party in November, 1948. How the majority of Communist leaders felt at the time was expressed on July 18 by Sid Stein, chairman of the New Jersey CP, when he said, in commenting on Bedacht's charges, "It is just as incorrect to think of the New Party as a capitalist party as it would be to think of it as an ex-

265

tension of the Communist party. It is neither. The third party movement in the United States is the beginning of a mighty people's coalition against imperialist reaction and war, and the defeat of the monopolies is a precondition of socialism in this country."

On the other hand, John Cotton Brown in his doctoral dissertation, *The 1948 Progressive Campaign: A Scientific Approach* (University of Chicago, December, 1949), quoted from a mimeographed sheet, "Turning Point," for November, 1948, put out by some other expelled Communists who thought that the leadership had been negligent in not espousing the Wallace cause earlier. The criticism read, in part:

"Here were people who for two and a half years, by indecision and doubletalk, by counsel now of 'too soon, premature, the masses aren't ready' and now of 'too late, the elections are too close,' did everything in their power to prevent the emergence of a correct Third Party until, through no fault of theirs, Wallace finally announced his candidacy. Now, with brazen effrontery, they insist on a major share of the credit for the organization of the Progressive party."

The credit-taking reference was to the draft resolution to be submitted to the national convention in August, 1948. The following section was widely interpreted as meaning that the party claimed to have been the principal factor in bringing the Progressive party into existence:

> The Communist party was the only force in American political life which instantly grasped the reactionary, imperialist issue of the Marshall Plan and without waverings and vacillations, undertook the struggle for its exposure and rejection. The Communist party from the earliest days after the end of the war understood that its traditional fight for a new people's party directed against the two-party system of the monopolies had once more been placed by events as an immediate practical question before the American people and, acting upon this understanding, it boldly proclaimed the need for such a new people's party. Because of its correct line, the party was able to carry on effective mass work and make significant contributions to the struggle for peace and democracy and to the forging of the new political alignment and people's coalition. The Communist party alone, long before it had become clear to wider sections of the people, signalized the rise of a fascist danger in the United States and exposed the ominous drive toward the transformation of our country into a police state.

Then, however, it added:

> In connection with the development of the third party movement, our party—despite its generally correct position—was slow in some respects in overcoming certain

doubts as to the advisability of an independent Presidential ticket, doubts and hesitancies which reflected influence of the lesser evil theory and which flowed from confusing the treacherous position of most of labor's top officialdom with the attitudes of the rank and file.

The last part was obviously a paraphrase of Dennis' earlier statement (see page 265).

On July 17, 1948 the *New York Times* used the headline "Communists Plan to Use Wallace" over an account of a statement by Simon W. Gerson, legislative representative of the New York Communist party, at the New York State CP convention as reported in the *Daily Worker* for that date. Gerson said:

> In building this great new coalition we Communists will do our share. Our Socialist outlook and firm conviction that only a Socialist reorganization of society can bring permanent peace, security and prosperity are no barriers to cooperation with persons of non-Socialist convictions in creating this great new realignment. We, of course, will freely advance our own fraternal criticism of policies within the great coalition. We seek no special position by reason of our advanced views and will of course oppose any special disabilities because of such views.

This statement meant, to the *Times* and some other newspapers, that the Communists considered themselves to be working for the first phase of socialism by supporting the Progressive party. In a formal statement, which the *Times* used on July 19, 1948, the CP disclaimed any intention of trying to run the Wallace movement for its own sake. Gerson, the spokesman, declared:

> The Wallace movement is by its very nature a great coalition of workers, farmers, Negro people, professional and small business people. The New Party is anti-monopoly, anti-fascist and anti-war. It is not by its very nature a socialist or communist party and we are not seeking to make it one. There is only one Marxist party in America and this is it, the Communist party. Any effort to exclude socialist-minded people from contributing their efforts to the New Party movement stems from those who are seeking to disrupt the third party movement. That is the real meaning of the persistent efforts to spread the tale that the Communists somehow seek to use Wallace.

To buttress the attitude of those who believe the Communists were just "talking big," this fact is pertinent: it is an old trait, which some non-Communist groups also possess, to claim as much credit as possible. In

1945 Earl Browder threw the Democratic party into a tizzy with a report to the Communist party National Committee in which he contended that the Communists had "contributed essentially" to the victory of the Roosevelt-Truman ticket in 1944. Here are two typical comments at the time, indicating the influence of predisposition on judgement: Sen. Scott Lucas (Dem., Ill.): "The Communists are on the wane. The only influence they had in the last election was adverse to the New Deal." Rep. Noah Mason (Rep., Ill.): "Browder, Hillman & Co. are riding high—certainly they won the election for Roosevelt."

Examination of Communist periodical literature during 1946 and 1947 provides clues as to why some elements in the CP were slow in recognizing the Wallace movement as "by its very nature a great coalition." Most penetrating of the Communist analyses of the developing scene were those of A. B. Magil in *The New Masses*. In the Oct. 8, 1946 issue, in comment upon Henry Wallace's retirement from the cabinet, he wrote, "No doubt about it: the Wallace episode has widened popular dissatisfaction with the two major parties. It has thereby provided an opportunity for accelerating a political realignment which, under labor's leadership, can in the post-election period bring this simmering discontent to a point where it boils up into a new vigorous people's party. The question is: how shall we today grasp this opportunity most effectively?"

In the months that followed, Magil failed to be encouraged by the progress that was being made, because the labor leadership which he deemed necessary was not developing. In the Dec. 3, 1946 issue he wrote: "Our objective should be to start building now a broad people's movement, a coalition of classes—workers, dirt farmers, small businessmen, professionals—of organized groups and of all those with the Negro people. The recent Conference of Progressives is the nucleus of such a coalition but it needs to be greatly extended to make it capable of developing, around the issues of domestic and foreign policy, a vast national effort culminating in a progressive victory in 1948."

The dim view that Magil took of the Conference of Progressives seemed positively glowing by comparison with what he thought of the Progressive Citizens of America. In the Jan. 14, 1947 *New Masses*, he wrote: "The launching of PCA helps bring into focus a number of problems that concern the further development of independent progressivism. In the first place, can PCA constitute potentially the whole of this movement and can it, when conditions are ripe, transform itself into a new people's political party? In my opinion it cannot. It has an indispensable job to do, but it would be a mistake to believe that PCA can replace or render superfluous the independent political activity of organized labor. . . To base this movement on the middle classes, whether of city or countryside, is to base it on quicksand." Later in the same article he lamented "the relative unreadiness of the labor movement for the leading role it must play in welding together the political elements that can become—and should become by 1948—a new antifascist, anti-monopoly people's party."

By the June 3, 1947 issue Magil was encouraged by the resolutions of the Packinghouse, Automobile and United Electrical Workers favoring

268

an ultimate third party; the primary victory of Charles A. Savage in Washington; the outcome of several municipal elections and the results of public opinion polls showing disapproval of certain aspects of American foreign policy. "All these victories," he wrote, "point in the direction of independent progressivism and are potential capital for a new party. True, they are only beginnings and it would be absurd to draw from them more than tentative conclusions. . . ."

In the Sept. 23, 1947 issue of *New Masses,* Magil struck a balance sheet of pros and cons in the third party movement and concluded, "It remains true that without the active participation of a substantial section of the trade union movement and without the support of large numbers of Democratic voters, no serious new party can be formed."

Examination of the files of the *Daily Worker* during the crucial fall, 1947 period reveals that the coverage given to Henry Wallace was no better than that given by other newspapers. There was no editorial campaign "whooping it up" for a third party, although the few references that were made to the developing movement were sympathetic. An example was an editorial, "Pepper's Stand," in the issue of Aug. 18, 1947, which chastised the Florida senator for his endorsement of President Truman and rejection of all third party ideas which, the editorial said, "can hardly sound sensible to those who recall his fiery criticism of the Administration." The *Worker* reasoned: "Third party advocates will naturally regret Pepper's stand because it harms the rising movement of a third party. But those who know the score will not be dismayed and they will still look to Pepper to play a progressive role. The progress of the third party movement must be gauged by the rising sentiment for independent political action among the workers and farmers in the country and by the practical steps being taken to organize it. It is the millions of common people who have no real political home (and no fear of losing it) who must be relied upon to build one."

In its Aug. 29, 1947 issue the *Worker* quoted from Wallace's Labor Day piece in the *New Republic:* "It is time for labor to 'come out fighting' and take the lead in a progressive political movement based on a far-sighted and well organized alliance between workers and the farmers." On Sept. 1, 1947 the paper made passing favorable mention of his suggestion; two days later it editorialized at length on Wallace's Labor Day speech in Detroit under the heading, "A Guide for Progressives." This editorial read in part:

"The present problem facing these [liberal] movements is to provide the groundwork for a progressive program and slate. Whether this will take place through an alliance with the Democratic party or through an independent third party cannot be determined until next summer and is not the problem now."

A one-paragraph editorial in the *Worker* for Oct. 7, 1947, was as follows:

"Progressives and American labor have the duty of keeping our country on a democratic peaceful course. The nation urgently needs a strong anti-monopoly, anti-war coalition based on the Roosevelt-Wallace line. The overseas resistance to Wall street reactionaries helps the democratic forces here in the United States."

In an editorial, "Thanks, Senator Bridges," on Oct. 20, 1947, the *Worker* commented on a Paris news story that Sen. H. Styles Bridges (Rep., N.H.) had warned the French government that "the speed and strength of American aid to France would depend on whether that nation stopped a wave of strikes." The next to last paragraph of this full-page piece read:

"Bridges' warning that American food will go only to strike-breakers and anti-Communists adds new weight to Henry Wallace's recent remarks that if this bipartisan 'get-tough' policy goes on, America will have to have a new political party, a peace party."

And that was the last important editorial mention of Wallace until after the Dec. 15, 1947, action of the PCA board to urge him to run for the Presidency. Then its editorial, "They Fear Wallace," in the Dec. 18 issue, was hardly a clarion call to arms. It began, "A frantic anxiety is beginning to make itself felt in certain quarters as the Wallace for President movement begins to assume practical form," and concluded: "The only genuinely practical course for any progressive or trade unionist in the United States today is to break with the bipartisan Hooverism which is ruining the nation's hope for peace and democratic progress. To adjust oneself to this bipartisan Toryism on the ground of 'practicality' is to help betray the nation to the march of pro-Fascist reaction. Wallace alone among the possible candidates speaks for the interests of the common man and a democratic America."

For American Communists the monthly magazine *Political Affairs* performs a *New York Times* type of service; that is, it publishes the complete texts of all important proceedings and statements. Six years later Frank Kingdon told me that the "blueprint" for the Progressive party of 1948 was contained in the May, 1947 issue of that magazine. What he had reference to was the May Day Appeal. Beginning "May Day this year must be a powerful demonstration of United Labor Action," after about 1,000 words on why all labor and liberal groups should oppose reactionary Big Business it concluded: "This unity is needed to build a broad democratic coalition for independent political action as an alternative to both major parties which are controlled by the trusts. Only in this way can the people register their will in the 1948 elections. May Day must be a giant demonstration of United Labor and People's Action." It was signed by the National Board, CPUSA, William Z. Foster, chairman, and Eugene Dennis, general secretary.

As early as its December, 1946 issue *Political Affairs* had editorialized in favor of "a people's party which will include the Communists," and referred to the recently-fired Henry Wallace as one who had "contributed a great deal toward checking the G.O.P. advance."

The January, 1947 issue carried the remarks of Eugene Dennis, at the December meeting of the CP National Committee, regarding the *Daily Worker's* first-day criticism of Wallace's speech of Sept. 12, 1946.

In its Sept. 13, 1946 editorial, "Wallace Evades Issue," the *Daily Worker,* after admitting that Wallace had not "agitated for war" as had

Governor Dewey and Sen. Taft, had written: "But if Wallace's address did not have the rampant jingoist imperialist overtones of American imperialist responsibility for world reaction. . . Wallace repeated the major fallacies advanced by most apologists for American imperialism and designed to cover up Administration policy."

In its news story in the same issue, it had said: "While expounding the peace ideals of the late President Roosevelt, Henry Wallace defended the policies which are undermining those ideals." By contrast it lauded Claude Pepper's "powerful speech."

In its Sept. 14, 1946 editorial, "Truman, Wallace and Pepper," the *Worker* had begun to be more friendly. It wrote: "While Secretary Wallace obscured the responsibility of American imperialism for world tension today, he advanced certain policies that are in opposition to the bipartisan program of Vandenberg, Byrnes and Truman."

The next day, Sept. 15, in its editorial, "Disowning Peace," the paper had declared:

"By slapping Henry Wallace in the face, President Truman has openly confessed his abandonment of the policies of the late President Roosevelt.

"He has actually slapped the American people in the face, because Henry Wallace's speech last Thursday night, despite all its shortcomings, was a reflection of the deep worry which pervades our people over the present war trend of the Administration."

Communists would say that the paper merely was reacting to developing news events. Others, however, cite an Associated Press account dated London, Sept. 14, as having swayed the editorial judgment of the American Communist newspaper. The AP story, as it appeared in the *New York Times* for Sept. 15, was as follows:

> The Moscow radio, in an English language broadcast today, gave this report on the New York address of Secretary of Commerce Henry A. Wallace:
>
> "The United States Secretary of Commerce and Senator Pepper urged the improvement of relations between the United States and the Soviet Union.
>
> "At a large political rally in New York City, the United States Secretary of Commerce and Senator Pepper demanded a return to Roosevelt's foreign policy. The audience loudly applauded Wallace's condemnation of imperialism but punctuated his remarks against the U.S.S.R. with cries of disapproval."

Eugene Dennis gave the Communist version in *Political Affairs:* ". . . neither the national Board nor the secretariat discussed or read in advance either the speech of Wallace or the *Daily Worker* editorial . . . the first editorial in the *Daily Worker* on the Wallace speech adopted such a completely negative attitude . . . (they) were disoriented by the unjust and harmful remarks by Wallace on the Soviet Union and the Communists. Because of this, the comrades failed to grasp the fact that

271

Wallace, in his own way and within the limitations of his position, was challenging the main line of the Byrnes-Vandenberg policy and in the first place the 'get tough with Russia policy.' "

In the February, 1948 issue of *Political Affairs*, William Z. Foster wrote:

"It is absolutely necessary to begin building the new mass party now . . . conditions are ripe . . . the political situation promotes it . . . there must be no illusion that the Democratic party as such can be won for the task that a people's party will perform . . . the Communists must form an active recognized section of the movement. From an immediately practical standpoint . . . there must be a progressive Presidential candidate in the field in 1948 without fail; if not on the Democratic ticket, then surely on an independent ticket. . . ."

The foregoing quotations, with the same deletions, are those which Americans for Democratic Action used in its mimeographed report, *Henry A. Wallace: The First Three Months*, the main section of which began:

"The American Communist party's campaign to promote and control a Third Party in the United States is revealed in CP documents published over the past three years.

"The third party objective figured in the abrupt demotion of Mr. Browder in the summer of 1945. Jacques Duclos, the French Communist leader who broke Browder and set the new line for the CPUSA, said in his manifesto that a major objection to the Browder policies was that they would end 'in liquidation of the independent political party of the working class in the U.S.'

"In the same article which spelled the end of Browder's leadership of the CPUSA Duclos generously and perhaps significantly quoted from Secretary of Commerce Henry A. Wallace."

News of the statement by Jacques Duclos, secretary of the French Communist party (in the April, 1945 issue of the official French CP paper *Les Cahiers du Communisme*), first reached American readers by means of an article by Nelson Frank in the *New York World-Telegram* for May 22, 1945. This forced publication of the news of what came to be called "the Duclos letter" in the *Daily Worker* for May 24 and stirred up such a controversy among American Communists that, on July 28, 1945, Browder was deposed, after 15 years of being the No. 1 American Communist. This happened simultaneously with the dissolution of the year-old Communist Political Association and the reinstitution of the Communist party with a new constitution.

The references to Henry Wallace in the Duclos letter were two, both near the end, as follows:

"In the United States the omnipotent trusts have been the object of violent criticism. It is known, for instance, that the former Vice President of the United States, Henry Wallace, has denounced their evil doings and their anti-national policy."

"The former Vice President of the United States, Henry Wallace, present Secretary of Commerce, said rightly that one cannot fight fascism abroad and tolerate at home the activity of powerful groups which intend to make peace'a simple breathing spell between the death of an old tyranny and the birth of a new'."

It was Browder's leadership in persuading the old CP to dissolve, on May 20, 1944, that Duclos had severely criticized, as a policy "straying dangerously far from the victorious doctrines of Marxian Leninism," and one which revised the principles of Marxism "through the conception of a long peace between classes in the United States, the possibility of suppressing class warfare in the post-war period and the establishment of harmony between labor and capital."

Publication of the Duclos letter confirmed the essential facts of a story which the *World-Telegram* had carried more than a year earlier, on March 9, 1944; Communist leaders, including William Z. Foster, had denied them at the time. The story pertained to a secret meeting, on Feb. 8, 1944, of the CP Political Committee, at which Foster was unanimously outvoted in an attempt to obtain condemnation of a report that Browder had made on Jan. 7, 1944, to the National Committee. The report pertained to the Teheran conference, held Nov. 28 to Dec. 1, 1943, at which Roosevelt, Churchill and Stalin, in a declaration, expressed their "determination that our nations shall work together in the war and in the peace that will follow."

Of the effects of the Duclos letter, Foster wrote in his *History of the Communist Party of the United States* (International, 1952), page 435:

"Undoubtedly, with events at home and abroad daily showing the stupidity of Browder's revisionism, the American Communists, without Duclos' intervention, would eventually have cleaned the party of this political poison. But it would have been a difficult process, probably involving a serious party split. As it was, his famous article greatly facilitated the smashing of Browder's opportunist system, for which the Communist party of the United States remains deeply indebted to Jacques Duclos and the French Communist party."

On June 18, 1945 the National Committee of the CP unanimously condemned Browder's viewpoint, agreed with Duclos and endorsed the Foster position, which it had scorned in February. Before this, in May, Frederick Woltman had said in the *New York World-Telegram* he could "state authoritatively" that the Duclos blast originated in Moscow, where the French leader was shown a copy of the Foster attack. He did not elaborate as regards his source of information.

Foster epitomized his case against Browder in his opening remarks at the Nov. 16-18, 1945 meeting of the National Committee of the CP in New York; which remarks became the foreword to the pamphlet, *America At the Crossroads,* by Eugene Dennis. In essence it was that Browder erred in foreseeing a post-war world in which the principles of Marxism-Leninism would no longer be valid. He thought that capitalism, rejuvenated and grown progressive, would work easily in peace and harmony with the Socialist world to heal the wounds of war. The United States would embark on a world program of industrialization of backward countries, to bring prosperity and democracy to them.

Foster contended that none of this happened. Instead, the United States became imperialistic, bent on world conquest, getting tough and trying to dictate to the Soviet Union. Since then it has become a frequent practice of self-evaluating Communists to trace party weaknesses to the Browder period of control. Inspiration for the policy, which culminated in the temporary dissolution of the American Communist party in 1944, was Georgi Dimitroff, general secretary of the Communist International; he had propounded the idea of a united front against fascism on Aug. 2, 1935, at the 7th world congress of the Communist International. His statement is to be found in his book, *The United Front*. The American "follow-up" was *The People's Front* (International, 1938) by Earl Browder.

Browder was correct, Foster admitted, in supporting FDR in his fight against reaction. "This correct policy, however," he says in his book (page 336), "as later events were to show, was eventually to be distorted by Browder into an unpermissible subordination of the CP to the bourgeois Roosevelt program in general."

Browder was not formally expelled from the Communist party until Feb. 14, 1946, but once the decision had been made to abandon his united front policies, Communists in 1945 and 1946 did not rush to join new movements; rather, they were skeptical of them. Witness, for instance, the words of Eugene Dennis in his report to the Nov. 16-18, 1945 meeting of the CP National Committee:

> There is increasing disillusionment among the masses with the Truman Administration and hence with the Democratic party. Within the CIO, within many Negro organizations and among the independent voters' groups, there is a deepening realization that it is necessary to strengthen and expand the independent political action of labor and the progressives. While the approach of most of these popular forces is to develop independent action along the line of PAC and NC-PAC, there is also a growing minority sentiment for building a national third party. Similar trends are to be noted in the La Guardia-Morris "No deal" grouping, as well as among many of the followers of Wallace in the Democratic party. In view of these developments and taking into account the imperialist course of the Truman administration, and the historic need of advancing independent political action, it is necessary to re-examine the question of a third party.

*Obviously, it was not the belief that such a third party, presumably entirely impossible as long as Browderism prevailed, could develop through such organizations as the PAC and the NC-PAC.* It is a known fact that it was the Left Wingers who opposed the merger of the NC-PAC and the ICC-ASP into the PCA in December, 1947. This goes entirely contrary to what many charged: that there was a Communist-directed step-by-step organizational development, culminating in the Progressive party in 1948. Rather, it would seem that widespread Communist support for the idea of a new party, from October or November, 1947 on, was either: (1) An act of desperation after it became apparent that no other organization of any importance, including—or, perhaps, especially—the CIO, was going to oppose the Marshall Plan and other aspects of the bipartisan "get tough" policy, or (2) enough Communists were swept up in the enthusiasm which Henry Wallace had engendered throughout the country during 1947 to become convinced that there was a possibility of success for a mass movement regardless of the opposition of the nominal leaders of labor and liberal groups, and its middle-class, rather than proletarian, origin.

I suspect that both factors were operative. Despite the many ups and downs of Communist policy, a desire to ultimately crack the two-party American political system was a longtime Communist ambition. Communists had played as large a part as they were permitted to play in virtually every earlier third party attempt. As the *Daily Worker* editorialized on April 30, 1948, in comment on Philip Murray's charges that the Progressive party was Communist-inspired: "The facts are that the Communist party has openly advocated a new, independent political party of the American masses for the past 30 years." The same editorial continued to remind Murray of a few other facts:

"Communists have also advocated and actively helped in organizing industrial mass industry unions now known as the CIO and for this the CIO was described as a 'Communist plot' by the open shoppers. It's an old story."

The record, as I have tried to compile it in this chapter, does not seem to indicate any clear-cut long-range plot to make Henry Wallace the standard-bearer of a new party in 1948; however, there are some who presumably have looked at the same record and firmly believe differently. Arthur Schlesinger, Jr. is one. In *The Vital Center* (Houghton Mifflin, 1949) he is convinced of the existence of an almost superhuman Kremlin-directed international conspiracy; as much so as Adolf Hitler or Joseph McCarthy ever were. In his zeal to "fit pieces into a pattern," or for other reasons, however, Schlesinger completely misinterprets Eugene Dennis' attitude toward the PAC and the NC-PAC. Whereas direct quotation shows that Dennis did not believe any third party effort could develop out of such organizations—a view which A. B. Magil and others shared—Schlesinger categorically states that exactly the opposite was true: that Dennis said in 1945 that those organizations would be used to build a new party. Henry Wallace's dismissal from the Cabinet, according to Schlesinger, was a "wind-fall" to the Communists. He explained: "This well-intentioned, woolly-minded, increasingly embittered man was made to order for Communist exploitation; his own sense of martyrdom was swiftly generalized to embrace all friends of Soviet totalitarianism."

According to Louis Budenz in *Collier's* for Sept. 18, 1948, the Communists decided to take Henry Wallace "into custody" not long after Wallace's return from his mid-1944 trip to Siberia, which he described in his *Soviet Asia Mission* (Reynal & Hitchcock, 1946). Budenz even named the Communist-approved cabinet and other appointments President Wallace would make: Frederick Field, Secretary of State; Lee Pressman,

275

Attorney General; Paul Robeson, Ambassador to the Soviet Union, and so on.

Reviewers of James A. Wechsler's *The Age of Suspicion* (Random, 1953) have written that the editor of the *New York Post* therein exposed the Communist origin of the Progressive party. Maybe he did, but I cannot find his evidence after three thorough readings, and several more cursory ones, of the book. All Jimmy Wechsler reveals is that many of the arguments used by Wallace to criticize American foreign policy were ones which Russians and American Communists also used; and that, traveling about the country with Wallace, he saw a number of persons whom he recognized from his own Communist days.

Similarly inconclusive is the evidence upon which Eric Goldman, in *Rendezvous With Destiny* (Knopf, 1952), based his statement that, "Indications were certainly plentiful that the Progressive party was deeply influenced by men who had long thought along Communist or fellow-travelerish lines." As will be revealed in later chapters dealing with the Progressive party's founding convention, Goldman's list of the most influential included names of persons either not even there, or playing little or no part.

About five months before any of the meetings of which Michael Quill spoke, another inveterate anti-Communist, Adolf A. Berle, Jr., former assistant secretary of state and chairman of the Liberal party, called upon President Truman to warn him that the third party talk which had been bandied about in recent months was entirely Communist-inspired. Press accounts for July 9, 1947 quoted Berle as saying he did not believe Wallace realized what was happening. Of the Communists, Berle declared: "They are trying to punish Mr. Truman for bucking them diplomatically. Surely, they know what they are doing, but we are in doubt about Henry himself." In the *New York Times* for Sept. 23, 1947, Berle was reported as saying that the Portland dispatch of Foster's endorsement of Wallace (see page 256) verified the "advance information" that the Liberal party had had of Communist intentions to use Wallace as a "front," so as to punish Truman and insure victory for Republican reactionaries.

Several times during 1948, Dorothy Thompson charged that the Progressive party represented typical Communist strategy—that of splitting the strongest party of the left by persuading some disgruntled leader to secede with his followers. In Italy, Poland and Czechoslovakia, the Social Democratic parties had been disrupted by similar tactics, she said.

Victor Lasky began his article, "Who Runs Wallace?" in the June, 1948 *Plain Talk*:

"The Communist party conceived, initiated, formed, staffed—and controls from top to bottom—the third party movement fronting Henry Agard Wallace's bid for the White House. The New Party, as the self appointed Gideon prefers to call it, is actually the Communist party with a New Look. The greatest political success Kremlin agents ever managed to pull off in this country, the New Party marks Josef Stalin's entrance into American politics in a big way—with no holds barred."

As evidence, Lasky claimed that in mid-1946 the Communist party

276

National Board specifically named Wallace as leader of a proposed new party. And then he named those whom he said "ran" Wallace: Beanie Baldwin, Lee Pressman and John Abt.

Of Beanie I have already said quite a bit in the preceding chapters. He was Sidney Hillman's right-hand man in the NC-PAC, for which position he was picked by Philip Murray. He then headed the PCA. Before that, he was called to Washington by Paul Appleby, assistant to Henry Wallace in the Department of Agriculture, and gives Rexford Guy Tugwell credit for having educated him in liberal ideas. No matter how strong in dislike of him any of them might be, the idea that Baldwin was an agent of the Kremlin is abhorrent to scores of persons who have known and worked with him closely for two decades. I know because I have asked them, including many who have no sympathy with the direction Beanie's activities have taken. Some of them even say that in the CIO-PAC in 1944 Beanie was called a red-baiter. His forte was said to be broad large-scale planning, rather than minute administrative details.

A word should be interjected here about Mrs. Baldwin who, until she married Beanie early in 1948, was Mrs. Lillian Traugott, field service director for the PCA. Incidentally, it would not be difficult or superfluous to have an entire chapter devoted to the roles of wives of men mentioned in this study. In widely different ways a number of them were extremely important, namely: Mesdames Abt, Kingdon, Imbrie, Pepper, Benson, Taylor and, especially, Wallace.

During the war years Lil served in Europe for the Office of Strategic Services. She worked for the NC-PAC before joining the office staff of the PCA. Hence, she was a liberal "doer" as well as thinker. Her liberalism dated from the depression days of the '30s, when she was forced to abandon her college training in becoming a chemical engineer to take a business course and go to work. It was reading Samuel Hopkins Adams' fictional *Revelry*, about the scandals of the Harding Administration, that caused her to become politically conscious and to revolt against her conservative Republican background.

When the Progressive party convention was held in July, 1948, Lee Pressman became prominent as secretary of the Platform Committee. Years later, Pressman admitted that he had been at one time a member of the Communist party, but everyone I've talked to who was in the know agrees that his role was negligible in the early moves to form a third party and that Pressman's influence during 1947 in persuading Wallace to head a third party was virtually nonexistent. In a few phone calls, to Beanie Baldwin and others, he did not disguise his sympathy for the developing movement; but he was still chief counsel for the CIO and right-hand man to Philip Murray, whose opposition to the new party idea was open and widely known. This reporter believes that if the contrary were the case someone, among the many whom he questioned on this point, would have given some clue. However, the same answer has come from Michael Straight, Helen Fuller, Lewis Frank Jr. and Viola Scott, Wallace's personal secretary, who noted those who visited the *New Republic* offices; Baldwin, Abt, Marcantonio, at least a half dozen others in secondary positions of importance, and, most significantly, both Wallace and Pressman themselves.

To anyone who gives the American Communists credit for being supermen, able to make plans years or decades in advance and then to carry out the strategy without a minor deviation, clandestinely and behind the scenes, this evidence may not be conclusive. An answer I received from several, however, including some violent anti-Communists, was: "American Communists just aren't that smart."

Certainly Pressman had no reason to feel any personal loyalty to Henry Wallace. In 1934 he had been one of the victims of the famous "purge" in the Department of Agriculture, when Wallace acceded to the wishes of Chester Davis, AAA administrator, and fired Jerome Frank as general counsel. Pressman was one of Frank's assistants and went out with him. Then Harry Hopkins made Pressman general counsel for the Works Projects Administration, telling him, Pressman recalls, "The first time you tell me I can't do something, you're fired." In 1936 Pressman became general counsel for the CIO and its biggest affiliate, the United Steelworkers of America. For years, before he resigned on Feb. 6, 1948, this was a $19,000 a year job. He prepared most of the important officers' reports to the annual conventions and was Murray's main support. Kermit Eby, educational director of CIO from 1943 to 1949, gives this as an indication of Pressman's importance: whenever Murray wanted to confer with anyone else, he summoned him to his presence, but when he wanted to see Pressman, he usually went to the latter's office.

Pressman's bitter enemy during his CIO years was James B. Carey, secretary; almost without exception, Pressman won their arguments. For one thing, Pressman is a Cornell and Harvard Law School graduate and a member of Phi Beta Kappa, which indicates that he possesses intelligence beyond anything Carey could ever approach. Furthermore, he had the support of 11 Left Wing CIO affiliates, approximately one-fourth of the representation on the National Executive Board. There are two sides to a "coin" such as this. If, from one angle, it can be said that Pressman represented Left Wing interests in high CIO circles, it can also be said that he was the agent by which Murray and others kept the Left Wingers in line. Who, in other words, can really be said to have used whom? I doubt if such a cold, calculating, keenly intelligent man as Pressman was conscious of being used by either. He had his own convictions, which later were shaken. When the long-secret conference which ended in his resignation from the CIO broke up on Feb. 6, 1948 observers noted that there were tears in his eyes, as there were in those of Philip Murray. In his public statement explaining his resignation. Pressman declared that it would enable him to participate in the Progressive party campaign. At Tugwell's urgent request, he became secretary of the Platform Committee, of which Tugwell was chairman. He was also the American Labor party candidate for Congress in the 14th Congressional District in Brooklyn. He was never on the PP payroll, nor a member of any of the high policy-making groups of the party.

Very much the same relationship that had existed between Murray and Pressman had existed between Sidney Hillman and John Abt. The latter, in other words, was the former's "legal brains" and his liaison man with the Left Wingers in the Amalgamated Clothing Workers, and both the CIO-PAC and the NC-PAC. A graduate of the University of Chicago Law School, Abt was also a lawyer in early New Deal days in both the Agricultural Adjustment Administration and the WPA. Then he became counsel for the famous Senate (La Follette) Civil Liberties Committee and also served as a special assistant to the Attorney General of the United States. On Jan. 5, 1948 the Executive Board of the Amalgamated gave Abt a leave of absence, from which he never returned, "in order to be free actively to participate in the campaign of Henry Wallace for peace."

During most of the summer of 1947, Abt had been abroad attending meetings of the World Federation of Trade Unions, but he was back in the fall to participate in the PCA meetings which considered Wallace's candidacy, and to personally urge Wallace to run. He became general counsel of the Wallace for President committee, and then of the Progressive party at Beanie Baldwin's personal request. Before the appointment was made, however, at Abt's own insistence there was a conference between the two and Henry Wallace. At it, Abt raised the question of whether his holding a high position in the Progressive party might be an embarrassment to Wallace. He told Wallace that his wife, Jessica Smith, was editor of *Soviet Russia Today;* that his sister, Marian Bachrach, was public relations director for the Communist party; and that he had been subpoenaed and had appeared before the Federal grand jury investigating subversion in southern New York in November, 1947. Wallace did not inquire of Abt if he was a Communist, but turned to Beanie and declared, "I guess we can carry that load," adding some strong remarks to the effect that it was necessary to meet "this sort of thing head on."

Neither Pressman nor Abt was mentioned in the indictments which the Federal grand jury returned on the eve of the Progressive party convention in July, 1948. The next month, however, Whittaker Chambers mentioned them in testimony before the House Committee on Un-American Activities. That was the same day that President Truman publicly called the committee hearing a "red herring," intended to divert public attention from the Republican failure to consider seriously his anti-inflation proposals to a special session of Congress. Truman said that all of the testimony presented by Chambers had been considered by the grand jury, the proper body under American law to make such investigations.

On Aug. 20, 1948 Abt, Pressman and Nathan Witt, former executive secretary of the National Labor Relations Board and Pressman's law partner in 1949, refused to answer questions put to them by a one-man subcommittee (Richard Nixon, later Vice President) of the House Committee on Un-American Activities, pleading the protection of the First, Fifth and Sixth Amendments. A week later Louis Budenz also mentioned the three men, along with Alger Hiss, in testimony before the committee. As a result of the publicity, John Abt made the suggestion that he resign his Progressive party position, but Wallace would not hear of it.

To understand Wallace's attitude, it is necessary to recall that before the postwar concern over Communism as an internal and external threat gathered momentum, only the *Chicago Tribune,* Gerald L. K. Smith, Martin Dies and similar critics objected to the presence in government of persons with leftist political views. It was not popular to be a Communist, but the concept of the existence of a conspiracy to bring about revolution in the United States had not yet developed. In Vol. I of *Roosevelt and Hopkins* (Harper, 1948), Robert Sherwood wrote, on page 55: "In the early days of the New Deal he [Hopkins] worked as he was to work later in war, with regard for nothing but the interests of the American people and of FDR which to him meant one and the same thing. In appointing men and women to positions of authority he was concerned only with consideration of their competence and zeal; he did not give a damn whether they were Methodists, Baptists, Catholics or Jews—and he was especially instructed by the President never to ask whether a person needing relief is a Republican, Democrat, Socialist or anything else." In 1936, as noted, Earl Browder had been invited to speak at the *New York Herald Tribune* annual forum. On July 17, 1936, he also spoke at the Institute of Public Affairs at the University of Virginia. In 1940, Joseph Barnes relates in *Willkie* (Simon & Schuster, 1952), the Republican party bought advertising space in the *Daily Worker* to appeal to Communist voters; the latter were strongly isolationist at the time, as a result of the Hitler-Stalin pact of Aug. 29, 1939, which was not broken until the Nazis invaded the Soviet Union on June 22, 1941. In July, 1945 Tammany Hall, the Democratic organization in New York, endorsed Benjamin J. Davis, Communist, for re-election to the City Council—until William O'Dwyer, mayoralty candidate, insisted the endorsement be withdrawn. On Nov. 10, 1947 Acting Mayor Vincent Impellitteri and Council Majority (Democratic) Leader Joseph T. Sharkey attended the funeral of Peter Cacchione, Communist member of the City Council.

It was not surprising that Henry Wallace either ignored or failed to be impressed by reports that some of his supporters were too far to the left of center. At the time, he agreed with Harry Truman that the hue and cry constituted a "red herring," although he thought Harry Truman was in no position to point the finger of scorn at others. Almost a year after he had broken with the Progressive party, in an interview with Edwin A. Lahey which appeared in the *Chicago Daily News* for March 31, 1951, Wallace said: :

> You know, I didn't actually realize how strong the Communists were in the Progressive party. I think now they were out to knife me.
>
> Back in September, 1948, after the nominating convention, Louis Adamic and Jess Gitt of York, Pa., came up here [Farvue] to see me.
>
> They said they had it from British sources that the Communists actually wanted to keep the vote for me as low as possible to show the world a reactionary influence in America. I couldn't believe it at the time.

Wallace voluntarily elaborated upon this story for me only to the extent that he thought Adamic's British source was some newspaperman who had written him a letter. Louis Adamic was mysteriously shot to death on Sept. 5, 1951, in his burning farmhouse at Riegelsville, N.J., a few days before his work *The Eagle and the Roots* (Doubleday, 1952) appeared; therefore I lost the opportunity to question him about it. I did talk at length to Gitt and to Lewis Frank, Jr., who was also present at the interview. Gitt, who engineered the visit after Adamic approached him, says positively that there was no mention of any British source of information and that if there had been any, he is certain Adamic, his very close friend, would have told him of it. He says that, partly as a result of conversations with Louis Bean, eminent agricultural economist and statistician, Adamic became convinced that Wallace should stress in his speeches the point that such policies as the Truman Doctrine and Marshall Plan were playing into the hands of the Soviet Union, by weakening the prestige of the United States throughout the world. If Communists wanted to strengthen their position, Adamic argued, they would encourage these and similar facets of American foreign policy, rather than oppose them, and he suggested that Wallace suggest as much in his speeches and statements.

With this version of the interview Frank is in agreement; both men are certain that Wallace was correct in his recollection to Lahey of having given the matter little attention at the time. Baldwin, to whom Wallace mentioned the incident some time after it occurred, confirms this fact also. Frank recalls Wallace as having declared that hard work by rank-and-file Communists had been an important factor all over the country in obtaining signatures on petitions to put the Progressive party on the ballot and that, for many reasons which he had been stating publicly for years, he refused to say anything which could be interpreted as red-baiting.

At Henry Wallace's request, within a week after he went to Farvue with Adamic, Jess Gitt wrote a 600 word letter to Wallace summarizing the conversation. It is proof positive of the extent to which Wallace's memory played tricks on him when he talked to Lahey three years later.

In the first place, the conversation took place during the last week of June, not in September. A typical sentence from Gitt's summary follows:

"Russia, if she is smart, and assuming she is convinced war cannot be avoided, would encourage our bipartisan policy even to the extent of opposing the policy for no other purpose than to cause Congress to vote the funds to carry it out."

There was absolutely no mention in the letter, any more than there is in the memory of either Gitt or Frank, of any of the points which Wallace mentioned to Lahey.

Pertinent here is the motivation of the Communists, once they became committed to participation in the Progressive party. Was it, as Wallace later came to believe, to "do a job on him," so as to demonstrate to the world the weakness of American liberalism? Or was it to do exactly the opposite, to "indicate the potentialities of Communistic strength," as Philip Murray declared at the CIO convention in Portland, Ore. on Nov. 22, 1948; that is, to build a strong people's movement, which they believed they would be able to control after 1948? Or was it a short-term policy of using a convenient medium whereby to condemn American foreign policy and/or promote that of the Soviet Union? In any case, was the object to split the liberal vote, confuse progressives, defeat Harry Truman and bring about the election of a reactionary Republican in the expectation that, after four years of Republican rule, the people would react violently in a politically leftward direction?

All of these explanations were advanced by supposedly reputable political observers. In the *Detroit News* for Dec. 18, 1947, for instance, Blair Moody (later a U.S. Senator) wrote:

> Extreme leftists, meaning Moscow's American agents and those who follow their line, are doing their best to split the American liberal movement and elect a reactionary president next November. That, according to the strategy the Communists think is canny, would be the surest way to wreck the country and bring a violent overturn via depression.

> Their immediate object is to make the re-election of President Truman impossible. What they will do if the Republicans come up with a progressive or middle-road candidate is a bridge they reportedly have not yet crossed. They do not appear to be worrying about that—yet.

> Step No. 1 in this campaign is to get Henry A. Wallace, the former Vice President, Secretary of Commerce and what-have-you, to run at the head of a third party ticket. They, and certainly Wallace, know he would have no chance. But he is being told, despite the current returns from America Speaks, that "Truman has no chance anyway," and Wallace had better place himself at the head of a "new party" which will "take over the liberal movement in 1952."

Somewhat similarly, Alfred Baker Lewis of Greenwich wrote to the Hartford, Conn. *Times* on Nov. 29, 1947: "In order to defeat Truman, the Communists want to put up Wallace as a third party candidate, hoping that he could take away enough votes from Truman to elect a reactionary Republican. In that event the Russian propaganda that the U.S. is imperialist and reactionary would be given greater plausibility."

According to a *Chicago Times* editorial, "PCA, Wallace and Zhdanov," of Jan. 16, 1948: "Wallace has the support of Communists because he gives prestige to their arguments." In his syndicated "Inside Labor" column for Dec. 24, 1947, Victor Riesel opined: "The Communists want that [a third party] so they can get off speeches which will sound in Europe like there's a great workers' and farmers' upheaval in America. That kind of propaganda pays off for the lefties."

What almost nobody was willing to admit was that the Communists

might actually have believed there was such an upheaval; or that, by lending their support to the movement Henry Wallace had started, they could
help bring it about, even though they had previously hoped and expected
that the third party they had long wanted must not have the kind of
middle-class roots the PCA provided. In *Political Affairs* for July, 1953
appeared the final text of the "Resolution on the Situation Growing Out
of the Presidential Elections," which had been adopted a short time
earlier by the CP National Committee. It contained the following:

> In the 1948 elections we were confronted with the task of
> finding the broadest united front electoral vehicle for bring-
> ing sharply before the American people the question of
> peace. From this arose the need for our party to help
> stimulate the formation of a united front peace ticket and
> even the formation of a united front party machinery to
> campaign for that ticket.
>
> However, the mistake our Party made was to confuse this
> task with the historic task of forming a new mass party
> of the people. As a consequence, there existed the wrong
> estimate that the formation of the Progressive party rep-
> resented more than the simple emergence of an important
> fighting force for peace; that it represented in fact the
> emergence of a great mass People's party.

Translated, this means about the same as what Lee Pressman told
me: "There was a hell of a lot of romanticizing at the time." And that
was true not only, *nor primarily,* of members of the Communist party.

Henry Wallace was never more sincere than when he concluded his
broadcast, on Dec. 29, 1947, announcing his independent candidacy for
the Presidency in 1948:

> Thousands of people all over the United States have asked
> me to engage in this great fight. The people are on the
> march. I hope that you who are listening to me tonight
> will lead the forces of peace, progress and prosperity
> throughout your communities and throughout our country.
> Will you let me know that you have come out fighting
> against the powers of evil?
>
> We have assembled a Gideon's Army, small in number,
> powerful in conviction, ready for action. We have said
> with Gideon, "Let those who are fearful and trembling
> depart." For every fearful one who leaves, there will be a
> thousand to take his place. A just cause is worth a hundred
> armies. We face the future unfettered, unfettered by any
> principle but the general welfare. We owe no allegiance
> to any group which does not serve that welfare. By God's
> grace, the people's peace will usher in the century of the
> common man.

# ¶14 ANNOUNCEMENT AND REACTION. *A compilation of the critical and defensive comments as regards some of the major issues raised by Henry A. Wallace's decision to run for President on a New Party ticket.*

Henry A. Wallace arrived in Chicago from Farvue, his farm near South Salem, N. Y., about noon on Monday, Dec. 29, 1947. He went directly to the Drake hotel, where Mrs. Emmons (Anita McCormick) Blaine had rented an entire floor for his use. Leaders of Progressive Citizens of America groups, labor unions and others, from 18 states and the District of Columbia, stayed there; all were in the city to be present at Wallace's 10:30 p.m. nationwide radio broadcast, over the Mutual Broadcasting System.

At 2 p.m. Wallace went to a suite at the Knickerbocker hotel and, with the press excluded, met with about 1,000 persons for over four hours; between 300 and 400 being able to crowd into the suite at one time. Ernest Di Maio of Chicago, district president of the United Electrical Workers, C.I.O., presented the former Vice President with a petition signed by approximately 100,000. It urged him to accede to the request, made to him a fortnight earlier by the PCA Executive Committee, that he run in 1948 as an independent candidate for the Presidency of the United States.

George Cermak, chairman, and Zalmon Garfield, director, of the Progressive party of Cook County, Ill., told of the campaign which had ended in November: the top man on a slate of 21 candidates for the Superior Court of Cook County had obtained 313,847 votes, 20,985 less than his nearest Republican-Democratic coalition opponent. As the day drew to a close, workers came to the hotel directly from the shops in their working clothes, to listen, express their views and meet their political hero.

An emotional interlude occurred when Paul Robeson, the famous Negro baritone, pushed his way to the front of the room. He spoke briefly on the need for a Presidential candidate who favored race equality without equivocation. Then he sang some of his most popular songs. There were tears in the eyes of both Robeson and Wallace—and of others too—when he finished.

Dinner was private, at the home of Mrs. Blaine. About 40 of Wallace's leading advisors and aides accompanied him to the MBS studio in the Chicago *Tribune* tower. No others in the Chicago area heard the speech which followed because WGN, the Chicago *Tribune* station and the local MBS outlet, did not carry it. Robert W. Kenny, former Attorney General of California and national chairman of the PCA; former Gov. Elmer A. Benson of Minnesota; and Robert Morss Lovett were there. So were Professors Thomas Emerson and Fowler Harper of the Yale law school, and Rexford Guy Tugwell of the University of Chicago, an early New Dealer who had served under Wallace in the Department of Agriculture. So was Mrs. Wallace.

There was no surprise when Henry Wallace began his peroration, "I announce tonight that I shall run as an independent candidate for President of the United States in 1948," and then followed with the reference to Gideon's Army with which the preceding chapter concluded.

During the preceding 20 minutes Wallace had, in one way or another, anticipated most of the adverse comments which filled the newspapers for several days thereafter. His comments (or rebuttals), and others that were added by some of his cohorts in the ensuing days, can best be presented in connection with the points (charges) themselves. The pros and cons of the most ramified issues were as follows:

1. *Effect upon the leading contenders for the Presidential nominations of both major parties.*

While making it clear they had no use for Henry Wallace, his supporters and ideas, Republican spokesmen predicted that the New Party (as it was called until the founding convention in July) would draw most of its support from the ranks of Democratic voters, and consequently insure the election of a Republican President and Congress in November, 1948.

Agreeing with the Republican appraisal, many others deplored Wallace's decision. They declared that not only would it mean the defeat of Harry Truman or almost anyone else the Democrats might nominate, but that, even more regrettably, the Republicans would be encouraged to nominate a reactionary candidate. In New York's *PM* for Dec. 30, 1947, Max Lerner wrote that "only a political miracle will prevent Dewey or Taft from being the President of the United States a year from now." Others went further and expressed the belief that Wallace's action would prove about as disastrous to the Presidential hopes of Dewey as to those of Truman. No longer, those who felt that way explained, would the Dewey forces be able to argue that only their man had a chance to carry New York State for the Republicans. With the Amalgamated Clothing Workers, 300,000 strong, certain to pull out of the American Labor party as soon as it endorsed Wallace, so much former Democratic strength would be destroyed that anyone running on the GOP ticket could carry the state, it was contended.

That a Republican victory in 1948 was the main objective of the Progressives was widely suggested. In a column entitled "What Makes Henry Run?" syndicated by the Newspaper Enterprise Association, James Thrasher recalled Wallace's remark, early in December, that he preferred Taft to Truman (see page 239); he then surmised: " . . . a good guess is that the self-appointed leader of the unborn third party hopes to swing them [three or four key states] to the GOP and that the GOP candidate will be Mr. Taft . . . Maybe he (Wallace) sees himself as the wise and benevolent leader whom the people will turn to in 1952 to rebuild a Republican-wrecked economy."

I have found this piece, signed by Thrasher, in the Gloversville

(N.Y.) *Herald* for Jan. 5 and the Ogdenburg (N.Y.) *Advance News* for Jan. 11. I have also found it, without Thrasher's signature, in 37 other newspapers as a local editorial on various days in late December, 1947 and the first three weeks of January, 1948. It may have been used in others, but even if not the strong nature of the journalistic opposition to the Progressives is indicated.

Of all the nationally prominent columnists, only David Lawrence, to the best of my knowledge, was skeptical from the start of the widely held belief that Wallace's New Party doomed the Democrats. In his column for Dec. 30, 1947, he called Wallace's action "relatively inconsequential in a political sense," and warned, "Republicans who think it is going to draw any large number of Democratic votes from Truman may be exulting a bit prematurely." As Lawrence saw it, the New Party might "deprive the Republicans of their apparent plan to try to pin the Communist label on the Democratic party." As a result, he wrote, "the Wallace movement will help the Democrats more than it will hurt them." In the Atlanta *Constitution* for Jan. 6, 1948, Ralph McGill took a similar attitude.

Democratic leaders, of course, said virtually the same, but their comments were probably generally accepted as examples of "whistling," to keep up their courage in the face of imminent disaster. Rep. John McCormack, of Massachusetts, leader of the Democratic minority in the House of Representatives, said publicly: "The voters we may lose will be more than offset by those voters who will vote the Democratic ticket because of Mr. Wallace's attempt to create confusion."

President Truman, the man presumably most affected, refused all public comment at the time on Wallace's announcement. He was reported by close advisors, however, as not much concerned; in fact, to be virtually "brushing aside" the whole matter as beneath his notice. The direct quotation, accredited to a White House spokesman, was, "He doesn't give a damn. Why should he?" This seemed to be merely a political pose or bravado at the time and later, when Truman took out after Wallace; nevertheless, I am convinced that Harry Truman always believed that he was going to be nominated and elected, despite Wallaceites, Dixiecrats, and the attempts of the CIO, ADA and others to obtain Eisenhower or some other candidate as the Democratic nominee. Five years later he told the person who interviewed him in my behalf that he at no time thought the Progressive party would seriously injure his chances. Jonathan Daniels, who worked closely with him during the summer of 1948 as a speech writer, has told me that he never heard Truman mention Wallace or the Progressive party.

Although Henry Wallace made no specific reference in his announcement speech to what effect he thought his venture would have on the comparative strength of the two major parties in 1948, in the months and years to follow he said what not only his own supporters but many others said at the time: *that Harry Truman seemed to be a "dead duck" politically anyway.*

Closely related to the question of what effect Wallace's candidacy would have on the Presidential chances of various major party aspirants was:

2. *Effect upon the 1948 Congressional campaigns.*

The orthodox viewpoint was the same as regards the Presidency: that a New Party would split the Democratic vote and improve the chances of a Republican victory. Not only that; just as it was argued that the Republicans would be encouraged to nominate a more reactionary candidate for President, so it was asserted that more liberal candidates for Congress, mostly on the Democratic ticket, would be injured if the New Party entered their contests. This would be particularly true, it was contended, in several of the states with the largest number of electoral votes, namely: New York, Ohio, Illinois and California.

Resigning from the PCA on Dec. 22, 1947, A. J. Liebling, author of *The Wayward Pressman* and frequent contributor to *The New Yorker* magazine, wrote, "The tactic of helping proclaimed reactionaries to take power, with the expressed hope that the people will eventually get sick of them, was tried out in Germany in 1932 and was a tragic flop." In *PM* for Dec. 18, 1947, Max Lerner opined that a 1948 victory for reactionaries was "exactly the purpose of the Communists who are today most vigorously plumping for a Third Party." He explained as follows: "The reasoning is that Russia will be better off in the cold war if it deals with an American government which is obviously reactionary and imperialist than with one which still has some substance of liberalism, along with the trimmings."

Before Wallace announced, the national leadership of ADA said that a new party "would spell sure defeat for the legislative objectives of liberals at home and would mean a retreat from American responsibility abroad, directly serving the worldwide interests of the Communist party." After Wallace's announcement the ADA said that his movement "would assure the election of a reactionary, isolationist administration."

The day after the PCA overture to Wallace was announced, J. Raymond Walsh, New York State chairman of the PCA, in his nightly commentary over station WMCA, predicted that a New Party would not poll more than 500,000 votes and that the poor showing "would kill the chances of progressive politics in America for a long time, possibly for the rest of your life." After Wallace announced, Walsh, having resigned from the PCA, declared in his broadcast: "What will probably happen now is this: Taft will go to the White House. And 40 or 50 fairly progressive congressmen who otherwise might win will be defeated."

One of the "fairly progressive congressmen" whom Walsh meant was among those who raised the "split liberal" argument even before Wallace's announcement. He was Rep. Chester Holifield (Dem., Calif.). In an open letter to him on Dec. 22, 1947, Beanie Baldwin set forth the New Party advocates' argument: "Mr. Wallace's candidacy will provide the stimulus essential to bring out a large vote, without which progressive Congressmen, particularly those in marginal districts, can not hope to be elected." Baldwin cited election statistics, which he said demonstrated that "the election of progressives to Congress is generally determined by the size of the vote cast." He pointed out that, in 39 of the 54 Congressional districts which the Democrats lost to the Republicans in November, 1946, the margin of defeat averaged less than 5,000 votes; while the drop in the number of votes, as compared to 1944, averaged 27,000.

A week after Wallace's announcement J. Howard McGrath, chairman of the Democratic National Committee, stated publicly, "Wallace's candidacy will help elect Democratic congressmen by bringing out a large vote." Wallace wryly commented: "For once I agree with Senator McGrath. It is estimated that millions of voters will now turn out to vote who would not otherwise have bothered to go to the polls."

In his Dec. 29 press conference in Chicago, Wallace emphasized that he intended to support liberal candidates for Congress regardless of their party. He particularly named Rep. Adolph Sabath (Dem., Ill.) as one whom he would endorse.

In his announcement speech Henry Wallace indirectly touched on the "split liberal" argument when he tackled the related problem head-on:

3. *From the liberal standpoint, what difference did it make whether a Democratic or Republican administration was elected in 1948?*

Wallace began by declaring that speaking to a half million Americans in all parts of the country over a period of 15 months had convinced him that there was widespread belief that both war and depression were imminent. He recalled that he had often declared, "If the Democratic Party continues to be a party of war and depression, I will see to it that the people have a chance to vote for peace and prosperity"; that he had stated the terms under which he would support the Democratic Administration, thus: "Let the Administration repudiate universal military training and rid itself of the Wall Street-military team that is leading us toward war." The Democratic response, he indicated, had been, "Henry Wallace, we welcome your support but we will not change our policies."

"Thus," Wallace said, "the leadership of the Democratic party would deprive the American people of their rightful opportunity to choose between progress and reaction in 1948. As far as the Republican party is concerned, there is no hope—as George Norris, Fiorello La Guardia and Wendell Willkie long ago found out . . . There is no real fight between a Truman and a Republican. Both stand for a policy which opens the door to war in our lifetime and makes war certain for our children."

In his Dec. 18 piece, Max Lerner denied the "Tweedledum-Tweedledee sameness of both major parties," especially regarding what he called the two major domestic issues of 1948: price-and-inflation policy and labor policy; but he went into no discussion of either. In his Dec. 28 reply, Baldwin did. He admitted that the Republicans killed the original OPA; but it was Truman, he said, who delivered the final *coup de grace* to price controls, in November, 1946. "It was Truman," Baldwin wrote, "who tossed out controls of building materials, thus wrecking the veterans' housing program. It was Truman who lifted the lid on steel and paved the way for more price rises. It was Truman who kept appealing to big business for 'voluntary' price reductions while prices zoomed, refusing to mention price controls (except to call them 'police state' measures) until the special session of Congress was convened."

In regard to Truman's labor record, Baldwin admitted he was "on record as having vetoed the Taft-Hartley law," adding, "but let us not forget that Truman himself invited this type of law by his own role in breaking the railroad strike and in calling for legislation to draft strikers—legislation so drastically anti-labor that even Senator Taft ran away from it." And he charged Truman with insufficient effort to obtain Democratic support for his Taft-Hartley veto.

Baldwin also lambasted Truman's loyalty program and his appointment of Wall Streeters to positions formerly held by New Dealers. "What liberal," he asked, "will prefer the author of the Loyalty Order to the man who has spoken out with such courage and clarity on the crucial issues of civil liberties? What liberal will prefer the man who sends guns to the Greek reactionaries to the man who calls for sending bread and clothing and milk to all people in need? What liberal will prefer the man who has surrounded himself with Wall Street and military men to the man who sacrificed his Cabinet post rather than submit to their plans?"

Baldwin pointed to the inability of John L. Lewis in 1940 to swing his miners to support of Wendell Willkie as evidence that the vote of labor's rank and file was uncontrolled. "The '46 elections showed it again," he wrote, "when the best efforts of labor leaders failed to move labor to make dum and dee choices."

4. *The value of waging a fight which even its strongest proponents knew could not be won.*

Probably the most-used editorial comment on the Wallace announcement was "Wallace knows he can't win," or its equivalent. As evidence of this fact, the candidate's reference to his following as a Gideon's Army was cited. Also the following passage from his speech:

> The lukewarm liberals sitting on two chairs say, "Why throw away your vote?" I say a vote for a new party in 1948 will be the most valuable vote you ever have cast or ever will cast.

> The bigger the peace vote in 1948, the more definitely the world will know that the United States is not behind the bipartisan reactionary war policy which is dividing the world into two armed camps and making inevitable the day when American soldiers will be lying in their arctic suits in the Russian snow.

This had been immediately preceded by the following:

> When the old parties rot, the people have a right to be heard through a new party. They asserted that right when the Democratic party was founded under Jefferson in the struggle against the Federalist party of war and privilege of his day. They won it again when the Republican party was organized in Lincoln's time. The people must again

have an opportunity to speak out with their vote in 1948.

And it was followed shortly by the following:

> Let us stop saying, "I don't like it but I am going to vote for the lesser of two evils."
>
> Rather than accept either evil, come out boldly, stand upright like men and say loudly so all the world can hear—"We are voting peace and security for ourselves and our children's children. We are fighting for old-fashioned Americanism at the polls in 1948. We are fighting for freedom of speech and freedom of assembly. We are fighting to end racial discrimination. We are fighting for lower prices. We are fighting for free labor unions, for jobs, and for homes in which we can decently live."

Although he used the word sparingly in public, in private Henry Wallace often referred to his venture as a "crusade," which it was better to go down fighting than not to have attempted. That he thoroughly believed such was the case I have no doubt; nor did even his most severe critics question the sincerity of his conviction.

Henry Wallace wanted to do his utmost to stop what he considered a trend toward American imperialism in foreign affairs and destruction of the social gains of the New Deal era at home. His fears for the future were partly expressed in the following section of his speech:

> Two years ago I denounced those who were talking up world war as criminals. Of course, the bulk of our people are not criminals, but it is possible for a little handful of warmongers to stampede them.
>
> As Mark Twain long ago pointed out, " . . . The nation will rub its sleepy eyes and try to make out why there must be a war and will say, earnestly and indignantly, 'For it is unjust and dishonorable and there is no necessity for it' . . . The handful will shout louder, and now the whole nation will take up the war cry and shout itself hoarse, and mob any honest man who ventures to open his mouth, and presently such mouths will cease to open. Next the statesmen will invent cheap lies, putting the blame on the nation that is attacked, and every man will be glad of those conscience-soothing falsities."
>
> This pattern, as Mark Twain saw it 50 years ago, is repeating itself on a scale so vast as to threaten the destruction of humanity. The rich monopolists have always been more ready to sacrifice their sons than their money, but now they have reached a point where they are willing to sacrifice both for the sake of world control.

It just doesn't make sense. The time has come for a new party to fight these war-makers. We say that peace is mandatory and that it can be had if we only want it.

Then he opposed universal military training as a first step toward militarization and stressed the need for a worldwide program of reconstruction.

In addition to considering it worthwhile to wage a crusade even in the expectation of defeat, Wallace and his supporters had some reason for believing that their cause was not entirely hopeless. Throughout 1946, 1947 and 1948, national public opinion polls to predict the outcome of elections were at the peak of their popularity. They indicated, at the time Wallace made his announcement, that the chances were good for him to make a creditable showing and establish himself as a strong political influence.

On the eve of Wallace's announcement, Dec. 21, 1947, the Gallup pollsters announced the replies of a national cross section of independent voters to the question: "Suppose you had a chance to vote for your favorite candidate for President in 1948. If such an election were being held today, which one of these men would you vote for?" In percentages, the results were: Eisenhower—18; Truman—17; Dewey—13; Stassen, Marshall and Wallace—10 each; MacArthur—8; Vandenberg and Warren—4 each; Taft—3.

Shortly after Wallace's announcement, on Jan. 21, 1948, a Gallup question was: "If a Presidential election were being held today, and Truman were running for President on the Democratic ticket against Dewey on the Republican ticket and against Wallace on a third-party ticket, how do you think you would vote—for Truman, for Dewey, or for Wallace?" The percentage results were: Truman—48, Dewey 41, Wallace—7. When the same questions was asked, with a different combination of possible candidates, the results were: Truman—40, Eisenhower—47 and Wallace—6. Also: Truman—51, Taft—31 and Wallace—8. For still another possible combination, announced Feb. 15, 1948, the results were: Truman—45, Stassen—41, Wallace—6. By states in a Truman-Dewey-Wallace race, results announced on Feb. 29, 1948 showed Wallace was favored percentage-wise as follows: New York—15, Pennsylvania—7, Illinois—8; Chicago only—13, California—11.

Not only the pollsters, but also newspapermen, politicians and others supposedly wise concerning voting behavior, regardless of their personal feelings, forecast Wallace's vote all the way from one to 10 million, the usual estimate being close to 5 million. In *PM* for Dec. 10, 1947, for instance, Jennings Perry said Wallace would get 5 to 8 million if he ran. At the CIO Executive Board meeting on Jan. 22, 1948, Harry Bridges said 4 million. In the *Amsterdam News* for Jan. 24, Lester Granger said 2 to 3 million. "My own guess," wrote Morris Rubin in the *Progressive* magazine for February, 1948, "at the moment is that he will roll up no less than 3 million, more likely 4 million and perhaps go as high as 5 million." Rubin extended a great deal of effort during the following months to explain that his magazine (which ultimately endorsed

Norman Thomas, the Socialist candidate) was the successor to the La Follette dynasty publication and in no way connected with Wallace's party. The letters he received condemning him for opposing the new Progressive party, he confessed in the issue of March, 1948, exceeded in bitterness any he had ever received before in connection with an important issue. In its May, 1948 issue, the *Progressive* declared: "The Wallace strength seems at flood tide now. Unusually dependable observers think he would get no less than 10 million votes if the election were held tomorrow."

On March 21, 1948, Norman Thomas predicted that Wallace would get 5 million votes. In the New York *Times* for March 7, James Hagerty, veteran political analyst, had predicted the same. James A. Farley, longtime chairman of the Democratic National Committee, had dumfounded experts in 1936 when he correctly predicted that FDR would carry all states except Maine and Vermont; on April 17, 1948 he was reported from Richmond as predicting that Wallace might get 6 to 7 million votes nationally, 1 million of them in New York State. Even Westbrook Pegler, easily Wallace's most vicious journalistic opponent, on May 5, 1948 forecast 5 to 8 million votes for the New Party nationally.

On the other hand Victor Riesel, not far behind Pegler in his vilification of Wallace, predicted in his New York *Post* column for Jan. 16, 1948, that Wallace would poll only 750,000 to 1 million votes. Similarly Frank Kingdon on Jan. 22, 1948, in the same paper declared that, whereas Wallace would probably get 5 million votes if the election were held at that time, by November his total would not exceed 1 million. Len DeCaux, longtime editor of the *CIO News*, who handled publicity for the labor division of the Progressive party in 1948, tells me he never expected that Wallace would get more than 1 million votes. On the other hand Mabel Cooney, Wallace's personal secretary, says that up to the end she thought the total would be 7 million. Early in 1948, Sen. Wayne More (Rep., Ore.) told a Wallace supporter that he thought 10 million would be a good guess. Lee Pressman, who resigned as general counsel for the CIO on Feb. 6, 1948, to become the American Labor party candidate for Congress from the 14th C.D. in Brooklyn, topped Morse's estimate, telling Kermit Eby that 11 million would not be too many votes to expect. Eby himself expected 5 to 6 million.

Regarding the Northwest, its foremost journalist, Richard Neuberger, reported in the March, 1948 *Progressive* that there seemed little doubt that Wallace would obtain as many votes, in several states, as had been the Democratic margin of victory in 1944: 23,270 in Oregon, 7,262 in Idaho and 5,012 in Nevada. Neuberger wrote of the powerful moral issues that Wallace sounded: Wall Street and the Army in government; anti-imperialism; "peace and prosperity" and so forth.

In February, James Roosevelt was reported to have told President Truman that the Wallace vote in California would probably be 500,000. In March, James Hagerty of the New York *Times* named the same figure as the Wallace strength in New York and, a month later, Jim Farley said 1 million. Clemens France predicted 120,000 votes and victory in Rhode Island, and other Progressive party leaders throughout the country allowed themselves to be similarly carried away by their initial enthusiasm. A great deal of the optimism stemmed from the surprising victory of Leo Isacson, running as a Wallaceite in the Feb. 17, 1948 by election in the Bronx 24th Congressional District, to be discussed in a later chapter. Suffice it to say here, by way of summary, that there was plenty of authority, other than that of starry-eyed Wallaceites, to assume that at the beginning of 1948 there existed a chance for a New Party to make a creditable showing.

Partly offsetting this, however, were the more practical observers who raised another issue, namely:

5. *The legal and financial obstacles with which a third major political party was confronted.*

William B. Hesseltine, professor of history at the University of Wisconsin, wrote in *The Rise and Fall of Third Parties* (Public Affairs Press, 1948) that in many states the old political parties were as firmly entrenched in 1948 as the Communist party was in Moscow. His book, an extension of a series of articles for the *Progressive* magazine, came out during the 1948 campaign and was so derogatory in its evaluation of the Wallace movement that it almost seemed to be aimed at it. Nevertheless, after taking three pages to list the legal obstacles faced by a new party state by state, Hesseltine concluded:

"The implication of these figures is clear. A new political party must rest upon a broad popular foundation. With mass support neither the financial nor the legal obstacles need prove insuperable. The practical work of organization cannot be neglected, but the major task before liberals and progressives is agreement on principles. Only after that agreement can the labor of organization begin." He did not believe any such agreement on principles existed on a wide enough scale to augur well for the New Party's attempt to qualify in a sufficient number of states.

Other scholars who have studied earlier attempts at national third parties have emphasized the extent to which state laws, setting up stiff requirements to qualify for a place on the ballot, militate against their chances for success. In *The Progressive Movement of 1924* (Columbia University, 1947), Dr. Kenneth Campbell MacKay wrote of the La Follette movement:

"The total effect of the state election laws was, first, to force La Follette to run under a variety of party labels: Progressive, Independent, Independent-Progressive and Socialist; and, second, to divert precious funds and campaign activity from the business of persuading voters to cast their ballots for La Follette to the less fruitful job of complying with the technical regulations of the conglomerate election laws. Indeed, the state election laws must be considered one of the most effective devices to discourage formation of a new party."

The 1924 Progressives had found it more difficult than the 1912 (Teddy Roosevelt) Progressives, because of the tightening of legal requirements which had taken place in several states after 1912, in order to discourage another Bull Moose attempt. After 1924 there was still further raising of the barriers, to make the 1948 Progressives' task even more difficult. In Chapter 7, "Legal Barriers," of *Discontent at the Polls: A Study of Farmer and Labor Parties, 1927-1948* (Columbia University, 1950), Murray S. Stedman Jr. and Susan W. Stedman explained their nature in the latter year. They included: inability of a new party to hold a primary election until it had participated in a general election and qualified by polling a certain percentage (usually 5 per cent) of the total vote; high number of signatures required of persons who hadn't participated in the new party on the ballot, the number sometimes being an arbitrary figure, with a certain geographical distribution required, or a proportion of the total vote for some office (usually Governor) at a preceding election; high filing fees for candidates and for petitioners; requirements that signature solicitors be residents of the same political districts as petition signers, that they present sworn affidavits, sometimes being required to notarize each signature obtained; unreasonably early filing dates, often quite a bit ahead of those for major parties' petitions; stiff legal residence requirements, poll taxes and similar discouragements to voting.

Speaking of the 1912 campaign, the authors of a report on "Legal Obstacles to Minority Party Success" in the *Yale Law Journal* for June-July, 1948 wrote:

> This experience puts the problem of the legal requirements of ballot legislation in a more realistic light. To compete successfully with the major parties a third party must organize and develop through time; it cannot stake all on one spectacular bid but must anticipate the exigencies of permanence. If this attitude is taken ballot legislation imposes no new demands. The collection of a given number of signatures within a specific time tests the strength of the new organization and can well become a possible means of giving the necessary contact with the individual voter. The requirement that such signatures be divided over a given number of counties is but a call to develop the extensive local organization without which a party cannot hope to win an election. The suspicion becomes all too strong, therefore, that complaints about legal requirements are either attempted shields for inadequacy or evidence of unwillingness to think realistically.

Another way of interpreting the situation described would be that the authors believe no new party should go before the voters until reasonably certain of victory.

In January, 1948 not even the most sanguine devotee believed the New Party would be on the ballot in 45 states the following November. In the New York *Sun* for Dec. 20, 1947, David Lawrence opined that it might be possible to do so in 27 states "but the red tape is substantial. In 21 others the difficulties make it seem impracticable." Milburn P. Akers, then political editor for the Chicago *Sun,* has told me that in 1944 Wendell Willkie told him that he investigated the state election laws and concluded that they made any third party attempt futile. To

John Abt, the New Party's chief counsel, to whom fell the responsibility of overcoming the legal obstacles in 1948, Paul Kern stated that study in the early '30s had convinced him that it would be foolhardy to try to get on the ballot in more than 30 states. No political commentator at the time mentioned any figure higher than 40 as within the realm of possibility for the Wallace crusaders.

Asked, upon his return to New York on Dec. 31, 1947, where the money was to come from, Henry A. Wallace said that the financing of his campaign would be up to the people. "I certainly don't know any other way," he said. "I don't think the corporations will finance it."

It had, of course, been the people who had paid for Wallace's extensive speaking trips during the preceding year. They had done so by buying tickets to hear him speak and by responding to the fund-raising speeches of Dr. Frank Kingdon, William S. Gailmor, Dr. Clark Foreman and local talent. The Wallace meetings, mostly PCA-sponsored, had been good drama, with effective use of lighting, scripts and dramatic entertainers. As a result of the "milk 'em dry" technique, which began by calling for large contributions such as $1,000 and ended with the waving of $1 bills in the air and the emptying of pocket change into containers distributed and collected by pretty girls, a $100,000 debt interited from the NC-PAC and the ICC-ASP had been wiped out, and $450,000 had been raised to operate the PCA national office during 1947. That there was truth in the theory that a ticket sale increased interest in an event was proved in October, 1946, when a free Madison Square Garden rally drew a disappointing crowd. Certainly the PCA and the Progressive party developed the technique of mass giving more than had ever been done before. At the Sept. 12, 1946 rally (the one which led to Wallace's firing from the Cabinet), 5,000 out of the 18,000 present gave $16,000. In October, 1948 virtually every one of another 18,000 in the same place gave $26,000—and that was a poorer response than had been obtained at any other rally during the interim. The March 31, 1947 rally to protest the Truman Doctrine, for instance, had brought $33,000; the May, 1948 Garden rally approximately $45,000 and the Yankee Stadium rally, on Sept. 10, 1948, close to $70,000.

Despite the tremendous financial success of the 1947 ventures, in November of that year the PCA had a balance of just $19,000, and there had been no pledges of big giving before Wallace went to Chicago for his announcement. A few days after his return, about 150 business and professional people, who had made financial contributions in the past, were called together for a dinner at the Essex House. The program there was limited to a political speech by Henry Wallace and a financial "talking to" by Michael Nisselson, president of the Amalgamated Bank; he told the moneybags that what they had given in the past was nothing by comparison with what he expected them to put up, that night and from then on. About $80,000 in gifts and pledges was obtained. Nevertheless, it took an almost all-night effort, less than a month later, to raise $13,000. The money was needed as a down payment, so that the national headquarters of the Wallace for President committee could be opened on Feb. 22, 1948, in the old Atterbury mansion at 39 Park Avenue, New York City.

Direct mail appeals, and advertisements in such publications as the *New Republic* and the *Nation,* brought in considerable money, but all of these efforts combined would have been inadequate to raise the $1,800,00 which the national office spent during 1948, or the approximately $3 million which was spent by state party and other groups throughout the country, in behalf of the Wallace-Taylor or local Progressive tickets. The financial angel for the Progressive party turned out to be Mrs. Emmons (Anita McCormick) Blaine of Chicago. Probably $800,000 of the total national expenditures was originally her money, which she distributed widely where needed from coast to coast. Nobody else came anywhere close to contributing as much as did Aunt Anita, or A.B. as we called her; and I don't know whether the $800,000 figure includes the expense of the luncheons, dinners and parties at her 11 East Erie Street mansion, or the hotel, chauffeur, telephone and other bills she paid, for Wallace and his entourage and others, on numerous occasions.

Anita McCormick Blaine, who died on Feb. 12, 1954 at the age of 87 years, was a fabulous person, at least during the last years of her life when I knew her. Our acquaintance began about 1940, when the Chicago chapter of the Union for Democratic Action, with Freda Kirchwey of *The Nation* as speaker, was organized at her home. The causes to which she contributed in her effort to "distribute the money where it will do the most good," as she put it, could be numbered in the hundreds, if not thousands. Whenever any group in Chicago got what it considered a liberal idea, it sent a delegation to have tea with Mrs. Blaine. Many of her largest gifts, however, were the result of impulse. Although A.B. had a deep distrust of institutionalized religion and of most clergymen (she cut off aid to the McCormick Theological Seminary, which her father started), she believed that she herself had revelations or inner urges which she was bound to obey. Well do I recall her relating how, sometime in 1949 or 1950, she saw an appeal for funds in a copy of the *National Guardian* which she had carelessly cast aside, and within a few minutes was on the telephone talking to a representative of the paper in New York, to promise economic security for a period of several months. I was present in her home on the evening of April 29, 1949, when she decided to put up $600,000 to help Ted Thackrey start the New York *Daily Compass,* although I wasn't fully aware of what was going on at the time. In an article, "The Compass Story—Some Lessons Learned in Failure," in the Dec. 26, 1953 *Editor & Publisher,* Thackrey related how Mrs. Blaine excused herself more than once for what he called a "private vigil" or "divine guidance," in order to make up her mind. Some of Ted's old friends think he was uncharitable in that article. I agree as regards his attempts to blame the American Newspaper Guild and others for part of his journalistic failure; but I do not think he exaggerated the behavior of Mrs. Blaine, however inappropriate it might have been to mention it.

At the time of her death, Mrs. Blaine still had $41,364,236.05 of the fortune left her in 1884 by her father, Cyrus H. McCormick, the famous inventor of the reaper. I recall her often telling with pride that her father made his fortune because he had faith in the dirt farmers of the middlewest and allowed them credit to purchase his machines. It was her desire to use his money, which she considered hers in trust, to continue doing good for the common people of the world.

Mrs. Blaine was the widow of Emmons Blaine, the son of James G. Blaine, the Republican "Plumed Knight" candidate for the Presidency, who lost the election in 1884 to Grover Cleveland. Her husband died in 1892 and their only son, Emmons Jr., died during World War I at 28, while working for the government in a ship-building plant in Lansdowne, Pa. A daughter, Anne (Nancy) Blaine, was born after her father's death, to the former Miss Eleanor Gooding, whom Emmons Jr. had married a year earlier. In characteristic fashion, Mrs. Blaine rented an entire floor of Henrotin Hospital for the new mother and baby. When she grew up, Nancy failed to share many of her grandmother's views. She was liberal, to the extent of working for the CIO-PAC Chicago office; she is married to Col. Gilbert Harrison, rightwing AVC leader, ADAer and publisher of *The New Republic*. It used to be pretty painful for Nancy to have to help play hostess to Henry Wallace, Paul Robeson and a number of other people whom her grandmother liked to have around.

Henry Wallace tells me that Mrs. Blaine was attracted to him following publication of his *Statesmanship and Religion* in 1934. Beanie Baldwin first met her in 1944, at an Amalgamated Clothing Workers convention. They were introduced by Sidney Hillman, who had "a good nose for money," according to Beanie, but probably never got more than $5,000 out of A.B. for the NC-PAC. The night after the failure of the Democratic convention to renominate Wallace in 1944, Mrs. Blaine came at midnight to the CIO-PAC headquarters and expressed high indignation. From then on she was the principal financial angel of the NC-PAC and later of the PCA and the Progressive party. When William H. Miller arrived in Chicago from New York to organize the Chicago branch of the NC-PAC, she embarrassed him by insisting upon paying all of his personal living expenses, including his newspapers, in addition to seeing that he got his salary.

Mrs. Blaine's will was drawn in 1937 and unchanged, even by minor codicil, since that time. When it was filed for probate, it was revealed that, after $11 million was given to Nancy and some other bequests were made, a trust fund of $20 million was to be administered by Nancy, Dr. Roger I. Lee of the Harvard Medical School and Richard Bentley, lawyer, to "advance thought" on six general subjects. These were: (1) the right of education for all children; (2) the relationship of life and the ethics of industry and commerce; (3) the institution and education toward a common ideal of public health; (4) possibilities of communication between seen and unseen worlds; (5) relations between peoples and nations and the avoidance of war; (6) growth of the spiritual as distinguished from the material elements of human life.

As a possible explanation of such a will, deemed to serve as flypaper for a host of crackpots seeking subsidy, James Brown IV, director of the Chicago Community Trust, told a group, "She was strongly under the influence of Henry A. Wallace at the time."

I have no way of knowing how accurate that surmise was. I do know that Anita Blaine greatly admired Henry Wallace, as she had Franklin Roosevelt, in whose behalf she furnished full page newspaper advertisements across the country in 1936. I do not think she measurably influenced Wallace's thinking during the 1948 campaign or at any time, despite the fact that she must have run up some tremendous telephone and telegraph bills keeping in constant touch with him. However, all of the attempts by some of her relatives and socialite friends to prejudice her against Wallace were completely wasted. She not only served as a national officer of the NC-PAC, PCA, Wallace for President Committee and Progressive party, but she also ran for University of Illinois trustee on the Progressive ticket in 1948. In her support of Wallace's One Worldism she was acting consistently, as after World War I she had been a strong advocate of American participation in the League of Nations.

Henry Wallace never wanted to talk money matters with A.B. Instead, whenever there had been a meeting of any kind in Chicago and it was deemed important to approach her financially, he would inform her that Beanie Baldwin would stay over a day to talk business, which he then did. Great care always was taken to give A.B. a minute report on how every cent of her money was used. As much as possible her unsolicited suggestions regarding campaign strategy were taken, but mostly she waited for ideas to be presented to her.

Anita McCormick Blaine's overwhelming passion was the brotherhood of man. She was a highly emotional person at times, when she felt herself being led in the direction of a contribution to the cause of peace and goodwill on earth. But she was an extremely shrewd woman, even in her last years. She turned down more requests for assistance than she granted, and she was the captive of no person or clique. Right in the middle of the 1948 campaign she announced a gift of $1 million to establish a Foundation for World Government; the trustees, in addition to herself, were to be Stringfellow Barr, Scott Buchanan and Harris L. Wofford Jr. At first it was reported that Henry Wallace might also become involved, but Mrs. Blaine kept her various groups "apart," as everyone who dealt with her knew. In September, 1954 the United States tax court ruled the $1,043,375 she gave the Foundation for World Government was not tax exempt because it "was not organized exclusively for educational purposes" and ordered her estate to pay $571, 674.

Mrs. Blaine was first cousin to Col. Robert R. McCormick, editor and publisher of the Chicago *Tribune,* and she stood for about everything "Bertie" was against. I don't know whether she ever tried to convert her cousin to her own way of thinking. I do know that a good many conservative executives of the International Harvester Company, and other business enterprises with which she was connected, must have run the risk of apoplexy more than once when they attended functions at her place in the company of some of her more liberal friends. It never occurred to her that it was possible to mix groups injudiciously, and her Right Wing associates apparently considered an invitation to one of her functions as tantamount to a royal command. Once she wanted to send her butler to Washington to obtain a White House appointment for her. When Rex Tugwell told her that this was not the way one went about seeing the President, she replied, "Everybody sees Mrs. Blaine."

And just about everybody who had any part in the civic or political life of Chicago for a half century *did* see her, and the majority of them wish that it were still possible to do so. She was a grand woman, whose Victorian tastes did not prevent her devotion to the best interests of the underdog, as she saw them.

Related to the procedural and financial difficulties which the New Party faced was:

6. *The problem of political organization and personnel.*

Following the second annual convention of the Progressive Citizens of America, Jan. 16-18, 1948 at Chicago, Doris Fleeson wrote in her syndicated column, as it appeared in the Chicago *Daily News* for Jan. 20:

"The Progressive Citizens of America have an internationally known candidate and are long on enthusiasm for him. PCA is short of practically everything else it takes to run a Presidential campaign, including political talent, experience, money and organization."

Of the same gathering Milburn P. Akers wrote, in the Jan. 19 Chicago *Sun:*

"The Knickerbocker hotel held, over the week-end, a strange medley of people; a considerable number of idealists, with their heads high in the clouds of political inexperience; a handful of practical (very practical) polititians; a number of fellow travelers and a few Communist party members."

And in his Jan. 23 column, Thomas L. Stokes summarized:

"Perhaps the most impressive thing about the Progressive Citizens of America convention in Chicago which initiated a third-party movement for Henry Wallace was that the bulk of its 500 delegates were what we call 'intellectuals.' "

It was, of course, absolutely true that there was an almost complete dearth of persons with practical political experience as elected officeholders, or at least campaign experience as candidates for office. Neither then nor at any other time during 1948 did any members of Congress openly support the Progressive party, with the exception of Sen. Glen Taylor (Dem., Idaho) who became the Vice Presidential nominee, Rep. Vito Marcantonio (ALP, N.Y.) and Rep. Leo Isacson (ALP, N.Y.) after his special election in February. All over the country there were mayors, state representatives and other state and local officials who were friendly, but there weren't many of them willing to risk being publicly photographed while shaking hands with a prominent Progressive.

As 1948 opened, PCA claimed 100,000 members in 750 communities across the country, with chapters in 24 states and individual members in all states. It probably had about half that many who kept up their dues, and in only New York, California and Illinois—as detailed in Chapter X—was there anything resembling a traditional political organization, with ward and precinct workers ready to go into action. That is, unless Elmer Benson succeeded in swinging the Minnesota Democratic-

Farmer-Labor party into the Wallace column. One of the best statements of the organizational weakness of the New Party was one prepared in self-criticism by Arthur Kahn, head of the nationalities division, in a report on June 19, 1948. It read in part:

> The listing of states on the ballot or engaged in petition drives does not provide a thorough picture of the conditions of the New Party, for outside New York City and a half dozen other cities in the nation, there is scarcely any political organization. This lack of organization is certainly one of the reasons why the New Party has not been able to react with sufficient vigor to attacks in states like Ohio and Oklahoma.
>
> So weak are most of the state organizations that were it not for the assistance of the national office it would have been impossible to collect the required number of signatures on petitions in states like West Virginia and Oklahoma. In the future in organizing ward clubs, in strengthening the New Party against ever-sharpening attacks and in ensuring an honest count of the ballots in November, the national office will not be able to offer adequate assistance to the states . . .
>
> The New Party is primarily a mass of sympathetic citizens still to be organized by a handful of enthusiastic Wallace workers, few of whom are experienced in political work . . . The New Party is called upon to accomplish in a few months throughout the nation what it has taken the American Labor party 12 years to accomplish in New York City.

As a partial offset to this lack of experienced leadership and rank and file organization at the grass roots level, the national office came to be staffed by an extremely competent group of workers. Almost all of those in positions of responsibility had had similar experience in the CIO-PAC, the NC-PAC and/or the PCA, and were well qualified for their jobs. They had also worked together in those previous positions. Any campaign headquarters always seems to be a beehive of disorganized and confused activity, and that of the Progressive party was no exception. Nevertheless, at the operational level the Progressive party was probably quite a bit above par in smooth efficiency. Whatever mistakes were made were those of a higher echelon on policy or overall strategy.

On Jan. 26, 1948, Henry Wallace made formal in writing his request that C. B. Baldwin resign his position as director of the PCA and become campaign manager, "to coordinate the work of the many groups which will be active in support of our progressive program." From then on Beanie had complete administrative authority. Probably his first acts were to retain the 15 paid PCA executives in as many states, and to hire field organizers to assist in organizing other states and setting up machinery,

300

including paid personnel, in them. Salaries of employees of new state groups were subsidized as long as necessary by the national office. The maximum number of paid employees on the national payroll at any one time was 155, almost all of them in the New York headquarters.

Those headquarters at 39 Park Avenue were later called "a big farce" by Vito Marcantonio, and similar opprobrious things by others, but such complaints related mostly to the retention of the lavish quarters after November, 1948. A four-story 40 room brownstone, the mansion had been built in 1863 by Samuel Atterbury, railroad magnate. It had high ceilings, marble-manteled fireplaces, crystal chandeliers and an elevator from the basement to the third floor. The Progressive party moved in on Feb. 22, 1948 and paid $1,500 a month rent. The original lease expired on Dec. 15, 1948, after which occupancy continued on a month-to-month basis until March 30, 1949; then, mostly for reasons of economy, the PP moved to 56 W. 45th Street, still later to 150 W. 46th Street, 17 W. 45th Street and 1133 Broadway, each time into smaller space at less money. A huge apartment house numbered 41 Park Avenue now stands where the Atterbury mansion once did.

During 1948 the top floor of 39 Park Avenue was used by the fund raisers, bookkeepers and the nationalities division. In eight rooms on the third floor were the offices of Baldwin and of John Abt, head of the legal division; George Murphy, assistant campaign manager; the speakers' bureau and the women's division. On the second floor were offices for Henry Wallace, his speech writers and the publicity department, including the music, art and other divisions. What was originally a ballroom on the main floor was used as a meeting place or conference room, capable of accommodating 75 to 100 persons. Also on the first floor was a big workroom for about 30 volunteers at a time, and small rooms for mimeographing machines and similar equipment. In the basement were the labor, youth, and Caravans for Wallace divisions and offices, and there was a small cafeteria and kitchen.

Formal announcement of the formation of a national Wallace for President committee and its officers was made to the public on Jan. 29 by Henry Wallace. The six "brain trusters," as they were promptly dubbed by some segments of the press, were: Elmer A. Benson, former Minnesota Governor and Senator, chairman; Jo Davidson, eminent sculptor, former chairman of the ICC-ASP and honorary chairman of the PCA, co-chairman; Paul Robeson, Negro actor and concert singer, co-chairman; Dr. Rexford Guy Tugwell, University of Chicago professor of political science and one-time undersecretary of agriculture and Governor of Puerto Rico, co-chairman; Angus Cameron, of Boston, editor-in-chief of Little, Brown & Co., book publishers, treasurer; C. B. Baldwin, campaign manager. The next day Mrs. Anita McCormick Blaine of Chicago was added to the list as another co-chairman. This group immediately issued a nationwide call for members and stated it planned to hold a national conference in April. At the end of a month another co-chairman, Albert J. Fitzgerald, president of the CIO United Electrical, Radio and Machine Workers of America, had been added and a list of 700 committee members was made public. It was quite an impressive

Who's Who of labor and liberal leaders, university professors, artists, actors and intellectual leaders in all walks of life.

Missing, however, were the top names in labor circles. From Washington on Jan. 6, 1948 William Green, president of the American Federation of Labor, called the Wallace venture "a great political mistake," and predicted that "labor generally will be opposed." He said that he had followed Wallace's speeches, "and I've got the impression from them that Russia is right and America is wrong. I'm against him." He forecast, "I think, as the picture unfolds it will be pretty clear that he is sponsored by Communists."

Following an interview with President Truman on Jan. 20, 1948, A. F. Whitney, president of the Brotherhood of Railway Trainmen—who in mid-1946 had promised to use the entire treasury of the brotherhood, if necessary, to defeat Truman—said that he had reached "complete understanding" with the President. He also said that he would not necessarily oppose all members of Congress who had voted for the Taft-Hartley act, because he believed that some had experienced a change of opinion. "Anyway, it depends on who opposes them," he said. Whitney told reporters that he had tried in December to persuade Wallace not to start a third party. Wallace told me that he has no recollection of any such attempt by Whitney.

According to press accounts at the time, the most recent visit of Philip Murray, CIO president, to the White House prior to Wallace's announcement was on Nov. 12, 1947, at a time when President Truman was conferring individually with a number of non-governmental leaders regarding his foreign policy. Murray was reported to have "pledged his organization's support of the program as it now exists." Three days later the press carried reports of a long memorandum from Murray to Truman in which he declared that labor "claims the right to participate fully in all phases" of the administration of the foreign aid program, which should be in the hands of men "free from the narrowness of view which characterizes certain segments of the business community."

That Wallace had considerable rank and file labor support was evident by the number of resolutions endorsing his action passed by locals all over the country. Most of these locals, however, were affiliated with the 11 CIO internationals whose presidents opposed the national CIO action condemning the New Party on Jan. 22, 1948. With the exception of Michael Quill of the Transport Workers the 11 stood their ground throughout 1948, although predictions that organized trade union support and campaigning effort would be meager were correct.

The PCA, which spearheaded the drive to persuade Wallace to run and provided the sole organizational structure on which the New Party could build, was primarily middle-class, intellectual and professional. Its membership did not consist of the type of persons used to getting out and ringing doorbells, or manning the polls as watchers on election day. Rather, they were the rally-attending, money-giving and petition-signing kind and altogether too many of them for the good of the political party valued their sense of respectability too much to engage in the rough-and-tumble of everyday political activities. Hence the disappointment, chagrin and/or horror that many of them experienced when they sought, for the first time in their lives, to be "practical" politicians at the lowest level was not surprising. That they would have experienced exactly the same sensations, or even worse, had they attempted to operate similarly within either of the major parties is beside the point, as far as building the down-to-earth strength of the New Party is concerned.

Many outstanding intellectuals were for Wallace. Albert Einstein, on March 30, 1948, hailed Henry Wallace as the only man who "can save us from the threatening domestic and international situation." Late in the campaign Thomas Mann, Nobel prize-winning refugee from Nazi Germany, wrote of Wallace:

"In the eyes of the whole world the millions who will give him their votes will represent the moral and intellectual elite of America. For no matter how grave the difficulties which could seem to block our way to an honest understanding with today's Russia, we cannot but recognize in the Russian-American conflict the one appalling obstacle to all human progress. The future of mankind depends on its solution and Wallace means to help solve it."

From Spring Green, Wis., the illustrious architect Frank Lloyd Wright wrote on Aug. 6: "We shall vote for you here at Taliesin and we hope our vote is sustained by millions." In an interview in the *Daily People's World* for Oct. 19, 1948, Sidney Burke quoted Norman Mailer, author of the celebrated novel *The Naked and the Dead*, as saying, "Wallace is the only national figure who is an obstacle to fascism in America." And from across the ocean, George Bernard Shaw gave the University of Michigan *Daily* a copyrighted statement for its Feb. 25 issue, saying that Wallace "is the only Presidential candidate whose election will allay Russian suspicion of America." In an interview on July 23 with Johannes Steel, Shaw called Wallace "the only American figure today who knows what it is all about."

In his press conference on Dec. 29 in Chicago, Wallace said he "supposed" Communists would vote for him, "because I'm sincerely in favor of peace." He added: "In the same way I believe I'll get considerable support from the Quakers and the Methodists who want peace also. I'm eager to have the support of all who want peace. I don't care who they are. I'd hope, though, that if the Communists in this country vote for me they didn't come out and say so in formal resolutions." Asked if he would formally disavow any such open Communist support, Wallace said, "I'm not going to be distracted by red herrings."

The next day in Milwaukee, according to the Milwaukee *Sentinel* for Dec. 31, 1947, Wallace again said he hoped the Communists would "have a heart and not come out with any resolutions" for him; but as for repudiating them if they did, he added, "I will keep my eye on the main ball and not be distracted by red herrings." During his Milwaukee interview Wallace was asked his opinion regarding the extent to which American Communists were agents of Russia. He replied that he didn't know. Although he hadn't known many Communists, he said, he made a point of asking every one he did meet "point blank" whether such was the case. The newspaper quoted Wallace further:

303

"They all answer that they don't seem to have any way of getting in touch with Moscow and that Moscow doesn't seem to want anything to do with them. They don't invite us to their parties in Washington, they say, and they sounded kind of pathetic, like poor lonesome souls."

In further answer to reporters' questions, Wallace got himself into what later proved to be an embarrassing situation. That was when he said he would answer the question of accepting or denouncing Communist support "exactly like Franklin D. Roosevelt." According to a United Press dispatch from Chicago, dated Dec. 29 and printed in the Philadelphia *Inquirer* for Dec. 30, Wallace said, "I'm going to do exactly what he would have done and you can look up the record on that."

The difficulty, from Wallace's standpoint, was that some newspaper men *did* look it up and found that on Oct. 5, 1944 FDR had said: "I have never sought and I do not welcome the support of any person or group committed to Communism or Fascism or any other foreign ideology which would undermine the American system of competitive enterprise and private property."

Confronted with this evidence at the PCA convention more than a fortnight later, Wallace was still evasive; he was quoted as repeating, "I'll have to look up the record and find out what FDR really did." As quite a few journalists and others predicted at the time, the "repudiate or not repudiate" issue plagued him throughout the entire campaign.

The presence of Communists as workers in the Progressive party was one of the main factors, though not the only one, conditioning the thinking of those who attempted, early in 1948, to appraise:

7. *The probable long-range effect of the New Party venture.*

Outside Progressive ranks most of the predictions as to the enduring effect of a New Party were not complimentary. Typical of the nastiest type was Victor Riesel's in the New York *Post* for Jan. 16, 1948:

"Come November, Wallace will count his 750,000 or 1 million votes and quit the new 'Progressive' combine. So will the innocents. And the activists who, it will be discovered, are the comradely type, will inherit the Progressive party in some 20 or 25 states. And live happily ever after peddling the class struggle over that push cart."

More politely, Max Lerner wrote in *PM* for Feb. 1, 1948:

"His campaign will be a futile insurgent gesture with the main organizational strength provided by the Communists, whose prize victim and trophy Wallace has become. And the movement he leads will go down in history as a valiant but mistaken fringe movement instead of part of the central current of American liberalism."

Still more politely the National Educational Committee for a New Party, headed by A. Philip Randolph, president of the AFL Pullman Porters, and Israel Feinberg, vice president of the International Ladies Garment Workers, declared:

" . . . Mr. Wallace is performing a distinct disservice to the cause of a peaceful world and a democratic America. His candidacy is also bound to have a deterrent effect on the formation of a genuinely democratic-farmer-labor-progressive party which the NECNP is anxious to see emerge on the American scene after the next Presidential election."